LEEDS METROPOLITAN UNIVERSITY

SOCIAL POLICY REVIEW 8

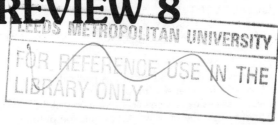

Edited by

Margaret May

Principal Lecturer in Social Policy
London Guildhall University

Edward Brunsdon

Principal Lecturer in Social Policy
London Guildhall University

Gary Craig

Professor of Social Policy
The University of Humberside

SPA

SOCIAL POLICY
ASSOCIATION

SOCIAL POLICY REVIEW 8

Published by the Social Policy Association
London Guildhall University
London E1 7NT

First Published 1996

British Library Cataloguing in Publication Data
Social Policy Review - (No.8) -
1. Great Britain. Social Policies
361.6'1'0941

ISBN 0 9518895 5 9

Typeset and produced by the University Printing Unit, University of Kent at Canterbury

Contents

International Developments

Contributors

Lynda Bransbury Free-lance Researcher and Policy Officer
Local Government Information Unit.

Mita Castle-Kanerova Senior Lecturer in Social Policy
The University of North London and
Honorary Professor, Charles University,
Prague

John Clarke Senior Lecturer in Social Policy
The Open University

Gary Craig Professor of Social Policy
The University of Humberside

Karen Clarke Lecturer in Social Policy
The University of Manchester

Hartley Dean Reader in Social Policy
The University of Luton

Tony Eardley Senior Research Fellow Social Policy
Research Centre, The University of
New South Wales, Sydney

Caroline Glendinning Senior Research Fellow National
Primary Care Research and
Development Centre, The University of
Manchester

Howard Glennerster Professor of Social Policy
The London School of Economics

Norman Ginsburg Professor of Social Policy
The University of North London.

Sylvia Horton Principal Lecturer
The University of Portsmouth

Linda J. Jones Dean of the School of Health and
Social Welfare, The Open University

Ruth Lister Professor of Social Policy
The University of Loughborough

Carey Oppenheim Lecturer in Social Security Policy
South Bank University

Gillian Peele Professor of Politics
Lady Margaret Hall,
Oxford University

Roland Petchey Lecturer in General Practice
The University of Nottingham

David Smith Professor of Social Work
The University of Lancaster

Robert Sykes Senior Lecturer in Social Policy
Sheffield Hallam University

Marilyn Taylor Reader in Social Policy
The University of Brighton

1 Introduction

Margaret May,
Edward Brunsdon and
Gary Craig

The Social Policy Review aims to provide an academic and practitioner audience with a review of contemporary debates and
developments in social welfare provision and policy analysis in
Britain and other countries. Last year's Review addressed the
shifting boundaries of social policy; this year we focus on some of
the core concerns of current provision and policy. The first section - 'Reorientations in social policy' - opens with John Clarke's
prescient call for a re-analysis of the role of the state after the welfare state. As he notes, social policy analysts, whether Fabian or
Marxist inspired, traditionally assumed an inextricable connection
between social welfare and the state. But the revival of neo-liberalism and governmental attempts to switch to non-statutory and
self-provision have called into question the idea of the welfare
state itself.

There has been a major intellectual investment over the last
decade in assessing the changing welfare landscape and the
concomitant shifts in the internal organisation of the state,
reflected in the new lexicon of the 'mixed economy of welfare',
'quasi-markets', 'Post-Fordism' and 'post-Fordist state forms'. For
Clarke, none of these notions fully capture the complexities of the
new welfare order. The focus on the reorganisation of finance and
delivery threatens to delimit current debates. It also obscures the
continuing significance of the state in the construction and management of welfare. He maintains that the state's role is better
seen as a process of dispersal, involving new relations of power
(and resistance).

Clarke's concerns are taken up in a variety of ways in Taylor's contribution to this section which analyses the issues facing the voluntary sector as state management of welfare is both fragmented and reformed. As she emphasises, the myriad forms of voluntary provision are subject to a range of contradictory expectations and pressures. Recent attempts to expand its service delivery role whilst empowering consumers, increasing accountability and securing new resources, have exacerbated this diversity. For Taylor, reconciling the resultant tensions and releasing new opportunities, is contingent on a structural framework in which the state plays an active role.

Similar concerns about the state and citizenry underpin Dean's chapter which focuses on another central concern in social policy analysis, the nature of welfare rights and redress. He considers the four key notions of adjudicative redress, consumer redress, case redress and declaratory address, and the rights they invoke. As he demonstrates, these are not only highly contested but entail different legal and administrative procedures with different power relations. Over the last decade he detects a shift away from adjudicatory and participative forms of redress to a new range of complaints procedures. Ostensibly this is in line with increased consumerism and the drive to a more pluralist welfare market. But for Dean, as for Clarke, changes in the forms of welfare delivery and redress are less significant than the underlying power relations between the state and the individual. His analysis of recent trends suggests the new, dispersed, routes to redress have not substantially shifted the balance between the two, but rather signify the emergence of a more fragmented, discursive approach to welfare rights.

Cognate issues emerge in the contributions to the second section which review recent developments in the core services of income maintenance, education, housing, health and social care. In a year marked by a plethora of pre-electoral proposals, stock-taking in each of these areas is not only timely but salutary. Oppenheim and Lister offer a retrospective analysis of social security over the last decade. Though promoted as creating a system for the next century, the 1986 Social Security Act inaugurated a period of unremitting change. Whilst recognising two distinct phases in this period in terms of Ministerial styles and strategies, the authors maintain that both were governed by a political agenda centred on questions of fraud, administrative downsizing, simplification, targeting, incentives, obligations, self-reliance, familism, and the containment of public spending. The resultant legislative upheaval has not as yet dismantled state provision, but it has led to a significant shift towards an American residualist approach to provision, and with it, rising inequality and poverty. Opposition proposals seem to rely on a similar strategy and thus the insecurities of the 'risk society' have yet to be fully challenged.

This somewhat sombre picture is confirmed by Craig et al's detailed study of the Child Support Agency (CSA). Having outlined the gestation of this new instrument for assessing and collecting child maintenance and its surprisingly smooth parliamentary passage, they focus on the Agency's controversial first years, the extensive criticisms which forced major revisions of the original legislation and lone parents' experiences of the new support system. What emerges is both a clear picture of the extent to which the Government's fiscal goals excluded other objectives and increased the insecurities and poverty experienced by lone parent families and the government's failure to learn from earlier policy fiascos.

Accessible, affordable child care presented one possible means of alleviating these insecurities as well as meeting the needs of all working parents. But, as Glennerster argues in the next chapter, the most significant recent initiative in this area, the Major government's pre-school voucher experiment, has been tailored to the needs of more affluent parents and local electoral concerns. It has failed to integrate day care with pre-school education. His analysis of the pilot schemes not only prefigures more recent experience, but also highlights the extent to which nursery school legislation demonstrates the wider use of vouchers and voucher-like arrangements throughout education and training.

A similar pattern can be traced in social housing. Here again the much vaunted 1988 Housing Act has been succeeded by a further spate of initiatives. In examining these, Ginsburg distinguishes between attempts to mollify public concern over rising repossessions and visible homelessness during the 1989-93 recession and the subsequent renewal of the campaign to either privatise or marketise the social housing stock, culminating with the 1996 Housing Bill. Focusing on developments since 1993 Ginsburg assesses the drive to: increase both council and housing association rents; restrict access to social housing, and restructure its management and ownership. He also provides a helpful guide to the controversial changes proposed in the 1995 White Paper and the amended 1996 Bill and points to the many constraints on wholesale privatisation.

Nevertheless, it is clear that in housing, as in social security and education, the Major government is proving as committed as its predecessors to reshaping Britain's welfare map. This process is, perhaps, even more pronounced in health care, where, as Petchey's review of recent developments indicates, the NHS is on 'the verge of a radical shift in its centre of gravity'. Whilst debate on the implementation of the internal market has tended to focus on the hospital sector, he suggests GP fundholding has become increasingly central to the government's health strategy. Though apparently conceived as an interim measure it is emerging as the government's preferred purchasing mechanism, heralding the advent of a new primary-led health care service. There is a real concern, however, that as with the community care reforms, current policy is based on an over-optimistic notion of the sector's caring capacity. Drawing on a wealth of recent research, Petchey's evaluation of the first tranches of fundholders leads him to conclude that, as yet , there are a number of unresolved issues constraining the emergence of a primary-care led NHS.

Bransbury's chapter on the implications of local government reorganisation for social care services raises rather different concerns. As she emphasises, welfare issues did not feature prominently in the reform agenda and local government restructuring now in train has been surprisingly neglected in mainstream policy writing. Yet the implications for social care and other services are profound and not confined to the transitional process. This, as her analysis of Wales and the first phase of reorganisation in England shows, imposed considerable strains on service delivery even where there was close liaison between outgoing and incoming authorities. Whether this will be avoided in areas yet to reorganise remains to be seen and, she argues, the experience of the new unitaries will require careful monitoring, particularly as the English review is leading to a messy, inconsistent and irrational local government map and adding further layers of variability to an already fragmented pattern of care.

The reform of local government was superimposed on a social service workforce already confronting sweeping changes emanating from other government policies, most notably in child and community care. The implications of these policy changes for users and for professional practice have attracted considerable debate. But the manifold changes charted earlier in this Review are not only re- casting welfare delivery, they are also affecting employee relations in state welfare agencies as Horton, in the next chapter, shows . Having outlined the traditional system of organised representation and collective bargaining, she surveys recent attempts to establish more individualised and localised structures and implement 'new' human resource management' strategies. Inherited practices have, it seems, proved highly resistant to change which has, in consequence, been uneven between and across services. Nevertheless, she argues, the public welfare workforce is being re-stratified and the 'model employer' notion, once prevalent among state employers, is giving way to commercial management strategies.

The performance-driven processes considered by Horton are further illuminated in Smith's wide-ranging review of the changing remit and role of the probation service. He maintains that from the mid-1980s to the early 1990s, a sustained attempt was made to incorporate the service into a 'modernised criminal justice system'. The changing penal climate and a renewed faith in imprisonment since 1993, however, herald more radical changes in its functions, training and recruitment. But, as Smith shows, these too are contingent on the performance-based controls of 'new managerialism', including, most recently and controversially, a proposal for performance-related pay.

The final contribution to this survey of recent developments in Britain raises another long-standing concern of social policy, namely, the analysis of the complex relations between different welfare policies and wider societal divisions. Drawing on this tradition, Jones calls for the inclusion of transport on the social policy agenda, pointing to the manifold ways in which current transport policy fuels social, gender and ethnic divisions, deprives many groups of social participation, and is likely to undermine attempts to foster 'community care'.

In our final section, 'International Developments', we return to some of the issues of social security design discussed by Oppenheim and Lister. In a wide-ranging and highly topical comparative study of OECD countries, Eardley considers the extent to which social assistance schemes have taken on less of a 'safety net' and more of a 'back to work' role. He suggests that while there has been a broad-based movement to limit welfare dependency, there is considerable policy variation with member countries clustering into one of four main groupings. Most significantly, clear associations between work 'incentive' schemes and unemployment rates are difficult to discern.

Though the country-specific surveys which follow focus on recent developments in very disparate societies (the Czech Republic, Italy and the United States), they also point to the disjunctures between rhetoric and policy implementation. Castle-Kanerova provides an overview of the Czech Republic's new social security system and the manifold pressures arising not only from economic transition, but also its contradictory pre-war and communist legacies. Whilst the new system has many affinities with social protection schemes elsewhere, she suggests its fragile financial and administrative base are a major source of concern, as is the government's underlying agenda.

Italy too has seen a series of attempts to realign not only its social security system, but welfare provision in general. On the surface the approach taken shares many of the features, as well as the vocabulary, of market-inspired initiatives in other parts of Europe. But, as Sykes shows, these have to be set against the particular configuration of welfare arrangements based on clientilism, regionalism and the inter-meshing of statutory and non-statutory welfare.

Whilst the complexities of Italian provision may have impeded comparative policy analysis, those of the United States have long been the focus of inquiry. Given its importance as the seedbed of neo-liberalist policies, it is fitting that this Review concludes with an assessment of recent developments in American social policy. As Peele's survey of Clinton's welfare initiatives suggests, radical reform is in many ways precluded by the structure and culture of American policy processes. It also indicates the extent to which America's market-based, voluntarist, system is still moulded by the state.

This volume is published as the United Kingdom begins to gear up for a general election in which many of the themes addressed in the Review are likely to feature prominently. We shall return to these issues in the next edition as we assess the prospects for further wide-ranging reform and the on-going debate over the future of welfare provision.

2 The Problem of the State after the Welfare State[1]

John Clarke

The last decade has seen extensive transformations of the organ-isation of social welfare in Britain which have called into question the idea of the welfare state itself. Social policy has developed a growing battery of phrases to describe this re-organisation: the mixed economy; welfare pluralism; quasi-markets; the contract state, etc. This chapter is concerned with the conceptual prob-lems of such terms and links these to the challenge of rethinking the form of the state itself. It starts from a double assumption: first, that the state itself is something worthy of attention and second, that it has not really been getting the attention that it deserves in the study of social policy. While there are pragmatic reasons for this neglect (the organisation of research funding, the attempt to keep up with the sheer scale and pace of change, etc.), this chap-ter argues that social policy needs to re-engage with the problem of the state. The first two sections locate the problem of the state associated with the rise of the New Right, while the next three examine the limitations of some attempts to conceptualise the shifts involved in the restructuring of social welfare. Sections six and seven address the use of ideas of post-Fordism in theorising changes in the welfare state and the final section presents an alternative analysis based around the notion of 'dispersed' state forms.

Posing the problem of the state in social policy

The study of social policy in Britain in the twentieth century has always assumed, even when it has not articulated, an inextricable connection between social welfare and the state. There are two polarised positions which may demonstrate the strength of this linkage. Most accounts of the discipline of social policy draw attention to its Fabian or social democratic origins in which the state is identified as the agency or engine of social reform. It is beyond the scope of this chapter to trace the genealogy of social policy, but the intersection of Fabianism, the 'social citizenship' of the new liberals and British labourism produced a unity built around a conceptualisation of social welfare as the province of the state. However much alternative sources of providing or enhancing social welfare were admitted, the state was seen to play the dominant or guiding role. For the most part, social policy as a discipline has been dominated by this conceptualisation of the state as the embodiment of social reform, through the application of expertise, promoting universalist social citizenship. While there has been attention to hiatuses, unevenness, failures and shortfalls the question of the advancement of social welfare has always been posed on the terrain of the state.

Marxism has provided an alternative approach to the study of the welfare state. Although different in many respects, it shared the terrain of the state and its inextricable connection with social welfare with its Fabian twin (Lee & Raban, 1988). While the roots of the dispute stretch back to the nineteenth century, the arguments between the two conceptions of the state within social policy became a major focus for the discipline from the early 1970s. However, crudely or complexly argued, the major distinction between the two lay in their conceptualisation of the state and its relationship to welfare. For Fabianism, the state represented a more or less transcendent social agency whose principles and powers were counterposed to, and limited the exigencies of market capitalism in a progressive way. For Marxism, the state was - more or less essentially - a capitalist state whose structural ties inclined it towards dominant class interests or ensured the reproduction of capitalist social relations.

The return of the repressed: welfare without the state?

I am aware that these brief formulations do not do justice to the complexity and richness of either position and there is not space here to give attention to the extensive work done on analysing the state (and the welfare state in particular) as a gendered and racialised structure (see, for example, Williams, 1989). Nor do they deal with the persistent problems of producing an adequate definitionion of the 'welfare state'.[2] What I want to concentrate on, however, is the way in which the shared assumptions about the centrality of the question of the state in these analyses were undercut by the 'return of the repressed'. Throughout the 1970s the political and theoretical arguments around social policy were conducted within a frame of reference in which the state was assumed to be the centre and where the most significant differences were to be found in the conceptualisation and evaluation of the state's role. Neither Fabianism nor Marxism contemplated the emergence of a different frame of reference - what Green (1993) has called 'welfare without politics'.

The revival of neo-liberalism as an economic theory and as a contributor to the New Right political project undermined the comfortable assumptions about the centrality of the state and its inextricable links with social welfare. Its arguments about markets, public choice, the inefficiency of state monopolies and the need to free the consumer-citizen from the tyranny of the state, combined with the welfare reforms of the Conservative governments, dislocated both the old regime of the welfare state and its academic satellite - the discipline of social policy. Both Fabianism and Marxism have encountered some difficulty in analysing capitalist states which seemed to have abandoned 'social progress' (on the one hand) and the 'best possible shell' for capitalism (on the other). The anti-statism of the New Right project thus destabilised core assumptions in the study of the welfare state and the welfare state itself.

So, how are we to go about conceptualising what now exists? It seems clear that, except totemically, the concept of the welfare state will not do as the basis for analysing the emergent welfare patterns. They simply do not look like what we previously understood the welfare state to be - even though we understood it in a variety of ways. What has been disrupted in the 1980s is the apparently inextricable connection between the words 'welfare' and 'state'. I do not mean that people (including academics) do not go on talking and writing about 'the welfare state' but this tends to be as a 'practical concept' used either descriptively to reference the social organisation of welfare provision or as a reference point from which to measure change or crisis. Beyond this, there are a number of different concepts which lay claim to capturing the new welfare order. Some of these are about processes (privatisation, marketisation, residualisation etc.); some are about new patterns of provision (mixed economics; welfare pluralism; quasi-markets) and some address the form of the state itself (post-Fordism, for example). In the following sections, I explore some of the limitations of these attempts to re-think the welfare state before offering some tentative alternatives.

The mixed economy of welfare

Although not exactly a new concept, the idea of the mixed economy of welfare has grown in popularity in the face of changed patterns of provision. In particular, it has been used to index the shift from provision dominated by state agencies to a situation of multiple providers located in different sectors. Typically, mixed economies are conceived of as being composed of service provision from public, voluntary (or not-for-profit), private (for profit) and 'informal' sectors (see, for example, Wistow et al, 1994 p32).

Fundamentally, the 'mixed economy' is only a descriptive concept, indicating little more than the fact that there are different sources of welfare supply. At this level, all national welfare regimes are 'mixed economies' since there is nowhere where the state is or was the monopoly or sole provider (Cochrane, 1993). It is, of course, possible to specify the concept empirically in a number of different ways. One might calculate the different volumes of provision contributed by the different sectors (although as usual the 'informal sector' remains rather difficult to quantify). One might also move to analysing different mixed economies of welfare within a national formation. We have argued elsewhere that there is no national mixed economy, since the mixes of providers are differentiated by welfare service as well as by sector, and spatially, in different and differently defined localities (Charlesworth, Clarke & Cochrane, 1996).

There are, though, a number of other problems which are not resolved by such empirical specification. In concentrating on provision, the mixed economy approach implies an equivalence between provider sectors. As Mishra has argued, the assumption of functional substitution is a rather optimistic one and obscures a number of possible sources of 'disentitlement' (1990, p111). While this criticism focuses on the possible effects of a 'more mixed' mixed economy, there are other analytical problems about the concept. The analysis of mixed economies relies on an essentialist definition of 'sectors' which has two important consequences. First, it reifies the difference between sectors, often with an implied motivational structure. So, distinctions are drawn between the public, independent, voluntary and informal sectors (or some equivalent set of distinctions - 'for-profit', not-for-profit', 'for love', etc.). Leaving aside for the moment the problem of the 'informal sector', such designations rely on a crude classification which overrides internal sectoral differences that affect their 'mar-

ket positioning', their approach to service provision and their relations to the central and local state. So, for example, the corporate
welfare provider has substantial differences from the 'independent
proprietor'; while large national or international voluntary organisations are not the same as local 'grass roots' provision. It also
leaves open the question of whether the trajectories of organisations within the different sectors will have the long (or even medium) term effect of blurring the boundaries between them.

More worryingly, the concentration on sectors tends to
draw attention away from the field of relations in which they are
emeshed. Most discussion about mixed economies of welfare has
focused on the movement outwards of tasks, duties and responsibilities from the state to other agencies - through divestment,
decentralisation, delegation and contracting. The stress has been
on reducing 'public' provision (if not financing) through the
enhancement of a variety of 'private' provisions. Nevertheless, it
is important to attend to the ways in which new relationships and
new flows of power are constructed in these processes. What
from one angle can be viewed as the diminution of the state's role
can be seen from another as the extension of state power, but
through new and unfamiliar means. At its crudest, this points to
new relations of financial dependency - evidenced by the anxieties
of the commercial residential care sector or by the fears in the voluntary sector about clientelism. More elaborately, it raises questions about the nature of power exercised through regulation,
contracting, monitoring and surveillance. While rhetoric may
stress 'independence', the relationships that are at stake in acting
as sub-contracted or delegated agents of the state require attention to the *expansion* of state power through such new modalities. It may be that we are so used to posing the question of state
power in terms of its direct action (through state institutions), that
we have found it difficult to track the shifts of power that have
gone along with a reduction in direct public provision. But by
treating sectoral boundaries as if they were essential and unchang-
ing features of the landscape of welfare provision, too little attention has been paid to the emergent relationships that organise
and re-organise them (see also Mackintosh, 1995 on the need for
'evolutionary analysis').

These problems are further increased by turning to the 'public
sector'. The phrase rather loosely designates direct provision of
benefits and services through state institutions, but leaves open a
problem about the relationship between the public sector and the
state. Clearly, the public sector cannot be the state (or even the
welfare state), since there are other public 'functions' - of politics,
policy and resourcing, for example - which are not integral to the

idea of public sector *provision*. The public sector itself now
embodies a variety of functions and forms which range from
direct provision through semi-autonomous organisations (trusts)
to 'enabling' or 'purchasing' non-providers. As with the other sectors, there are salient issues both of internal differentiation and
new fields of relationship (both service specific and spatial, not
least in the relations between the central and local state). Even if
we take this as one sector in a new mixed economy, there remain
questions about the relationship between the state and public sector provision. At the very least, the concept of the mixed economy requires a notion of a state which organises the structure of
and relationships within specific mixed economics of welfare
(including the scale, scope and responsibilities of the 'public sector') as well as the more obvious functions of policy formation and
financing.

   One might see this as the split forced by the New Right: marking the separation of the command structures of the state from
the operational/service functions of the public sector, embodied
in a variety of forms (agencies; quangos; purchasers etc.).[3]
Nevertheless, the 'policy/implementation' distinction has always
been a rather unstable and contested line and there is little reason
to think that its current incarnation (as the distinction between
strategic and operational management) is any more robust or reliable.
To go back to a more archaic language, it might be more appropriate to treat the mixed economy as a 'structure in dominance'
in which one element of the combination (the state) both performs its own function (providing through the public sector) and
allocates the places of other elements within the combination.
However this is understood (and there is no necessary reason to
go back to Althusserian structuralism), the mixed economy
urgently requires us to think in terms of a field of power relations
and not just the distribution of tasks or functions as part of the
'organisation of service delivery'.

The public/private divide

A rather different set of problems is raised by an alternative conception of the 'public' as one side of the binary distinction
between public and private realms. This has taken on greater
salience with the concern over forms of 'privatisation' in relation
to public services (Swann, 1988). Three forms might be identified. First, 'privatisation' as the direct sale of public assets to the
private/commercial sector as in the case of public utilities like gas,
water and electricity. Although it is possible to identify elements
of such processes at the margins of social welfare (and attempts

to create larger scale shifts, such as with pensions), this first sense of privatisation has not been the dominant feature of British welfare policy.[4]

The second is the process of blurring the boundaries between public and private sectors by means of sponsored competition and restructuring. Such changes form the core of the arguments around whether the NHS has been 'privatised'. It clearly has not in the first sense of privatisation but the changes in competition, financing, trading rules and organisational structures have had the effect of blurring the boundaries between 'public' and 'private'. In part these are the result of introducing marketising or pseudo-competitive relationships into service provision, but they are also the consequence of isomorphic injunctions that the public sector should learn to 'become businesslike' in more general terms (see, for example, Pollitt, 1993; and Waine & Cutler, 1994). Assessments of the consequences of these changes vary - depending on how much weight is given to the policy and regulatory constraints on NHS organisations. This second sense of privatisation involves a degree of *de-differentiation* - a reduction, though not necessarily removal, of some of the distinctions between the state and the market (or the public and private sectors).

The third sense of privatisation is the shift of responsibilities from public to private understood as the familial domain. This is most visible in the fields of health and social care, but is part of a wider agenda about the transfer of resources (via taxation policies), choices (the 'consumerist' model) and duties away from the state. However, as with the delegation of service responsibilities in the mixed economy model, this cannot be understood as movement in a single direction. It is more than a shift towards expanded roles for the family and reduced responsibilities for the state. The redrawing of the public/private distinction has also produced greater state involvement in the 'private' domain. The shift of responsibilities to 'families' has been accompanied by the subjection of households to greater state surveillance, regulation and intervention. For example, the Child Support Act, while being rhetorically defined as making parents 'responsible', has also created an apparatus of investigation and regulation. Similarly, the 'criminalisation' of parents of delinquent children subjects familial relations to juridical processes. The assessment of carers as well as users within social care extends the reach of the state at the same time as increasing the responsibilities of primary carers.[5] Like the dual movements of centralisation and decentralisation, the reshaping of the public/private divide is a complex, not a simple process. While the state has withdrawn in some ways, its powers and apparatuses have been extended in others - transferring 'responsibilities' but simultaneously creating the capabilities of surveillance and enforcement to ensure that such responsibilities are being fulfilled. The reification of the public-private divide, though undoubtedly helpful to the ideological project of the New Right, is one that is dangerous for social policy analysis, not least because it draws attention away from the state's role in articulating and repositioning that boundary.

Markets and quasi-markets

Although the binary opposition between the state and the market (Loney et al.1986) has not proved to be quite the absolute choice that neo-liberal ideology suggested, it is nevertheless clear that 'markets' in a variety of forms have been central to the process of restructuring the state over the last fifteen years. Different aspects of the state have been subjected to a variety of marketising processes, ranging from competitive tendering and 'externalisation' to forms of internal trading with various points in between. Market processes - and particularly the workings of 'quasi-markets' in social welfare - have been a recent focal point for social policy inquiry (Le Grand & Bartlett, eds 1993; Taylor Gooby & Lawson, eds 1993; Hudson, 1994; Johnson, ed 1995). Although such studies have been productive in demonstrating the conditions of such markets and the central role played in them by 'proxy customers', they are limited in a number of significant ways.

The first is the tendency to abstract the market or quasi-market as a focus for analysis from the wider field of social relationships within which that market is embedded. As a consequence, forms of relationship and forms of calculation which are not competitive/contractual tend to disappear or to be treated marginally as exogenous to the model (a phenomenon not unknown in economic analysis). As we have argued elsewhere in relation to social care, this may make the analysis tidier, but it does mean that critical dimensions are often absent (Charlesworth, Clarke & Cochrane, 1996; see also Mackintosh, 1995). Unfortunately, being exogenous to models does not guarantee being exogenous in practice. While quasi-markets were undoubtedly introduced as a means of disrupting and dislocating old forms of relationships in the welfare state (the nexus of political, professional and bureaucratic modes of control), their arrival has not meant the disappearance of such relationships. Rather, these changes pose the question of how to rethink the structuring of different forms of relationship in new welfare regimes (Clarke & Newman, forthcoming).

It is possible to pick up this problem in a number of different ways, but I want to focus here on one particular example - t he problem of 'motivation'. For instance, Le Grand & Bartlett (1993a, p35) comment that in quasi-markets 'there are commonly non-prof it providers, whose motivation is unclear' in the context of competitive relations which are supposed to be driven by profit-maximising strategies. Such concerns with motivation replicate the problem of essentialism that I raised in the context of the mixed economy, since it assumes that motivation is sectorally specific. Despite more elaborate attempts to find 'proxy' motivations for profit maximisation (e.g. avoiding deficits or being subjected to hard budget constraints, Le Grand & Bartlett, 1993b, pp212-3), the question of motivation tends to be framed within an 'economic calculus' which presumes that some motivational structures (the pursuit of profit) are 'naturally occurring' phenomena (Mackintosh, 1995 pp34-37). More importantly, the abstraction of quasi-markets from their social and political contexts misses the coterminous 'mixed messages' that are embedded in policy formulations: for example, where 'competition' is supposed to coexist with forms of 'collaboration' (Clarke & Newman, 1993b; Charlesworth, Clarke & Cochrane, 1996). Market relations are not the only ones that are politically intended to operate, even in quasi-market settings. As a result, the analysis of quasi-markets gets into interesting tangles about 'anti-competitive' behaviour which might be better understood as embedded in other forms of relationship (collegiality; co-operation; non-economic values or ethics, etc.).

A second problem concerns the bracketing of the question of 'need' in much quasi-market analysis. While recognising that this issue is the subject of considerable epistemological, theoretical and empirical difficulty, it ought to be a central issue for the study of quasi-markets. They were, after all, introduced in the name of consumer choice and justified by reference to the non-transparency of professional representations of need in the old welfare regime (Clarke, 1994). Le Grand & Bartlett address this problem a s follows:

> 'Need', of course, is itself far from unproblematic as a term; here we shall regard it as the resource requirements of the individual concerned, with the specific implication that the more care resources an individual requires to bring his or her level of welfare up to some predetermined level, the greater is his or her need.
> (1993, p19)

There are a few difficulties condensed here, not least the cir-
cularity of an argument that says the more resources someone
needs, the more needy they are. However, my main concern is
that this view of need does not address the problem of representation. If the old regime was flawed by professional domination of
representations of need (which depowered the service user), what
forms of representation rule in the new quasi-markets?
Speculatively, it is possible to suggest that the old bureau-professional forms of representation have been compounded with managerial representations and calculations within quasi-market settings in rather unstable formations. The (unevenly) decentralised
distribution of budgets and/or resources is part of what we have
called a 'dispersed managerial consciousness' - the establishment
of frames of reference and calculation articulated around budgetary 'ownership' or responsibility. In this mixture one is likely to
find the conflation of old professional representational systems
('client centred'), new marketised systems ('customer centred') and
new managerialised systems ('budget centred'), in which the last is
likely to exercise a constraining, if not decisive, interest - the bottom line calculation (see also Clarke, 1994 and 1995a).

The significance of these new conditions for representing need
is intensified by their co-existence with shifts towards organisational decentralisation and devolution - processes which multiply
the sites of decision-making and which are likely to condense the
professional and managerial representations in the same individual or group (e.g. in fund holding practices or care management
teams). Although such movements may place some types of decisions 'closer to the customer', they simultaneously locate budgetary or resource consciousness and constraints there too.

The analysis of quasi-markets in social welfare has illuminated
some dimensions of the new shape of welfare provision, but has
tended to abstract them from wider sets of relationships which
exist alongside - or, more accurately, are articulated with -
competitive and contractual forms. These include the residues of
older forms of professional, administrative and political structures
and cultures - as well as new patterns of organisational dispersal,
pressures towards collaboration, partnership and 'synergy'. As a
result, the over attention to quasi-markets leaves open important
questions about the political and organisational formations in
which the newly marketised processes have been put to work.

A post-Fordist welfare state?

The clearest alternative to the theoretical agnosticism of the 'mixed economy' and the over-narrow focus of 'quasi-markets' has been the attempt to apply regulation theory and the idea of post-Fordism to the restructuring of the welfare state (see, for example, Burrows & Loader, eds 1994). The arguments about the transition from Fordist to post-Fordist regimes in capitalist economies have reopened questions about the role and character of the capitalist state. Although these arguments are highly contentious, they do raise important issues about the relationship between changes in social policy and the state and wider patterns of social and economic restructuring. As a result, they may offer one route out of the problems of focusing too closely on the field of party politics (and Conservative welfare reforms, in particular) or of giving too much attention to specific new patterns of welfare organisation. There are two ways in which regulation theorists have attempted to draw links between post-Fordism and welfare restructuring. The first is pitched at the level of welfare policy (what are the priorities or tendencies of welfare policy in post-Fordist societies?). The second is directed to the structures of the state itself (Is there a post-Fordist form of welfare state?).

In relation to the first of these, Jessop (1994) has drawn a hypothetical distinction between the old Keynesian Welfare State (KWS) and the possibly emergent Schumpeterian Workfare State (SWS), which might be the form of welfare policy allied to post-Fordist economic development. The SWS is characterised as having a commitment to promoting innovation, flexibility and economic competitiveness and social policies are subordinated to economic objectives. It promotes market development and market forms and its welfare agenda is subordinated to 'the interests of capital':

> the combination of the late Fordist trend towards internationalisation and the post-Fordist stress on flexible production has encouraged states to focus on the supply-side problem of international competitiveness and to attempt to subordinate welfare policy to the demands of flexibility (1994, pp26-7).

Pitched at this sort of general level and informed by a few examples, the post-Fordist argument looks relatively plausible. So, too, does the claim that the nation state is being progressively hollowed out by a double movement of power away from it - on the one hand by decentralising forces towards regional and local institutions and on the other hand by the appropriation of power by supranational institutions (such as the European Union).

I have two rather different, although overlapping reservations about this model. The first concerns problems of empirical detail. If the British welfare state has failed to promote innovation, flexibility and the like does this mean that it is not post-Fordist? Jessop's answer to this is that Britain represents a 'flawed post-Fordism' but this seems to rule out the possibility that there are other ways of understanding the formations of contemporary capitalism than 'post-Fordism'. Despite his tentative (and hypothetical) adoption of post-Fordism as a framework, Jessop seems to work rather hard to close off alternatives. More significant, however, is the problem of how to identify 'post-Fordist' trends in social policy. It is one thing to demonstrate that social objectives have been subordinated to economic objectives - by reference to public spending constraints or 'job creation schemes, but social policy over the last fifteen years has a rather more complex character. How, for example, can the Child Support Act be construed as a post-Fordist welfare policy?

Jessop himself is somewhat cavalier about such problems, suggesting that:'(m)any other current changes, of course, are irrelevant, marginal, or contradictory to the consolidation of post-Fordist societalisation' (1994, p33). This replicates one of the continual problems of 'post-Fordist' analyses - the readiness to overlook those elements of the present that do not fit the model.[6] But it also glosses over the issue of contradictions that might be thought central to such analyses, given how much attention has been given to the contradictions which brought on the 'crisis of Fordism'. By contrast, post-Fordism appears as a contradiction-free zone . In consequence, I would suggest that one central task for the analysis of the new welfare order is to understand the contradictory movements that have been taking place. Not the least of these problems is the tension between neo-liberal and neo-conservative social agendas articulated around freedom and discipline and often 'resolved' through the question of the family. So the CSA might be seen as framed by multiple objectives (reduction of welfare costs; the regulation of deviant family forms; the restoration of 'responsibility' via the agency of the state, etc.). Similarly, community care involves not just the transfer of responsibilities to the private sphere of the family but builds 'carers' as well as 'users' into the system of state surveillance and discipline. As Williams (1994) and others have argued, post-Fordist analyses seem to have difficulty 'remembering' that there are social relations other than class. I have suggested elsewhere that the concept of Fordism can only make sense if there is an understanding of the gendered economy of the family as the essential linkage between mass production and mass consumption

(Clarke, 1991, chapter 4). Quite what the family is doing in post-Fordism remains unclear. Is serial monogamy the flexible family form of post-Fordism? Is lone-parenting the site of a new multi-skilled worker? In what ways has consumption been 're-gendered' in the supposed move away from mass consumption?

These issues mark the point at which empirical worries about the accuracy of post-Fordist analyses meet the theoretical anxieties. Especially, but not only, in the field of social policy, Marxist analyses of the capitalist state have been challenged, tempered and displaced by others which gave greater centrality to other social relations, in particular those of 'race' and gender. Post- Fordist arguments proceed as if none of this had happened, giving analytical centre stage to class interests and relations - and often in rather crude and functionalist forms.

Post-Fordist state forms?

The second axis of post-Fordism concerns more than the direction of social policy, opening up the question of the form of the state itself. For example, Jessop argues that the 'nation state' has been 'hollowed out' - and that this process can be seen in trends towards decentralisation and devolution of various kinds in social policy. However, it is also essential to take account of the ways in which power of different kinds has been 'recentralised' at national level - over the national curriculum, over local government, over the rules and financing of quasi-markets in welfare, and so on.

Equally, there are important issues about the nature of some aspects of 'devolved' power in the current shape of social welfare. While not wanting to go as far as Taylor Gooby and Lawson's argument that: '[p]ower over the essentials is retained centrally while management of inessentials is decentralised' (1993, p133) since it assumes that what is essential is known in advance,[7] it nevertheless emphasises the tendency to centralisation that has been visible in social policy. In addition, the structures through which power has been decentralised or devolved have not remained untouched. Indeed the traditional intermediate institutions of the local state have been much reduced and, to a large extent, supplanted by new forms of control: particularly non-elected boards and agencies (TECS, Trusts, Housing Associations, etc.). As before, this raises questions about the nature of state power as it is exercised through indirect rather than direct agency.

A rather different perspective has been developed which examines the changing organisational forms of the state through an analysis of the shifting forces of production, looking in particular at ways in which new technologies of control have created the conditions for new organisational forms. For example, Hoggett (1990) has argued that we have seen a shift from bureaucratic forms of organising welfare towards post-bureaucratic forms, which may be analogous to the move from Fordist to post-Fordist forms of organising production. Hoggett's work has been both imaginative and suggestive - and has the undoubted merit of focusing on the relations of control of bureaucratic and professional modes of organisation within the changing state formation (and parallels discussions elsewhere about the changing patterns of regulation of 'expert knowledge' see, interalia, Reed, 1994; Prichard & Willmott, 1995).

There are two difficulties associated with this analysis. One concerns the Fordist analogy and the consequent designation of old welfare state forms as 'bureaucratic monoliths' (constructed by Murray, 1991, as the form of equivalence between Fordist mass production and consumption and state welfare). It is, I think, highly arguable whether the welfare state was ever Fordist (except possibly by virtue of existing in Fordist economics). Certainly, many of its organisational structures and labour processes remained resolutely 'pre' or 'non' Fordist (Clarke, 1996; see also Rustin, 1994). Equally, I am not convinced that the delivery of universalist welfare services can be constructed as an equivalent to mass consumption, since they also involved the elaborate construction of complex forms of differentiation and categorisation of users, needs and 'treatments'.[8] In part, of course, these differences were constituted in the form of bureaucratic categorisation but they were also the product of professional classification and judgement. That is, the 'bureaucracies' of state welfare worked through the (more or less autonomous) discretion of 'street level bureaucrats': professionalised workers or 'bureau-professionals' (Clarke, 1995a). This is not to argue that there have been no changes in either the forms of social regulation or the forms of categorisation that operate within social welfare (see, for example, Wlllliams' arguments about varieties of diversity, 1994). But, again, I am not convinced that these can be encompassed by a simplifying binary division between old and new.

In more mundane ways, the limits of the productionist analogy with Fordism and post-Fordism can be demonstrated in Lawson's attempt to apply Hoggett's analysis to social services departments. She argues that 'a core-periphery model is emerging in local authorities in the 1990s, with decentralisation of production to area offices, and the core tasks of strategic planning, design and control remaining at the centre' (1993, p82). Even if one accepts that the concept of 'production' is transferable to social work (what is the product?), it is rather difficult to work out where such production used to take place if not in social work teams. In the process, issues about spatial decentralisation and the devolution (or more properly, *delegation*, as Birchall et al., 1995 have recently argued) of managerial rather than production functions become entangled.

We have argued elsewhere about the conditions and processes of managerialisation in relation to social welfare and I do not intend to detail them here. Instead I want to assert some of the main arguments in an abbreviated form (Clarke, Cochrane & McLaughlin, eds 1994). Rather than marking an epochal shift, the processes of managerialisation involve an attempt to realign a series of relationships - between the state and the citizen; between the state and the economy; and between the state and its institutional or organisational forms (including its labour processes). Even if these realignments take place in the context of a global recomposition of capitalism, it remains necessary to understand their specific national and political conditions, processes and outcomes rather than treat them as epiphenomenal reflections of 'deep' processes elsewhere. While the tendencies of these realignments may draw on ideas and models that are the 'practical theories' of contemporary capitalist organisation, their mobilisation and implementation still require political work. In the British context, that means paying attention to the way that managerialism has been taken up as a means of restructuring the state. In particular, this points to four domains. First, managerialism offered itself as the lever through which tighter financial control could be exercised over the 'burden' of public spending through the pursuit of intra-organisational efficiencies (Pollitt, 1993). Second, managerialism represented a means of organisational co-ordination which could dislocate and subordinate the old bureau-professional regimes of state welfare organisation. Thirdly, managerialism and its cognate discourse - consumerism - were adopted as a representational system through which the state-citizen relationship could be reworked (Clarke, 1994 and 1995b). Finally, managerialism provided a mode of inter-organisational co-ordination through which the complex dispersal of 'agency' from an institutionally centralised state could potentially be held together (Clarke & Newman, forthcoming). In each of these domains, managerialism has been articulated with the New Right's programme of state restructuring in Britain which has gained the legitimation of an isomorphic and technocratic view of 'management' as the natural mode of organisational co-ordination (Clarke, 1995a). At the same time, managerialism has had its social 'reach' extended beyond the terrain of corporate capitalism, at least in its American and British varieties.[9]

What sort of state?

This final section of the paper is deliberately tentative because it reflects my own uncertainty about how best to make sense of current tendencies and trajectories. It attempts to draw together issues raised in the preceding sections in the context of some thoughts about the different levels of abstraction that may be involved in analysing the state.

The first - and most abstract - of these concerns what might be called the 'epochal' continuities. The issue here is one of studying a state which is structurally capitalist, patriarchal and racialised - in that it is articulated with a social formation (nationally and internationally) which is 'structured in dominance' around those relations. This is, of course, to say everything and nothing. But to move beyond that level - towards studying how the state plays a role in the (contradictory) reproduction of such social formations poses problems about periodisation and comparison. These issues are beyond the scope of this chapter, so I will merely note that one might treat the 'Keynesian' or expanded welfare state that is primarily associated with the 1945-1975 period as one formation within a longer periodisation (dating from the late nineteenth century) in which the state takes on, substantial and complex welfare functions within capitalist societies.[10] At the same time, the comparative analysis of welfare regimes alerts us to the possible 'structured diversity' of the ways in which states may perform that role (Esping-Anderson, 1990; Ginsburg, 1992; Cochrane & Clarke, eds 1993; Sainsbury, ed 1994).

Overlaying such questions of historical periodisation and the comparative study of welfare regimes should serve as a reminder that questions of state form are not the same as issues of the reach or direction of welfare policy. For example, commitments to managed full employment, the social insurance of unemployment or to the centrality of the family form have been exercised within fairly diverse forms of state organisation. The restructuring of the British 'welfare state' since the mid-1970s needs to be thought about on (at least) two dimensions. One is the changing social character of welfare policy towards residualism or minimalism; towards recommodification; towards 'methodological familialism'; towards an intensified racialisation and so on. The other concerns the state form - how social welfare is organised by and through the state. The two are not identical. It is possible to imagine an unreconstructed state apparatus (old bureau-professionalism) being treated as the machinery through which to implement residualism and recommodification - or any of the other contemporary trends. Equally, it is possible to imagine trusts administering a higher level of de-commodified 'citizenship rights'. This is not to say that affinities between policy direction and state form cannot be seen in both politics and practices - for example, quasi-markets have an ideological affinity with re-commodification - but these are not inextricably or inevitably linked.

As we have argued elsewhere (Newman & Clarke, 1994), the New Right onslaught on the welfare state was not only a matter of changing social policy but was also driven by the political objective of dislocating the institutional arrangements in which British social democracy was embedded and through which it was symbolised. The 'welfare state' settlements of post-war Britain articulated both relationships and representations of citizenship, the public good and public service which constituted a key element of the social democratic 'power bloc' that threatened the programme of economic, social and political recomposition (Clarke, 1995a and 1995b). In that respect, the 'anti-statism' of the New Right was not just a rhetorical cover for either the greater centralisation of power or the unleashing of market forces but an identification of the relationship between the form of the social democratic state and its ideological and political effects.

The issues make the question of state form a central one. As indicated earlier, I have reservations about whether the formulations of post-Fordism or the Schumpeterian Workfare State are adequate for these purposes, but their elaboration does point to some of the tendencies that must be addressed. However, these need to be assessed alongside other (and potentially contradictory) directions in the recomposition of the British state. So, the post-Fordist concern with the 'hollowing out' of the nation state needs to be set alongside the concentration of executive power; decentralisation (both spatial and delegatory) alongside new forms of centralisation; 'contracting out' alongside monitoring, surveillance and evaluation and so on. One dominant concept for talking about shifts in the form of the state and its associated organisational forms has been that of 'fragmentation'. Like other post-Fordist concepts such as 'flexibility', I find fragmentation a little imprecise in that it attempts to unite a number of processes (decentralisation, delegation, devolution, sub-contracting, and more) in an overly general category. As a result, it is difficult to see anything but fragmentation (just as the world is full of flexibilities). But fragmentation as a concept gives a specific weight to centrifugal directions - the processes of splitting away from the centre (whether the nation state or the corporate 'core'). Hoggett's work stands as a reminder that there are also centripetal directions that need to be considered - the means by which strategic integration is exercised (or at least attempted).

I have a preference for thinking about these processes of reconstruction as *dispersal* rather than fragmentation for two reasons. The first is that it signals such processes as the effect of strategic calculation rather than natural or inevitable occurrences. That is to say, these are processes through which 'agency' is being distributed from and by a strategic centre. The state 'delegates' - through a variety of means - its authority to act in specified ways to subaltern organisations that are 'empowered' to act. The second reason for exploring the idea of dispersal is that it does not carry the intrinsically disintegrative connotations of fragmentation. It acts as a reminder that what is at issue are the relations of power that both underpin and act through the processes of dispersal (not least the means by which the centre attempts to maintain command while distributing power to the periphery). This stress on the 'relations of power' means that it is necessary to examine not just what sorts of power are 'held' in different places but also what the flows of power are that allocate positions and places in this field. It may, for example, be possible to trace the shifts in who exercises different types of decision-making power in specific policy fields (e.g. Winstanley et al., 1995), such redistributions need to be contextualised in the larger field of relations between the state and its subaltern organisations. It also means thinking about the power flows involved in enforcing and monitoring the exercise of such delegated agency.

Dispersal as a strategy of reconstruction has had a number of objectives. It aims to either by-pass or discipline the old institutional sediments of state organisational power - the 'bureau-professional' organisations of the welfare state. It subjects them , where they persist, both to power dispersed *beyond* them to the 'citizen-as-consumer' and to new forms of control from the centre through both fiscal discipline and methods of evaluation. It also aims to recruit them to the practice of 'self-discipline' through t he internalisation of financial and performance 'targets'. Finally, it aims to subject them to a field of relationships (usually quasi-competitive) which ensure behavioural, if not attitudinal, compliance with policy directions. There have been both vertical and horizontal shifts in the field of power. Each organisational 'agency' is positioned in a field of forces. The vertical axis aligns agencies as delegated authorities between the centralised power of the nation state and the 'consumer' power of the periphery while also subjecting them to more rigorous forms of financial and performance evaluation. The horizontal axis characteristically repositions them in a nexus of marketised or quasi-competitive relationships. Within this field of forces, agencies are typically given the 'freedom to manage' (Birchall et al., 1995).[11]

The 'freedom to manage' is a reminder that the dominant organisational agency and practical ideology of this dispersal is managerialism. Managerialism represents the intra- and inter-organisational mode of co-ordination that 'makes sense' of such dispersed power in a practical way. It actively seeks 'responsibility' and seeks to further disperse it as a corporate and individual good. It promises 'transparency' within a complex field of intra- and inter-organisational decision-making and performance. It is committed to the production of 'efficiency' in the pursuit of super-ordinate objectives. Managerialism is presented as the 'cement' that can hold together this dispersed organisational form of the state and, in its 'customer' orientation, claims to be able to rep-resent and service an individuated 'public' (Clarke, 1995b). Managerialised relations aim to provide the 'discipline' necessary for efficient organisation, particularly in relation to the claims of welfare professionalism for 'discretionary judgement'. They simul-taneously articulate a new basis for 'discretion' as a managerialist rather than professional calculus - the freedom to 'do the right thing' (Clarke & Newman, 1993a; Clarke, 1995a).

We have witnessed striking changes in the organisational form of the state and the way state power works. Much analysis has framed these changes in terms of the retreat or withdrawal of the state - pointing to a diminished public sector operating in the context of a mixed economy. In this view, the 'state' is now main-ly conceived of as a combination of policy making and financing functions increasingly separated from 'service delivery'. Nevertheless, I think it can be argued that far from being shifts towards a 'rolling back' of the state, these changes involve a 'rolling out' of state power but in new, dispersed, forms. These new forms have the objective of promoting integrative relation-ships which both cross and reorganise the conventional bound-aries of public and private (or state and non-state). Dispersal engages more 'agencies' and 'agents' into the field of state power, 'empowering' them through its delegatory mechanisms and sub-jecting them to processes of regulation, surveillance and evalua-tion. This process brings the contemporary state form closer to what might be described as the 'Foucauldian' ideal, relying less on direct control through state apparatuses of the conventional kind and more on 'productive subjection'.[12]

At this point, though, it is important to stop and insert a brief health warning. The Foucaldian ideal does have some dangerous tendencies towards idealism. Too many of the analyses of the pro-ductivity of power and discursive subjection have tended to treat such strategies as though they worked rather than as *attempts to achieve* their desired results. It is, I think, important to insist that 'intentions' are not always realised, attempted 'subjections' are not always accomplished and 'discursive strategies' do not always achieve their objectives. This is an issue at the micro-level (organisations persistently fail to produce the 'ideal' worker and new technologies still have a few 'bugs') and at the macro-level. If this is a new field of state power, it is also a rather 'leaky system'.

It is, then, important to treat dispersal and managerialised co-ordination as strategies rather than accomplishments. I have tried to stress 'aims' and 'objectives' rather than assuming too readily that these are outcomes since they are both contested and contradictory. Not everyone wishes to be empowered through these processes of dispersal, while others treat being empowered all too seriously or assert that the empowerment being experienced is all too partial. Managerialisation has only achieved partial and uneven 'disciplining' of the old bureau-professional regimes, effecting localised sites of (particularly professional) resistance to corporate incorporation (Prichard & Willmott, 1995). Neither the attempt to delegate responsibility nor the effort to represent decision making as the domain of technocratic managerialism have been entirely successful - particularly, but not only, in the case of the NHS. The perverse consequence of dispersal is that while it aims at the breaking up of the institutionalised centres of power (and power bloc formation) characteristic of the old state form, it also multiplies new sites of resistance through the increase in the number of decision-making nodal points. I do not wish to end by overstating the significance of such resistances, since they are often localised and fragmentary (dispersed, in fact). Although they may fall some way short of a 'counter-hegemonic bloc', they are a necessary reminder that the recomposition of the form of the state is less than smoothly functional.

One way of thinking about the achievements and limitations of these processes of state restructuring is through the idea of 'conditional indeterminacy' - the bounded spaces in which agents are 'empowered' to act. The managerialised dispersal of state power clearly aims to construct new spaces and boundaries of indeterminacy: those arenas of decision-making now allocated to 'consumer choice' (or the choices of proxy consumers) and to the 'managerial prerogative' rather than being defined by centralised policy-making or professional judgement. These 'freedoms' are conditional - framed by policy and resource constraints from the centre and acted upon within a 'managerial calculus'. Nevertheless, there are other conditions which make such sites of decision-making more unstable and these have more to do with the relationships between the state and the 'social' rather than the internal structure of power relations within the state. To use a military metaphor, one might view dispersal as the establishment of 'salients' (or bridgeheads) beyond the walls or boundaries of the 'old state': the creation of new sites of articulation between state power and civil society. In this process, the delegation of state power 'empowers' a range of agents who are not themselves part of the formal institutions of the state - they are associations, groups, corporate entities and individual 'consumers' who are located in civil society (and who gain part of their legitimacy precisely from not being the state). Nevertheless, these 'salients' are also vulnerable to co-option by local alliances and interests. In part, this has to do with the limitations of managerialism itself. Notwithstanding its penchant for missions and visions, managerialism is essentially a subaltern function, plying its trade in the service of others' super-ordinate goals. As a consequence, it is vulnerable to competing definitions of the 'service' mission that may be articulated by professional groups, user groups or other 'lay' perspectives.[13] The attempt to control the conditions of 'indeterminacies' in these new forms derives in part from the perception that the old institutional arrangements had themselves become co-opted or corrupted by undesirable social objectives or ideologies.

One objective of the recomposition of the state was to discipline and control the 'liberal' tendencies of welfare bureau-professionalism, in particular the vulnerability of 'front-line' workers to the demands of different groups for rights or services. In part, the break-up of the old welfare settlements was driven by movements which insisted that forms of inequality that had previously been consigned to the status of 'extra-social' (for example, ethnicity, gender, sexuality, disability) were, in fact, social phenomena and required social reparation.[14] Welfare policy and practice was unevenly co-opted by such 'socialising' analyses and demands (for example, in commitments to 'anti-discriminatory practice' and equal opportunities policies). Becoming business-like was expected to restrain this socialising tendency towards 'ologies and isms' that was visible in the old welfare state. Managerialised dispersal may have changed some of the conditions in which such issues now appear (subjecting them to the requirements of business planning , market positioning and fiscal rectitude). It may also have produced a new dominant form of constructing the relationship between welfare services and social differentiation as one of 'managed diversity'. Despite these shifts, the tensions involved remain potent ones for the organisation of social welfare, as well as for the analysis of social policy. In particular, they are the basis for continuing resistance to the conception of an individuated - or consumerised - public as the recipient of welfare services.

What I have tried to sketch in this last section is a way of rethinking the relationship between the state and social welfare after the welfare state. It has focused on the reorganisation of state power in the processes of dispersal, involving new relations of power along vertical and horizontal axes in which it is possible to make sense of the combined presence of centralisation and decentralisation, more 'mixed' economies and marketised conditions of welfare provision. Managerialism is a central feature of this process of dispersal as the practical ideology - or organisational cement - that embodies the ideas and practices that sustain integration alongside dispersal. Managerialism is also central to the construction of new sites of 'conditional indeterminacy', since it provides the decision-making calculus which is supposed to frame the choices made by newly empowered agents. Nevertheless, the strategy of dispersal is more unstable in practice than in its conception. In part this derives from the limits of managerialism but also from the inability of the strategy to resolve underlying tensions about the nature of the 'social' in social welfare.

These tentative suggestions about the shape and direction of welfare state restructuring are, in one sense, less important than the overall argument of this paper about the centrality of the state to social policy analysis. The breaking up of the 'old' welfare state has drawn attention away from the problem of the state towards more limited analyses of policy, finance and service delivery. However, I have tried to argue that changes to the form of the state should not be subsumed under the heading of 'changes to service delivery systems'. Mishra has warned of the dangers of taking such organisational changes at their face value, arguing against 'talking about 'management', 'adaptation' and 'flexibility' as if these were politically neutral measures through which policy managers could operate a 'rational', if somewhat circumscribed, social welfare system' (1990, p107). It is important for the analysis of social policy to avoid treating such changes as if they were simply new technical solutions to the problems of organising social welfare provision. If they are detached from the analysis of the state and state power, whether as sectors or quasi-markets, it becomes increasingly hard to make sense of the relationship between forms of 'service delivery' and the 'social' character and consequences of social policy. There is a danger that two decades of New Right 'anti-statism' will leave the analysis of social policy unable to pose questions about the changing form and strategies of state power. The promise of 'welfare without politics' is a neo-conservative illusion and one which should not be reproduced in the study of 'welfare without the state'.

Notes

1. This is a slightly revised version of the paper presented at the Social Policy Association annual conference in Sheffield, July 1995. It has benefited from comments made there and subsequent suggestions from the editors of this volume. It arises out of collaborative work with a number of people and I am particularly grateful to Janet Newman, Allan Cochrane and Eugene McLaughlin for their continued support for my obsessions (although they are, of course, not responsible for them). This is also one of a series of working papers which explores a number of ideas in the transition between the arguments of Clarke, Cochrane & McLaughlln (eds) Managing Social Policy (Sage, 1994) and a forthcoming book being written by Janet Newman and myself.

2. At the very least, there is a continuing difficulty about whether this refers to a type of state or states which have taken on so me welfare functions. Since welfare states are not clear - or unified - organisational entities (involving some but not all of the state apparatuses or agencies as well as different 'levels' of the state) such conceptual clarity is rather difficult to achieve. See also Cochrane (1993).

3. This has been one of the ways in which the new right populism has been manifested in practice, allowing the use of political power to 'represent' the people against an over-powerful state by turning the 'public sector' into the object of discipline, reform and greater control (Clarke, 1995b).

4. It has, though, performed a significant ideological function, providing a reference point against which welfare reforms have been measured. Such measurements are various, ranging from neo-liberal complaints about the 'failure' to privatise to social democratic warnings of 'creeping' privatisation. I am tempted to suggest that its main effect has been to make reforms which fall short of full blown privatisation look like 'reasonable compromises'. Such a combination of threatened reform and less dramatic policy has been a recurrent feature of neo-conservative 'ideological politics' in recent times.

5. It may be that such shifts are better identified as potential rather than real, given the relatively limited capacity of state agencies to operationalise them. Nevertheless, the elaboration of 'packages of care' around the assumption of the availability of

informal care carries the potential of extending 'labour discipline' through 'contracting' carers, assessing the 'quality of care' and even 'certifying' carers.

6. Although this is not the place to go into it, there are enormous difficulties about making both past and present fit the formulations of such binary theorising, see inter alia, Sayer & Walker, 1992; and Clarke, 1996.

7. It thus misses one of the main conditions for the oscillations between 'hands off' and 'hands on' government, visible in both the NHS and the Prison Service, in the shifting definitions of what counts as 'operational management'.

8. One need not be a Foucauldian to recognise that the field of the social in social welfare was composed out of complex and cross-cutting classificatory schemas (or discourses) which produced - as well as reproduced - a multiplicity of 'subject positions'.

9. The managerialism that we have come to know and love is one which has its roots in specific national formations (particularly the USA, see Clarke & Newman, 1993a) and which, despite its undoubted globalising ambitions, is not universal.

10. For reasons of brevity, I am not repeating the phraseology of 'capitalist, patriarchal and racialised' on each occasion but see no reason to think that they do not apply, albeit in the context of specific national formations.

11. There are a number of side benefits that are also sought in these changes - in particular, the dispersal of decision-making responsibilities away from the centre through the language of 'operational autonomy' and 'managerial freedom'.

12. Although this should not be taken so far as to suggest that more old-fashioned methods, not least key features of what we used to call 'juridico-repressive apparatuses,' have been abandoned.

13. It should be noted that this is not a claim about the 'progressive possibilities' of managerialism, since this indeterminacy is, at least, equally open to co-option by representatives of local or national capital (especially in the 'partnership' mode).

14. Some of these arguments about the crisis of the 'social' in social welfare are taken up and expanded in Clarke (1995b). I am particularly grateful to Gail Lewis for encouraging me to think about them.

References

Birchall, J. Pollitt, C. & Putnam, K. (1995) 'Freedom to manage? The experiences of NHS Trusts, grant-maintained schools and voluntary transfers of public housing', Paper to UK Political Studies Association Annual Conference, York, April.

Burrows, R. & Loader, B. (eds) (1994) Towards a Post-Fordist Welfare State, London, Routledge.

Charlesworth, J. Clarke, J. & Cochrane, A. (1996) 'Tangled webs? Managing local mixed economies of care' Public Administration, vol. 74, pp67-88.

Clarke, J. (1991) New Times and Old Enemies: Essays on Cultural Studies and America, London, Harper Collins/Routledge.

Clarke, J. (1994) 'Capturing the customer? Consumerism and social welfare', Paper for ESRC seminar on 'Conceptualising Consumption Issues', University of Lancaster.

Clarke, J. (1995a) 'Doing the right thing? Managerialism and social welfare', Paper to ESRC seminar on 'Professionals in Late Modernity', Imperial College.

Clarke, J. (1995b) 'Public nightmares and communitarian dreams: the crisis of the social in social welfare', Paper to Theory, Culture and Society Conference, Berlin.

Clarke, J. (1996) 'After Social Work?', in N. Parton (ed) Social Theory, Social Change and Social Work, London, Routledge.

Clarke, J. Cochrane, A. & McLaughlin, E. (eds) (1994) Managing Social Policy, London, Sage.

Clarke, J. & Newman, J. (1993a) 'The right to manage: a second managerial revolution?', Cultural Studies vol.7 no.3, pp427-441.

Clarke, J. & Newman, J. (1993b) 'Managing to survive: dilemmas of changing organisational forms in the public sector', in N. Deakin & R. Page (eds) The Costs of Welfare, Aldershot, Avebury.

Clarke, J. & Newman, J. (forthcoming) The Managerial State: Power, Politics and Ideology in the Remaking of Social Welfare, London, Sage.

Cochrane, A. (1993) 'Comparative approaches and social policy.', in A. Cochrane & J.Clarke (eds) Comparing Welfare States, London, Sage.

Esping-Anderson, G. (1990) The Three Worlds of Welfare Capitalism, Cambridge, Polity Press.

Ginsburg, N. (1992) Divisions of Welfare, London, Sage.

Green, D. (1993) Reinventing Civil Society: Rediscovering Welfare without Politics, London, Institute of Economic Affairs.

Hoggett, P. (1990) 'Modernisation, political strategy and the welfare state', Studies in Decentralisation and Quasi-Markets, No.2, Bristol, SAUS.

Hudson, B. (1994) Making Sense of Markets in Health and Social Care, Sunderland, Business Education Publishers.

Jessop, B. (1994) 'The transition to post-Fordism and the Schumpeterian workfare state', in R. Burrows, & B. Loader (eds) Towards a Post-Fordist Welfare State, London, Routledge.

Johnson, N.(ed) (1995) Private Markets in Health and Welfare: an International Perspective, Oxford, Berg.

Lawson, R. (1993) 'The new technology of management in the personal social services', in P.Taylor-Gooby & R. Lawson (eds) (1993) Markets and Managers, Buckingham, Open University Press.

Le Grand, J. & Bartlett, W. (1993a) 'The theory of quasi-markets', in J. Le Grand & W. Bartlett (eds) Quasi-Markets and Social Policy, Basingstoke, Macmillan.

Le Grand, J. & Bartlett, W. (1993b) 'Quasi-markets and social policy -the way forward?', in J. Le Grand & W. Bartlett (eds) Quasi-Markets and Social Policy, Basingstoke, Macmillan.

Lee, P. & Raban, C. (1988) Social Theory and Social Policy, London, Routledge.

Loney, M. et al., (eds) (1986) The State or the Market? London, Sage.

Mackintosh, M. (1995) 'Competition and contracting in selective social provision', European Journal of Development Research vol.7, no.1, pp26-52.

Mishra, R. (1990) The Welfare State in Capitalist Society, Hemel Hempstead, Harvester Wheatsheaf.

Murray, R. (1991) 'The State After Henry', Marxism Today, May, pp22-27.

Pollitt, C. (1993) Managerialism and the Public Services, Oxford, Basil Blackwell (second edition).

Newman, J. & Clarke, J. (1994) 'Going about our business? The managerialization of public services', in J. Clarke, A. Cochrane & E. McLaughlin (eds) Managing Social Policy, London, Sage.

Prichard, C. & Willmott, H. (1995) 'Tactics and targets: the managerial challenge to professional locales in UK universities', Paper to ESRC seminar on 'Professionals in Late Modernity', Imperial College, London.

Reed, M. (1994) 'Expert power and organisation in high modernity: an empirical review and theoretical synthesis', Paper presented to ESRC seminar on 'Professionals in Late Modernity', Cardiff.

Rustin, M. (1994) 'Flexibility in higher education' in R. Burrows & B. Loader (eds) Towards a Post-Fordist Welfare State London, Routledge.

Sayer, A. & Walker, R. (1992) The New Social Economy, Oxford, Basil Blackwell.

Sainsbury, D. (1994) Gendering Welfare States, London, Sage.

Swann, D. (1988) The Retreat of the State: Deregulation and Privatisation in the UK and the US, New York and London, Harvester Wheatsheaf.

Taylor-Gooby, P. & Lawson, R. (1993) 'Where we go from here; The new order in welfare', in P.Taylor-Gooby & R. Lawson (eds) Markets and Managers, Buckingham, Open University Press.

Waine, B. & Cutler, T. (1994) Managing the Welfare State, London, Berg.

Williams, F. (1989) Social Policy: A Critical Introduction, Cambridge, Polity Press.

Williams, F. (1994) 'Social relations, welfare and the post-Fordism debate', in R. Burrows & B. Loader (eds) Towards a Post-Fordist Welfare State, London, Routledge.

Winstanley, D. Sorabjl, D. & Dawson, S. (1995) 'When the pieces don't fit: a stakeholder power matrix to analyse public sector restructuring', Public Money and Management, April-June, pp. 19-26.

Wistow, G. Knapp, M. Hardy, B. & Allen, C. (1994) Social Care in a Mixed Economy, Buckingham, Open University Press.

3 The Canary in the Coalmine: Issues Facing the Voluntary Sector

Marilyn Taylor[1]

Introduction

The voluntary sector has been the poor relation of social policy analysis since Beveridge wrote his treatise on Voluntary Action in 1948. And yet, as the boundaries between public and private shift, an understanding of a sector which 'is neither public nor private ' (Rein, 1989) becomes increasingly important. It is not only its position as a non-profit, non-governmental sector between state and commerce which makes it pivotal in the analysis of social policy, but also its position between the public, organised world and the personal, informal networks of family and friendship, which are essential to welfare. As such, it can be seen as the 'canary in the coalmine' of social policy - an indicator of the feasibility and consequences of change.

To generalise about the voluntary sector is a hazardous business. It contains within it everything from the large household name charity, through the major environmental campaigning organisations, to a local arts centre run by a minority ethnic group, the darts team or the lunch club round the corner. It is a sector whose diversity - of motivation, role, activity, values and structure - defies any neat categorisation (Kendall & Knapp,

1995). This diversity has given it an ambivalent role throughout the history of welfare: as the carrier of established power and status but also as the instrument of dissent; as innovator but also as a source of resistance to change; as advocate of state intervention but also as the guardian of independence; as benevolent 'do-gooder' but also as a vehicle for solidarity against oppression (Taylor & Kendall, forthcoming).

Evers (1993) has described the voluntary sector as the place where the different rationales of market, state and community intersect . As a consequence of its intermediate position, the voluntary sector[2] is a place of contradictory forces and rationales, mediating between multiple stakeholders, whose interests have to be continually renegotiated. Operating across political, economic and social spheres, many of its organisational and political dilemmas are likely to be more widely shared as networks and alliances are forged across organisational and sectoral boundaries to produce a complex and multi-layered picture of welfare for the twenty-first century.

This chapter will take three of the issues that are central to the reformulation of welfare policy at present - consumerism, accountability and resources. It will examine them from the point of view of the voluntary sector, not as a special case, but as an indicator of challenges that are likely to face welfare as a whole.

Consumerism

The disenchantment with what were seen as 'producer-led' public services by the end of the 1970s is well-documented, as is the argument for consumer- and 'needs-led' provision which has influenced many of the reforms since that time. The resulting challenges for welfare have been delivering choice in new welfare markets and strengthening the user voice.

Delivering choice

The introduction of compulsory competitive tendering in some services and contracting out in others has offered opportunities for the voluntary sector to develop a major role in service delivery, opportunities that analysts of the voluntary sector had themselves been urging on government for some time (Wolfenden, 1978; Gladstone, 1979; Hadley & Hatch, 1981). These analysts saw 'welfare pluralism' as a way of combining universalism (through state funding) with the values they associated with the voluntary sector: choice, flexibility and being close to the consumer and community.

For many organisations in the UK, the reforms offer an opportunity for grants to be turned into properly costed service agreements. Some see opportunities to expand into new areas. Others, who have felt excluded from the patronage of the grants system, e.g. black and minority ethnic groups, may find new systems more accessible and transparent. New markets in welfare have also opened the way to a range of user-led services in the form of community-based housing associations, centres for independent living and other services and facilities run by service users themselves.

But the new 'quasi-markets' in welfare have raised a number of questions (Taylor & Hoggett, 1994a), reflecting longer-standing experience in the US (Smith & Lipsky, 1993). Firm evidence is hard to find as yet, but there is concern, for example, that markets in the UK will favour the larger providers, or will transform the smaller provider into a more professionalised, mainstream organisation, away from the business it knows best and is best equipped to provide (Prins, 1995). Commercial markets - from newspapers to beefburgers - demonstrate the power of the large enterprise over the small and the power of advertising to manipulate preferences. Baldock (1993) reports that those welfare systems in Germany and elsewhere where the state has long financed non-profit organisations to deliver services are dominated by large 'semi-monopolies'. In the UK, larger charities have the advantage in the new markets of being better known, better able to bring in the necessary expertise and better able to bear the considerable transaction costs attached to contracting. New not-for-profit trusts, formed by local authorities to move their own provision into the independent sector, are potentially even more powerful competitors.

Does this matter? If diversity, support and choice for the consumer are real goals for welfare, it does. Little will be achieved for the service user if large statutory service empires are replaced by large independent empires, whether they represent the diversification of commercial empires, the reconstitution of public bodies in independent clothing or the expansion of traditional charities. Also at risk in a welfare market are the 'complementary' roles played by voluntary organisations against a background of state provision. Prevention, mutual support, development and a 'watchdog' role have been supported by government funders in the past and taken the pressure off mainstream services. Will they continue to find support?

Hoyes et al. (1993) suggest that devolved purchaser structures are the most likely to achieve easy access for smaller providers. There is a strong argument for purchasers to take some responsibility for the development of their local voluntary sector 'market'. Although market development was a major feature of early government guidance to local authorities in the field of community care, however, financial constraints have pushed this to the edge of purchaser agendas (Lewis et al., 1995). There are exceptions (Deakin, 1994), but they are most likely to be in authorities which have already invested in their local voluntary and community sectors. Where there is no history of such investment the prospects for choice and diversity are much bleaker.

Managing and supporting diversity - of size and function - will require organisational innovation with and beyond the voluntary sector. Structures and networks are needed which support smaller, community-based organisations by delivering economies of scale, expertise and support, while allowing organisations to remain participative, responsive and light on their feet (Taylor et al., 1995). This, of course, is the challenge that the 'management gurus' of industry have been addressing for some years in their search for consumer responsiveness (Peters & Waterman, 1982). It is not a new challenge to a sector which already has within it a diversity of federal organisations. The model of national professional umbrella bodies, like Age Concern, offering support to autonomous local organisations run largely by volunteers, is relatively common. Recent years have also seen a growth in franchising within the sector. But changes in charity law and the pressures of contracting have raised issues about legal liability which could act as a counter pressure towards centralisation of structure and direction.

The language of future welfare delivery is one of networks and alliances as opposed to bounded organisations with a clearly defined 'inside' and 'outside' (Clegg, 1990; Taylor & Hoggett, 1994b) - a new and flexible way of approaching old co-ordination problems. There are new opportunities for joint working both within and across the new institutional environment in welfare, while models of 'flexible specialisation' in the private sector suggest that successful enterprises can be developed through supportive networks. The sector also has a long tradition of co-ordinating agencies - councils for voluntary service and similar bodies - which have provided support to smaller organisations and a forum for co-ordination across the breadth of the sector. Larger charities could play an important role in supporting and sub-contracting to smaller independent local groups. Local authorities are well-placed to play a crucial 'enabling' role. It is also important that as purchasers, they and health authorities recognise the interdependence of local organisations (Taylor et al., 1995). The failure of one organisation to survive or the diversion of key actors, from whatever sector, into new roles and activities can destabilise complex networks of provision.

Strengthening voice

Effective choices require informed and confident users. The voluntary sector has enhanced the user voice through providing information and support, one-to-one advocacy and through campaigning. The outlook for these activities is uncertain. Taylor Gooby (1994) and Kendall and Knapp (forthcoming) variously suggest that funding for advice, self-help and community development in the voluntary sector is in decline. But there is evidence of some new money to support user involvement and the growth of user-based organisations has led to innovative new practice in self-advocacy and independent living schemes.

Service delivery will not be transformed solely through market choice, however well-informed and confident the user. As well as choice, service users want more control over the services they eventually receive. Purchasers and other funders (including the Lottery) are reinforcing this challenge by demanding that voluntary organisations have in place adequate user involvement policies.

But what exactly is user involvement? Recent research[3] suggests that, for many charities, it is the adoption of consumer policies based on best practice in business and aimed at increasing individual consumer rights. These are a considerable step forward and have forced a re-examination of service and professional cultures, especially where they are designed by and with service users and backed by advocacy services. But the consumerism of the market alone is inadequate to the demands of complex services that rely on trust and continuity between provider and user and that are often purchased through an intermediary. Contracting out lengthens chains of accountability and consumer preferences are still often defined, interpreted and analysed from above. A focus on individual consumer rights runs the risk of substituting contractual redress for effective service delivery (Clarke et al., 1994), with fear of litigation inhibiting creativity and risk - 'suer'- rather than user - led services. While consumer policies should be required, there fore, as a base-line of good practice, they are likely to be most effective in the context of strategies which give users a collective voice and encourage a continuing dialogue between user and provider.

Wann (1995) calls for policies which will put self-help at the core of the twenty-first century welfare state. Such policies require more fundamental changes yet in the nature of service delivery, with users involved in decision-making and governance, with more opportunities for user and community-led services, and with an emphasis on support and information which will allow service users to make their contribution as genuine partners rather than recipients. Ultimately, as users gain confidence, it is possible to envisage a future where many of the large charities will be moving towards user control.

Such policies will challenge the professional control of services but they also force traditional charities to re-examine the place of altruism in their mission, and to find ways of rechannelling, even confronting, the commitment of people who have given time and energy over many years to their cause. Some organisations have begun to pick their way down this thorny path and there is considerable scope for 'promoting a general sense of common interests between service providers and service users' (Morris, 1994). For others - Gutch (1995) cites the medical research charities - the issue has scarcely surfaced.

In some policy areas, user-led organisations have now established a track record alongside traditional providers: community-based housing associations are one example (although still very much in the minority among housing associations). We do not all wish to run the services we use, however. There is also the ever-present danger of 'dumping' where money is tight - devolving not power but responsibility for diminishing budgets. Services run on the margins of the labour market will not empower users. User organisations often prefer to focus on providing the support, information and advocacy which is vital to allow users more control in existing welfare provision and which takes a 'whole-person' view rather than focusing on a particular service.

Like many small but successful entities, user-based organisations have to face the challenges of growth and professionalisation if they decide to take on new roles, and of changed relationships with their own highly diverse service users (Taylor et al., 1995). Many of the larger charities were started by carers and some by users, but they have grown almost beyond recognition and are now being challenged by their own user constituency.

The challenges of user involvement and control are likely to require organisational innovation, with fundamentally new approaches to decision-making and organisational structure offering service users a variety of routes to empowerment. The structures required by Charity Law seem increasingly ill-suited to this imperative, not only because they exclude potential beneficiaries from trusteeship but because of the difficulty of dispersing liability, authority and power.

Accountability

In the perfect market, the provider of services and goods is regulated by demand. If an organisation does not provide what enough consumers want, it goes out of business. In the imperfect reality of welfare provision, services cannot be regulated in this way. The service user is not necessarily the purchaser - demand is mediated through third parties, e.g. the care manager or the GP. Continuity or complexity of care may preclude a simple 'exit' to another service; services are most urgently required when potential users are at their most vulnerable. For these and other reasons, some form of accountability is required beyond the individual service user.

Under the welfare state umbrella, the professional ethos was seen as a neutral guarantee of safety, quality and protection at times of vulnerability (operational accountability), the democratic system as the ultimate authority for choices about priorities (political accountability). Post-1979 that confidence has been abandoned and both systems have been replaced largely by a managerialist ethos (Clarke et al., 1994). A quangocracy of unelected bodies has been created to take on many public functions; direct service provision has been replaced by an increasing emphasis on regulation; an audit explosion (Power, 1994) has, with astonishing effectiveness, established efficiency and economy as the ultimate values in welfare provision. Where does this leave the voluntary sector?

An old law

Those voluntary organisations which are charities - some 180,000 - are subject to Charity Law. This has the function of protecting the donor, by ensuring that the money given goes to the cause for which it is given and not to profits, to activities outside the Trust Deed or charitable purposes as defined under the legislation, or to fraudulent purposes. Since charities benefit from tax privileges, it also protects the taxpayer, through all the above and through some restrictions on political activity. Voluntary organisations constituted as Industrial and Provident Associations or Friendly Societies do not have the same tax privileges, but probity and accountability to members are protected under the relevant legislation.

Recent reforms have tightened accountability, reduced grey areas and raised awareness of the liabilities that Trustees have. However, a law designed in the sixteenth century and amended only partially since that time is ill-suited to meet current needs.

Changes in fund-raising methods coupled with a concern to avoid potential restrictions on political activities have led respectively to the proliferation of trading companies and campaigning arms. Private competitors, whether against charity shops on the high street or unfair competition in the care market, have begun to question the tax exemption privileges of charities; and service users are questioning a law which, insofar as it prevents potential beneficiaries from becoming trustees, can exclude user-led organisations from tax privileges.

Mulgan and Landry (1995) discuss these anomalies in detail and propose that charitable status be attached to activity rather than organisational form. Beyond that they argue that the demands of probity are equivalent to those made of business - no more but no less. There is certainly an argument for separating tax exemption issues from issues of protecting the donor and ensuring probity, and requiring different forms of accountability for each. However, this proposal begs questions about the nature of public accountability in the twenty-first century welfare state and the definition of public benefit. What should the tax payer and citizen require?

Accountability to purchasers

Government, national and local, provides 40 per cent of voluntary sector income (Salamon & Anheier, 1996). With the move from grant- aid to contracts, the financial relationship between statutory agencies and voluntary organisations has moved from one of investment or endowment to one of purchase which has the potential to transform the nature of statutory voluntary relations. It is still too early to reach confident conclusions, but there is some concern that the dismantling of service empires may be confounded by the growth of regulation empires as authorities try to contain the element of risk in third party relationships or bow to increasingly centralised agendas.

In the US, Bardach comments that regulation appears to be 'governed by a ratchet mechanism that allows it to move upward but never downward'. He argues that protective regulation is by its nature clumsy and 'unprepared to deal with the new, the subtle, the ambiguous or the unusual - and it will .. be oppressively constricting and costly when it does make the attempt' (1989, pp223-4). The new, the subtle, the ambiguous and the unusual (and the risky) are the territories where the best of the voluntary sector operates and which are essential to a social ecology that can respond to change (Harman, 1993). Tensions between safety and flexibility will need to be resolved imaginatively if we are to

avoid a welfare environment of clones, either as a result of purchaser and inspectorate demands (what DiMaggio & Powell
(1983) refer to as 'coercive isomorphism') or through a 'mimetic'
or 'normative isomorphism', whereby organisations adjust their
operations in order to become more attractive to funders.

The evidence on specification and regulation is mixed so far.
Richardson (1995) finds heartening evidence that purchasers are
prepared to involve providers in specification and that contracts
with voluntary sector providers are not forcing them to change
their operations, but there are also counter-examples (Lewis,
1993). Voluntary organisations have taken the initiative in developing processes of evaluation, monitoring and quality assurance
on their own terms. Research in the commercial world has
demonstrated that trust can be built into flexible contract relationships (Ring & Van de Ven, 1992; Kenney & Florida, 1988), while
debates about the new economics and social audit may offer
authoritative alternatives to current monitoring systems. Deakin et
al. (1994), in the most comprehensive survey so far, report a
spectrum of contract relationships across public authorities from
tight to loose. Nonetheless , the success of the new managerialism in the public sector (Clarke et al., 1994), the advance of cer-
tification, new European regulations, and even patient and consumer charters (especially those designed by government departments or purchasers), have the potential to bring in by the back
door the trappings of bureaucracy that were so publicly thrown
out of the front. They can also be insensitive to the resource constraints under which many small organisations operate and the
possibility that different standards may apply to different kinds of
organisation.

Public accountability, Day and Klein (1987) argue, requires a
common currency of explanations and assumptions between
those who give and those who hold to account. The new forms
of accountability are based on assumptions which are rarely, if
ever, placed under public scrutiny (Power, 1994). Lukes' third face
of power (1974) now wears the guise of the auditor. For voluntary
organisations, this creates enormous tensions. Voluntary organisations can be described as 'value-rational' organisations
(Rothschild-Whitt, 1979), which ultimately justify their actions,
not by the bottom line, nor by the mandate of the electorate and
the legislature, but by appeal to common values among their multiple stakeholders. The search for 'common currencies of expla-
nation' or shared frameworks of meaning and ways of converting
them into committed practice is a central organisational task
(Paton, 1996), and one that cannot be suborned to the new
managerialism without changing the nature of the organisation
and its potential to mobilise resources and energies.

The appearance of corporate responsibility policies and social audit in parts of the private sector suggests an increasing recognition of multiple accountabilities and values even in the commercial world, while the expansion of shareholding through the public utilities has begun to bring some diversity of values into the annual shareholders' meeting (as, for example, in the 1995 AGM of British Gas), although very much at the margins and against considerable resistance. The challenge of reconciling increasingly diverse interests also emerges from post-Fordist and post-modernist analysis. In a political climate which lays increasing emphasis on 'partnership', handling a volatile and dynamic set of interests is likely to become commonplace both within and beyond the individual organisation (Taylor, 1996). A recognition of multiple accountability offers a new transparency and new possibilities for learning and growth. But it is not a panacea. It can be horrendously difficult to manage and negotiate, as the experience of many a voluntary organisation will testify. It is easy to lose sight of 'the task' in managing the process (Landry et al., 1985; Batsleer, 1995). Nor does the notion of multiple accountability change the fact that partners go into such arrangements with very different powers and resources. The rhetoric of partnership will not cause these imbalances to disappear.

Accountability to citizens

Day and Klein (1987) identified two major sources for the common currency that they see as a prerequisite for accountability: stewardship (rooted in medieval systems of estate management) and the Western democratic system. The previous section demonstrates the persistent appeal of stewardship. Democracy on the other hand seems to be in chronic decline. The globalisation of capital, along with New Right ideologies which see democracy as an outdated project, offers the prospect of a 'society of possessive, alienated, isolated individuals, at the mercy of capital' (Curry & Zarate, 1995, p151). Post-Fordist and post-modernist analyses highlight the rise of interest group politics divorced from a 'grand narrative' which can weigh their competing claims (Taylor Gooby, 1995). They further underline the growth of an identity politics which, in confronting marginalisation and exclusion, may risk colluding with their recreation in another form, trapping excluded groups into the competitive expression of disadvantage or channelling them into the provision of highly specific, poorly resourced services (Meekosha, 1993).

Voluntary organisations can be seen as an embodiment of a system of special interests. If welfare is to move into the indeterminate area between public and private, then the particularism of the sector, with its potential for exclusivity and schism (Taylor & Hoggett, 1994b) will be reflected on a much wider level. But the other face of particularism is diversity and as participants in a broader democratic structure, voluntary organisations have had a valuable role to play in stimulating and informing public debate, and in giving a voice to dissent and to 'outgroups' in society. Mulgan and Landry (1995) define this role in a market framework: as contributing to the free competition of ideas and social innovation, making it more likely that society will innovate, evolve and discover truth. On this basis, they argue for the removal of political constraints on charity. Others argue that, as voluntary organisations become 'agents' of government and providers in the marketplace, their political role is being compromised and they are being transformed into a new breed of not-for-profit organisations without the roots and values generally associated with the sector (Knight, 1993).

The depoliticization of the voluntary sector, whether by law or incorporation, is a denial of one of its essential features. But the apparent depoliticization of the state adds a further dimension. How is the political voice of the sector to be heard when power and agency are increasingly dispersed (see the chapter by Clarke in this volume)? The political vacuum left by the erosion of demo cracy, especially at local level, means that, rather than being a champion of diverse interests in a democratic state, the sector is likely to be turned in on itself in a cacophony of competing interests. There will be little hope of locating the sources of power which need to be addressed for real change to take place and even less potential for developing the more widely shared frameworks of meaning against which political progress can, with however much difficulty, be made and measured.

There is an alternative scenario. In the 1970s and 1980s, the state, especially at local level, played a role in developing political pluralism, by supporting many of the new organisations that were pressing for change - tenants' and community organisations, black and ethnic minority organisations, women's organisations, and so on - either with funding or development workers. Over the years, a variety of initiatives have been introduced to encourage participation in aspects of local government. The early 1990s have given voluntary sector, community, and user and carer involvement a new impetus through demands for 'partnership' in fields as diverse as community care planning and commissioning, area-based regeneration (through City Challenge and then the

Single Regeneration Budget Challenge Fund), and local Agenda 21 strategies (following the Rio summit).

Voluntary organisations have always been embedded in local policy networks (consider, for example, the local Round Table or Rotary). But experience suggests that the new opportunities for partnership carry within them many tensions. First, there is evidence that some voluntary organisations are defined out of planning and commissioning processes in community care because, as potential providers, they have a vested interest and can potentially capture the market. While this is undoubtedly a danger that needs addressing, the baby should not be thrown out with the bathwater. Such a policy reduces the role of many organisations to its economic dimensions, ignoring the political and social dimensions which they bring to a rounded concept of welfare. As sole guardian of consumer and community interests, the purchaser becomes very powerful. User organisations sometimes need other allies.

Secondly, the rhetoric of partnership belies the reality. Partnership is difficult and time-consuming. Many voluntary organisations lack the resources and status 'to be present in the intensive, regular contact points through which policy communities are knitted together' (Kendall & 6, 1994), especially if they are smaller organisations with limited resources (Russell et al., 1995). For many small organisations, opportunities to participate in consultations and partnerships are a mixed blessing. They make heavy demands on organisations whose limited resources are already stretched, especially where organisations which are seen as the only route of access to excluded populations. For many community representatives there is also the very real danger of co-option into official agendas and away from community priorities.

Thirdly, as we have seen, partnership tends to reproduce existing patterns of power. Although voluntary organisations are increasingly involved in the growing number of 'collaborative' and consultative networks which influence and legitimate policy, they are unlikely to be in the more 'entrepreneurial' networks where the real action is (Reid & Iqbal, unpublished) and may feel with some justification that the returns have been far less than the energy expended (Hastings et al., 1996). Official procedures, perceptions, expectations and language dominate partnerships and disadvantage community and voluntary sector partners (Roberts et al., 1996). The drive to consensus disempowers the diverse (Hastings et al., 1996). Whatever power local authorities have lost, they still retain considerable power in comparison with others around the partnership table.

The positives of new partnership and participation opportunities are that they have raised expectations and organisational
capacity - although the costs of disappointed expectations can be
high. There has been real progress in the development of consul-
tati on with users in some areas. Some urban regeneration partnerships have also given people 'hands-on' power, in providing
the opportunity for them to develop and implement projects of
their choice and become local social entrepreneurs (MacFarlane,
1993). It may be that the language of 'partnership' has been best
realised by local authorities in areas where they have limited competence - criminal justice, health, environmental planning and
quango watch initiatives - perhaps because the balance of power
is more even and existing vested interests are slight (Martin et al.,
1995). On this basis, it is possible to imagine a new political
power growing out of the ashes of the old. But turning local government inside out in this way requires a major leap forward
(Stewart & Taylor, 1993).

Criticism of partnership should not be laid solely at the door of
local government. Central government, with the expectations it
creates and the limits it places on local discretion and finance,
remains the ghost at the feast. A terminally damaged local state is
unlikely to transform itself: change requires confidence and the
autonomy to mobilise resources in the most effective way. But this
does not mean going back to a paternalist and producer-led state.
Rather it requires that the control of central over local government be loosened with more autonomy over services and budgets
at local level - the sort of system that is taken for granted in many
other countries. It also requires a re-examination of competences
at local level which would encourage imaginative forms of investment where it is most needed. The kinds of trust that this chapter
has already recommended as the basis for the purchaser-
provider relationship at local level are famously lacking in the
relationship between central and local government.

The moral crisis

The clarion call of the New Right and successive conservative governments has been the need to reduce 'dependency' - a condition
for which charity and indiscriminate giving used, ironically, to be
blamed (Mulgan & Landry, 1995). But both right and left have
also criticised the moral vacuum left by the market and an indi-
vidualist ethos (Green, 1993) which increasingly leaves the individual to make ethical decisions that in the past were guided by
the community or tradition to which the individual belonged. The
post-modern society appears to have eroded confidence in any
authority (Taylor Gooby, 1995).

Pinker remarks that: 'There is always trouble in store for the ordinary run of people when doctrines of moral improvement rise too high on the agenda' (1995, p86). Those calling for a return to morality often assume that morality is an uncontested concept, that the morality of the powerful is that of the masses. Communitarianism does make the case for morality to be constructed by communities - there are clear links here with the concept of value-rationality discussed earlier. But there is still an assumption, at least in the popular version of communitarianism, that moralities can be constructed which will be universally acceptable. And yet the history of 'associative democracy' (Hirst, 1994) in the voluntary sector is of competing moralities, schism, moral indoctrination and sometimes oppressive regimes (Taylor & Hoggett, 1994b; Taylor, 1996). Without a concept of overarching democracy, which can at least attempt the difficult task of reconciling the particular with the universal (Tester, 1992), the individual, to borrow Meekosha's term, is either cast adrift on a sea of relativity or caught in 'an alternative of regressive communities based on ethnic & other exclusive identities, which are internally repressive or externally hostile' (Curry & Zarate, 1995, p162).

From the 'active citizen' of the 1980s to renewed calls for community service across party lines, the voluntary and community sectors have been conscripted into revitalising concepts of moral responsibility. But this is too often conceived as an alternative to the overemphasis on rights that was associated with state welfare (viz. the 'active citizen debate of the mid-1980s) and as such represents a simplistic understanding of a sector which has a long tradition as a champion of individual and collective rights. A third way which has the potential to reconcile rather than oppose these two demands is to develop concepts of reciprocity (Gouldner, 1960; NCVO, 1990), arguing not only that rights depend on responsibility but that responsibility can only be exercised on the basis of rights and inclusion. The challenge thrown down by users and excluded communities to rethink altruism is part of this debate as are the much more fully developed debates about citizenship and exclusion in the social policy arena.

Resources

Clarke et al. (1994), as well as other commentators, associate the new managerialism with the 'affordable' welfare state, downsized, leaner and meaner. In the face of rising demand, the voluntary sector has obvious attractions as a vehicle for mobilising energies and resources outside the state or the market. But can it fill the gap?

Government itself contributes a significant proportion (about a third) to the total income of the sector. Central government funding seems to have passed its peak, however, with the disappearance of the special employment schemes of the past, the absorption of the Urban Programme and Section 11 funding into the Single Regeneration Budget and cuts in funding to housing associations. Current evidence is that local authority funding is holding up, surprisingly well (Mocroft, 1994), despite anecdotal evidence of local hardship. However, Richardson (1995) reports that voluntary organisations find themselves subsidising contract payments, something that larger organisations are best equipped to do. Local government reorganisation and the creation of new unitary authorities are likely to affect this picture. Voluntary organisations outside the main metropolitan areas or serving areas larger than the new authorities are particularly vulnerable. While government is likely to remain a significant contributor, therefore, it is unrealistic to see it as a significant source of new funds, especially outside its own mainstream agendas. The challenge for the sector, no less than for society as a whole, is to find ways of generating significant new resources to meet social goals in the twenty-first century.

New resources are not likely to come from traditional sources. Corporate giving has not yet lived up to initial hopes. Individual giving has stalled, and it has yet to be seen what effect the Lottery will have. The fundraising market is as likely to favour the larger and well-known organisations as the contracts market (Taylor Gooby, 1994). Cahill (1995) argues that, with the privatisation of lifestyle that characterises today's society, traditions that in the past mobilised large numbers of people to communal effort and work for the common good are seriously depleted. Although volunteering seems to be holding its own - studies suggest that half the population have recent experience of volunteering - there is little evidence of significant untapped resources or that those groups of the population who now have time on their hands - the unemployed, the early retired, for example - can be recruited into public service. Women have long been a central resource within the sector, which offered them a route to self-expression, public life and education, when few others were available. But both the market and the state are now looking to women to fill other agendas: in a flexible labour market, for example, or alternatively at the centre of family care and responsibility.

Volunteers, especially as traditionally defined, are often in the wrong places and even in communities where volunteering is part of the culture, population imbalance may mean that demand outstrips supply - in rural areas, for example (Taylor & Lewis, 1993).

An increased awareness of Trustee liability, along with competition for local volunteer managers from schools, may further diminish the pool from which local management committees can be drawn.

Pinker describes the informal sector (also heavily dependent on women) as 'the last Eldorado of unexplored altruism to be quarried and rendered more cost-effective' (1995, p86). Many community-based and self-help organisations lie at the boundaries of organised and informal activity and the line between informal caring, mutuality and volunteering is very fine. But these boundaries are also precarious. Mainstream services cannot depend on such precarious foundations and increasing regulation may well exclude many traditional sources of help, because they cannot or will not be regulated.

If this appears a pessimistic view, it is important to remember the voluntary sector's considerable capacity for survival and financial innovation - some of today's major financial institutions owe their existence to the mutual societies of earlier centuries. Early social housing was financed through offering the opportunity to combine philanthropy with investment, albeit at a low return (Owen, 1964). More recently, disadvantaged communities have developed credit unions in the face of discrimination from financial institutions, while LETS schemes offer new approaches to marginalised local economies. New ideas about social investment and charity bonds (Mulgan & Landry, 1995) offer the prospect of a revolution in individual giving, with traditional donors transformed into small (social) investors. The rise of social audit has the potential to transform business ideas of what 'counts' and what is worth investing in. The repertoire of options is likely to be further enriched by experience in developing countries, following the decision of some international aid agencies to tackle poverty in the UK. Mulgan and Landry (1995) have explored the possibility of innovative new forms of private investment, borrowing ideas from other countries in the developing and 'developed' world, such as community banks, while ideas of social audit have the potential to transform our ideas of 'what counts'. The rediscovery of poverty in this country by international aid organisations offers the potential for some creative cross-fertilisation between developing countries and economically marginalised localities in the UK.

Leat et al. (1986) found that far from discouraging income generation, voluntary organisations with government funding were more likely to raise additional funds. While the state itself is unlikely to provide new resources for welfare directly, especially in the context of tax cuts and cuts in public spending, it is possible to envisage new approaches to public finance which emphasise its leverage as a financial institution. Mulgan and Landry (1995) offer a range of suggestions, from hypothecation to government bonds, as to how this might happen. State leverage is also likely to have a role to play in developing social and investment in areas where potential entrepreneurs are unable to raise finance on the private market (Taylor, 1995; Thake, 1995).

Conclusions

The welfare reforms of recent years were designed to deliver a system that was more responsive to users, that could call on more resources and whose energies could be co-ordinated by the mechanism of the market. As a result of these reforms, voluntary organisations in the late twentieth century face many contradictions: between partnership and competition; between empowerment and altruism; between rights and responsibility; between the particular and the public interest; between fragmentation and social cohesion; between a rhetoric of decentralisation, on the one hand, and the globalisation of the economy and the centralisation of state power, on the other.

Their response to these contradictory pressures has been shaped by their own complex character, situated across the shifting boundaries between public and private. The picture presented above is one of both opportunities and dangers - it is still too early to say what the outcome will be. This chapter has called for organisational innovation, new forms of democracy and new forms of finance and audit if these tensions are to be addressed and the contribution of the voluntary sector, in all its diversity, is to be maximised. The dilemma of reconciling the particular with the general interest is an enduring one: Tester (1992) argues that this polarity is irreconcilable. Although there are many different interpretations of the phrase, the notion of a 'stakeholder' society which has momentarily captured the political imagination as this book goes to press suggests that there is some momentum behind an attempt to mediate between the particular and the general, self-interest and mutual interest. The diversity of the voluntary sector, its ability to release individual energies to address collective needs and, on occasion, to mobilise diverse constituencies around common interest s is an essential part of any reconciliation. But it is not sufficient. An overarching framework - but one which allows for the expression of separate interests - is essential to any concept of society.

It is hard to see how this can be done other than by the democratic state. And yet, there are many reasons to resist this conclusion, given the experience of the state, central and local, as a power which itself inhibits and excludes. Past experience may make us sceptical of the ability of the state to resist being co-opted itself by the most powerful interests - there are too many cautionary tales to tell. Nonetheless, in the UK and elsewhere, the increasing use of the term 'local governance' suggests an alternative model whereby the local state acts as a co-ordinating and generating force for a variety of local actors. It is the image of an ' open' state, as against the paternalism and secrecy for which governments in the UK are so often criticised, and one which recognise s the difficult transformation that partnership requires. It is also an image of a state which, to use Taylor Gooby's terms (1995), is neither 'retreating' by leaving the problem of co-ordination to the 'invisible hand of the market' nor 'extending its influence' through the 'invisible hand' of the regulator.

To transform the state requires a new and robust conception of citizenship which does not founder on the sterile see-saw between rights and duties of many recent debates but which is built on reciprocity and an understanding that a democratic state is all our responsibility. Insofar as the voluntary sector brings a broad range of people into public life, it has a major contribution to make to that vision. Its experience in trying to make sense of its own dilemmas - dealing with uncertainty and ambiguity, reconciling different interests around common causes, finding new ways of understanding altruism in response to community and user criticism, releasing new resources in new ways - will be essential if that vision is to be turned into a reality. But without the shared meanings that are delivered, however painfully, of the political process, we face a scenario of the 'survival of the fittest' on the one hand or increasing conflict between fragmented interests on the other. A coherent system of welfare, effective use of resources and dependable, let alone equitable, networks of provision are unlikely to be the result.

Notes

1. Parts of this chapter are drawn from reviews carried out with the financial support of the Joseph Rowntree Foundation's Committee on Central-Local Government relations and of the Commission on the Future of the Voluntary Sector. I am also grateful to Michael Cahill for his comments on an early draft.

2. The concern of this chapter is with the contribution of the sector as a whole to welfare, in all its diversity and with all its

contradictions. Individual organisations may not display all the characteristics discussed here. It is becoming more common now to refer to the voluntary and community sectors. For ease of reading, the term voluntary sector is used here, but encompasses community-based and user-based organisations as well as those based on service to others.

3. I am grateful to Mike Locke for permission to use some of the initial findings from his research with Paul Robson. The completed research will be summarised in a Joseph Rowntree Foundation Findings in early 1996.

References

Baldock, J. (1993) 'Patterns of change in the delivery of welfare in Europe', in P.Taylor Gooby & R. Lawson (eds) Markets and Managers: New Issues in the Delivery of Welfare, Buckingham, Open University Press.

Bardach, E. (1989) 'Social regulation as a generic policy instrument ', in L. M. Salamon (ed) Beyond Privatization: The Tools of Government Action, Washington, DC, Urban Institute Press.

Batsleer, J. (1995) 'Management and organisation', in J. Davis Smith, C. Rochester, & R. Hedley (eds) An Introduction to the Voluntary Sector, London, Routledge.

Beveridge, W. (1948) Voluntary Action, London, Allen & Unwin.

Cahill, M. (1995) 'Beyond consumerism: reworking welfare for the 21st century', paper prepared for the Social Policy Association Annual Conference, Sheffield Hallam University, July.

Clarke, J. Cochrane, A. & McLaughlin, E. (1994) 'Mission accomplished or unfinished business? The impact of managerialism', in J. Clarke, A., Cochrane & E. McLaughlin (eds) Managing Social Policy, London, Sage.

Clegg, S. (1990) Modern Organizations: Organizational Studies in the Post-modern World, London, Sage.

Curry, P. & Zarate, 0. (1995) Machiavelli for Beginners, Cambridge, Icon Books.

Day, P. & Klein, R. (1987) Accountabilities: Five Public Services, London, Tavistock.

Deakin, N. Thomas, N. Smith, P. Hearn, T. & Walsh, K. (1994) 'The devils in the detail: some reflections on contracting for social care by voluntary organisations', paper prepared for ESRC seminar: 'Challenges for Voluntary Agencies in a Changing Social Policy Environment', Centre for Voluntary Organisation, London School of Economics.

DiMaggio, P. & Powell, W. (1983) 'The iron cage revisited: institutional isomorphism and collective rationality in organisational fields', American Sociological Review, vol.48, pp147-60.

Evers, A. (1993) 'The welfare mix approach: understanding the pluralism of welfare systems', in A. Evers & I. Svetlik (eds) Balancing Pluralism: New Welfare Mixes in Care for the Elderly, Aldershot, Avebury.

Gladstone, F. (1979) Voluntary Action in a Changing World, London, Bedford Square Press.

Gouldner, A. (1960) 'The norm of reciprocity: a preliminary statement', American Journal of Sociology, vol.91 no.3, pp481-510.

Green, D. (1993) Reinventing Civil Society: the Rediscovery of Welfare Without Politics, London, Institute of Economic Affairs.

Gutch, R. (1995) 'Benefits of user-led research', Trust Monitor, October/November.

Hadley, R. & Hatch, S. (1981) Social Welfare and the Failure of the State, London, Allen & Unwin.

Harman, W. W. (1993) 'Rethinking the central institutions of modern society: science and business', Futures, pp1063-70.

Hastings, A. McArthur, A. & McGregor, A. (1996) Less than Equal: Community Organisations and Estate Regeneration Partnerships, Bristol, The Policy Press.

Hoyes, L. Jeffers, S. Lart, R. Means, R. & Taylor, M. (1993) User Empowerment and the Reform of Community Care, Bristol, SAUS Publications.

Hirst, P. (1994) Associative Democracy: New Forms of Economic and Social Governance, London, Polity Press.

Kendall, J. & Knapp, M. (1995) 'A loose and baggy monster', in J. Davis Smith, C. Rochester & R. Hedley (eds) An Introduction to the Voluntary Sector, London, Routledge.

Kendall, J. & Knapp, M. (eds) (forthcoming) The Voluntary Sector in the UK, Manchester, Manchester University Press

Kendall, J. & 6, P. (1994) 'Government and the voluntary sector in the United Kingdom', in S. Saxon-Harrold & J. Kendall (eds) Researching the Voluntary Sector, Volume II, Tonbridge, Charities Aid Foundation.

Kenney, M. & Florida, R. (1988) 'Beyond mass production: production and the labour process in Japan', Politics and Society, vol.16, no.1, pp121-58.

Knight, B. (1993) Voluntary Action, London, Home Office.

Landry, C., Morley, D. Southwood, R. & Wright, P. (1995) What a Way to Run a Railroad, London, Comedia.

Leat, D., Tester, S. & Unell, J. (1986) A Price Worth Paying? a Study of the Effects of Government Grant-Aid to Voluntary Organisations, London, Policy Studies Institute.

Lewis, J. (1993) 'Developing the mixed economy of care: emerging issues for voluntary organisations', Journal of Social Policy, vol. 22, pp173-92.

Lewis J. Bernstock P. & Bovell V. (1995) 'The community care changes: unresolved tensions in policy and issues in implementation', Journal of Social Policy vol.22, no.2, pp173-92

Lukes, S. (1974) Power: a Radical View, London: Macmillan.

MacFarlane, R. (1993) Community Involvement in City Challenge: A Good Practice Report, London, National Council for Voluntary Organisations.

Martin, L., Gaster, L. & Taylor, M. (1995) Clients Purchaser and Enabler Roles, Luton, Local Government Management Board

Meekosha, H. (1993) 'The bodies politic - equality, difference and community practice', in H. Butcher, A. Glen, P. Henderson & J. Smith (eds) Community and Public Policy, London: Pluto Press.

Mocroft, I. (1994) 'A survey of local authority payments to voluntary and charitable organisations, 1992/3', in Charities Aid Foundation, Dimensions of the Voluntary Sector, Tonbridge, Charities Aid Foundation.

Morris, J. (1994) The Shape of Things to Come: User-led Social Services, London, National Institute for Social Work.

Mulgan, G. & Landry, C. (1995) The Other Invisible Hand: Remaking Charity for the 21st century, London, Demos.

NCVO, (1990) Directions for the Next Decade: Understanding Social and Institutional Trends, London, National Council for Voluntary Organisations.

Owen, D. (1964) English Philanthropy: 1660-1960, Cambridge, Ma., Harvard University Press.

Paton, R. (1996) 'How are values handled in voluntary agencies?', in D. Billis & M. Harris (eds) Voluntary Agencies: Challenges of Organisations and Management, Basingstoke: Macmillan.

Peters, T. & Waterman, R. (1982) In Search of Excellence, New York, Harper and Row.

Pinker, R. (1995) 'Golden ages and welfare alchemists', Social Policy and Administration, vol. 29, pp78-90.

Power, M. (1994) The Audit Explosion, London: Demos.

Prins, M. C. (1995) 'Organisational change in small voluntary organisations: a study of twelve day centres and luncheon clubs for elderly people', paper presented to 'Researching the Voluntary Sector', National Council for Voluntary Organisations, 7-8 September.

Reid, B. & Iqbal, B. (1996) 'Redefining housing practice: interorganisational relationships and housing networks' in P. Malpass (ed) The New Governance of Housing, Harlow, Longman

Rein. M. (1989) 'The social structure of institutions: neither public nor private', in S.B. Kamerman & A.J. Kahn (eds) Privatization and the Welfare State, Princeton, Princeton University Press

Richardson, J. (1995) Purchase of Service Contracting, London, National Council for Voluntary Organisations.

Ring, P. & van de Ven, A. (1992) 'Structuring cooperative relationships between organisations', Strategic Management Journal, vol.13 , pp483-98.

Roberts, V., Russell, H., Harding, A., & Parkinson, M. (1996) Public/Private/Voluntary Partnerships in Local Government, Luton, Local Government Management Board.

Rothschild-Whitt, J. (1979) 'The collectivist organisation: an alternative to rational-bureaucratic models', American Sociological Review, vol.44, pp509-27.

Russell, L., Scott, D. & Wilding, P. (1995) Mixed Fortunes: the Funding of Local Voluntary Organisations, Manchester, University of Manchester.

Salamon, L.M. & Anheier, H. (1996) The Emerging NonProfit Sector: An Overview, Manchester, University of Manchester.

Smith, S. R. & Lipsky, M. (1993) Non-profits for Hire: the Welfare State in the Age of Contracting, Cambridge, Ma., Harvard University Press.

Stewart, M. & Taylor, M. (1993) Local Government Community Leadership, Luton, Local Government Management Board.

Taylor, M. (1995) Unleashing the Potential: Bringing Residents to the Centre of Estate Regeneration, York, Joseph Rowntree Foundation.

Taylor, M. (1996) 'Between public and private: accountability in voluntary organisations', Policy and Politics, vol.24, pp57-72.

Taylor, M. & Lewis, J. (1993) 'Contracting: what does it do to voluntary and non-profit organisations', paper prepared for 'Contracting: selling or shrinking?', National Council for Voluntary Organisations and South Bank University, July.

Taylor, M. & Hoggett, P. (1994a) 'Quasi-markets and the transformation of the independent sector', in W. Bartlett, C. Propper, D. Wilson & J. Le Grand (eds) Quasi-markets in the Welfare State, Bristol, SAUS Publications.

Taylor, M. & Hoggett, P. (1994b) 'Trusting in networks? The third sector and welfare change', in P. 6 & I. Vidal (eds) Delivering Welfare: Repositioning Nonprofit and Co-operative Action in Western European States, Barcelona, Centre d'Initiatives de l'Economia Social.

Taylor M. & Kendall J. 'The history of the UK voluntary sector', in J. Kendall & M. Knapp (eds) (forthcoming) The Voluntary Sector in the UK, Manchester, Manchester University Press.

Taylor, M. Langan, J. & Hoggett, P. (1995) Encouraging Diversity: Voluntary and Private Organisations in Community Care, Aldershot, Arena.

Taylor Gooby, P. (1994) 'Charities in recession - hard times for the weakest', in S. Saxon-Harrold & J. Kendall (eds) Researching the Voluntary Sector, Volume II, Tonbridge, Charities Aid Foundation.

Taylor Gooby, P. (1995) 'In defence of second-best theory: state, capital and class in social policy', plenary session paper, Social Policy Association Annual Conference, Sheffield Hallam University, July.

Tester, K. (1992) Civil Society, London, Routledge.

Thake, S. (1995) Staying the Course: the Role and Structures of Community Regeneration Organisations, York, York Publishing Services .

Wann, M. (1995) Building Social Capital: Self~help in the Twenty-First Century Welfare State, London: Institute for Public Policy Research.

Wolfenden Committee (1978) The Future for Voluntary Organisations, London, Croom Helm

4 Who's Complaining? Redress and Social Policy

Hartley Dean

State governed welfare provision in Britain presents a bewildering and changing array of mechanisms for the redress of grievances (see Figure 1). Understanding the role of redress in relation to social policy requires a grasp of the competing and shifting discourses through which rights of redress are constituted and the developing forms of legal and administrative regulation to which the recipients of welfare services and benefits are subject.

In this context, recent trends may be construed as a shift away from rights of appeal towards rights of complaint. In place of forms of redress based on a monolithic rule-book, we have forms of redress which establish diverse circuits of blame. It might be argued that this shift is commensurate with what is described by some (Burrows & Loader, 1994) as a transition from a 'Fordist' to a 'post-Fordist' welfare state. By itself, this idea has insufficient explanatory power to account for recent developments. This chapter therefore sets out to distinguish different modes or forms of redress, before discussing the emergence and the apparent exhaustion of the tribunal as a means of redress; the emergence and the partial eclipse of ombudspersons and mechanisms for public participation; and the emergence and perhaps illusory ascendancy of complaints procedures. The paper will conclude with a discussion of the problematic nature of redress in relation to the exercise of social rights and the propensity for mechanisms of redress to constrain resistance by the subjects of the welfare state.

Figure 1: Specified statutory procedures for individual redress in relation to state welfare provision[1]

Social Security	Social Security Appeal Tribunal Medical Appeal Tribunal Disability Appeal Tribunal Child Support Tribunal Social Security Commissioner Child Support Commissioner Social Fund Inspector Parliamentary Commissioner for Administration Housing Benefit Review Board Local Commissioner for Administration
Personal Social Services	Complaints Procedure under NHS & Community Care Act 1990 (a three stage procedure, culminating in a review panel) Complaints Procedure under The Children Act 1989 (a three stage procedure culminating in a review panel) Local Commissioner for Administration
Health	New NHS complaints procedure (a common two stage procedure, culminating in a review panel, which from April 1996 should supercede the various family health servi ce, hospital and community unit procedures) Mental Health Review Tribunal Health Service Commissioner
Education	Education Appeals Committee Special Educational Needs Tribunal National Curriculum complaints procedure Local Commissioner for Administration

[1] This therefore does not include:remedies available to private providers (e.g. Registered Homes Tribunal) or relating to the state regulation of private provision (e.g. Rent Assessment Committee); nor does it include the voluntary and/or extra-statutory schemes and procedures operated, for example, by certain local authorities.

Forms of redress

Notions of redress are dependent on the character of the rights they seek to assert. There is not one form of redress, but many. I propose for heuristic purposes to identify four: adjudicative redress; consumer redress; case redress; and declaratory redress.

Adjudicative and consumer redress are founded on a doctrinal conception by which rights inhere in the individual as proprietor; rights in the mould of classical jurisprudence and liberal governance. They owe their origins to the ascendancy of 'man-made' law (which guards the interests of property) over 'natural' law (which had guarded the privileges of crown and aristocracy) (Fine,1984). From their opposing perspectives, both Hegel (1821) and Marx (1887) recognised that the origin of modern rights lies in ownership and that, under capitalism, people must recognise and relate to each other as the owners of the property, goods or labour power which they exchange between each other. Even when it comes to rights to welfare benefits, it has been argued, the 'government largesse' to which citizens may be entitled may be regarded as a form of property or commodity, subject to the same rules and forms of redress as other kinds of property (Reich,1964). Though both are informed by the same doctrinal conception, adjudicative and consumer redress are very different from one another. Adjudicative redress constitutes the individual as a juridical subject, for whom redress lies in an appeal to judicial (or quasi-judicial) authority, and in the right to have a disputed entitlement adjudicated under prescribed rules and procedure. Consumer redress, constitutes the individual as a transacting customer, for whom redress lies in the right to arbitration over the standard and quality of goods and services.

Case redress and declaratory redress are founded upon a conception of rights as claims upon the state (cf. Spicker,1993); rights which are strictly the creatures of policy decisions and priorities (Hirst,1980), or else which are rhetorical demands based on conviction and realised by and through struggle over policy. Both forms owe their origins to the rise of the machinery of the state and its power to administer, not only the 'proportional justice' of classical jurisprudence, but the 'creative justice' (Titmuss,1971) of beneficent experts and administrators; and its capacity to satisfy human needs outside the market on a 'decommodified' basis (Esping-Andersen,1990). Though informed by the same claims-based conception of rights, case redress and declaratory redress are, once again, quite different from one another. Case redress constitutes the individual as a client, for whom redress lies in mounting a challenge to discretionary decisions taken by welfare administrators or professionals upon the deserts or merits of her/his individual case. Declaratory redress, constitutes the individual as a citizen, for whom redress lies in the assertion of a political challenge by voicing grievances through public channels.

The development of redress mechanisms in relation to state welfare has always been subject to a tension between doctrinal and claims-based conceptions of rights. In what might be characterised as the 'Fordist' age of the welfare state, this was reflected in debate about the respective merits of entitlement over discretion as the basis of rights to welfare (Donnison,1982); between adjudicative redress and case redress. In the 'post-Fordist' age the same tension is reflected in debate about the respective merits of managerialist and democratic interpretations of 'quality' (Pfeffer & Coote,1991); between consumer redress and declaratory redress. I shall first flesh out this general model (see Figure 2), before turning to a more critical examination of the relations of power which are underpinned by different mechanisms of redress.

Figure 2 Social Rights & Forms of Redress: A Model

Conception of rights	Associated forms of redress	Implied status of individual actor	Corresponding mechanism for redress	Appropriate body or agency
doctrinal	adjudicative redress	juridical subject	appeal	tribunal
	consumer redress	transacting customer	personal complaint	complaints/ quality assurance system
claims-based	case redress	'client'	case review	case committee
	declaratory redress	'citizen	petitionary complaint	participative forum or ombudsperson

Case committee vs. adjudicative tribunal

The basis of rights to state organised welfare have been contested since the nineteenth century Poor Laws. In Scotland aggrieved applicants for poor relief had rights of appeal to the local Sheriff and, in the final instance, to the Court of Session. One of the philanthropists who agitated for such rights had argued that a reasonable level of support was or should be the legal right of the poor against 'the more opulent and fortunate classes' and, in accordance with 'the laws and practices of all civilised nations', the resolution of a disputed claim for relief should therefore be impartially conducted: it 'must not be left to the final adjudication of the parties who are burdened with the assessment' (Sir Archibald Alison, Principles of Population, 1840, cited in Webb & Webb,1963, p1034).

In England, however, the only redress available to a person who had been refused poor relief lay to the Relief Committee of the Board of Guardians. It was a right to a case review by the authority responsible for the disputed decision. Chadwick, the Benthamite architect of the English Poor Law, insisted that the administration of poor relief should not be clogged by the intervention of the courts. The courts, he argued, were concerned only with the claims of individual subjects and not the 'large classes of cases and general and often remote effects, which cannot be brought to the knowledge of judges' (cited in Finer,1952, p88)

No form of independent adjudicative mechanism relating to the administration of welfare was introduced in England until the 1911 National Insurance Act established the curiously-named Court of Referees to adjudicate disputed claims for unemployment benefit . Throughout the twentieth century, while rights of appeal have been extended in relation to many welfare benefits, policy makers have continued to insulate the administration of welfare from scrutiny by the ordinary courts, preferring instead to set up administrative tribunals (Cranston,1985).

In practice, tribunals represented a compromise between doctrinally 'pure' adjudicative redress and pragmatic claims-based case redress. Hoggett has argued that the welfare state itself has been a 'mongrel' form of organisation, involving 'an uneasy marriage between a pre-Fordist craft (professional) productive system and a Taylorised (rational bureaucratic) system' (1987, p223). In a sense this has been reflected in the tension between on the one hand the kind of tribunals before which 'clients' might seek a review of the way in which professionals and experts had handled their case, and on the other the kind of tribunals before which juridical subjects might seek an adjudication as to whether decisions had been properly and rationally made. The compromises struck within this uneasy marriage were not always the same. In the case of the Court of Referees (later to become the National Insurance Local Tribunal [NILT]), 'fair play' was ensured by a legally qualified chairperson assisted by a trade union and an employer's representative: its jurisdiction was closely defined by legislative rules. Other tribunals were differently constituted and had greater scope to exercise discretion. The Unemployment Assistance Tribunal created in the 1930s (later to evolve into the Supplementary Benefit Appeal Tribunal [SBAT]) was not legally chaired and, originally, its membership included a representative of the benefit awarding authority.

Ultimately, it was the adjudicative tribunal which achieved ascendancy. As tribunals proliferated into other areas of welfare and government business, the Franks Committee (1957) asserted that tribunals should be regarded as 'the machinery provided by parliament for adjudication rather than as part of the machinery of administration'. Franks established three guiding principles for tribunals: 'openness, fairness and impartiality' (1957, para. 41) and the reforms to which his recommendations gave rise were intended to apply new standards to the work of tribunals. Tribunals with jurisdictions affecting, amongst other things, social security, health services, education and housing were brought under the supervision of the Council on Tribunals. Perhaps the high point in the development of the adjudicative tribunal came with the eventual merger in 1984 of the SBAT - much criticised for its tendency still to act as a 'case committee' rather an adjudicative forum - and the NILT, to form the Social Security Appeal Tribunal (SSAT), which promised to bring a new level of rigour and sophistication to social security adjudication. The reform seemed to signal a victory for those who had been advocating a welfare system based on entitlement and adjudication rather than discretion and review (Adler & Asquith,1981). The ideal of an appeal to an independently constituted tribunal represented a mechanism of redress appropriate to the universal scope and complex nature of the modern welfare state.

However, Franks had also declared that the advantages of tribunals over courts, was their greater 'cheapness, accessibility, freedom from technicality, expedition and expert knowledge' (ibid, para. 38). These expectations, Genn & Genn (1989) have suggested, conflict with Franks' guiding principles. The commitment of tribunals to judicial standards may be compromised if 'cheapness' means appellants are not guaranteed legal representation; if, because of the complex nature of welfare legislation, 'accessibility and freedom from technicality' are limited to 'such matters as the atmosphere of proceedings and tribunal documentation' (Genn & Genn 1989, p114); or if the volume, diversity and intricacy of appeals makes 'expedition and expert knowledge' difficult in practice to sustain.

If the 1980s marked the ascendancy of the adjudicative tribunal, they may also have marked the beginning of its decline. In 1982 when housing benefit was introduced and its administration entrusted to local authorities, the government refused to introduce an independent appeal mechanism, preferring instead to provide a two stage internal review procedure. Claimants wishing to challenge a benefit determination may first ask the local authority officers responsible to re-examine the disputed decision and, if still then dissatisfied, may have the matter referred to a Housing Benefit Review Board composed of local councillors. Research into the functioning of Review Boards (Eardley & Sainsbury,1991) has recommended that their role would be better entrusted to the SSAT. However, not only has the government declined to add to the jurisdiction of the SSAT, in 1988 it removed elements of that jurisdiction. Whereas the SSAT had adjudicated on appeals against the refusal of special one-off payments under the old supplementary benefits scheme, when responsibility for such payments was transferred to the discretionary social fund, no right of appeal was provided. Once again a two stage internal review procedure was introduced. Applicants wishing to challenge the decisions of Social Fund Officers may first ask for the decision to be re-examined at local level and, if still dissatisfied, may then have the matter referred to a regionally-based Social Fund Inspector (see Dalley & Berthoud,1992).

In these instances in place of rights of appeal there has been a reversion to rights of case review. Ostensibly against this trend there are other instances in which new tribunals have lately been created: the Child Support Tribunal (CST) under the Child Support Act 1991 and the Special Educational Needs Tribunal (SENT) under the Education Act 1993. Significantly, both tribunals will function more as case-review bodies, than 'pure' adjudicative bodies. Although this was not initially so in the case of the CST, recent proposals will allow discretionary variations in the application of the child support formula (DSS,1995a) and this may yet radically affect the nature of the CST's jurisdiction. The SENT is specifically charged with responsibility for reviewing the decisions of local education authorities in circumstances in which authorities themselves must exercise discretion within the broad parameters of a non-binding Code of Practice (DFE,1994). To this extent these new tribunals will be required, not so much to determine entitlement, as to regulate discretion. The pendulum is swinging back again and we may be witnessing the beginning of an erosion of adjudicative redress in favour of case redress. These, however, are not the only changes afoot.

Petitionary forum vs. complaints system

There is in Britain little in the way of a tradition of what I have termed declaratory redress. Foucault (1980) has argued that the transition from feudalism to modernity involved an inversion of the process of justice. Where once, supposedly, the subject enjoyed a right to declare his/her grievances and demand justice of the sovereign or the sovereign's representative, and the latter was under an (albeit wholly unenforceable) obligation to listen or to arbitrate, the modern subject has an obligation to submit to the decisions of those in power, whose right it is to determine and impose what they determine to be just. The nature of the process by which 'constitutional' power over subjects has been negotiated has been different in Britain compared with continental Europe (Mann, 1987).

Ombudspersons

The early development in England of highly centralised political and administrative structures - the 'Westminster model' - may account for Britain's failure until recently to develop mechanisms of declaratory redress such as the people's champions or 'ombudspersons' which had for some 200 years characterised the more decentralised administrative systems of Nordic countries (Lewis & Birkinshaw, 1993). Classical ombudspersons in the Nordic mould wield independent investigatory powers and may 'dig where the courts and tribunals cannot trespass' (ibid, 78). A petitionary complaint to an ombusperson may result in an exposure of systemic weaknesses in policy and administration and proposals for reform.

In Britain we have so far done little more than flirt with the idea of ombudspersons. Following the Whyatt Report (1961), three ombudsperson schemes were eventually introduced - the Parliamentary Commissioner for Administration (with power to investigate complaints about central government departments), the Local Commissioners for Administration (with power to investigate complaints about local government) and the Health Service Commissioner (with the power to investigate complaints about the National Health Service). However, compared with ombudsperson schemes in other countries (not only Scandanavian countries, but also Austria, France, New Zealand, Australia and Canada), the powers of the British versions have been significantly compromised. First, they may only investigate in response to complaints addressed specifically to them (and, in the case of the Parliamentary Commissioner, complaints may be referred from the public only by Members of Parliament). Second, they are prevented from investigating if a complainant has any alternative means of redress. Third, they are embargoed from investigating matters encroaching on organisational, personnel or contractual matters. Finally, they may only investigate complaints relating to 'maladministration'; to technical and procedural matters rather than the substantive merits of decision making and policy. Adapted to co-exist with the Westminster model, the ideal of an accessible people's champion was not so much emasculated, as subverted to a different purpose; to serve the interests of rational administration.

Public participation

Similarly, Cockburn (1977) has argued, innovations in the 1960s and 1970s to increase public participation in local government in fact served, not as a check upon the functioning of large 'corporate' style local authorities, but as a part of the process by which these monoliths extended power into the environment in which they had to function. The Redcliffe-Maud Commission (1969) had sought to create, beneath the massive bureaucracy of local government, a tier of parish and community councils, whose powers were to be minimal, but which were to fulfil a primarily consultative role. In the event, these were provided only in rural areas and it was left to independent campaigners and 'progressive' local authorities to introduce extra-statutory neighbourhood councils in just a handful of inner-urban areas. Here again was a potential if limited mechanism for declaratory redress; a forum outside the machinery of representative government through which petitionary complaints and challenges could be mounted against local functionaries and elected politicians. In the same spirit Redcliffe-Maud also proposed that all local authorities should introduce comprehensive complaints procedures, a recommendation which until the 1990s was poorly observed (Lewis et al.,1986) and tended at best to generate mechanisms which were more defensive than responsive (McCarthy et al., 1992).

The vogue for participation which was evident in the policy rhetoric of the 1960s and 1970s was similarly reflected in the Skeffington Report (1969) which urged planning departments to develop mechanisms for consulting local people on development proposals, and in the Seebohm Report (1968) which portended the ways in which public participation could provide a community orientation to the functioning of new and larger social services departments. It has been suggested, however, that British local government in this era was 'busily engaged in adopting the form of the modern industrial democracy precisely at the moment when in the private sector it was entering a period of crisis and supercession' (Hoggett, 1994, p42). That said, the Seebohm Report was rather prescient in the way it illustrated the ambiguity which can underpin a discourse of public participation. Having argued that citizen participation should ameliorate the distinction between 'clients' and service providers, Seebohm added, 'The whole community 'consumes' the social services, directly or indirectly, as well as paying for them through taxation, and consumers have an important contribution to make to the development of an effective family service' (1968, para. 492).

Here on the one hand is an essentially Fordist notion of a universal public service that is centrally produced for the benefit of the 'community' as a whole; a vision which would seem to be rooted in a claims-based conception of rights and which would imply that the purpose of public participation is to facilitate some element of declaratory redress. On the other hand Seebohm, himself a businessman, also insinuates the language of the supplier-consumer relationship and a rejection of the kind of case redress which might have been available to the 'clients' of paternalistic services. Implied here is the possibility that public participation might presage a form of consumer redress that could admit, not only petitionary complaints by members of the 'community', but personal complaints by individual consumers.

New public management

In the event, it was another businessman, Griffiths (1983; 1988), who played a seminal role in the radical remoulding of the welfare state in the 1980s and 1990s. This entailed the introduction of business techniques or what has been called 'new public management' (Hood, 1991) particularly to the health and social services. The techniques employed have mimicked certain of the management processes which are developing within an increasingly 'globalized' economy: their object is to stimulate efficiency through competition between service providers at the local level, while at the same time centralising control over resource allocation. This has resulted in organisational change within welfare state institutions through, for example, the creation of internal and/or 'quasi' markets in which welfare providers must compete for public funds, and the institution of 'arms-length' executive agencies governed by politically determined performance targets

(Gray & Jenkins, 1993; and see Clarke's chapter in this volume). What has been insinuated into the organisation of state welfare is a managerialist doctrine or ideology that is as concerned to promote a change of culture as it is to change the substantive content of services. This, and its consequences for notions of 'redress', is most clearly manifested in the Citizen's Charter.

Launched in 1991, the Charter did not so much create new rights as reiterate the established priorities of government policy towards the public sector (Miller & Peroni,1992). To a list of initiatives which included 'more privatisation' and 'wider competition', was added 'more effective complaints procedures' and 'better redress for the citizen when things go badly wrong' (Prime Minister's Office 1991, p5). Central was a belief that it is not administrative or judicial authority which will make welfare providers take complaints seriously, but the fear of competition (Pirie,1991). The citizen of the Citizen's Charter is not the social democratic subject of the Fordist welfare state, but the 'heroic consumer' (Warde,1994) of post-Fordism: s/he is not a helpless client, but a discriminating customer. In this way the 'business' of service provision is uncoupled from the 'politics' of welfare. Service providers are driven by individualised incentives and the need to attract and retain customers, not by policy considerations or professional vocation. When things go wrong, customers are encouraged to blame local service providers, not policy makers or power structures.

In the Citizen's Charter and the new complaints procedures of the 1990s the right to redress is linked to a particular notion of 'quality'. Pfeffer & Coote have made the point that 'we are all in favour of quality, as we are all against sin' (1991, pi), yet it is a slippery term which, in the context of the new public management, has been elevated to the status of a doctrine: quality is a function of organisational performance, and the measure of quality is customer satisfaction; quality may and must be continually improved through organisational review and assiduous customer care. In such a context, the handling of complaints 'should be a positive part of the customer-supplier relationship rather than simply a damage limitation exercise' (CCCTF,1994a, p1).

While the customers of public services are therefore encouraged to blame providers, the new managerialist ethos is subtly geared to dissipate blame and so prevent political recrimination. This is demonstrated in a discussion paper series produced by the Citizen's Charter Complaints Task Force, which defines redress in terms of 'the whole range of responses which organisations can offer to the user who has suffered sub-standard service. Redress heals the breach with the user that poor service has caused.'

(CCCTF 199 4b, no.6, para.1.1). To this end, it is important for organisations to turn grievances into complaints if they are to root out and deal with dissatisfaction. Staff must share the goal or mission of their organisation and they should be empowered through training to deal expeditiously with complaints. Complaints and the information they generate are important management tools, and skilful complaint handling is an important means of demonstrating commitment and disarming aggrieved customers. Of paramount concern is, not the apportionment of blame, but the realisation of system aims: 'Organisations have to recognise that complaints may often arise not from any breach of regulations by a member of staff but from a shortcoming in the system, which they need to know about if they are to correct that fault' (ibid, no.4, para. 2.4.2). Accountability attaches to everybody and nobody and can be absorbed.

Complaints systems

What also tends to be absorbed by this form of consumer redress are the precepts of those participatory mechanisms of declaratory redress dating from initiatives of the 1970s and early 1980s. Local authorities which had sought to democratise their structures through equal opportunities policies, decentralisation initiatives and experiments with local charters and service contracts (Thomson, 1992) have had their efforts subjected to a rather different gloss: their objectives have been subverted or at least eclipsed by a discourse which is 'system' rather than 'community' oriented. While some commentators continue to advocate the ideal of the 'responsive authority' with a 'bottom-up' rather than a 'top-down' view of citizens' grievances (McCarthy et al., 1992), or a 'democratic' as opposed to a managerialist approach to quality (Pfeffer & Coote,1991), the nature of the complaints procedures now emerging is primarily informed by a concept of consumer redress.

The main examples are the social services and NHS complaints procedures. The official guidance on the community care complaints procedures enjoins social services departments to seek out and welcome complaints 'as a measure of user satisfaction and performance' (DH 1990, para. 6.6). The Wilson Report (1994), which recommended the new NHS complaints procedure, drew explicitly upon the example of private sector organisations. In defining the objectives of the complaints procedure, the report stresses that complainant satisfaction may 'enable the relationship between patient and practitioner to be restored'; that 'complaints can be used positively to improve services'; that

ensuring fairness to practitioners and staff and avoiding unnecessary litigation should allow complaints handling to become less
negative and defensive (ibid, pp18-19).

None of this should be divorced from the policy context in
which the new procedures are being introduced. Recent policy
changes mean that the overall allocation of resources for health
and social care is centrally determined while substantive responsibility for rationing decisions is devolved to the local level.
Commenting on the operation of community care complaints
procedures Simons (1995, p88) has observed that in many parts
of Britain 'complaints procedures are being used to soak up the
tensions generated by t he need to ration scarce resources'.

However, research by Simons (op cit) and by Dean, Gale &
Woods (1996) has revealed considerable inconsistency in the way
the community care complaints procedure is operating in practice. Social services departments have been interpreting their
responsibilities in different ways. What is counted as an 'informal'
first stage complaint and the numbers of complaints which are
then 'registered' for a second stage investigation vary between
authorities. The research in which this author was involved concentrated on the third stage of the procedure where unresolved
complaints are considered by a review panel chaired by an independent person. We detected considerable confusion on the part
of review panels as to their precise role and functions and differing expectations on the part of the complainants. On occasions
we detected vestiges of each of the four forms of redress discussed
in this paper. Sometimes panels appeared to function as a case-
review committee, sometimes as a petitionary forum, sometimes
as an adjudicative tribunal and only sometimes as a personal com-
plaints/quality assurance panel.

At the time of writing, proposals for a two stage NHS complaints procedure to replace the complicated assortment of complaints and appeals processes which have applied within the various parts of the NHS have still to be implemented. However, if
the experience of local social services departments is anything to
go by, there is likely to be an extended period in which health care
providers and authorities struggle to come to terms with their
responsibilities for managing locally-established complaints procedures. The ascendant official rhetoric may be clear about what
that role should be, but the aspirations of those involved are more
complex. What is more, apparently undaunted by 'the practical
difficulty of separating service from benefit-related grievances'
(DSS,1995b), the Social Security Benefits Agency is currently
evaluating the possibility of introducing a customer complaints
procedure to run alongside established social security adjudication
machinery.

Social rights, subordination and redress

Previous attempts to provide theoretical models or ideal-type taxonomies (for example, Mashaw,1983) in order to describe mechanisms of welfare redress have characteristically been concerned with notions of administrative or bureaucratic 'justice'. To this extent, such accounts are themselves located in a doctrinal conception of rights and do not draw the distinction made here between doctrinal and claims-based rights. The endemic tension between these concepts provides the fulcrum around which debates and discourses about redress conventionally occur: debates about the relative 'fairness' of independent adjudication as opposed to administrative case review; discourses about the rights of 'customers' as opposed to the rights of 'citizens'.

The history of redress within the welfare state is not a simple story of progression from claims-based to doctrinal rights. It is a story of transition at the level of both kinds of rights. Although it never quite existed in such a form, the grand 'Fordist' welfare state might be characterised by its emphasis on adjudicative redress at the level of doctrinal rights and declaratory redress at the level of claims-based rights. A more highly flexible 'Post-Fordist' welfare state might be characterised by its emphasis on consumer redress at the level of doctrinal rights and a reversion to case redress at the level of claims-based rights. This may partly describe current changes. More fully to explain such changes we should also consider what is distinctive about redress within the context of social policy; and what is the nature of the power that is exercised or resisted through redress?

The subordinate nature of social rights

The redress with which this paper is concerned relates specifically to the enforcement of the social rights of citizenship, in the sense which Marshall (1950) has distinguished social rights from the civil and political rights of citizenship. More recently, Plant has argued that social rights 'are not in fact categorically different from civil and political rights' (1992, p17). The opportunities underwritten by social rights should be no less constitutive of citizenship and they need be no less affordable or contestable than the freedoms underwritten by civil and political rights. However, Plant acknowledges that 'if the idea of rights is linked to the idea of enforceability, then Marshallian social rights are actually a bit of a sham' (ibid, p26). Social rights entail claims on scarce resources and this may require rationing and the exercise of administrative or professional power which may be countered only by the idea that citizens have rights in the public sector as they do in the private sector. To this end Plant advances a large-ly rhetorical claims-based notion of citizen empowerment while urging a strictly piecemeal and pragmatic approach to redress.

This argument is taken up by Coote (1992) to advocate the enactment of a British social charter. This would specify sub-stantive rights to welfare and provide a framework within which to interpret and develop social legislation. According to Coote, however, such a charter should not be directly enforceable by way of individual redress and it should not be constitutionally entrenched in the way that she would like to see a bill of civil and political rights entrenched. Coote's argument is that it is only through the democratic process (i.e. guaranteed political rights) that social rights can be won, and that the function of a social charter should be to provide a 'supportive environment' in which to promote 'procedural' rights to welfare (i.e. rights founded doc-trinally within the civil sphere). Even the most articulate champi-ons of social rights refrain from asserting them on an equal foot-ing with civil and political rights. Social rights seem destined to remain constitutionally subordinate (see Dean,1996). Civil rights may be enforced through the courts and political rights through the electoral process. Redress in respect of social rights in con-trast is exercisable not of itself but subject only to legal or political authority.

If we are to understand welfare redress from the perspective of a claims-based conception of rights, then redress for any claim to the conditions necessary to satisfy the needs of social existence must assume either a declaratory or a case-oriented character. It must be asserted politically, or it must amount to a challenge to those with power over the distribution of resources. Where the definition of social rights and the administration of welfare are subordinate to political processes redress may take on the char-acter of resistance. Such redress requires mechanisms of expres-sion which, though they lie outside the immediate realm of elec-toral politics, must be sanctioned from within it (participative forums or ombudspersons), or which may establish special plead-ing before some administrative or professional authority which parliament has empowered (case review committees).

If we are to understand welfare redress from the perspective of a doctrinal conception of rights, then redress for an entitlement to welfare benefits or services must assume either an adjudicative or a consumer form. It must conform to the processes of civil law or the norms of the market. Where social rights are subordinate to contractual processes, redress may take on the character of liti-gious proprietorship. Such redress is channelled either into quasi-judicial forums (tribunals) or quasi-market systems (complaints procedures).

The subordination and resistance of welfare recipients

Not only are social rights constitutionally subordinate, but the recipients of state welfare are themselves subordinated. The mechanisms of redress associated with social rights can be implicated in this process. I have argued elsewhere that, in the development of the modern welfare state, the 'case approach' and 'legalisation' represented two complementary disciplinary techniques for the subjection of welfare recipients (Dean,1991).

By the 'case approach' I refer to those methods of surveillance and classification which were developed in nineteenth century England by organisations such as the Charity Organisation Society as a means, not only of distinguishing the deserving from the undeserving, but of influencing the character and habits of 'the poor'. Such methods have since been refined to provide the basis of social casework practice on the one hand, and some surviving precepts of social assistance administration on the other. While case redress may be understood as a way of challenging or resisting the use of case approach techniques by welfare administrators, ultimately it requires complicity with such techniques. Complainants or appellants must constitute themselves as supplicants or as individual cases with special or deserving circumstances. While this tendency has been condemned in the past in relation to social assistance tribunals (for example, Adler & Bradley, 1975), it can be witnessed today before community care review panels, not least because of the ways in which complainants may feel constrained when challenging needs assessments by social services professionals to 'act the part' of the deserving supplicant (Dean, Gale & Woods,1996).

By 'legalisation' I refer to the definition of rights which ensured on the one hand that official decision makers were constrained by predetermined rules, but on the other, that the objects of decision-making were constituted as individual juridical subjects - as the bearers of such rights. In this way, the burden of vigilance against the undeserving supplicant was transformed into a burden of proof laid upon the subject in need of state assistance. To qualify for assistance, the subject must not only submit to official scrutiny but must demonstrate compliance with the relevant rules and conditions. Such rules and conditions appear, not as coercive impositions, but as correlative duties to the rights of citizenship upon whose acceptance the status and identity of the subject depends. Adjudicative redress requires that the appellant submits to the jurisdiction of the tribunal. The tribunal has power, not only to interpret and determine appeals in accordance with substantive law, but to regulate the conduct of the appellant in accordance with procedural rules (Dean, 1991, ch. 6). Once again, we have more recently observed such tendencies at community care review panel hearings, some of which function in spite of guidance to the contrary with at least a hint of the trappings of the adversarial traditions of the English legal system (Dean, Gale & Woods,1996).

The various public participation initiatives which characterised policy developments of the 1960s and 1970s gave rise to forms of declaratory redress which were ostensibly liberating rather than disciplinary. Reference, however, has already been made to the work of Cockburn (1977), who has suggested that the effect of such initiatives was often to disable protest and to co-opt the most vocal complainants. Where complaints forums or committees were developed as part of such initiatives these often provided a mere 'ritual of participation' (Mathiesen, 1980) through which criticism was orchestrated only as a means to control it. None the less, after observing one such committee, McCarthy et al commented that it had succeeded in creating opportunities for 'vox pop' to be heard and, on at least one occasion, had resulted for a chief local government officer in 'an uncomfortable grilling' by a member of the public: they assert that 'Cynics may dismiss this as little more than a bureaucratic tableau vivant staged for the benefit of an angry citizen, but the fact that it took place at all is in many ways significant' (1992, pp94-5).

This raises questions about what people hope to achieve by way of redress. Mulcahy & Lloyd-Bostock, on the basis of research on hospital complaints procedures, have observed that some complaints are probably better seen as ends in themselves than as instrumental or goal-directed. Where the complainant does 'want something' it may well be an appropriate social response' (1992, pp63-4). Research on community care complaints procedures in which the author was involved encountered complainants who plainly had nothing to gain materially. One man, complaining on behalf of his mother - who had since died - about a disputed disabled facilities grant, told the review panel 'I'm going to make sure this cannot happen to anyone else' (Dean, Gale & Woods 1996). What he clearly sought was vindication, but the procedure cast him in the role of a petitionary representative of the community interest. He was made to act out his personal anger as altruism. This ritual of participation resulted neither in complainant satisfaction, nor any perceptible change in council policy or procedure: the panel concerned did not and perhaps could not identify any generalisable or lasting lessons to be learned from a particular and isolated complaint.

The emerging forms of consumer redress are enmeshed within their own relations of power. The ideological fiction from which they draw authority assumes, not merely parity of status between the suppliers of services and their customers, but that the customer and her/his wishes are sovereign. However, even the CCCTF acknowledges that 'The 'customers' of the Inland Revenue and the prison service, for instance, may well feel it unfair that they are 'customers' at all' (1994b, no.3, para. 1.2) and the same might be said of those who as a result of powerlessness or vulnerability become 'customers' of welfare agencies.

The managerialist approach to 'quality' in service provision is dedicated, not to complying with customer's wishes, but to maximising customer satisfaction or 'goodwill', to which end communication - through promotional materials, customer care protocols and complaints procedures - plays a vital part in shaping the expectations and perceptions of the customer. The Wilson Committee commissioned consultants to review complaints procedures in both the public and private sectors. Among the 'lessons' to be learnt from the review was 'that levels of satisfaction were affected by the time and the number of contacts taken to close a complaint' (Wilson 1994, p29). The advice to organisations is to be pre-emptive; to use the telephone to contact complainants immediately; even to solicit complaints before transactions are completed. The emphasis is on 'empowering' front-line staff and training them, for example, in the use of eye contact, body language and listening skills. Acknowledging that it can be difficult for public sector staff to deal with complaints about policy matters over which they have no control (for example, benefit levels), the CCCTF emphasise the role which such staff have in overcoming the 'misunderstandings' which the public may have:

> Organisations might usefully look at training for staff on how to handle complaints about policy positively (such as explaining the policy, or suggesting a further option for the person to pursue their complaint, rather than 'Sorry mate, nothing I can do')
> (CCCTF, 1994b, no.4, para. 2.1.8).

In effect, welfare organisations are urged to manipulate their customers' perceptions and, if not actually to deceive, to create a favourable impression of the organisation and the policy context in which it operates.

We should not decry the idea of empowering and enhancing the skills of front-line staff, but neither should we be immune to the implications if this should be achieved at the expense of relatively powerless and vulnerable service users. This has been clearly illustrated in the work of Ungerson and Baldock (1994) who found that the users of social care services could be significantly disadvantaged if they had neither adopted the ethos nor mastered the skills necessary to negotiate provision as consumers within a mixed economy of care. The research on community care complaints procedures in which this author was involved suggests that complainants who appear before review panels may seldom play the part of the dissatisfied sovereign customer. Well-intentioned review panels, far from empowering the complainant, exhibited a certain Procrustean tendency to fit the complainant and her/his problem to the limitations of their own jurisdiction and to reinforce the authority of the departments whose decisions they reviewed (Dean, Gale & Woods,1996).

Conclusion

This paper has sought to demonstrate that welfare redress is a complex issue, underpinned by competing ideas about where rights come from. When people complain about welfare services or appeal against the allocation of welfare benefits they do so often for complex reasons and with a variety of expectations, which are not well understood.

Redress is concerned, not only with rights, but with the exercise of power. To demand redress is to offer resistance, though ironically resistance is itself necessary to the exercise of power (Foucault, 1981). Mechanisms for redress provide diverse points of resistance to the state yet have been consistently deployed to insulate, nourish or extend the authority of policy makers, to defuse anger and protest, and to define the recipients of welfare as 'cases', as legal 'subjects', as 'citizens', or as 'customers'. Recent developments may represent a move away from adjudicative and participative forums in favour of case-review and complaints systems, although the trend is not necessarily decisive. When it comes to who complains, it is not only the heroic consumers of quasi-market provision and the helpless clients of residual discretionary mechanisms, it is also litigious subjects and angry citizens who continue through their resistance to constitute the welfare state.

References

Adler, M. & Asquith, S. (eds) (1981) Discretion and Welfare, London, Heinemann.

Adler, M. & Bradley, A. (eds) (1975) Justice, Discretion and Poverty: Supplementary Benefit Appeal Tribunals in Britain, Abingdon, Professional Books.

Burrows, R. & Loader, B. (eds) (1994) Towards a Post-Fordist Welfare State? London, Routledge.

Citizen's Charter Complaints Task Force (CCCTF) (1994a) Complaints: Literature Review, London, Cabinet Office.

Citizen's Charter Complaints Task Force (CCCTF) (1994b) If Things Go Wrong ... A Discussion Paper Series: no.1 Access, no.2 Simplicity and speed, no.3 Fairness, no.4 Attitude and motivation, no.5 Information, no.6 Redress, London, Cabinet Office.

Cockburn, C. (1977) The Local State: Management of Cities and People, London, Pluto Press.

Coote, A. (1992) 'Introduction' in A. Coote (ed) The Welfare of Citizens: Developing New Social Rights, London, Rivers Oram/IPPR.

Cranston, R. (1985) Legal Foundations of the Welfare State, London, Weidenfeld and Nicolson.

Dalley, G. & Berthoud, R. (1992) Challenging Discretion: The Social Fund Review Procedure, London, Policy Studies Institute.

Dean, H. (1991) Social Security and Social Control, London, Routledge.

Dean, H. (1996) Welfare, Law and Citizenship, Hemel Hempstead, Prentice Hall/Harvester Wheatsheaf.

Dean, H., Gale, K. & Woods, R. (1996) 'This isn't very typical I'm afraid: Observing community care complaints procedures', Health and Social Care (in press).

Department for Education (DFE) (1994) Special Education Needs Tribunal: Consultation Paper on Draft Regulations and Rules of Procedure, London, DFE.

Department of Health (DH)(1990) Community Care in the Next Decade and Beyond: Policy Guidance, London, HMSO.

Department of Social Security (DSS) (1995a) Improving Child Support, Cm. 2745, London, HMSO. Department of Social Security (DSS) (1995b) Social Research Branch Newsletter, Autumn 1995.

Donnison, D. (1982) The Politics of Poverty, Oxford, Martin Robertson.

Eardley, T. & Sainsbury, R. (1991) Housing Benefit Reviews: An Evaluation of the Effectiveness of the Review System in Responding to Claimants Dissatisfied with Housing Benefit Decisions, Department of Social Security Research Report Series, no. 3, London, HMSO.

Esping-Andersen, G. (1990) The Three Worlds of Welfare Capitalism, Cambridge, Polity.

Fine, B. (1984) Democracy and the Rule of Law: Liberal Ideals and Marxist Critiques, London, Pluto Press.

Finer, S. (1952) The Life and Times of Sir Edwin Chadwick, London, Methuen.

Foucault, M. (1980) 'On popular justice: A discussion with Maoists' in C. Gordon, (ed.) Power/Knowledge, Brighton, Harvester Press.

Foucault, M. (1981) The History of Sexuality: An Introduction, Harmondsworth, Penguin.

Franks, O. (1957) Report of the Committee on Administrative Tribunals and Inquiries, Cmnd. 218, London, HSMO.

Genn, H. & Genn, Y. (1989) The Effectiveness of Representation at Tribunals, London, Lord Chancellor's Department.

Gray, A. & Jenkins, B. (1993) 'Markets, managers and the public service: The changing of a culture', in P. Taylor Gooby & R. Lawson, (eds) Markets and Managers: New Issues in the Delivery of Welfare, Buckingham, Open University Press.

Griffith, Sir Roy (1983) National Health Service Management Inquiry, London, Department of Health

Griffiths, Sir Roy (1988) Community Care: An Agenda for Action A Report to the Secretary of State for Social Services, London, HMSO.

Hegel, G. (1821) Philosophy of Right, 1942 edition, Oxford, Oxford University Press.

Hirst, P. (1980) 'Law, socialism and rights', in P. Carlen & M. Collison (eds) Radical Issues in Criminology, Oxford, Martin Roberts on.

Hoggett, P. (1987) 'A farewell to mass production? Decentralisation as an emergent private and public sector paradigm' in P. Hoggett & R. Hambleton (eds) Decentralisation and Democracy, Occasional Paper 28, Bristol, School for Advanced Urban Studies.

Hoggett, P. (1994) 'The politics of the modernisation of the UK welfare state,' in R. Burrows & B. Loader (eds) Towards a Post-Fordist Welfare State?, London, Routledge.

Hood, C. (1991) 'A public management for all seasons?', Public Administration vol.69 no.1 pp3-19

Lewis, N. & Birkinshaw, P. (1993) When Citizens Complain: Reforming Justice and Administration, Buckingham, Open University Press.

Lewis, N. Senevratne, M. & Cracknell, S. (1986) Complaints Procedures in Local Government, Sheffield, Centre for Criminological Studies.

Mann, M. (1987) 'Ruling class strategies and citizenship', Sociology, vol.21, no.3, pp339-354.

Marshall, T.H. (1950) 'Citizenship and social class', reprinted in T.H. Marshall & T. Bottomore (1992) Citizenship and Social Class, London, Pluto Press.

Marx, K. (1887) Capital, vol.1, 1970 edition, London, Lawrence & Wishart.

Mashaw, J. (1983) Bureaucratic Justice, New Haven, Yale University Press.

Mathiesen, T. (1980) Law, Society and Poltical Action: Towards a Strategy under Late Capitalism, London, Academic Press.

McCarthy, P. Simpson, B. Hill, M. Walker, J. & Corlyon, J. (1992) Grievances, Complaints and Local Government: Towards the Responsive Local Authority, Aldershot, Avebury.

Miller, S. & Peroni, F. (1992) 'Social politics and the citizen's charter,' in N. Manning & R. Page (eds) Social Policy Review 4, Canterbury, Social Policy Association.

Mulcahy, L. & Lloyd-Bostock, S. (1992) 'Complaining - what's the use?', in R. Dingwall, & P.Fenn (eds) Quality and Regulation in Health Care: International Experiences, London, Routledge.

Pfeffer, N. & Coote, A. (1991) Is Quality Good for You? A Critical Review of Quality Assurance in Welfare Services, London, Institute for Public Policy Research.

Pirie, M. (1991) The Citizen's Charter, London, Adam Smith Institute.

Plant, R. (1992) 'Citizenship, rights and welfare', in A. Coote (ed) The Welfare of Citizens: Developing New Social Rights, London, Rivers Oram/IPPR.

Prime Minister's Office (1991) The Citizen's Charter: Raising the Standard, Cm. 1599, London, HMSO.

Redcliffe-Maud, Lord (1969) The Report of the Royal Commission on Local Government in England, Cmnd. 4040, London, HMSO.

Reich, C. (1964) 'The new property', Yale Law Journal, vol.73, no.5, pp733-787

Seebohm, F. (1968) Report of the Committee on Local Authority and Allied Personal Social Services, Cmnd. 3703, London, HMSO.

Simons, K. (1995) I'm Not Complaining But ... Complaints Procedures in Social Services Departments, York, Joseph Rowntree Foundation.

Skeffington, A. (1969) People and Planning, London, HMSO.

Spicker, P. (1993) 'Needs as claims', Social Policy & Administration, vol.27, no.1, pp7-17.

Thomson, W. (1992) 'Realising rights through local service contracts', in A. Coote (ed) The Welfare of Citizens: Developing New Social Rights, London, Rivers Oram/IPPR.

Titmuss, R. (1971) 'Welfare rights, law and discretion', Political Quarterly, vol.42, no.2.pp

Ungerson, C. & Baldock, J. (1994) Becoming Consumers of Community Care, York, Joseph Rowntree Foundation.

Warde, A. (1994) 'Consumers, consumption and post-Fordism', in R. Burrows & B. Loader, (eds) Towards a Post-Fordist Welfare State? London, Routledge.

Webb, B. & Webb, S. (1963) English Poor Law History, vol.2, London, Frank Cass.

Whyatt, Sir John (1961) The Citizen and Administration: The Redress of Grievances, London, Stevens.

Wilson, A. (1994) Being Heard: The Report of a Review Committee on NHS Complaints Procedures, Leeds, Department of Health.

5 Ten Years after the 1986 Social Security Act

Carey Oppenheim and
Ruth Lister

Introduction

The 1986 Social Security Act was billed as carrying the social
security system into the next century. Yet since 1986 the reform
of social security has been almost continuous. The 1986 Act
embodied central strands in Conservative social security policy,
each of which received different emphasis at particular points
over the decade. We begin this chapter by focusing on the Act
itself, its implementation and aftermath. We then look back over
the ten years, identifying the key policies, contexts and approaches of different Secretaries of States and review the broad themes
underlying the changes since 1986 (fraud, incentives, obligation,
self-reliance, the shift from state to family, targeting and the relationship between social security and economic policy).The penul-
timate section of the chapter considers the combined impact of
these changes and how far they amount to a shift in the nature of
this part of the welfare state. We conclude with some thoughts
about the current debate on social security.

The 1986 Social Security Act and its aftermath

The first Conservative government's radicalism was not primarily focused on the welfare state (Timmins, 1995). However, the early 1980s contained the seeds for future policies (Lister, 1991). Most important was the breaking of the link between long-term national insurance benefits and pensions and earnings, not only because of substantial expenditure savings, but also because it represented a rejection of the view that benefits should reflect increases in national prosperity. The changes made in the early 1980s were, in Timmins' words, 'driven by a desperate determination to reduce spending [rather] than by any ideologically coherent approach to means- testing or incentives' (1995, pp376-7).

In contrast, the 1986 Act encapsulated an all-encompassing approach to social security reform. Norman Fowler described the reforms as 'the most fundamental review of social security since the Second World War' (DHSS, 1985, preface). In fact the parameters of reform were limited by two important factors - it was a nil-cost review and taxation was not included.[1] In practice, the Green Paper's focus was dominated by means-tested benefits and pensions rather than the social security system as a whole. It drew on carefully selected parts of the Beveridge legacy, arguing in particular that 'social security will be based on the twin pillars of provision - individual and state - with stronger emphasis on individual provision than hitherto' (DHSS, 1985, para.6.6). It also emphasized the dangers that the cost of social security posed to the economy.

The Act's objectives remain at the core of the government's social security strategy today: that social security policy should be consistent with economic objectives, direct resources to those in the greatest need, simplify the benefits structure, improve the administration of benefits and reinforce 'personal independence rather than extend the power of the state' (DHSS, 1985, para 6.6) (See Figure 1 for the main changes in the Act).

The changes amounted to what researchers at the LSE Welfare State programme have called 'churning' rather than targeting: money has shifted between groups of claimants, with families with children, sick and disabled people and the very elderly benefiting at the expense of the unemployed and in particular the young (Evans et al., 1994). Moreover, within broad categories of gainers there were significant proportions of losers. Importantly the LSE research found that the reforms appeared to make no difference to the numbers falling below the poverty line.

The 1986 Act's significance, in the view of some commentators was much exaggerated; the Financial Times argued

Figure 1 The 1986 Social Security Act: central changes

Income support replaced supplementary benefit premia for certain groups such as families, lone parents, pensioners and disabled people replaced the old additional payments for extra needs.
Social fund replaced regulated system of single payments; it is composed of two parts: the regulated fund for maternity, funeral and cold weather payments and the discretionary fund which administers both community care grants and loans. The latter is budget limited and discretionary. A system of internal reviews and appeals to social fund inspectors replaced the legal right of appeal.
Family credit replaced family income supplement; it is more generous than its predecessor, but free school meals were withdrawn from working families at the same time.
SERPS based on life-time earnings rather than best 20 years, fiscal incentives to opt out of SERPS and occupational schemes into private pensions.

that 'historians are likely to regard the 'Fowler' reforms as little more than a penny-pinching stopgap. They do not address the real problems, not least because of the narrowness of their scope' (5 April 1988). Certainly the Act did not match the rhetoric of a 'new Beveridge' ; many experienced no change as a result of the legislation and the reforms' radicalism was tempered by political expediency. For example, child benefit was not means-tested despite earlier media predictions, and the original proposal to abolish SERPS was dropped in the face of opposition from the pensions industry among others. However, as the embodiment of a number of themes which have continued to drive social security policy (see below), the Act did represent something of a milestone.

Ten years on

Thus, far from marking an end to reform, the 1986 Act heralded what has sometimes felt like an era of permanent revolution. It is possible to divide this ten year period into two phases: the first, from 1986 to 1993, shifts between ideology and pragmatic consolidation under the respective reigns of John Moore and Tony Newton; the second is dominated by Peter Lilley's sector-by-sector review of social security spending, and by important changes in the parameters of debate about the challenges facing social security which be gin to cross party political lines.

When Moore took over as Secretary of State in 1988 it was clear that he saw the 1986 Act as the first step towards a radically reformed welfare state. His overtly ideological approach, influenced by the New Right, was very different from the pragmatic style of his predecessor, Norman Fowler. He put a new gloss on the Fowler reforms, borrowing the language of 'welfare dependency' from the United States. The ideological deployment of this language was to become increasingly dominant in the politics of social security during the 1990s. Means-testing was seen not only as a means of focusing on the poorest and curbing the scope of public expenditure but as fulfilling a more overtly ideological purpose 'to change the climate of opinion on welfare' (1987).

Moore oversaw two important pieces of legislation which were directed towards young people and the unemployed. The first of these, the 1988 Social Security Act, replaced the right of sixteen and seventeen year-olds to income support with a guarantee of a youth training place for each young person. Severe hardship payments were available in particular circumstances for young people who were not in work, training or education. Second, the 1989 Social Security Act brought in the 'actively seeking work' test for unemployed people. This followed closely on the heels of a toughening up of the availability for work tests. However, Moore's legacy, exemplified by his speech 'The end of the line for poverty', which rejected the concept of relative poverty, was in Timmins' view, more about the language and rhetoric of welfare than about specific measures. 'It is from around this time that the words 'welfare state' began to lose some of their traditional feeling of being a positive good' (1995, p452).

Moore's replacement by Newton promised a return to more pragmatic policies and style. He oversaw changes to disability benefits which brought in a mixed package of improvements to existing provision including the introduction of Disability Living Allowance and Disability Working Allowance. It was also under Newton that, despite the long-term opposition of Margaret Thatcher, child benefit was once again uprated after being frozen for three years in the mid to late eighties. In the run-up to the election Major's 1991 Budget signalled an important turn-around - child benefit was to be uprated annually in line with inflation. Newton spurred on by Mrs Thatcher, also presided over the introduction of the Child Support Act which, once implemented, was to be a highly contentious piece of legislation.

Lilley's arrival at the DSS coincided with a sharp deterioration in government finances. While public expenditure featured strongly in debates around the 1986 Act, it acquired an overriding importance in this period, triggered by the Portillo Reviews of Public Spending. But Lilley has tackled social security very differently from Fowler - rather than one big open review and a single social security act - he has proceeded sector-by-sector behind closed doors. Pirie, president of the Adam Smith Institute, argues that such an approach is likely to gain greater public acceptance and that while each change appears to be 'relatively minor', the final result is a 'radical' change (Sunday Times, 7 September 1995).

The sector-by-sector approach has led to a series of far-reaching changes. The two most important structural reforms have been the introduction of incapacity benefit and the job seekers allowance, both of which embody radical changes to the national insurance scheme. Entitlement to incapacity benefit, which replaces invalidity benefit, is limited by a functional test of incapacity. Alongside other cutbacks this reduces the numbers of claimants by 300,000 a year, creating annual savings of £2 billion by the end of the century (Social Security Committee, 1995). The job seeker's allowance replaced unemployment benefit and income support for the unemployed in 1996. It reduces the length of time contributory benefit is received from twelve to six months and lowers benefit for eighteen to twenty-four years olds in line with income support. A new job seekers agreement is a condition of receiving benefit and tougher availability and actively seeking work tests and sanctions are introduced. Savings are estimated at £0.7bn by the end of the century (Social Security Committee, 1995). Lilley's reforms follow over a decade and a half of steady erosion of the scope and cost of benefits for these key contributory benefits (Atkinson and Micklewright, 1989; Lynes, 1992; Lynes, 1994).

Other policy changes under Lilley include equalising the pension age at sixty five, further long term cuts to SERPS, reductions in housing benefit and help with mortgage interest for income support claimants, as well as restrictions on benefits for foreigners and asylum seekers. As a whole the sector-by-sector approach will have, according to his estimates, pruned some £5bn a year from the social security budget by the year 2000 (DSS, 1995b).

Themes underlying social security policy change

The emphasis given to the various themes underlying social security policy has thus varied with different Ministers. These themes, while not exclusive to the Thatcher and Major period, have been highlighted during it reflecting the economic and ideological preoccupations of the era (Lister, 1991).

Fraud and 'abuse"

The anti-fraud refrain has been heard frequently both before and since 1986. However, under Lilley the drive against fraud has become a central source of budget savings with new measures announced annually. Anti-fraud initiatives are estimated to yield £2.5 billion by 1998/99 (DSS, 1995a). Lilley's crusade against fraud and 'abuse' has also focused on asylum seekers and people from abroad: 'We all want to help genuine refugees. But Britain should be a safe haven, not a soft touch' (Lilley, 1995a). A raft of measures has restricted benefits for this group including the introduction of the habitual residence test in 1994 which, although aimed at 'benefit tourism', has had a particularly detrimental effect on Black and minority ethnic groups (Allbeson, 1996). More recently, the rules on 'public funds' and sponsorship have been tightened up and the rights of asylum seekers have been drastically curtailed, in effect barring many groups of people from abroad from access to nearly all social security benefits. The Social Security Advisory Committee concluded that while the task of dealing with growing numbers of asylum seekers was difficult for the Government, it did not believe that:

> it is acceptable that a solution should be sought by putting at risk of destitution many people who are genuinely seeking refuge in this country, amongst whom may be some of the most vulnerable and defenceless in our society (SSAC, 1996 para 88).

Social security fraud is indeed an important issue, although its extent and the actual savings from anti-fraud work are subject to considerable uncertainty (Deacon, 1994). An important distinction has to be made between organised and individual fraud. The latter has to be examined in the context of the complexity, inflexibility and inadequacy of many social security benefits (Deacon, 1994; Field, 1995) as well as a highly casualised labour market (Dean, 1996). The drive against fraud has not been accompanied by a parallel commitment to increase the take-up of benefits. The association in DSS press releases and announcements between benefit 'abuse' and people from abroad is particularly worrying in the context of a political debate which is preoccupied with 'race'. Measures such as the proposals to fine employers who employ illegal immigrants as well as the cutbacks in social security touch not only those most directly affected - people from abroad - but ripple outwards to affect many other people from black and minority ethnic communities (Gordon & Newnham, 1985; Amin with Oppenheim, 1992).

Shedding responsibility and cutting civil service numbers

The increase in the number of staff working on anti-fraud initiatives has taken place in the context of an overall reduction in DSS civil servants, as part of the drive to reduce expenditure. Several measures have led to a shifting of responsibilities. In the social security area three government agencies have been created: the Benefits, Employment and Child Support Agencies which function at arms-length from ministers. The creation of government agencies raises an important issue about ministerial accountability. The introduction of housing benefit has bestowed responsibility upon local authorities for administering, subsidising in limited areas and policing a major social security benefit. Employers too have taken on growing responsibility for administering both Statutory Maternity Pay and Statutory Sick Pay. In 1991 the subsidy received by employers for SSP was reduced from 100 per cent to 80 per cent. Since that date it has been reduced still further with the exception of small firms.

There is some evidence from the National Association of Citizens Advice Bureau (NACAB) that some employers refuse to pay Statutory Sick Pay (SSP) or pay at a reduced amount or sack employees who become sick (NACAB, 1990). However, according to larger scale research (Middleton et al, 1994) the growth of employer involvement in SSP does not appear to have affected employer practice. As far as Statutory Maternity Pay (SMP) is concerned research by the Policy Studies Institute suggests that a small proportion of women are not receiving their entitlement (McRae and Daniel, 1991).

The most recent and dramatic measure is the proposed cut of 25 per cent in the running costs of social security over the next two to three years. Suggestions of self-assessment for claimants have been floated alongside a purchaser/ provider split in the administration of benefits (Guardian, 8 February 1996).

Simplification

Simplification has been another means of reducing civil service numbers. The need to simplify the social security system is all too apparent. There has been a degree of administrative simplification within the means-tested system itself. All three benefits are now based on 'common provisions,' that is, broadly similar rules for assessing entitlement (with some exceptions for example, lone parents) and premia for particular categories(see Figure 1 above) replaced the complex additional requirements which met a multitude of different needs; although Hill (1996) notes that some of the complexity has shifted into the housing benefit scheme. However, administrative simplification is not equivalent to simplification for the claimant. While there is evidence of an increase in take-up of the main means-tested benefits, it is still low for some groups and remains well below 100 per cent in most cases (Piachaud, 1996).

However, there are other aspects of means-tested benefits which have become far more complex. The introduction of severe hardship payments has added a discretionary layer into a means-tested scheme. Young people have to satisfy not only a means-test, but also a test of hardship. Despite the increase in the number of payments, many young people are ill-informed and find it very difficult to make a claim (three offices have to be visited) (COYPSS, 1995). The array of welfare to work schemes which include various earnings disregards, rolling up earnings over a period of time (the Back to Work Bonus) in-work premiums for family credit and childcare disregards are useful, albeit modest, attempts to provide footholds in the labour market. However, they also highlight the difficulties of a means-tested scheme encompassing changing economic and social conditions in a straightforward and simple way.

Above all, given the centrality of the targeting strategy - whether it is greater means-testing or conditionality or discretion - administrative complexity inevitably follows. The much higher administrative costs of means-tested benefits (in particular the social fund which incurs administrative costs of 61 per cent of its overall expenditure) in comparison with most other kinds of benefits, bear witness to this (Piachaud, 1996; DSS, 1995b).

Targeting

The spiralling complexity of the social security system principally stems from the commitment, expressed most clearly in the Fowler reforms, to targeting help on those most in need. Until 1993, targeting was interpreted and implemented as means-testing, which had been seen as largely unproblematic by the Government. However, since 1993 there has been some recognition of the impact of means-tests on the incentive to work and save. In his Mais Lecture Lilley argued that 'means-testing is not the only way of targeting benefit more closely on need' (1993). He outlined other ways of focusing help, which have been implemented as policy: categorisation (eg raising the retirement age for women to sixty five), defining need more narrowly (eg limiting incapacity benefit through a change in the definition of incapacity), tighter enforcement (eg, the rules for Restart), conditionality (eg, the new job seekers agreement) and contributions tests (tightened up considerably for unemployment benefit). In fact, many of these alternative measures for focusing on need more closely will in turn result in greater means-testing.

Means-tested benefits have multiplied over the decade (Field, 1995; Piachaud, 1996). The Government itself estimates that nearly a third (30 per cent) of individuals are in households in receipt of one or more of the main means-tested benefits (DSS, 1995b). Piachaud (1996) shows that expenditure on means-tested benefits has grown from 17 per cent of all benefits in 1979 to 33 per cent in 1993, but that the growth of means-testing has not been uniform or consistent. 'The politically vulnerable and expendable' such as the unemployed have received harsher treatment to save on public money. Crucially, he reveals that the strategy has not resulted in better targeting. Taking the bottom two quintiles together, he shows that in 1979 they received 63 per cent of cash benefits where as by 1993 this had fallen to 59 per cent.

As the Social Security Committee (1995) has emphasised means-testing conflicts fundamentally with other tenets of government policy: it diminishes incentives, increases complexity, acts as a disincentive to take out private provision, creates greater scope for fraud and flies in the face of the goal of increasing self-reliance.

Incentives

This concern with incentives has always been a feature of social security policy but under the Conservatives it has become an oft-cited and explicit objective. A variety of tools has sharpened incentives to work. These fall broadly into four categories: reducing benefit levels, subsidising low wages, increasing sanctions and welfare to work measures as described above.

In relation to the first, Lilley states that he does not want to improve incentives by cutting benefits for the unemployed but rather 'to ensure that our benefit system overall makes people better off in work than out of work' (Lilley, 1995b, p34). Despite this claim, a series of measures has chipped away at the benefits side of the equation: ending earnings-relation and dependency additions, reducing benefit for young people getting job seeker's allowance (JSA), the restriction to 6 months for contributory JSA and reducing help with mortgage payments for income support claimants.

The second tool which encourages people into low paid work encompasses family credit, disability working allowance and the piloting of an earnings top-up (equivalent to family credit for people without children). Alongside these benefits are changes in hours rules to encourage claimants, especially lone parents, to move into part-time work. The third approach involves both a toughening of the obligation to be available and seek work as well as a sharp increase in the sanctions for not doing so.

The strategies for increasing incentives have a number of problems. First, some have attempted to straddle the gap between benefits and work by reducing the living standards of some groups of claimants. Second, the subsidisation of low wages removes the obligation of employers to pay adequate wages themselves in the absence of a minimum wage. Third, a policy of increasing sanctions may also be counter-productive - the threat of subsequently losing much or all of benefit militates against taking the risk of entering employment. In addition, research on the actively seeking work test found that employers did not want to employ people they thought were applying for jobs simply to comply with the test (Jacobs, 1994). More generally, the effectiveness of measures to increase incentives is doomed in a means-tested system. The poverty trap may have lost its worse excesses (no one now has a withdrawal rate of over 100 per cent), yet as means-tested benefits proliferate so too does the poverty trap; the numbers in a poverty trap of 60 per cent marginal tax rates or more has increased from 450,000 in 1988 to 620,000 today (Piachaud, 1996).

Obligations

Intertwined with the concern with incentives is a deeper philosophical shift from a language of rights to obligations - reflecting new Right thinkers in the United States, but now increasingly used by the centre-left (Lister, 1996). Moore (1988) spelt out clearly what he called the balance of the citizenship equation:

In a free society, the equation that has 'rights' on one side must have 'responsibilities' on the other. It has to. it will not stay free for long unless it does. For more than a quarter of a century, public focus has been on citizens' 'rights' and it is now past time to redress the balance.

The language of responsibility and obligation is central to the discourse of two major pieces of legislation - the Child Support Act and the Job Seekers Allowance. At the heart of the CSA is the obligation of absent parents to support their children. This enforcement of responsibility is stated explicitly in relation both to the power to deduct benefit from the caring parent who refuses to name the father and in relation to the deduction from the absent parent on income support. The notion of personal responsibility is over-riding (Oppenheim & Lister, 1996). The Job Seeker's Allowance White Paper, with its introduction of a Job Seeker's Contract, argues:

> Changes are needed to make clear to unemployed people the link between their receipt of benefit and the obligations that places upon them (DSS & DEG, 1994, para.2.7).

Fleshing out the concepts of responsibility and obligation in practice is fraught with difficulties. In relation to the CSA, in many cases absent parents have felt that the obligation that the state is imposing upon them is inappropriate - hence high levels of non-payment.[2] The enforcement of family responsibility highlights the difficulty of extensive state involvement in a complex area of people's lives and contrasts with the rhetoric of reducing the power of a coercive state (Oppenheim and Lister, 1996). In the case of unemployment, it is more difficult to enforce an obligation to seek work in a climate of high unemployment - in such situations, stricter sanctions are simply experienced as punitive. Despite little evidence of their success, the government has continued to expand its mandatory training and job search programmes of which 'Project Work', a compulsory work experience programme, is the latest (Murray, 1996). Rights and obligations can be understood as standing in a relationship of broad reciprocity, but there is a distinction between measures which accept that unemployed people have responsibility to be available for work which it is reasonable to expect them to do, and at a reasonable wage, and measures designed to force the unemployed into inappropriate and unacceptably low paid jobs (Lister, 1996a).

Self-reliance and independence

Both the themes of incentives and obligations feed into another central tenet of Conservative ideology:

> I came to office with one deliberate intent. To change Britain from a dependent to a self-reliant society - from a give-it-to-me to a do-it-yourself nation' (Thatcher, quoted in Timmins, 1995, p497).

The vision of promoting independence incorporates a number of aspects including reducing the 'dependency culture' and encouraging private provision. The concept of a 'dependency culture' owes much to debates in the United States, where Novak and others argued that'behavioural dependency' is 'at the heart of the poverty problem' (1987). In this view, the welfare state is seen as generating the very problems it is designed to solve. This analysis was taken up by a number of Ministers and most passionately by Moore. Perhaps the most graphic illustration of this is his frequently quoted contrast between the 'sullen apathy of dependence' and the 'sheer delight of personal achievement' (1987).

Two examples of policy were presented explicitly with reference to this ideological pre-occupation. The social fund was directly concerned with reducing 'dependence' on the state and weakening the culture of 'welfare rights'(Lister, 1991). Its introduction provoked widespread criticism from a range of organisations - official, academic and voluntary. It has resulted in a reduction in claimants' living standards with many falling below the income support level while they pay back loans, without meeting its objective of concentrating help on those facing greatest difficulties (Huby & Dix, 1992). Research by children's charities has shown how badly families with children have been affected by the change (eg, Barnardos, 1990). The reduction in access to help from the state has simply displaced dependency into other spheres - family, friends, charity and loan companies, often charging very high rates of interest.

The removal of income support from young people was justified along similar lines. According to a DHSS press release (1987) it was 'designed to avoid the damaging effects for young people of moving straight from school into the benefits culture'. But as several reports have documented, substantial numbers of young people fall through the safety-net (MacLagan, 1993) and the exposure of young people to crime, homelessness, abuse and exploitation is a far cry from the government's aim of increasing independence (Craig , 1991).

The goal of self-reliance has also been pursued in relation to increasing self-provision for social security needs through the private sector. Private provision is seen as enhancing individual choice and responsibility, as a way of increasing incentives to work and save and as a means of reducing public expenditure (Lilley, 1995b). The changes to SERPS under the 1986 Act (and more recent changes) and the encouragement of private pensions by providing fiscal incentives represent a significant redrawing of the boundary between public and private. More recently the reduction in help with mortgage costs is specifically geared to encourage prospective owner occupiers to provide their own cover in case of unemployment. The 'No Turning Back Group' of MPs has suggested that self-provision could be extended much further with the state withdrawing from other benefits such as the basic pension, unemployment and disability benefits (1993).

However, the growth of private provision is associated with important limitations and dangers. First, private provision come s with a cost to the state - by 1993/94 £9.1billion had been spent on providing national insurance rebates to encourage people to take out a private pension (Hansard, 2 February 1996, col.137). Secondly, the private sector cannot cater for the most vulnerable groups who come with the highest risks - those with repeated bouts of unemployment and sickness will either not be able to obtain cover or be unable to afford the higher premiums. The danger is that such initiatives will tend to create two-tier provision. Thirdly, the example of overselling by some pension companies who encouraged certain clients to leave good occupational schemes, highlights the difficulty of making informed judgements in a highly complex field. Fourth, while private provision is partly promoted on the ground s of enhancement of choice, it is not clear that people rate choice over and above security (Gray, 1994). The Social Security Advisory Committee in its analysis of private provision concluded: 'We foresee a continuing need for the current range of state benefits and any enhanced involvement of the private sector should be seen as an addition to, rather than an alternative to, the state scheme' (SSAC, 1994, para 1.6).

Finally, the rhetoric of self-reliance suggests that independence is distinct from and thus incompatible with reliance on state support and yet very often support from the state, whether in the form of cash, services or regulation can act as an important tool for achieving independence (Oppenheim, 1990).

Redrawing the boundaries between state and family

The promotion of independence has involved a significant redrawing of the boundaries of responsibility between state and family. A number of policies have contributed to this shift such as the repeated reductions in state support for young people which have been geared to encouraging parents to support older children, the social fund and most clearly the Child Support Act (CSA). The extent of the Treasury clawback of maintenance (£450m of a total of £530m anticipated savings in the first year was earmarked for the Treasury) is a direct expression of the substitution of private for state support. It comes at the cost to the majority of lone parents who are on income support and receive no financial benefit from the changes, unless they move into work (Garnham and Knights, 1994; Millar, 1994; Craig et al. in this volume).[3]

In this shift of responsibilities the 'family' ideal is a traditional one composed of a married couple with children. The anxiety on moral and economic grounds about both the future of the traditional family (Morgan, 1995) and the rise in lone parenthood punctuates social policy debates, whether it is in the latest Housing Bill or in the 1986 Budget (Lister, 1996b). The latter proposed freezing the lone parent premium and one parent benefit as part of a new policy: 'my intention over time is to continue to narrow the gap between the benefits which go to lone parents and those which go to couples' (Lilley, 1995b). But these latest measures are at odds with research that shows that lone parents face higher costs than couples with children (Dickens et al, 1995) and the Government's own earlier recognition of this. While the social security system does favour lone parents in some modest ways, decisions about family formation are complex, and not simply about the amount of state support available.

Control of Public Spending

Underpinning all the other themes has been the partly economic, partly ideological, goal of reducing public spending and thereby the role of the state. Given the government's view that 'public expenditure is at the heart of Britain's present economic difficulties' (Public Spending White Paper, 1979), it is not surprising that social security with the largest departmental budget, has featured centre stage in the attempts to bring spending down. The nil-cost remit of the 1986 Act looks rather modest in comparison with the approach since 1993 which has been dominated by the need to reduce public spending under the aegis of the Portillo Reviews.

The Growth of Social Security (DSS, 1993a) and Containing the Cost of Social Security (DSS, 1993b) are both central documents in putting the argument that social security spending is outpacing growth in the economy and that many other industrial countries are attempting to reduce spending in this area. Since then, the projections of spending have been revised downwards by £8bn, taking the share of social security spending as a proportion of GDP down from 12.6 per cent in 1994/5 to 11.7 per cent in 2000/2001 (Social Security Committee, 1995). The present Secretary of State attributes half of this reduction to policy changes, £2bn to falls in unemployment and the remainder to changes in forecasts.

The consensus that spending is out of control appears to be almost universal. However, a number of commentators have argued that the figures contained in The Growth of Social Security (DSS, 1993a) do not by themselves support the case for dramatic restructuring. They show that, assuming a relatively modest fall of a quarter in unemployment, social security spending would continue to represent a broadly stable share of GDP (Hills, 1993; Oppenheim, 1994). While the international picture does indeed show a widespread attempt to restrict social security spending, in many cases it is from a much higher base. The UK still has relatively low expenditure in this area in comparison with its neighbours. Moreover, social security spending is in part a reflection of external changes, including in some cases other areas of government policy. The three major causes of increased expenditure - increases in unemployment (and associated rises in benefits for sickness and invalidity), lone parenthood and the deregulation of rents - are largely beyond the control of social security policy itself. More fundamentally, the issue of the sustainability of the budget can only be answered , as the recent Social Security Committee Report suggests, in the context of 'the most fundamental of all questions namely the purpose of welfare itself.' (Social Security Committee, 1995, para 2). The Social Security Advisory Committee came to the conclusion that spending was not out of control and crucially that social security embodies 'the underlying values which society places on its care for fellow citizens in time of need. It is therefore a vital element in the social cohesion of the nation' (SSAC 1993, para.6.23).

The almost exclusive concentration on reducing the budget neglects the long-term costs to social solidarity of expenditure cuts. A number of commentators, including the former Thatcherite, Gray (1993), have become increasingly concerned that the pursuit of the individualistic neo-liberal economic goals have had unacceptably high costs. There is now a growing body of material on the centre-left which suggests that inequality, far from being a spur to economic growth, hinders it (Glyn & Miliband, 1994). This is not to argue that there is no crisis in social security, but that it is of a different order - which is only partly related to the question of public expenditure (Lister, 1996a).

Understanding the changes

How should we understand a decade of almost continual change in social security policy? Many of the policy goals have been contradictory or self-defeating - in particular the concentration on means-testing has clashed with the desire to increase incentives, to simplify and to promote personal independence. The control of public spending has been the touchstone of Conservative policy, and yet social security would appear to have trounced that strategy decisively. The budget soared from £46.5bn in 1978/9 to £85.2bn in 1994/5 (1994/5 prices) - a real increase of 83 per cent. The budget is, as we have discussed earlier, in part a reflection of broader social and economic trends which lie beyond the boundaries of social security. However, rises in expenditure cannot themselves be read as an indication of what Page (1995) has called the 'resilient welfare state thesis'.

In the Joseph Rowntree Inquiry into Income and Wealth, Hills (1995) found that key changes in benefit policy, in particular the breaking of the link between some benefits and earnings, and discretionary tax changes played an important role in undermining the effectiveness of the welfare state in narrowing income differences [4]. Some would argue that this is not an appropriate role for the welfare state. But if, as in our view, the reduction of inequality is an important goal for welfare the Rowntree finding provides important counter-evidence to the view that the welfare state was entirely 'resilient'.

Conservative policies have affected different sections of society in different ways (Oppenheim & Harker, 1996). For those who are in a weak position in the labour market, in particular women, minority ethnic groups and the unskilled and semi-skilled, the changes have reinforced market inequalities. For example, the changes to SERPS and the promotion of private pensions will be detrimental to those who have little bargaining power in the market. The overall shift to means-testing has particular implications for women, corroding their economic independence, as benefits are assessed on joint incomes (Lister, 1992). For minority ethnic groups increased emphasis on means-testing combined with exclusionary policies towards immigrants and asylum-seekers aggravates their already lower rates of take-up. As a whole the changes tend to reinforce exclusion: they exacerbate differences between the weak and strong in the labour market; they move towards the creation of two-tier provision in certain areas of social security policy as choice is offered only in a relatively unregulated private sector; and they inevitably begin to exclude the more afflu-ent as the system orientates itself more firmly around means-test-ed benefits.

In Esping-Andersen's (1994) tripartite model of post-war wel-fare states, the UK is portrayed as a hybrid which has elements of universal social rights and flat-rate benefits associated with Scandinavian welfare alongside greater private provision domi-nant in the US. He argues that despite changes over the 1980s European states are not moving closer to the US model. However, in a note (referring to the earnings de-indexation of the retirement pension in the UK) he states that 'the seeds of much more radical change are currently being sown' (p183). We would argue that there have been important shifts in welfare policy that do not, as is sometimes argued, amount to dismantling, but to a restructuring that does bring the UK closer to a US residual model in certain areas.

First, the boundary between state and private provision in both an economic and domestic sense has been redrawn - the changes to SERPS and the Child Support Act are central features of that change. The effect is a lowering of expectations of what the state will provide and what has to be met by family, kin or the private sector. Second, the marked shift to a means-tested strategy represents a re-orientation away from a model premised on uni-versal social rights and social insurance to one founded on pro-viding a minimum safety-net, where need has to be proved. Third, the extension of a more punitive approach to social security, seen in the tightening of work conditions (which Walker (1991) has argued are as tough as some of the compulsory workfare schemes in the US), the extension of sanctions and more recently the pilot-ing of workfare schemes, pushes us towards a more conditional rather than rights-based approach to welfare. And finally, the ide-ologically charged discourse of 'dependency', the 'underclass' and the 'benefit culture' imported from the United States has gained widespread currency. While the language and ideology are still at odds with the overall structure and balance of the British social security system, they filter into public debate changing the para-meters of how problems and solutions are defined.

Crucially, the social security system has faced a decade marked by major economic upheavals, compounded by the government's fierce adherence to de-regulation. There have been two recessions with unemployment reaching around three million in 1986 and again in 1991. The shape of the labour market has been radically altered with the persistent rise in non-employment (much less responsive to economic growth), the continued decline in male full-time work and the growth of female part-time work especially among married couples (Balls & Gregg, 1993) and the unprecedented dispersion of earnings (Hills, 1995). Each of these changes reverberates through the social security system as it tries to cope with sharply rising numbers of claimants whose hold on the labour market has become increasingly tenuous. Thus the re-drawing of the economic map has shaped and constrained the social security policy agenda in crucial ways.

The state of the debate

The challenges and possible solutions faced by social security policy are increasingly at the forefront of political debate (Lister, 1996a). A series of centre/left reports about the future of the welfare state from the Commission on Social Justice (1994), the Joseph Rowntree Foundation (1995), the Dahrendorf Commission (1995) and Frank Field (1995) share important common features. They stress a welfare to work strategy, the importance of social solidarity to economic growth, life-time learning and re-skilling, a revamping of social insurance to include marginal workers such as part-timers and a re-thinking of pension strategy (though with different solutions). All (with the exception of the Rowntree Report which is not as extensive in its policy proposals) largely reject means-testing as a way forward.

The reports embody important shifts in thinking about social security policy from the centre-left. They attempt to refashion welfare in the face of a society transformed by both broad economic and social changes and a decade and a half of neo-liberal policies. In his *Progress after Mais* speech, Lilley declared that the debate is no longer about whether social security should be reformed but about how. He suggests that there is greater recognition of four factors in social security policy: cost, welfare dependency, the need to modernise the system, and that private welfare strengthens the economy while taxpayer-financed welfare weakens it (1995b). Lilley's analysis of the state of the debate is partly correct, even if there remain important differences of emphasis particularly in relation to the role of the private sector. The reports on the future of welfare mentioned above, and other bodies, recognise the difficulty of cost, accept the need to look at incentives and also see a greater role for a regulated private sector in the area of pensions, which offers funds for much-needed investment (Hutton, 1995; Dahrendorf Commission, 1995).

Much in this consensus is positive. However there are also dangers. The focus on a welfare to work strategy runs the risk of creating a false dichotomy between welfare and work, marginalising those who have to remain on benefit because of caring responsibilities, disability, old age or entrenched unemployment (McCormick and Oppenheim, 1996). Some of these groups are trapped on benefits precisely because of other welfare/economic 'shortfalls'. The frequency of the use of the label 'welfare dependency' in many quarters tends to re-emphasize personal failing rather than broader social causes. This is not to say that individual motivation and perverse incentives within social security play no role, but to argue for an appropriate balance in the debate. The extension of the role of private pension provision brings with it the risk of entrenching the inequalities in people's working lives in their old age. The new visions of welfare have a strong faith in the future of employment growth; if such employment growth fails to materialise there is some radical re-thinking to be done, a point emphasised in particular by supporters of a Citizens Income scheme.

The pace of change in social security policy has been unremitting. Fowler declared in 1986 that 'social security system had lost its way' (DHSS, 1985); the same could be said in 1996. Reforms have not been able to grapple with the underlying challenges to the social security system - the transformations in family, lifecycle and work (Esping-Andersen, 1994). The growth and persistence of poverty and inequality over the decade with a quarter of the population living in poverty in 1992/93 could not be a clearer testament to this.

Notes

1. Fowler's attempts to include taxation within the scope of the reviews were firmly rejected by the Treasury (Lawson, 1993)

2. Recent reports suggest that the introduction of incapacity benefit has brought much lower savings than anticipated by the government (Financial Times, 15 April 1996).

3. Maintenance covers the parent with care as well as the children.

4. Hills found that between 1978 and 1984 cash benefits slowed the rise of inequality in market income but that after 1984 this trend was reversed and inequality of gross incomes, which includes benefits, rose faster than inequality of market incomes.

References

Allbeson, J. (1996) Failing the Test, CAB Clients' Experience of the Habitual Residence Test in Social Security, London, NACAB.

Amin, K. (with Oppenheim C.) (1992) Poverty in Black and White, Deprivation and Ethnic Minorities, London, Child Poverty Action Group Ltd.

Atkinson A.B. (with Micklewright, J.) (1989) 'Turning the screw: benefits for the unemployed 1979-1988', in A.B. Atkinson (ed) Poverty and Social Security, Hemel Hempstead, Harvester Wheatsheaf.

Balls, E. & Gregg, P. (1993) Work and Welfare, Tackling the Jobs Deficit, London, Institute for Public Policy Research.

Barnados (1990) Missing the Target, London, Barnados.

Coalition on Young People and Social Security (COYPSS) 6 Years Severe Hardship, An Update, London, COYPSS.

Commission on Social Justice (1994) Social Justice, Strategies for National Renewal, London, Vintage.

Craig G. (1991) Fit for Nothing: Young People, Benefits and Youth Training, London, The Children's Society.

Dahrendorf Commission (1995) Report on Wealth Creation and Social Cohesion in a Free Society, London, The Commission on Wealth Creation and Social Cohesion.

Deacon, A. (1994) 'Investigating fraud', Poverty, no.87.

Dean H. (1996) 'What sort of problem?' The New Review, Jan/Feb.

Dickens, R., Fry, V. & Pashardes P. (1995) 'The cost of children and the welfare state', Findings, Social Policy Research 89, Joseph Rowntree Foundation

DHSS (1985a) Green Paper, Reform of Social Security, Cmnd. 9517, London, HMSO.

DHSS (1987) Press Release, 23 October. DSS (1993a) The Growth of Social Security, London, HMSO.

DSS (1993b) Containing the Cost of Social Security - The International Context, London, HMSO.

DSS (1995a) Uprating Statement, 29 November. DSS (1995b) Social Security Departmental Report, The Government Expenditure Plans 1995-96 to 1997-98, London, HMSO.

DSS & DEG (1994) Job Seeker's Allowance, Cmnd. 2687, London, HMSO.

Esping-Andersen, G. (1994) 'Equality and work in the post-industrial life-cycle', in D. Miliband (ed) Re-inventing the Left, Cambridge, Polity Press.

Evans, M., Piachaud, D., & Sutherland, H. (1994) Designed for the Poor - Poorer by Design? The Effects of the 1986 Social Security Act on Family Incomes, WSP/105, London, Suntory Toyota International Centre for Economics and Related Disciplines.

Field F. (1995) Making Welfare Work: Reconstructing Welfare for the Millenium, London, Institute of Community Studies.

Garnham A. & Knights E. (1994) Putting the Tresury First, The Truth about Child Support, London, Child Poverty Action Group Ltd.

Glyn A. & Miliband D. (1994) Paying for Inequality, London, Rivers Oram.

Gordon, P. & Newnham A. (1985) Passport to Benefits? Racism and Social Security, Child Poverty Action Group & The Runnymede Trust.

Gray, J. (1994) The Undoing of Conservatism, London, Social Market Foundation.

Hill, M. (1996) 'The 1986 Social Security Act: ten years on', Benefits, Issue 15, pp2-4.

Hills, J. (1993) The Future of Welfare, A Guide to the Debate, York, Joseph Rowntree Foundation.

Hills J. (1995) Joseph Rowntree Foundation Enquiry into Income and Wealth vol.2, York, Joseph Rowntree Foundation.

Huby, M. & Dix, G. (1992) Evaluating the Social Fund, DSS Research Report no.9, London, HMSO.

Hutton, W. (1995) The State We're In, London, Jonathan Cape.

Jacobs, J. (1994) 'The scroungers who never were, the effects of the 1989 Social Security Act', in R. Page & J. Baldock (eds) Social Policy Review 6, Canterbury, Social Policy Association.

Joseph Rowntree Foundation Enquiry into Income and Wealth (1995) vol.1, York, Joseph Rowntree Foundation.

Kempson, E., Bryson, A.,& Rowlingson, K. (1994) Hard Times, How Poor Families Make Ends Meet, London, Policy Studies Institute.

Lilley, P. (1993) Benefits and Costs: Securing the Future of Social Security, Mais Lecture, City University Business School.

Lilley, P. (1995a) Speech to the Conservative Party Conference.

Lilley, P. (1995b) Winning the Welfare Debate, London, Social Market Foundation.

Lister, R. (1991) 'Social security in the 1980s', Social Policy & Administration, vol.XX, no.2, pp91-107

Lister, R. (1992) Women's Economic Dependency and Social Security, Manchester, Equal Opportunities Commission.

Lister, R. (1996a) 'The welfare state', in D. Halpern et al. (eds) Options for Britain, Aldershot, Dartmouth.

Lister, R. (1996b) 'Back to the familiy: family policies and politics under the Major government', in H. Jones & J. Millar (eds) The Politics of the Family, Aldershot, Avebury.

Lynes, T. (1992) The Wrong Side of the Tracks', Factsheet on Unemployment and Benefits, London, Child Poverty Action Group Ltd.

Lynes, T. (1994) 'In sickness and in poverty', Poverty no.89.

McCormick, J. & Oppenheim, C. (1996) 'Options for change', New Statesmen/Society 26 January.

MacLagan, I. (1993) Four Years Severe Hardship, London, Barnados & Youthaid.

Middleton S. et al., (1994) Statutory Sick Pay, The Response of Employers to the 1991 Changes, DSS Research Report no.24, London, HMSO.

Millar, J. (1994) 'Lone parents and social security policy in the UK', in S. Baldwin & J. Falkingham (eds) Social Security and Social Change, New Challenges to the Beveridge Model, Hemel Hempstead, Harvester Wheatsheaf.

McRae, S. & Daniel W.W. (1991) Maternity Rights: The Experience of Women and Employers, First Findings, London, Policy Studies Institute.

Moore, J. (1987) Speech on the Future of the Welfare State, Conservative Political Centre Conference, 26 September.

Moore J. (1983) Speech to the 105th Conservative Party Conference, Brighton, 12 October.

Morgan, P. (1995) Farewell to the Family? Public Policy and Family Breakdown in Britain and the USA, London, Institute for Economic Affairs.

Murray, I. (1996) 'Compulsion is not working', Working Brief, January.

National Association of Citizens Bureau (1990) Hard Times, London, NACAB.

'No Turning Back' Group (1993) Who Benefits? Re-inventing Social Security, London, Conservative Political Centre.

Novak, M. (1987) The New Consensus on Family and Welfare, London, American Enterprise Institute for Public Policy Research.

Oppenheim, C. (1990) Poverty the Facts, London, Child Poverty Action Group Ltd.

Oppenheim, C. & Harker, L. (1996) Poverty the Facts, London, Child Poverty Action Group Ltd.

Oppenheim, C. & Lister, R. (1996) 'The politics of child poverty', in J. Pilcher & S. Wagg (eds) Thatcher's Children, Politics, Childhood and Society, Brighton, Falmer Press.

Page, R. (1995) 'The attack on the British welfare state - more real than imagined, a Leveller's tale', Critical Social Policy, vol. 15, Autumn pp220-228.

Piachaud, D. (1996) 'Means-testing and the Conservatives', Benefits Issue 15.

Social Security Advisory Committee (1993) The Ninth Report, London, HMSO.

Social Security Advisory Committee (1994) State Benefits and Private Provision, The Review of Social Security Paper 2, Leeds, BA Publishing Services Ltd.

Social Security Advisory Committee (1996) The Social Security (Persons from Abroad), Miscellaneous Amendments regulations, Report from the Social Security Administration Committee, Cmnd. 3062.

Social Security Committee (1995) Third Report, Review of Expenditure on Social Security, Session 1994-95, London, HMSO.

Timmins, N. (1995) The Five Giants, A Biography of the Welfare State, London, Harper Collins.

Walker R. (1991) 'Fares to Workfare', Benefits, Issue 2, pp22-23.

6 Policy on the Hoof: The British Child Support Act in Practice

Gary Craig, Caroline Glendinning & Karen Clarke

The 1991 Child Support Act is one of the most complex and controversial pieces of recent British social policy legislation. It raises important issues about the state and family policy, income maintenance, the relationship between work and the benefits system and gender relations. It is also controversial enough to be regarded in some quarters as the 'second Poll Tax'. In the three years since its implementation in 1993 it has been the subject of three highly critical House of Commons Social Security Select Committee reports (HC, 1993; 1994; 1996) and damning indictments of maladministration from the Parliamentary Ombudsman (HC, 1995a; 1995b) and National Audit Office (NAO 1994; 1995). Two major revisions in regulations associated with the Act, followed by further amending legislation (DSS, 1995), were introduced within two years of its implementation. Even internal Child Support Agency reports have been critical (CAS, 1994; CSA, 1994). This level of controversy is all the more remarkable as the

Act passed through Parliament with no significant political divisions. Moreover, research has shown (Clarke et al. 1993; 1994; 1996) that very few lone mothers are hostile to the principle of parental maintenance.

This chapter traces the origins and early history of the Act and its executive arm, the Child Support Agency (CSA). It raises preliminary questions as to what the outcomes, as opposed to the stated objectives, of the legislation may be. The early history of the Act suggests that in making one objective - the reduction in welfare benefit expenditure on lone parents - paramount, the possibility of meeting other objectives of the legislation has been seriously compromised. A further consequence of the drive for benefit savings has been that the Agency has been slow to develop good administrative practice in an extremely sensitive area of policy. The government both failed to appreciate the complexity of the task involved and learn the lessons of relevant experience from within the UK and elsewhere.

The origins of the legislation

Two trends informed the publication in 1990 of proposals to change arrangements for assessing and collecting child maintenance (DSS, 1990). The first, demographic, trend was the increase in the number of lone parents since the early 1970s. Between 1971 and 1991 the number of lone parent families rose from 0.6 million to 1.3 million, the latter containing 2.2 million children. The increase in single (never-married) mothers was most dramatic. Their numbers quadrupled between 1971 and 1989, coming to constitute over one-third of all lone mothers (Burghes, 1993). The level of lone parenthood in the UK is the third highest of all OECD countries (Whiteford and Bradshaw, 1994).

The second trend was the dramatic increase in the numbers and proportions of lone parents dependent on social security benefits as their principal source of income and the consequent rise in public expenditure on this group. In 1971, only 37 per cent of lone parents claimed means-tested supplementary benefits, but by 1989 the proportion claiming Income Support (IS) had risen to 70 per cent (Bradshaw and Millar, 1991). This growing dependence on benefits partly reflected a decline in the numbers of lone parents in paid employment, especially part-time work. It also reflected the fact that the fastest-growing group of lone mothers, those who were unmarried, were least likely to be receiving maintenance from former partners which could be offset against means-tested benefits; where they did receive maintenance, it was usually at significantly lower levels than that received by divorced lone parents (Burghes, 1993). In 1981-82, spending on income-related benefits for lone parent families was £1.4 billion; by 1988-89 this had increased to £3.2 billion (DSS, 1990, vol.1). Yet despite this growth in public spending to support lone parent families, they were increasingly at risk of long-term poverty. By 1989 more than half of all children in poverty came from lone parent families (Utting, 1995, p34; see also Holtermann, 1993; JRF, 1995).

Before 1993, the systems of awarding and collecting maintenance through the Courts and DSS 'liable relatives' officers were characterised by adversarial negotiations between former partners; the use of wide discretion in determining maintenance awards; the absence of regular, systematic up-rating of maintenance payments in line with inflation or with improvements in a former partner's earnings; and apparent ease in avoiding compliance with court maintenance orders. In addition, the trend from 1984 onwards towards ' clean break' divorces meant that former partners were increasingly encouraged to give up claims on the matrimonial home in return for very low or no on-going maintenance payments in respect of a former partner and children (Land, 1994). Consequently it was argued that the Court system resulted in differences in the maintenance received by lone parent families which bore little relationship to their needs or to the circumstances of former partners (DSS, 1990, vol.1). Additionally, the living standards of 'second' families tended to be protected in maintenance assessments, whereas the majority of 'first' families - lone mothers and their children - lived on means-tested benefits. The Act therefore aimed to create greater equity between 'first' and 'second' families.

Given wider government concerns to find ways of halting the rise in public expenditure, it is not surprising that attention should have been drawn to the growing social security budget for lone parents. Thus, in a 1990 speech by Margaret Thatcher to the National Children's Home, references to the burden on 'abandoned' mothers and issues of childcare were overshadowed by a preoccupation with the financial dimensions of child support:

> No father should be able to escape from his responsibility and that is why the government is looking at ways of ... making the arrangements for recovering maintenance more effective (cited in Garnham and Knights, 1994, p1).

This concern to curb public spending meshed with other concerns over the growing fluidity of family relationships and with assertions from right-wing theorists that men were increasingly absent from family life (Dennis and Erdos, 1992).

The Child Support Act was also one of a wider range of measures put forward by the government to increase financial work incentives. Other moves in this direction included changes to the rules of eligibility for Family Credit (FC), a means-tested benefit which supplements the incomes of those on low wages. In 1992, the hours threshold for eligibility for FC was lowered from 24 to 16 hours per week. This meant that any lone parent who worked 16 hours a week or more could no longer claim IS. However, research evidence (Burghes, 1993; Holtermann, 1993; Clarke et al, 1994) suggests that other major obstacles are faced by lone mothers who wish to work. These include a significant 'poverty trap' in moving from IS to FC, because of the associated loss of many 'passported' benefits; and the lack of adequate training opportunities and child care facilities. A disregard towards the costs of childcare was introduced in 1993 for those on FC, worth up to £28 weekly to mothers able to use registered childminders. However, early evidence suggests that the conditions attached to this disregard (which rule out the use of relatives as childcarers) and its low level relative to the cost of formal childcare provision, will considerably limit its usefulness to lone mothers (Clarke et al, 1996).

Child maintenance was, however, seen by the government as the main vehicle for encouraging lone parents to move off IS, either into paid work or supported by higher maintenance alone. This was in line with the general argument that many long-term benefit claimants needed to be helped out of a 'culture of dependency', an argument supported by vigorously ideological attacks on lone parents in the early 1990s. The White Paper which preceded the Child Support Act predicted that 'up to 200,000 more lone parents will receive maintenance regularly', roughly doubling the total numbers in receipt of maintenance; and that about '50,000 caring parents will no longer be dependent on Income Support', roughly 6 per cent of those then on IS (DSS, 1990, Vol.1).

Reaction to the initial legislation

The main provisions of the Act and its associated regulations were to:

(a) Establish a new body (the Child Support Agency - CSA) responsible for assessing and collecting child maintenance payments;

(b) Create a universal but complex formula to calculate mainte-
    nance liabilities. The formula, originally linked to IS levels, did
    not take into account an 'absent' parent's actual expenditure,
    other than some housing costs. Lone parents on IS have all
    maintenance deducted, pound for pound, from their benefit;
    for lone parents on FC, £15 maintenance is 'disregarded' in
    calculating their entitlement;
(c) Oblige all lone parents claiming IS, FC or disability working
    allowance (DWA) to co-operate in the recovery of mainte-
    nance. The only exemption is where a lone parent can show
    'reasonable grounds' for believing this would cause her or any
    children living with her 'harm or undue distress'. Failure to co-
    operate without 'good cause' can lead to reduced benefits for
    up to 18 months.

Non-claimants of means-tested benefits would also be able to
ask the CSA to assess and collect maintenance, where there was
no existing Court Order. It was also planned that the Agency
would, from 1996, offer a universal service by taking on the
reassessment of maintenance in cases where a Court Order or
formal agreement was already in place but needed revision. For
lone mothers who were not claiming means-tested benefits, the
use of the CSA to assess and collect maintenance remained
optional (though as the Courts would no longer have powers to
assess maintenance, the only alternative would be a private, voluntary arrangement). The legislation was to be phased in over
three years, starting with new claims for FC and IS in April 1993
and gradually taking on all existing lone parent claimants.

The Act thus removed virtually all discretion in the assessment
and collection of child maintenance for lone parents receiving
means-tested benefits. Lone parents not on benefit might chose
between using the CSA or coming to a private agreement. If they
opted for the former, then the same complex formula was used to
determine an 'absent' parent's maintenance liability. The Act thus
sought to impose a financial solution (epitomised by the formula)
on the complex problems faced by separating and former partners. This solution provided in part for the reallocation of private resources between parents (largely from men to women)
through a state-sponsored mechanism. Arguably, this was an
entirely appropriate policy response to the widely varying levels of
maintenance received by some lone parents and to the failure of
some former partners to contribute to their children's financial
support. However, the Act did nothing to address the issue of
child poverty resulting from lone parents' long-term dependency
on IS; it also did not address any of the non-financial barriers to

the labour market for lone parents wishing to work. In essence, it imposed a social security response on a much broader set of social policy issues by means of a rigid, highly-regulated formula-based administrative mechanism.

The legislation's passage through Parliament was relatively uncontroversial and rapid. This was partly because it followed the pattern of much contemporary social security legislation in containing only the broad outline, with most of the detail being published later in the form of regulations. This led to concern in the House of Commons about the restricted opportunities for debate on detailed clauses and amendments. Several Peers also expressed reservations about the extent to which the Act allowed the state to intervene in intimate situations. The legislation received the Royal Assent only five months after the Bill had first been published.

It was left to national childcare and welfare rights organisations to voice the disquiet felt outside Parliament about some of the Act's provisions, particularly as these were likely to impact on lone mothers on benefit and their children. This concern included anxieties about the compulsion on lone parents on benefit to co-operate with the CSA and the linked financial penalties for non-co-operation; the fact, even if they did co-operate, one parent families on IS would not benefit financially; and the legislation's overall emphasis on financial rather than social objectives, which put it at odds with the spirit of the 1989 Children Act. Simultaneously, organisations led by 'absent' parents began vocal campaigns against the stringency of the maintenance formula.

Two years of chaos

The Child Support Agency is one of the semi-autonomous, executive Next Steps Agencies, created to reduce the numbers of directly-employed civil servants within the DSS. These Agencies are not directly answerable to Parliament but are responsible for the day-to-day management and administration of most social security tasks on the government's behalf. As the CSA's early experience showed, the political and managerial 'distance' between these Agencies and the government could be helpful in deflecting political criticism. Having recently experienced considerable embarrassment over the introduction of new benefits for disabled people, the DSS took some care with the establishment of the CSA and the training of its staff. However, the Agency was set stringent performance targets including, most controversially, the recovery of high levels of maintenance which could be offset against social security payments to lone parent families. In its first year, the Agency aimed to make benefit savings of £530 millions while incurring administrative costs of only £115 millions; in the long term, savings of £900 millions a year were expected to accrue (Garnham and Knights, 1994).

Despite these preparations, criticism of CSA administration quickly appeared. Allegations soon began to emerge that the CSA was prioritising so-called 'easy targets' - men in paid employment who were already paying maintenance to a former partner - on the grounds that these cases would prove administratively straightforward and yield considerably enhanced maintenance income to offset against social security payments. The CSA's Chief Executive responded that the Agency had no discretion to determine the composition of its caseload (a target of one million cases, half of them new lone parents and half existing lone parent benefit claimants in the first year). However, a leaked Agency memorandum indicated that staff had been instructed to pursue those cases which would make the biggest contribution to the 1993-94 savings target of £530 million:

> This is not the time for the cases we know should get early attention
> ... The name of the game is maximising the maintenance yield - don't
> waste a lot of time on non-profitable stuff! (CSA, quoted in Garnham
> and Knights, 1994, p70).

Regardless of how far the Agency actually was prioritising these cases, this allegation was widely believed by lone parents and former partners alike. Among the lone mothers interviewed in our part-longitudinal, qualitative study (Clarke et al, 1993; 1995; 1996) there was widespread endorsement of the principle that fathers had continuing financial (and other) responsibilities towards their children; and, conversely, that children had rights to share in the quality of life enjoyed by their fathers:'I think he should pay towards the children. I mean, they're his kids - he should help me clothe them and that' (Clarke et al, 1994, p.105). However, growing suspicions that the Agency was prioritising 'easy' cases and leaving those cases where former partners would prove harder to trace were borne out by the lone mothers' experiences: 'It] is a good thing in theory, but I think they're targeting the people who are obvious, as opposed to chasing the men that aren't paying up' (Clarke et al, 1994, p.106).

This 'targeting' was perceived to be in direct contradiction to the basic objective of the Act - the enforcement of parental responsibilities on the part of men who were hitherto evading them. Indeed, lone mothers considered it profoundly unfair that

men (whether their own former partner or not) who had continued to provide financial and other support for their children were
being singled out for priority investigation by the Agency, while
those who had avoided paying maintenance were able to continue doing so: 'They're penalising the honest ones, not the dishon-
est ones, if you like' (Clarke et al, 1994, p.107).

This tension between two of the main underlying objectives of
the Act - enforcing 'absent' parents' financial responsibilities and
recovering maintenance which could be offset against social security expenditure - quickly became apparent. Moreover, these
conflicting objectives became linked to criticisms of the stringent
formula used to calculate maintenance under the new legislation,
which often resulted in very large increases in maintenance liabilities. The formula was perceived to be profoundly unfair in a number of respects. First, it failed to take into account any previous
transfers of resources between former partners, particularly
where men had already transferred capital or relinquished equity
in joint property to a former wife and children as part of a comprehensive 'package' of measures on separation or divorce.
Former partners who had already transferred capital or housing
in this way were considered to be doubly penalised when they
were then also assessed to pay considerable increases in maintenance.

Secondly, the formula was felt to be unfair because it was
believed to have been devised to enable the Agency to maximise
its maintenance yield from 'responsible' fathers in order to com-
pensate for its failure to claim maintenance from the non-payers:

> I really think they've got to get the balance right; it's no good just
> catching the people that are working that can afford it, that's wrong,
> taking double the amount of money off them when there are so many
> that are trying to avoid it (Clarke et al, 1994,
> p107).

Some lone mothers expressed outrage at the levels of maintenance now being demanded from former partners, which they felt
were unrelated either to their children's actual needs or to the
actual weekly benefit levels with which they were expected to feed
and clothe their children:

> They've got to stop asking for so much. The weekly amount for a
> child under 11 on income support is about £15, but they're asking
> for sums beyond belief (Clarke et al, 1994, p.109).

Thirdly, the formula was unfair because it drew children into difficulties between mothers, fathers and their new partners over the new levels of maintenance which were likely to have an adverse effect on the father's living standards. Lone mothers reported that fathers had stopped buying their children treats and taking them out in anticipation of an increase in maintenance. Similarly, fathers and their new partners were reported to have accused lone mothers, in front of their children, of responsibility for the CSA's intervention:

> He [ex-husband] says his [new] wife and he may separate because he couldn't afford to pay [the higher maintenance] and run a home ... I know they are having difficulties and the children get the rough end of it. The CSA decision has definitely affected our situation, though I tread very carefully (Clarke et al, 1994, p.57).

However, despite the alleged prioritising of 'easy' cases, the actual benefit savings achieved by the Agency fell dramatically short of its target. The National Audit Office's first annual report on the CSA noted that a forecast of £110 million revenue for 1993-94 had translated into actual receipts of £5.7 million. The corresponding figures for its precursor organisations had actually been considerably higher, at £283 million in 1991-92 and £313 million in 1992-93.

Evidence of administrative difficulties became increasingly alarming. The first Chief Executive of the CSA resigned sixteen months after the Act came into operation and was replaced by a senior career civil servant. This allowed supporters of the legislation to claim that the poor quality of service provided by the Agency was largely a product of managerial style, rather than that of the legislative framework within which it was required to operate or the performance targets which it had been set. Nevertheless, criticisms of the Agency's performance continued to emerge from Parliamentary Select Committees, the Ombudsman and other quarters. These criticisms included long delays in processing assessments, high levels of inaccuracy in maintenance assessments, incomplete collection of relevant evidence and, most seriously of all, the failure of the Agency to enforce and collect the maintenance due from former partners. While citing the pressure to maximise benefit savings, the Chief Child Support Officer's first Annual Report acknowledged the widespread delays at each stage of the maintenance assessment process compared to the Agency's performance targets; and admitted that a substantial proportion of assessments had been made without 'sufficient relevant evidence' (CAS, 1994). The

National Audit Office (NAO) also expressed concern over widespread errors in the calculation of maintenance assessments and, once assessments were completed, delays in recovering the maintenance due (NAO,1994).

Despite large-scale restructuring of the Agency, revision of its internal procedures, enhancement of its computer systems and increased staffing, significant administrative problems remained. Two years after the Act became operational, the NAO (1995) found that financial inaccuracies still affected between 40 and 50 per cent of maintenance assessments; that half the Agency's cases were not completed within twelve months of being started; and that maintenance amounting to £535 million (of which some £87 million was due to go to 'parents with care') was still uncollected. The Social Security Select Committee's judgement of the first eighteen months of the Agency's performance was that it had been 'dire' (HC, 1996).

Lone mothers' experiences reflected these problems. They found themselves placed under considerable pressure to complete a Maintenance Application Form (MAF) but thereafter found it very difficult to obtain accurate and consistent information from the Agency on the progress of their cases and more difficult still to obtain the maintenance due to them. Some lone mothers were under the impression that the whole of their benefit payments would be stopped if they did not complete the MAF; others (including some who had experienced violence in a former relationship) were unaware of how they could legitimately withhold their consent for the Agency to approach a former partner. Delays of a year after a completed MAF or a request to withhold consent had been returned to the Agency were common:

> Marion was sent a MAF in April 1993. After receiving a letter 'stating that if I didn't fill it in they would deduct money from me payment... I filled it in and posted it straight away and I've never heard nowt since, so what were the point?' When re-inter viewed in 1995, Marion had still not heard whether her ex-partner's maintenance had been reassessed (Clarke et al, 1994, p92).

Lone parents who were anxious about the reaction of a former partner to a maintenance (re)assessment found these long delays particularly problematic:

> Jane was sent a MAF in April 1993. She wrote back describing her former husband's violence, because she did not want the Agency to contact him. She waited eleven months for a reply: 'I've got evidence, solicitors, courts, everything ... He'd start on me again, I know he would' (Clarke et al., 1994, p93).

When interviewed almost two years after the introduction of the Act, none of the 53 lone mothers who had been on means-tested benefits at the start of the study was now better off as a result of receiving maintenance through the CSA. Some lone mothers reported knowing that money was now being deducted from the wages or benefits of a former partner but were still not receiving it, despite sometimes heroic efforts to trace payments (Clarke et al, 1996). Indeed, many lone mothers argued that there was little point in co-operating with the CSA as they would be unlikely to gain financially. At worst, they faced both a deteriorating rela-tionship with their ex-partner and the loss of informal help towards the costs of their children from ex-partners who were no longer able to afford it:

> Things were ticking along nicely and he gave me £25 a week; if there was anything I couldn't afford like clothes or shoes, he'd buy that .. You can imagine what upset it has caused ... He knows that I had no choice and that I'll probably be worse off (Clarke et al., 1994, p.68).

All parties - 'parents with care', 'absent' parents and children of the relationship - could thus end up financially worse off. These experiences contrast starkly with promises made before the Act was introduced, that the Agency would provide a 'simple, fast and efficient' service (Garnham and Knights, 1994, p.59). The Agency's administrative difficulties were resented particularly deeply by those couples who had had their earlier, mutually acceptable maintenance arrangements summarily overturned. Not only had they had no choice about the new system; they had also experienced an arrangement which had worked well for both them and their children being replaced by one which seemed chaotic and unable to deliver maintenance as intended:

> for those who do [pay maintenance] and are happy with it, you should be left alone on both sides. He [former partner] feels the same. He knows he's got to pay for his children and has no disagreement. It's the way they're doing it (Clarke et al, 1994, p107).

In response to growing criticisms of the Agency's perfor-mance, DSS Ministers attempted to distance themselves by emphasising that these were executive, not policy difficulties. However neither the House of Commons Social Security Committee nor the Parliamentary Commissioner for Administration was convinced by this argument, pointing out that the DSS was responsible for both the policy implemented by the Agency and for its resource base. The Select Committee on the Parliamentary Ombudsman opened its report thus:

The Disability Living Allowance was introduced in April 1992 ... The serious delays which ensued in the processing of claims and the provision of benefit are well-known ... It was, therefore, with great concern that we witnessed maladministration on a similar scale in the introduction of the Child Support Agency ... For [two such events] to emanate from the same department within two y ears raises the most fundamental question as to the competence of [the DSS] and its ability to plan administration effectively (HC, 1995b, para.1).

Recent changes

Most of the public opposition to the Act has been orchestrated by 'absent' parents who have experienced or anticipate considerable hardship because of large increases in the maintenance they would have to pay for children from earlier relationships. Their lobbying of MPs, especially in marginal parliamentary constituencies, has proved highly effective. From September 1993 onwards, as 'absent' parents began to receive their first maintenance demands, campaigns developed against the new levels of maintenance being assessed. High maintenance demands were alleged to be encouraging some men to give up work (unemployed 'absent parents' were required to pay a maximum of only £2.20 - 1993-94 figures). Most of the changes which have been made in the provisions of the Act largely reflect the concerns of this particular lobby.

Thus amendments to the maintenance formula were announced in December 1993, to take effect from February 1994. This added further to the Agency's administrative burden, as completed assessments had to be recalculated. However, the complaints continued, prompting a second investigation by the House of Commons Social Security Committee (HC, 1994). In response both to the Committee's report and to more widespread criticisms of the Act, the Secretary of State introduced further regulatory and legislative amendments. In December 1994 it was announced that further work by the Agency on two groups of lone parents would be shelved indefinitely: those of 'parents with care' who had been contacted by the Agency before July 1994 but who had not responded to initial enquiries; and those lone parents who were already on means tested benefits when the Act came into effect but who had not yet been contacted by the Agency. Early in 1995 it was announced that the Child Support Agency's financial targets would be considerably downgraded for the foreseeable future. These announcements were followed by a White Paper (DSS, 1995) which proposed the introduction of phased amendments to the legislation and some further administrative reforms. These amendments included, with effect from

April 1995, a ceiling on the proportion of normal net income payable in maintenance by 'absent parents'; an adjustment to the formula to take account of past property and capital settlements made by separating couples; and further adjustments to the formula in acknowledgement of certain travel-to-work and other costs relating to new partners and step-children of 'absent' parents. Further discretionary provisions introduced during 1996 will allow some deviations from the standard maintenance assessment formula in certain specified circumstances.

The government also announced the indefinite deferment of those cases due to be taken on by the Agency from 1996-97, of lone mothers not in receipt of means-tested benefits who already have a maintenance agreement in force. These women and their former partners will therefore continue to use the Courts for the reassessment and enforcement of maintenance. Finally, from 1997 'parents with care' will be able to build up a maintenance credit of £5 a week which will be paid as a lump sum when the recipient starts work of at least 16 hours per week. Only the last of these provisions addresses the needs of 'parents with care' and it consists of 'jam tomorrow'. For reasons discussed earlier, it may offer little incentive for lone mothers wishing to work now.

In early 1996, the third report of the Social Security Select Committee on the CSA (HC, 1996) addressed some of the continuing administrative difficulties reported in the Agency's first three years. Among its recommendations were that 'parents with care'should receive more accurate and frequent information on the progress of their case; that the procedures for dealing with changes in circumstances and for liaison between CSA officials and the Benefits Agency should be reviewed; and that the Agency should give priority to parents with care on FC. However, despite the stream of administrative and legislative changes, the poverty experienced by lone parent families (largely female-headed) has remained untouched.

Compromises and concessions

It is likely to be some time before it is clear whether the original objectives of the Act can be met through the latest reforms. The 1995 amendments go some way to addressing some of the criticisms of the original legislation. However, these changes generally benefit more affluent 'absent' parents, rather than 'parents with care'. The very partial nature of the concessionary amendments to the legislation is illustrated by the announcement in the November 1995 budget that the poorest 'absent' parents, those who are themselves on Income Support, are to see their minimum maintenance payment more than doubled, from £2.35 to

£4.80 a week. The only concession to the poverty of lone parent families has been the planned introduction of a maintenance credit to benefit those moving from Income Support to Family Credit.

The government may have weathered the storm, at least until the next General Election, by tempering the opposition of better -off men at the expense of poorer and politically less popular lone parent families. The Labour Party's position remains unclear. What is clear, however, is that the government has had to resolve a chaotic situation largely of its own making.

First, the government had detailed knowledge of the Australian arrangements before it when it drafted the legislation. In the form in which the UK scheme was first introduced, there were significant differences between it and the corresponding Australian scheme. These differences have been at the root of much of the opposition to the UK scheme. For example, lone parents on social assistance in the UK have all maintenance off-set pound for pound from their benefit; neither they or their children benefit from maintenance payments so long as they remain on social assistance benefits. In Australia, entitlement to the equivalent Sole Parent Pension is only reduced by 50 cents for every dollar of maintenance received above a threshold amount. Maintenance paid in kind (for example help with school fees or property transfers) is also taken into account in assessing a former partner's maintenance liability. Furthermore, the UK scheme originally involved overturning all existing maintenance arrangements and also disregarded earlier property and capital settlements which had been made through the courts. In contrast, the phased introduction of the Australian scheme helped to reduce discrepancies between old and new maintenance assessments (Rhoades, 1995). Finally, the Australian maintenance assessment formula does not include an element for the lone mother as carer, whereas the UK scheme does, irrespective of her marital status (Land, 1994). This has caused ill-feeling amongst mothers wishing to avoid any sense of financial dependency on male ex-partners (Whiteford, 1994).

Of these differences, only the issue of pre-existing capital settlements is addressed by the recent reforms to the UK Child Support Act. 'Parents with care' still fail to benefit financially from the successful collection of maintenance from their ex-partners, so long as they remain on Income Support. The UK scheme also remains able to overturn pre-existing maintenance arrangements, many of them, as our research illustrated, constructed after years of difficult negotiations between ex-partners attempting to place the needs of their children at the centre of those negotiations. The

UK maintenance formula also still contains a substantial element for the carer, thus replacing dependence on the state with dependence on (largely male) ex-partners (Land, 1994).

Whilst the uproar against the Australian scheme was relatively muted, at least by British standards, it gave some indication as to where the most likely difficulties would arise (CSEAG, 1992). The amending 1995 Child Support Act implicitly acknowledges this failure to learn from the experiences of others. The experience of the Poll Tax during the 1980s might also have warned the UK government of the political backlash which might be expected from legislation which impinged negatively on so many of its 'natural' supporters. Finally, in terms simply of the management of complex new administrative arrangements, the earlier introduction of the new disability benefits scheme might have counselled caution in the introduction of difficult and sensitive new legislation.

The stated objectives of the White Paper which preceded the 1991 Act were to 'enhance parental responsibility' (by which was meant financial responsibility); create a 'fair balance' between the responsibilities of different parents; ensure that maintenance payments reflected changing circumstances; reduce dependence on IS; encourage parents to work; and provide a fair, consistent and efficient service from the Child Support Agency. In reality, the implementation of the Act has been driven most of all, not by the claim that 'Children Come First', the soundbite title of the White Paper, but by the need to cut benefit expenditure. In order to reduce opposition both within and outside Parliament, the government appears to have sought a new settlement between competing pressures, particularly that of the drive to cut public expenditure versus the hostility of middle and upper income men. To date, it has relieved to some degree the financial burden on the latter and slowed the phasing-in of the Act's provisions (thus considerably reducing the likely financial savings from the legislation), whilst giving virtually no ground to the needs of lone parent families. A further compromise has arisen between the objective of introducing consistency and equity into the assessment of maintenance and the need to limit the political damage caused by the continuing poor administrative performance of the Child Support Agency. Thus, in order to enable the Agency to deal more efficiently with its existing caseload of newly separated lone parents and lone parents on means-tested benefits, plans to extend the Agency's services to all lone parent families from 1996 have been abandoned. Non-claimant lone parents who already had a maintenance order when the legislation came into force in April 1993 will therefore continue to use the Courts to reassess and collect maintenance.

Whether these compromises represent a 'fair balance' between the responsibilities of different parents is debatable. Certainly, a fair and efficient service has not been delivered by the Agency to date; indeed, the ideal of consistency may be further away following the introduction of some discretion to 'depart' from the standard maintenance assessment formula. There may be a marginal reduction in the dependence of lone mothers on IS but the work incentive effect is likely to be small until wider barriers to lone parents' employment are addressed (Bradshaw and Millar 1991). The aim of adjusting maintenance payments to reflect the changing circumstances of former partners is likely to continue to provoke conflicts between the competing needs of 'first' and 'second' families.

After three years, some of the key objectives of the Child Support Act appear to have been seriously compromised. Initial ambitious targets for recovering maintenance and reducing public spending on social security benefits for lone parent families have been drastically scaled down and abandoned as a key CSA performance indicator. The 'targeting' of cases likely to yield increased maintenance relatively easily has meant that those 'absent' parents who the Act was ostensibly aimed at - those paying no maintenance to their children - are less likely to have been affected by it. The priority given in phasing in the legislation to lone mothers claiming means-tested benefits means that those lone parent families who stood to gain most from the Act - those in work who could keep most or all of their maintenance - are less likely to have had their cases dealt with. Indeed, with the indefinite postponement of those cases where the lone parent is not receiving benefit and already has a formal maintenance agreement, the prospects for some lone parent families of benefiting from the Act have receded even further. The consistent and equitable treatment of lone parents has been undermined by the Agency's deferment of work on any new cases of long-term lone parent benefit claimants who were already on benefit when the Act came into effect. The treatment of lone mothers who refuse to co-operate without 'good cause' has also been inconsistent, depending on when their case was dealt with. Some have had money deducted from their benefit for a period of eighteen months; others have simply had their cases shelved by the Agency for a year or more.

The aim of introducing greater equity through the use of a standard maintenance assessment formula has been thrown into question by proposals for discretionary 'departures' from the formula. The goal of treating equitably 'first' and 'second' families has also been undermined, as a series of changes to the formula have made increasing allowances for 'absent' parents and their new commitments while lone parent families on IS still receive none of the maintenance collected by the Agency in their name. Perhaps most serious, the goal of creating a uniform system of assessing and collecting maintenance for all lone parents, whether in receipt of means-tested benefits or not, has been indefinitely deferred. For the foreseeable future, two parallel systems of assessing and enforcing maintenance remain. The CSA will continue to deal with its existing caseload, plus any newly-separated lone parents (whether or not in receipt of means-tested benefits); while non-claimant lone parents who already have formal maintenance agreements will continue to use the Courts for the reassessment and collection of maintenance, with all the opportunities for discretion and inequity which that allows.

Although the most vocal opposition to the Child Support Act has come from organisations of 'absent' parents, many lone parents have also been highly critical of the legislation. Indeed, one unexpected consequence of the Act has been to generate similar levels of hostility from groups whose interests would appear, in theory, to be in direct opposition to each other. Many lone mothers on benefits, 'absent fathers' and their respective new partners all appear to be highly critical of the Act and its implementation, albeit for somewhat different reasons.

It is important to point out that these criticisms do not, on the whole, extend into opposition towards the principle that both parents should contribute towards their children's support, whether or not they live together. Lone mothers overwhelmingly expressed support for this principle (albeit with some qualifications about the circumstances in which it may be inappropriate to enforce it); many also reported support for the principle from their former partners (Clarke et al 1993; 1994; 1996). However, the manner in which the Act has been implemented has led most of those affected to conclude that the principle has not been fairly enforced.

In particular, the emphasis in the first two years on public expenditure savings targets have profoundly skewed the implementation of the Child Support Act and the outcomes for those affected. Consequently, the Act is perceived to be unfair because it has hitherto had the greatest impact on the 'wrong' men. 'Responsible' parents, those already paying maintenance, have been targeted for reassessment; those who have never paid maintenance regularly are believed to be of less interest to the Agency and so able to continue to evade their responsibilities. The Act is also seen as unfair because of the failure to allow any maintenance disregard for lone mothers and children on IS. This may have reduced the motivation of both lone mothers and 'absent' fathers to co-operate with the CSA and thereby added to the Agency's administrative problems. It is far from certain whether the planned maintenance 'credit' scheme will mitigate this particular concern.

The maintenance assessment formula is itself widely perceived as grossly unfair by men and their new partners because of the risks which it can pose to their living standards. The lone mothers in our studies (Clarke et al, 1993; 1994; 1996) also saw the formula as unrealistic, unfair and impacting adversely on relationships with their former partners and between children and their fathers. Finally, the uncertainty and confusion which have been caused by the chaotic administration of the CSA are perceived to be unfair, especially among those couples who had established amicable and mutually satisfactory financial arrangements which were subsequently overturned.

It is indeed arguable that the overwhelming emphasis during the Act's first two years on achieving benefit savings has so distorted its implementation that none of its other objectives have been attained. Indeed, the most recent administrative and legislative changes may lead the Act even further off course. It is salutary to speculate on how the Child Support Act might have been framed and implemented had it not been driven by this particular financial priority. The legislation might not have had such a narrow fiscal focus, but might instead have introduced a range of inter-related measures aimed at improving the employment opportunities of lone parents, relieving the poverty experienced by their children, and sustaining relationships between separated parents and their children, regardless of their financial or living situations.

References

Bradshaw, J. and Millar, J. (1991) Lone Parent Families in the UK, DSS Research Report no.6, London, HMSO.

Burghes, L. (1993) One-Parent Families: Policy Options for the 1990s, London, Joseph Rowntree Foundation/Family Policy Studies Centre.

CAS (1994) Annual Report of the Chief Child Support Officer, 1993-4, Central Adjudication Services, London, HMSO.

Clarke, K., Craig, G. and Glendinning, C. (1993) Children Come First?, London, Barnardo's.

Clarke, K., Glendinning, C. and Craig, G. (1994) Losing Support, London, Children's Society.

Craig, G., Clarke, K. and Glendinning, C.(1995) 'Savings or service?', Benefits, no. 13, pp8-12.

Clarke, K., Craig, G., and Glendinning,C. (1996) Small Change: The Impact of the Child Support Act, London, Joseph Rowntree Foundation/Family Policy Studies Centre.

CSA (1994) Child Support Agency: the First Two Years, Annual Report 1993/4 and Business Plan 1994/5, London, Child Support Agency.

CSEAG (1992) Child Support in Australia: Final report of the evaluation of the Child Support Scheme, Canberra, Australian Government Publishing Service.

Dennis, N. and Erdos, G. (1992) Families without Fatherhood, Choices in Welfare 12, London, Institute of Economic Affairs.

Department of Social Security (1990) Children Come First, Cm. 1264, vols.1 and 2, London, HMSO.

Department of Social Security (1995) Improving Child Support, Cm 2745, London, HMSO.

Garnham, A. and Knights, E. (1994) Putting the Treasury First, London, Child Poverty Action Group.

House of Commons (1993) The Operation of the Child Support Act, HC69, Social Security Committee First Report 1993-4, London, HMSO.

House of Commons (1994) The Operation of the Child Support Act: Proposals for Change, HC470, Social Security Committee, Fifth Report 1993-4, London, HMSO.

House of Commons (1995a) Investigation of Complaints against the Child Support Agency, Parliamentary Commissioner for Administration, Third Report 1994-5, London, HMSO.

House of Commons (1995b) The Child Support Agency, Select Committee on the Parliamentary Commissioner for Administration, Third Report 1994-5, London, HMSO.

House of Commons (1996) The Performance and Operation of the Child Support Agency, HC50, Social Security Select Committee, Second Report, 1995-6, London, HMSO.

Holtermann, S. (1993) Becoming a Breadwinner, London, Daycare Trust.

Joseph Rowntree Foundation (1995) Inquiry into Income and Wealth, vols.1 and 2, York.

Land, H. (1994) 'Reversing 'the inadvertent nationalisation of father-hood': the British Child Support Act 1991 and its consequences for men, women and children', International Social Security Review, vol.47, 3-4/94, pp91-100.

National Audit Office (1994) Appropriation Accounts 1993 - 94, vol 9, HC 670-ix, London, HMSO.

National Audit Office (1995) Memorandum: Child Support Agency, London, HMSO.

Rhoades, H. (1995) 'Australia's Child Support Scheme - is it working?' Tolley's Journal of Child Law, vol.7, no.1, pp26-37.

Utting, D. (1995) Family and Parenthood, York, Joseph Rowntree Foundation.

Whiteford, P. (1994) 'Implementing child support - are there lessons from Australia?', Benefits, no.11, pp3-5.

Whiteford, P. and Bradshaw, J. (1994) 'Benefits and incentives for lone parents: A comparative analysis', International Social Security Review, vol.47, 3-4/94, Geneva, pp69-89.

7 Vouchers and Quasi Vouchers in Education

Howard Glennerster

This chapter seeks both to raise general questions about the move towards vouchers and voucher-like arrangements in education and to discuss the more specific proposals for nursery vouchers announced in the Summer of 1995 by John Major, legislated in the Nursery Education and Grant Maintained Schools Bill (given its second reading in January 1996).

In the Summer of 1995 Mr Major announced an experiment in nursery school vouchers. The government would give parents the equivalent of a luncheon voucher or ticket with which they would be able to buy nursery education in private or state nursery schools or other pre-school facilities. This was a promise given against the advice of the Secretary of State for Education, it seems. Local authorities were asked to volunteer for an experimental year or 'Phase One' as the Government chose to call it. We return to the pilot scheme in more detail later to discuss its merits and problems. Yet before doing so it is important to be clear about the more general principles involved in voucher-type strategies for human services including education. This was not a sudden departure from previous Conservative policy. During the 1980s in the UK a whole series of measures had been taken which introduced voucher-like schemes into the education and training system. This was merely one more step in that direction, though an important one.

The origins of vouchers

The true origin of any notion is almost impossible to divine but some trace the notion of vouchers to Tom Paine. In The Rights of Man he discussed the burden of indirect taxation on poor families - 'a fourth part of (a labouring man's) yearly earnings' (Paine 179 1/2, 1969 Edition p262). It would be much more sensible, he argued, to reduce the taxes on the poor and pay poor families four pounds a year to help them bring up their children and require them to send their children to school. The local minister in each parish would inspect the children to make sure they were attending. This might be seen as an early proposal for a mixture of child benefit and an education voucher. It was merely part of a revolutionary package of constitutional reform for which Paine was accused of treason and escaped to join the revolution in France and thence to the newly independent American States!

Nevertheless, the key inspiration for the modern version of the idea is clearly Milton Friedman in Chapter VI of his highly influential Capitalism and Freedom (1962). This begins with a powerful statement of the case for small government and its importance for sustaining political freedom. Large government, employing numbers of state employees who can be bribed to pursue a party political agenda, endangers political freedom. If the state employs teachers and runs schools the system will run the risk of becoming totalitarian with politicians determining what children are taught. Given the interference of politicians with the National Curriculum in the United Kingdom since the 1988 Education Reform Act, who is to say this is a far fetched fear? The extreme Right in the United States are insisting on fundamentalist biblical interpretations of science and evolution in public schools in their localities. So it is not a fear to be taken lightly or confined to Communist totalitarian countries.

Friedman did accept that young families were not well placed to finance the expensive business of educating their children before they had a chance of saving the considerable sums that involves. Nor need they wish to spend on their child what the wider society or that child might in its later life consider optimal. State support to ensure adequate education for each child was therefore justifiable in Friedman's view, but that did not require state provision of education. The state merely needed to pay parents enough to enable them to educate their children up to the level society considered appropriate but choose which school would do it best - precisely Paine's proposal. The state, or voters, might be suspicious that parents would not spend cash on schools. It might be spent on things voters did not want to subsidise. Hence the notion of giving a tied form of enhanced purchasing power -

the voucher. This could only be spent on approved educational provision of a standard acceptable to the taxpayers' representatives - OFSTED or Her Majesty's Inspectors in the British case. Friedman's purpose is clear. The aim is to rid society of state schools and state employed school teachers in the name of political freedom.

Later followers of Friedman developed additional arguments. Parents want very different levels and kinds of education. But state systems of education tend to provide homogeneous education of the same level and kind. The state may want to insist that children receive at least a minimum standard of schooling for a minimum length of time. For the good of the child it may insist the child is not sent to work at the age of ten and that it must reach certain educational levels, because the child will be unable to be a fully independent being without those skills. But many parents may want their children to learn more than the local taxpayer is prepared to fund - to learn a another language, to learn music and play an instrument or to be taught in class sizes of ten. In a state system that will be just too bad. The median voter has decided enough is enough. The parent may purchase such extras but only outside the state schooling system. The virtue of vouchers, these reformers argued, was that those with high preferences for education could top up their base state funded voucher from their own pockets and take them to institutions that did have after-school clubs, violin lessons and modern languages and classes of ten. This would produce a better fit between parental preferences and outcomes for their children. The theoretical proof of this case was first advanced by Stubblebine (1965) in an economic efficiency argument.

A somewhat different case was advanced by two American lawyers from Berkeley - Coons and Sugarman (1980). They were not in favour of some children being able to get better education than others partly at the state's expense but they did think that parents ought to be able to choose the kind of schooling they wanted for their children. Education was such a personal thing that some parents might want informal child-led play as the basis of schooling. Others would want their children taught to read at three and dealt with in an atmosphere of strict discipline. No one could say that one set of parents was right and the other wrong. It was all a matter of opinion and parental preferences. Vouchers would enable those parents who wanted sand and water for their children to take them to sand and water dispensing schools and others to schools that did not spare the rod. The amount spent per child would have to be the same in their scheme of things, though it could be spent differently - lots of sand or thick canes!

The fact that much of this discussion originated in the United States is no accident. School Boards in most states used to insist that parents went to a particular school set by a given catchment area. In a society as dedicated to consumer sovereignty as the USA, this was a source of frustration for parents. For some religious groups, especially Catholics, the rule that no religion should be taught in school meant that many Catholics felt they must send their children to private Catholic schools. They received no state help if they did so. There was nothing equivalent to the settlement with the churches in 1944 in the UK under which denominational schools received state support. That would be unconstitutional in the USA. The Catholic church has long supported the idea of vouchers in the US as a way of enabling poorer Catholics to gain a schooling that fits their faith. At root, then, the Coons and Sugarman type case is one of enhancing parental choice of type of school not necessarily expanding the private sector and certainly not infringing equality of opportunity.

A fourth case is different again. It begins from a general critique of state monopoly. All monopolies tend to exploit the consumer who cannot object to what he or she is offered. They are powerless to transfer their custom. Such schools become unresponsive to parental concerns. Parents can only rely on parents meetings or elected governors to tell the school what they dislike or want added. There is no reason why the school should take any notice - parents have to send their children to the school anyway. The capacity of parents to 'exit' and choose another school would force schools to respond and improve their standards. This is an institutional efficiency argument and is a standard quasi market position similar to that which, for example, underlies the British health reforms of the 1990s.

All these arguments have their critics, of course, but it is important first to recognise that they are very distinct and lead to very different kinds of education voucher. Alan Maynard (1975) made this clear in an Institute of Economic Affairs pamphlet many years ago. A Friedman type voucher is designed to be cashable at private or state schools, and the purpose is to encourage the growth of private schools and a wider range of schools offering schooling of different kinds and qualities to parents of differing means and interest in their children's education. The kind of voucher advocated by Coons and Sugarman and Jencks (1970) would have confined the choice of school at which to cash the voucher to state schools and non-profit schools with a social purpose, perhaps catering for deprived children and certainly not able to charge top up fees. Jencks and others would have the voucher supplemented for children from poor homes. In theory, then, there are a considerable number of possible combinations of characteristics voucher schemes might take on - topped up or not, positively discriminated or not, extended to the private sector or not or any combination of all three!

Objections to the voucher principle

Each of the arguments above has its objections, and more significantly, critics hold other educational goals as more important than those espoused by voucher advocates. Yet the balance of argument shifts depending on what level and type of education is under consideration and this is well illustrated in the contemporary debate in the UK.

Friedman's view that extensive private provision is a bulwark against an authoritarian government can be questioned. Government control over the curriculum in schools in the UK was probably at its greatest in the period after 1861 when there were no state schools and the Government paid private schools on the basis of the examination results the pupils gained in tests set by Her Majesty's Inspectors. Such a system of payment by results meant a very narrow curriculum imposed centrally by politicians worried about educating the masses beyond their station. Probably the greatest freedom was given to schools in the period after the second world war when governors of state schools left head teachers and staff to teach much as they wished. A much greater degree of politicisation followed the introduction of the National Curriculum for schools, coincidentally with the attempt to introduce the voucher-like regimes we describe below. The fact that direct grant schools were private yet received state support in a voucher like way up to the 1970s did not prevent the Labour Government in 1976 saying they must go comprehensive and cease to be grammar schools or lose state money. If the state is giving the money it may be tempted to use its potential power unless such interference is thought unacceptable, as it was until 1988 in the UK. What matters, its seems, in preserving a society from authoritarian rule and political interference with schools is the vigilance of the population and its political system not the form of cash support schools receive. The Friedman case for vouchers can be challenged, therefore, on its own terms.

The second argument for top up vouchers comes in two parts. The first is that higher preference education spenders will been couraged to spend extra on top of the basic voucher financed by taxpayers and this will mean that more is spent on education overall. It turns out that this is proposition depends on a very restricted and questionable set of assumptions, notably that in a much more fragmented and private school-based system voters would continue to be prepared to pay just as much in taxes to support education . This is a pure assumption. A change in voters' perception of education from a public to a private good could change their willingness to support an education budget that essentially went to parents not the local school. It cannot simply be assumed that no change would take place, especially over the long run.

Top-up vouchers would be designed to produce a much wider spread in the levels and quality of education available - high preference high income families would be even more able to get better education for their children. Why not? We do not object to them buying much better hi-fi equipment. It is here that values and purposes become the deciding factor. If you think that it is important for children to begin life with as equal a set of opportunities as possible you will find the top-up voucher objectionable. If you view education like any other consumption good you will not see there is a problem.

The most powerful case to many is that choice and competition between schools may force relatively unresponsive, parent and child-unfriendly institutions to wake up and take notice. The choice or exit capacity gives parents a feeling of greater power and this may hold them in the state system. Critics argue that this choice model is one shared by few parents and is middle class based. Working class parents have no such view of schools. They want a good local school and for it to get on and do its professional job. Parental choice is pushing schools to respond to middle class values. Yet, if schools wish to retain middle class parents, they may have to.

The real problem with pure competition between profit seeking schools is the tendency for this to produce selection by schools rather than choice by parents. What distinguishes education from the production and sale of candy bars is that the quality of the output depends as much, indeed more, on the ability of the purchaser as it does on the producer. The single most important factor in pupil achievement is the capacity of the child and its home background. Any school that wishes to gain good results and hence keep a high demand for its services from parents with able children or with aspirations for them, has a strong incentive to 'cream skim' - attracting the most able and receptive pupils. Economic theory suggests that given a flat-value voucher, schools will become segregated competing to rid themselves of the most costly and difficult children to teach (Glennerster, 1991). Empirical evidence from Belgium, which has had a voucher scheme for many years, supports this thesis (Vandenburghe 1995).

This might not matter if segregated or highly selective schools proved better at educating children from all ability levels on the same per capita expenditure, ignoring social cohesion arguments for the moment. The evidence, however, suggests that this is not the case. Peer group effects tend to be important, the presence of more able or better motivated children have important effects on the average performance levels in a school. If this is so, and recent British research reinforces older research (Rutter, 1979; Hanusheck, 1986; Robertson and Symonds, 1995), the positive externality from having able and less able children and those from different social backgrounds taught in the same school means that competition which leads to school polarisation can reduce the human capital of a country. This argument, however, is one that is directed against a certain kind of voucher - one that is of the same value for every child. This encourages competition for the least expensive or most able child. It is possible to envisage a voucher or a funding formula which compensated schools generously for taking less able children or those from deprived areas. Local authority schools who take children who need special education are already treated in this way (Glennerster 1995). The administration of such schemes might be complex, however.

Clearly, then, the case for vouchers in education is most questionable where we are dealing with common statutory schooling aimed at a national curriculum, and where we hold values that give weight to social cohesion and equal opportunity. Where education is diverse and selective, as with higher education the case for a voucher type system is strongest. Pre-school education and day care present a similarly different balance. Before discussing those issues and the new government scheme for pre-school vouchers it is important to note that though the economic literature tends to talk of vouchers in their pure form, in the real world there are very few vouchers in this sense, but there are arrangements which are vouchers in all but name.

Quasi vouchers

In the early 1980s the Conservative Government flirted with the conception of vouchers when Sir Keith Joseph was Secretary of State for Education. The Department's civil servants managed to persuade him, much to his disappointment, that there were serious practical difficulties with the idea (Seldon, 1986). Instead the Government went ahead with a series of steps that introduced a number of quasi-, or voucher-like schemes both for schools and higher education. Extending other steps taken in the early eighties the 1988 Education Reform Act enshrined and extended parents' rights to send their child to the state school of their choice not just in their own local authority area but beyond it - 'open enrolment'. In practice, there are limits to parental choice that derive from the fact that popular schools have physical limits to the number of pupils they can take and there is no way schools can get ready approval to raise capital to expand or for other schools to enter this 'market'. Nevertheless, a parent does have the capacity to choose schools within these limits and schools are under considerable pressure to take children whose parents have put them as first choice. There is an elaborate appeals process, ultimately to the Secretary of State. At the same time, as choice was extended, schools funding was changed. A school now gets a devolved budget and the amount it gets is fixed by a formula which is essentially the number of pupils signed on at the school times a sum of money. Taken together these two features of the post 1988 scheme - open enrolment plus per pupil formula funding, constitutes a voucher, albeit one that is confined to state schools as in Jencks' original scheme.

The additional feature of the 1988 Act that made it more like the Coons and Sugarman version was the policy of encouraging some schools to opt out of local authority control altogether - Grant Maintained Schools. They are funded by a central government agency on a formula basis. Though formally state schools this brings them half way towards the Friedman ideal. Some future Conservative Government might well be able to float them off into the private sector altogether, funding all schools, including private ones, on a common formula basis. There is a small precedent for doing just that - the assisted places scheme introduced in 1981 by the Conservative Government which permits approved private schools to take pupils and charge them fees on an income tested scale recovering the difference from the real fee from the Government. This scheme is to be doubled in size and extended from secondary schools to primary schools, it was announced in the November 1995 Budget.

In exactly the same way the decision to finance universities by giving them a basic grant and then permitting them to compete for as many students as they could take, was essentially to create a student voucher scheme. Universities are private not-for-profit institutions. They can charge 'home fees' that are fixed by government at a fairly low level and well below the average cost of educating students. Yet this set fee for UK undergraduates is then paid by the student's local education authority. This arrangement has all the essential characteristics of a voucher-student choice of institution which then triggers a payment by the state when he or she enrols in the university. This was always the basis of funding for the polytechnics. This 'fees-only' policy, as it came to be called, produced remarkable results. Universities rapidly expanded to gain the extra revenue, competing furiously for the extra custom and adapting courses to meet student demand. The Government soon put a stop to this expansion, however, by limiting the number of home students universities could take. Competition for voucher-type funding nonetheless continued.

During the 1980s, then, the Conservative Government had been able to move a long way towards what we can call a system of 'quasi ' vouchers for both state and private schools and publicly funded independent universities. Yet this was still a long way from fulfilling Friedman's vision of a system of private schools funded with state vouchers. The complicated mess that is pre school provision offered the Conservatives a chance to move a little further towards this vision.

Vouchers for pre schools

While virtually all French, Belgian and Dutch four-year olds attend some kind of pre-school and so do most Scandinavian children, only just under three quarters of children in the UK attended pre-school in 1991 and only a third of three-year olds (CSO, 1995, Table 3.4). The UK provision of public day-care is minimal compared to other countries - only 28,000 places in the whole of the United Kingdom in 1993. These are provided by social services departments in quite separate establishments from local schools and are mainly for children in high risk categories. Most day-care provision is in private profit or not-for-profit establishments. There is widespread self-help activity with pre-school play groups run for a few hours a day by mothers with some trained help. This absurd bureaucratic separation between day-care and education results in an extremely inconvenient service for mothers and parents who wish to work. State schools are usually only open for hours that do not match working hours, and usually only provide places that are part time . They show almost no recognition of the needs of working mothers. Working mothers are driven into the private education sector for want of anything convenient in the state sector. This is extremely expensive and a political constituency of young working women is growing that would like state help with pre-school provision. Tax relief has been advocated to offset day care fees against the woman's tax though this would help high earners most.

Why is it that state schools have been so reluctant to adapt? There are some examples of joint school and day-care facilities in some local authorities but they are rare. Partly it is a matter of resources but mainly it is a reflection of the typical state sector problem - there is no reason why schools should respond to consumers' needs. They have no incentive to do so. To extend the school day, to provide facilities when parents want it, for whatever periods they want it, happens in American day-care when parentspay. In a UK local authority school it means complicated negotiations between chief officers who are jealous of their budgets. The unions see problems. It means putting together staff with different training and union contracts who will not take orders from staff who have different training. Why should any head take on all that pain when they can keep their 9-4 job and peace and quiet, too, if they only leave well alone. It is just the mothers who will suffer and why should that bother state school teachers or social service directors? If, on the other hand, mothers have purchasing power there is a thriving market willing to respond in remarkably flexible ways as anyone who has experienced it in other countries and in the UK private sector will attest. For more formal research evidence on this from the UK see Holterman (1995). One interesting study from Norway recently showed that even in that relatively well endowed tax rich and socially aware country, private fee paying nurseries were much better adapted to the needs of working mothers than municipally provided ones (Rongen, 1995).

There is, therefore, a strong case for giving working mothers a voucher that would enable them to purchase a combination of child care and education in whatever form they want at an approved standard, topping it up with fees paid by the working partner. This would provide just the incentive public providers need to introduce flexible services geared to working parents. If they fail the private or voluntary sector will do so (Glennerster 1995). Day-care in the public sector is already offered on a fees-for-service basis. Strangely perhaps the present Government scheme fails to incorporate the feature that might encourage a better integration of day-care and education. It is designed to largely benefit well off families living in Conservative local authorities who have refused to do anything on their own to provide pre-school education. This is a clever electoral ploy. It has little to do with the social needs of the broader range of families.

The Conservative pre school voucher experiment

The Government have proposed that parents of children aged four should receive a voucher which could be cashed at any pre school facility approved by Government, public or private. Parents would apply to a local agency separate from the local authority and receive a termly piece of paper worth the equivalent of £1,100 a year. Each of these vouchers would be divided into five parts, exchangeable for a half day of education and would be applied for termly. The parent would have to present these vouchers to its local authority school or to an approved private establishment. The school would then send them to the 'pre school agency' and in time receive a sum of money in return. If the mother lost the paper voucher the school would get no money.

The institutions that would be free to receive cash for such vouchers would be local authority schools, private nursery schools, play groups, local authority day nurseries and child minders who formed themselves into a group. They would initially be approved on paper but would then be inspected 'with a light touch' by OFST-ED-appointed inspectors some time later. Children would follow an early years curriculum - count up to ten, tie shoe laces and know their colours. Parents could top up the value of the voucher in private establishments but not in state schools. If a school failed to collect the vouchers it would not get paid by the agency. If a local authority wished to spend more than £1,100 on its pre-school children, and most spend much more than this, it would have to make up the difference itself. The unit cost of a full time place in a nursery school in England in 1993/4 was £3,320 and £2,600 for a place in a nursery class of a primary school. The £1,100 voucher would buy a place in a play group half time. The total extra money the Government was proposing to spend on new places in the scheme will be only £165 million with an extra £20 million spent on ad ministration. The remaining cost will be recovered from the grants which would have gone to local authorities - about £545 million.

The money to be distributed in this way was to be taken away from the standard assessment calculations which set the total central government grant local authorities receive. Those who currently spend most money on pre school facilities will have most taken away. The money will then go to the local agency who will give £1,100 to every parent with a 4 year-old child. The gainers will be those authorities who have spent least in the past and those parents who can afford to spend money educating their child privately who will now have part of the cost defrayed.

If parents opted to take up places in the private sector local authorities would lose that financial support. The scheme was to run as a pilot from April 1996 for a year and come into full operation in 1997. The only four authorities that agreed to collaborate in the pilot were Westminster, Wandsworth, Kensington and Chelsea - all with strong Conservative pedigrees - and Norfolk the

Secretary of State's home territory. Local authorities that already have widespread pre school provision will not be any better off but may lose resources to private nurseries. Those parents that can now afford to pay will find their bills reduced.

The scheme is thus tailored to appeal to Conservative councils and relatively well off parents of 4 year-olds. However, the most disappointing feature of the scheme is that it fails to address the main problem we have discussed above - the division between day-care and pre-school education and the highly inconvenient form of pre-school provision for parents who are at work. It thus misses what might have been an opportunity to tailor state pre-school facilities to the needs of working families and target such help especially generously on those on income support.

The main deficiency of the scheme is, then, that it was a missed opportunity:

1. It was confined to 4 year-olds
2. It was very mean in the value of the voucher,
3. It gave no incentive to local education authorities and schools to be more flexible in the hours they were open and the kind of care they provided,
4. The inspection and registering provisions were very weak raising fears about quality.
5. The checks on possible abuse by parents selling vouchers to others seemed very weak, too, as the Audit Commission complained (Audit Commission, 1995).

If parents could top up the voucher and pay for additional day care provision at state schools at hours that met the needs of parents or if those on income support could receive enhanced vouchers or quasi-vouchers that would enable them to get back into the labour market the scheme would achieve a much broader range of objectives and help a much wider range of families than the restricted group of richer people that will gain from the present proposals. This would mean changes to current legislation - to enable state schools to charge for non-educational provision from the age of 2, to transfer day-care powers from social services departments to education authorities and to give education departments the statutory duty to provide care and education for children of pre-school age at times convenient to parents. A voucher scheme that enabled parents to take their children to play groups or voluntary and private facilities would force local authorities to respond to the preferences of families not the other way round.

References

Audit Commission (1995) Counting to Five, London, HMSO.

Central Statistical Office (1995) Social Trends, London, HMSO. Coons, J. & Sugarman, S. (1980) Education by Choice: the Case for Family Control, Berkeley, C. A. University of California Press.

Friedman, M. (1962) Capitalism and Freedom, Chicago, University of Chicago Press.

Jencks, C. (1970) Education Vouchers: a Report on Financing Elementary Education by Grants to Parents, Washington D.C., Centre for the Study of Public Policy.

Glennerster, H. (1991) 'Quasi-markets for education?', Economic Journal vol.101, no.408 pp1268-86.

Glennerster, H. (1995) 'Opportunity costs', New Economy, May, pp110-114.

Hanushek E.A. (1986) 'The economics of schooling: production and efficiency in public schools', Journal of Economic Literature , vol .XXIV, pp1141-1171.

Holtermann, S. (1995) Investing in Young Children, London, National Children's Bureau.

Maynard, A (1975) Experiment with Choice in Education, London, Institute of Economic Affairs.

Paine, T. (1791/2, 1969) Rights of Man, Harmondsworth, Middlesex, Penguin.

Robertson, D. & Symons, J. (1995) Do Peer Groups Matter? Peer Group Versus Schooling Effects on Academic Attainment, London, LSE Centre for Economic Performance.

Rongen, G. (1995) 'Does the division of labour between private and public suppliers lead to higher productivity? Evidence from the Norwegian nursery sector?', Local Government Studies, vol.21 no.1 pp130- 149.

Rutter, M. (1979) 15000 Hours, Secondary Schools and their Effects on Children, London, Open Books.

Seldon, A. (1986) The Riddle of the Voucher, London, Institute of Economic Affairs.

Stubblebine, W. (1965) 'Institutional elements in the financing of education', Southern Economic Journal, July pp15-34.

Vandenburghe, V. (1995) 'Education and quasi-markets: the Belgian experience', SAUS Quasi-Markets research seminar, Bristol, March 1995

8 Recent Changes in Social Housing

Norman Ginsburg[1]

Ever since May 1979, Conservative government policy towards social rented housing has sought its privatisation. It is seen as an area of public spending which is not politically, economically or socially necessary for a modern capitalist state. However, privatising it has not proved as simple or as swift as privatising the utilities. The proportion of British housing in the social rented sector has fallen from around 35 per cent in 1979 to around 25 per cent in 1996. The actual number of social rented dwellings in England fell by only 19 per cent in the period 1979-1993. The terms 'social housing' or 'social rented housing' cover housing which has attracted central government subsidies and is rented from not-for-profit organisations, principally local authorities, New Town corporations, the Northern Ireland Housing Executive and housing associations. The latter are not of course in 'the public sector' and they are increasingly funded privately, so in some senses the housing association stock is already privatised. There is often no clear boundary between 'public' and 'private' provision of welfare services, but a continuum from one extreme to the other with housing associations somewhere in the middle but moving towards the private sector.

Some readers may be surprised to learn that the total real cost of social rented housing to the taxpayer (including both capital and current expenditure as well as housing benefit to tenants) was the same in 1992-93 as in 1980-81, around £13.8 billion at 1991-92 prices, although it reached a low of £9 billion in 1988-89 and is currently falling slowly (Hills, 1993, Table 47). Of course the allocation of this expenditure has changed very considerably. Subsidies to council housing and capital spending on local authority new building have fallen away sharply. However, capital spending on renovation of the council housing stock and spending on housing benefit have both increased considerably. Real capital spending by housing associations financed through the Housing Corporation remained fairly constant throughout the 1980s. It was increased very sharply in the early 1990s, as the government helped the house builders by buying up unwanted developments during the acute recession in the owner occupier market. Currently, however, public capital investment in housing associations is slipping back to the levels of the 1980s with private finance accounting for around 40 per cent of housing associations capital finance in 1995/6 (Wilcox, 1995, Table 52). The Chief Executive of the National Federation of Housing Associations recently pointed out that '1995/6 will see the worst level of combined housing association and local authority starts since 1945' (Coulter, 1996, p9). In the early 1980s the policy of privatising social rented housing was implemented by the sale of local authority homes to sitting tenants under the Right to Buy (RTB), encouraged by considerable discounts and also by significant increases in council house rents. These policies continue of course to the present day, but their impact has waned as the most attractive RTB deals are long gone and because housing benefit insulates most tenants from the effect of rent increases. Then in the mid 1980s the government developed schemes for the sale or transfer of estates to private bodies, mostly housing associations but also to private developers and Housing Action Trusts. Housing associations were also forced to raise more and more of their capital finance from private sources. Some but by no means all of these policies are very much alive, as documented below. Currently in the mid 1990s, further thrusts to the privatisation drive are being developed, most notably in the form of Compulsory Competitive Tendering (CCT) of local authority housing management, Local Housing Companies (LHCs) to take over housing management and development functions from local authorities and the extension of RTB arrangements for all housing association tenants. Assessment of the shape and impact of CCT would be premature given that only the initial stages of contracting have been reached, but the other measures are discussed below.

Analyzing the past six years of government policy for social rented housing, the period seems to divide into two. From 1989, policy took something of a turn to the left, while since around 1993, policy has moved visibly to the right. The period 1989-92 was dominated politically by the eclipse of Thatcherism and economically by recession. There was a certain amount of panic about the collapse of house prices, the repossessions crisis and also about the visibly increasing presence of homeless people on city streets. All this resulted in government committing more resources to housing association activity, as well as initiatives specifically targeting resources towards homeless people such as Private Sector Leasing for homeless families (replacing much bed and breakfast) and the Rough Sleepers' Initiative. Early in 1993, in the wake of the ERM debacle and the strengthening of right wing Euro-scepticism within the Conservative Party renewed enthusiasm for attempting to cut public spending, to privatise public services and thus to reduce taxes emerged.

The first public announcement of the new turn in government policy came in a speech in February 1993 by Michael Portillo, then Chief Secretary to the Treasury, which called for a special review of social spending programmes with a view to distinguishing 'essential' from 'avoidable' spending. Malcolm Dean was correct to describe this initiative as marking: 'the third stage of the Thatcher revolution ... redefining the boundary between public and private provision' (Dean, 1993, p23). This shift to the right also included renewed proclamation of basic family values involving attacks on lone mothers and on people under 25 who seek support from the welfare state rather than their parents. Kenneth Clarke's first November 1993 Budget has also been identified as a significant turning point for the welfare state by Hartley Dean (1994), and not just another incremental erosion. It demonstrated more clearly than ever before that the government: 'is prepared in varying degrees to abrogate its mediating role between the private individual and the market' (Dean, 1994, p115), notably in the areas of housing, sick pay and higher education.

During 1993 and early 1994 housing ministers canvassed some pretty radical, long-term ideas including the end of social house building, competing market rents in all sectors, the abolition of all subsidies including housing benefit and their replacement with a personal housing allowance covering owner occupiers as well as tenants (see Carter and Ginsburg, 1994, p101). January 1994 saw the publication of a consultation paper setting out proposals to severely restrict the access of homeless families to social rented housing (DoE, 1994). The latter provoked a very hostile reaction across a wide spectrum of opinion, but the Department of the Environment continued its internal review of policy. Eventually the White Paper Our Future Homes (DoE, 1995a) was published in June 1995 and a Housing Bill in January 1996. The White Paper and the Bill develop the proposals to restrict access to social rented housing particularly for homeless families, and also make new proposals for the further privatisation of ownership and management of the sector. Meanwhile throughout the last three years policy-making on housing investment, rents and housing benefit has been led by the Treasury and announced in Kenneth Clarke's November Budget speeches.

The principal policy shifts in the past three years are therefore the proposals to repress demand by withdrawing the right of homeless families to permanent accommodation in the sector, alongside a sharp fall in capital investment for housing association new building. And yet, illustrating the confusions and divisions within the government, the housing White Paper says that social rented housing 'continues to have an important role' because 'for people who are likely to have low incomes in the long term, social housing is the most cost-effective way to ensure that they have access to a decent home' (DoE, 1995a, p26). The government here concedes that below market rents in the sector save on housing benefit costs, improve work incentives and reduce the employment trap. It is almost a ringing endorsement. The market-led vision of 1993/4 seems to have given way to a more pragmatic, more collectivist one in 1995, but it is not unheard of for a government to face in two directions at once, keeping its options open ahead of an election.

In concentrating on the most recent period (1993-96), it seems appropriate to discuss the policy changes under three headings, housing benefit and rising rents, access to tenancies, and ownership and management of the social rented sector.

Housing benefit and rising social rents

Since the election of the third Thatcher government in 1987, policy for all sectors of rented housing has arguably been dominated by one principle - raising rents. The rationale is that driving rents towards market levels will generate increasing private investment in rented housing, facilitating the withdrawal of public funding to social rented tenures as well as improving quality and supply in the private and housing association sectors.

In the social rented sectors, recent rent rises have not been quite as spectacular as in the private rented sector, but they have nevertheless been substantial. Local authority rents rose in real terms by 36 per cent between 1988/9 and 1993/4 having remained fairly steady through the mid 1980s after the 51 per cent real rise between 1979/80 and 1982/3. Housing association fair rents (for pre 1989 tenancies) rose 27 per cent in real terms between 1989/90 and 1993/4 while housing association assured rents (for post 1988 tenancies) rose by 43 per cent in the same period (Newton, 1994, Table 125).

Under the rent and subsidy regime for council housing intro-duced in 1990, government subsidy comes in two forms - the housing element and the housing benefit element. In crude terms, as rents have risen the housing element subsidy has been pro-gressively reduced. The housing element of subsidy for each local authority is calculated annually by the Department of the Environment (DoE) with reference to an average guideline rent calculated on the basis of the estimated capital value of the stock according to right-to-buy valuations. Where the government con-siders the housing service costs less that its determination of the rental income, the housing element subsidy disappears and the 'excess' rental income subsidises housing benefit costs, thereby reducing the housing benefit element of subsidy. Effectively better off tenants are supporting those on benefit. In other words, coun-cils in this situation are making a 'profit' out of their housing, though only a notional one because of the cost of housing bene-fit. The majority of councils in England are now in this position, with the aggregate 'surplus' rental income now exceeding the aggregate cost of the housing element of subsidy (Newton, 1994, Table 86).

Under this system, the DoE have almost direct control of local authority rents. The system was introduced in 1989 by Nicholas Ridley so that, as he put it at the time, council rents would vary in a way: 'which takes more account of the geographical spread of housing, its type and the demand for it', (quoted by Hills,1991, p101). By tying subsidy to capital values, the government was clearly hoping to move towards a form of market rents or at least a 'market-like pattern of rent differentials' according to the Housing Minister in 1989 (quoted by Hills, 1991, p103). To implement this would have required a doubling of rents in affluent areas and a halving of rents in poorer areas, so a permanent 'damping mechanism' exists to smother the variations produced by the policy, leaving the DoE with complete discretion. Hills (1991, p104) estimated that this system would eventually lead to a post 1989 doubling of local authority rents in real terms, though the government has maintained a silence on how it sees the even-tual outcome. In 1994/5 the guideline rent increase was 4 per cent in real terms, that is 4 per cent above general price inflation.

The rise in housing association rents is of course also a direct consequence of policies implemented in 1989. Since the beginning of 1989 rents for all new housing association assured tenancies have become significantly higher than the 'fair rents' determined by the Rent Officer Service (ROS) for pre 1989 ten-ancies. Since 1989 the government have pursued a policy of steadily decreasing the proportion of the Housing Association

Grant (HAG) contribution to the capital cost of new housing association developments. In 1990/1 HAG contributed on average 78 per cent of the cost of mixed-funding finance, falling to 63 per cent in 1993/4. The Housing Corporation is planning to reduce this ratio to 55 per cent in 1995/6.

In effect then the capital subsidies being withdrawn from the social rented sectors are being partially replaced by a revenue subsidy in the form of housing benefit accompanying the greatly increased rents. About 60 per cent of tenants in the social rented sectors are receiving housing benefit. So in respect of the social rented sectors, the rise in housing benefit costs is largely a reflection of the reduction of other subsidies. Government concern about the rising cost of housing benefit expressed in recent ministerial pronouncements ignores the fact that the net effect of these changes on public expenditure is much smaller when the withdrawal of other housing subsidies is taken into account (see Oppenheim, 1994, p8 and Hills,1993, pp68-71).

Affordability

When the new system for housing association finance and tenancies was established in 1989, the government introduced the notion of 'affordable rents' to describe the new rent regime. However, neither the government nor the Housing Corporation supplied an operational definition of the concept. For example, in 1989 the Housing Corporation insisted that 'rents must be set and maintained within the reach of people in low paid employment' (quoted by Hills, 1991, p128) but this is obviously very vague. The situation has remained unresolved and unchanged since, the determination of affordable rents being left to individual associations who must balance the affordability criterion with strong pressures to maximise rental income.

Amongst policy analysts, a common way of operationalising affordability is to examine the ratio between rents and average male earnings. This affordability ratio remained very steady for all the rented sectors in the 1980s, but has risen sharply since 1989. In 1989 the affordability ratio for council housing was 9 per cent and for housing associations 12 per cent. By 1993 these ratios had risen to 14 per cent for council housing and 19 per cent for housing association assured tenancies. The use of male average earnings as a parameter understates the affordability problem, because there is a growing divergence of incomes between tenants in the social rented sectors and the average (Ford and Wilcox, 1994, pp67-8). The majority of social renting tenants receive housing benefit and are therefore largely protected from the affordability problem. Nevertheless increasing numbers of households with incomes just beyond eligibility for housing benefit are finding their incomes (net of rent) considerably reduced. The rising rent regime has also obviously exacerbated the housing benefit poverty trap. For example:

> a lone parent paying the 1993 average housing association rent for a new letting of a two bedroom dwelling, £52.29 per week would need gross earnings of some £200 per week before they escaped the housing benefit poverty trap. This is more than £20 per week above the prevailing level of average full-time female earnings (Ford and Wilcox, 1994, p70).

A family household with two children and a rent of £50 a week is only £12 a week better off earning £230 than earning £60, without taking into account the cost of school meals and travel to work. In this way, arguably the rising rent regime keeps more people on the dole, thereby sustaining public expenditure on the benefits system.

The inflationary consequence of rising rents is another critical aspect of the rising rent regime. According to Meen (1994) a ten per cent increase in all rents leads to a 0.4 per cent increase in the RPI, which will in turn trigger rises in pensions and benefits, while a ten per cent increase in social sector rents would reduce GDP by between 0.1 and 0.2 per cent. Hence the rising rents regime imposed by the government has adverse macro economic effects on the economy as a whole.

Recent Changes

The government began to recognise the problems created by its rent raising policy in the 1995 White Paper, which announced that in future guideline rent increases for local authorities will be brought in line with inflation, with the aim of maintaining affordability by establishing: 'a stable and sustainable level of guideline rents in real terms' (DoE, 1995a, p27). In future the guideline rent increases will come down to the general level of inflation and councils who raise rents beyond the guideline will be penalised by loss of housing benefit subsidy. According to Malpass (1996, p13) 88 per cent of councils currently charge rents in excess of the guideline in order to finance more repairs and maintenance work. The net effect of the new policy will be to delay repairs and maintenance in exchange for mitigation of the planned rent increases. On housing association rents the White Paper is much more cautious merely commenting that Housing Association

Grant levels: 'are reviewed each year and take into account the long term impact our decisions have on public expenditure [i.e. including housing benefit] and work incentives' (DoE, 1995a, p27). Naturally the government is keen to continue increasing the proportion of private sector capital finance underpinning housing associations which pushes up their rents. Having relinquished regulation of housing association rents in 1989, the government does not have any direct means of holding down rents should it want to do so. Nevertheless recent policy suggests some increased hesitancy in government about the wisdom of moving towards market or capital value rents in the social rented sector.

Access to Social Rented Housing

The January 1994 Consultation Paper on access to local authority and housing association tenancies (DoE, 1994) was widely viewed as an attack on both homeless people and lone mothers. The issue of young lone mothers in council housing was first raised by John Redwood in the summer of 1993 and was taken up by housing minister, Sir George Young, at the 1993 Conservative Party Annual Conference. He expressed concern about housing queue jumping by 'the unmarried teenager expecting her first, probably unplanned child'. In fact the Consultation Paper made only one minor reference to young single mothers, perhaps because only a tiny proportion of social rented tenancies are allocated to this group. The ensuing policy shift is clearly a response to feeling in Conservative circles that the present legislation is too generous to homeless families in general and to single mothers in particular. Hence the White Paper says that allocation schemes for social rented housing:

> should reflect the underlying values of our society. They should balance specific housing needs against the need to support married couples who take a responsible approach to family life ... The Government proposes to prescribe only the key principles on which allocation schemes should be based (DoE, 1995a, p36).

Never before has central government taken such an explicit view on eligibility for social rented housing, nor sought powers to prescribe principles on which it should be allocated. The implications for all unmarried people are clear - they are less deserving, they are second class citizens. The issue of teenage single mothers has been used as a wedge to soften up public opinion for undermining the rights to social housing of all homeless families in priority need. In recent months the Minister for Housing, David Curry, has been backpedalling furiously on this issue. On several occasions he has denied that the government wants to bash unmarried mothers, declaring that 'the Housing Bill is not about pursuing "a moral agenda"' (Curry, 1996, p9).

There is no evidence of 'queue jumping' by homeless families over others on the waiting lists despite allegations in the White Paper that they get priority treatment (DoE, 1995a, p36). The Consultation Paper cited evidence from Prescott-Clarke et al. (1994) which found that homeless people in temporary accommodation were allocated permanent accommodation more quickly than other waiting list applicants, but this ignores the very important differences in circumstances between the two groups. According to the Association of Metropolitan Authorities (AMA) around 25 per cent of local authority lettings are made to homeless families, who tend to be allocated and accept the least desirable properties through simple desperation (AMA, 1995, p8). The AMA (1995, p10) found that 82 per cent of local authorities made fewer offers of tenancies to homeless applicants than to other applicants. According to another survey, 59 per cent of homeless households are already on a waiting list prior to losing their accommodation (Butler et al, 1994, p20). Equally some homeless households who lose their accommodation suddenly would have had no reason to go on a waiting list prior to their crisis.

The allocation of social rented housing has always been at the discretion of local authorities and housing associations, though the latter have no statutory obligations to homeless people. The present homelessness legislation (Housing Act, 1985) says that homeless people in priority need through no fault of their own should be provided with suitable accommodation by local authorities and should get 'reasonable preference' in the allocation of secure tenancies. In practice this usually means that homeless households stay for months or even years in temporary accommodation (bed and breakfast, hostels, private sector leasing etc.). The legislation has been interpreted as giving such households the right to permanent, secure accommodation in the social rented sector, albeit after an indefinite period in temporary accommodation. However, ten days after the publication of the White Paper in the summer of 1995, apparently as a bolt from the blue, the Law Lords handed down a judgement which undermined the above interpretation of the law quite drastically. In the case of R. v. Brent ex parte Awua, the Lords interpreted local authorities' duty as being merely to provide suitable accommodation which need not be permanent or secure. Lord Hoffman reminded the court that the Act is not intended to enable local authorities 'to make inroads into [their] waiting list of applicants for housing' (quoted by Campbell, 1995, p17). There is obviously a remarkable symmetry with the thinking behind the White Paper. According to Holmes (1995, p11) there is so far 'very little evidence that authorities are using Awua to justify restricting the accommodation they provide' but they will have to change their policies in the light of forthcoming legislation.

Proposed New Policies

The Bill published in January 1996 makes the following proposals affecting the access of everyone, including homeless people in priority need, to social rented tenancies:

> Local authorities will only make permanent lettings (or arrange them through other social landlords) from a single waiting list or housing register; all local authorities are required to keep such a register. Homeless people (if eligible) have to join the single queue.

> The government will regulate who is eligible to go on the waiting list and how tenancies are allocated, through regulations yet to be published; possible criteria include means testing, age limits, family structure, residency requirements and waiting time on the list.

> Local authorities will have a duty to provide eligible homeless households with accommodation for twelve months, but only if there is no alternative, suitable accommodation available i.e. in temporary accommodation or in the private rented sector. After the twelve month period a review is required, and any right to accommodation within the social rented sector expires after two years unless it is a hostel place or a private sector lease.

The single housing register is a reasonable proposal as long as it is set up to assess households' housing needs fairly and flexibly. This is a hugely complex task given the diversity of housing needs and circumstances. Local authorities' past record has hardly been immaculate; there has been a long history of discrimination in housing allocations, not least against ethnic minorities and lone mothers. Eligibility criteria such as time on the waiting list and residency requirements have been shown to be racially discriminatory. The introduction of a minimum age for going on a waiting list would be consistent with government policy of restricting young people's welfare rights, for example to housing benefit and income support. They are being pressurised to remain dependent on their parents rather than the welfare state even up to the age of 25. The introduction of means testing to determine eligibility for social rented housing is also fraught with possible injustices. For example as Shelter (1995, p12) point out 'people who have disabilities , serious illnesses, or who are HIV positive may not be able to secure appropriate accommodation for themselves even if they do not have relatively low incomes'. According to Shelter (1995, p12) 15 per cent of the households accepted as homeless in 1994/5 were fleeing domestic violence. The new proposals will make their existence much more precarious and insecure. One of the principal reasons for the introduction in 1977 of homeless families' right to accommodation in the social rented sector was to prevent children coming into care as a result of homelessness. The current proposals will surely increase that likelihood.

In general, the proposal to refer homeless families and vulnerable single people to the private rented sector must in many cases compound their problems. Less than benign local authorities may interpret their responsibilities as very limited. It is not difficult to imagine a situation in which applicants are simply referred to newspaper advertisements or private accommodation agencies. Perhaps there will even be a return to serving travel warrants to other parts of the country or abroad just on the strength of a phone call to a letting agency. Landlords of quality properties are unlikely to let them to homeless people, particularly with children. As Shelter (1995, p13) says 'short-term tenancies in the private rented sector cannot be a substitute for a secure affordable home. The proposals would create potential or actual disruption every six or twelve months, and would make settled family life extremely difficult'. Finally, a great irony of these proposals is that the better the quality of temporary accommodation occupied by homeless families, the less likely they are to be permanently rehoused from a housing register, if priorities are determined by current housing conditions.

Responding to and anticipating such criticisms, the government published a consultation paper on housing allocation alongside the Housing Bill in January 1996. The tone of the document is tentative and the government seems content to leave the bulk of local authorities' discretion intact. It concedes that:' there is a case for giving everyone accommodated under the new homelessness duty the right to appear on the register' (DoE, 1996, p5). This would to an extent restore the rights of statutorily homeless people to permanent accommodation in social rented housing. In the document the government even considers the possibility of allowing: 'everyone over 18 (and people under that age in pre-scribed circumstances)...who has a local connection...the right to register' (DoE, 1996, p5) with the exception of people from abroad including asylum seekers. This would go well beyond the conditions for entry onto housing waiting lists established by many local authorities. The consultation paper also recognises that people with pressing, specific needs referred from Social Services Departments and/or the National Health Service would continue to get exemption in the new allocations regime. Extremely vulnerable people who: 'cannot reasonably be expected to find settled accommodation for themselves ... [will get] preference over all other applicants' (DoE, 1996, p13). However it is made clear that the numbers of people covered by such prioritisation will be very small, and the implication is that most applicants will be expected to find their own accommodation in the private sector. The government propose in the consultation paper to amend Section 22 of the Housing Act, 1985 which requires local authorities rather vaguely to give reasonable preference in housing allocation to people in insanitary or overcrowded houses, people living in unsatisfactory housing conditions, people with large families and people accepted as statutorily homeless. The latter two categories are dropped, while the first two are to be retained, with four more groups of people proposed for 'reasonable preference', namely:

> people living in conditions of temporary or insecure tenure; families with dependent children or who are expecting a child; households containing someone with an identified need for settled accommodation; households with limited opportunities to secure settled accommodation (DoE, 1996, p10).

These categories would surely cover a very significant proportion of statutorily homeless people. Such uncontroversial and wide-ranging criteria for determining and prioritising needs are justified in the document thus:

> Recognising the importance of a stable home environment to children's development, the Government believes that local authorities should give priority to ensuring that families, particularly married couples, with dependent children or who are expecting a child have access to settled accommodation (DoE, 1996, p11).

Here the document appears to be echoing the sentiments behind the original legislation giving rights to homeless families in 1977 and the concern about children coming into care due to homelessness. It is some considerable distance from the more punitive views about queue-jumping lone mothers expressed by ministers in 1993 and yet the privileging of 'married couples' still has echoes of that discourse. Looking at the policy discourse as it has unfolded from the summer of 1993 to the spring of 1996, at the time of writing it is dangerous to guess the final outcome, but it would seem that the government has drawn back from interfering substantially with local authority discretion in the allocation of social rented housing.

Other proposals in the Bill restricting the rights of homeless people include:

A person will be homeless if there is no accommodation anywhere in the world which they can occupy, or if that situation is likely to arise within 28 days; previously this was confined to the UK. This proposal will write into statute the 1988 decision of the House of Lords in the cases of British people of Bangladeshi origin from Tower Hamlets. They were denied accommodation under the homelessness legislation, because they allegedly had family accommodation in Bangladesh despite having lived in Britain for between 16 and 2 8 years (CRE, 1988).

Asylum seekers and their dependants will be ineligible for assistance if there is any accommodation in the UK they can occupy, no matter how temporary. They are not covered by the 28 day threat as above. There is no intimation in the White Paper as to how the housing problems of asylum seekers will be tackled and how they will be able to compete for private rented tenancies with statutorily homeless people.

The impact of both these measures will clearly be felt most by people of ethnic minority origin, whose status within the welfare state is thus further diminished. Finally, local authorities will have the power to establish one year 'introductory tenancies' for all their new tenants. Local authorities will be able to regain possession from introductory tenants who behave 'anti-socially' without formal, legal grounds. Shelter (1995, p36) believes that the deterrent effect on anti-social behaviour will be minimal and that this measure will add to the insecurity of homeless people who are eventually offered council housing. Existing tenants could use this measure to impose their prejudices on newcomers. Introductory tenants who are evicted will be intentionally homeless, leaving them and their children with few rights to assistance. At the very least there is considerable scope for injustices to occur under this measure, dependent as it is on local authorities' discretion.

All the way since 1993 the fundamental aim of these policy proposals has been to reduce the visible demand for social rented housing by further restricting the rights of homeless families to accommodation and by pressuring them into the private rented sector. Despite apparent softening on some details, at the time of writing there is little indication that the government is moving from that hard line.

Privatising Ownership of Social Rented Housing

In pursuing its mission to privatise local authority housing, Conservative governments since 1979 initially relied on the success of the right to buy legislation of 1980. This generated the sale of over 1.6 million homes to sitting tenants in the period 1981-1993. Then in the 1988 Housing Act, the government introduced two new schemes to encourage the transfer of whole council estates out of local authority ownership, namely Tenants' Choice and Housing Action Trusts (HATs). In the event neither of these initiatives prospered. Tenants' Choice gave tenants the power to bring in private developers to take over their estates. The idea was not attractive to tenants, worried about the possibility of getting a Rachmanite landlord and it was not financially attractive to private developers . HATs involved the transfer of an estate to a public agency which would implement an investment programme to prepare the estate for subsequent private ownership (see Karn, 1993). Again this was rejected by tenants up and down the country. Subsequently, four HATs were established in the early 1990s in Waltham Forest, Hull (North), Liverpool and Birmingham (Castle Vale). These schemes were initiated by the local authorities as a means of generating very considerable investment funds for these rehabilitation projects, which could not financed by other means because of public spending restrictions. HATs and Tenants' Choice are not mentioned in the 1995 White Paper and Tenants' Choice is explicitly abandoned in the Bill.

Large Scale Voluntary Transfers

Beyond the right to buy, the most significant form of privatisation of council housing has been what are called large scale voluntary transfers (LSVTs). This means the voluntary disposal by a local authority of its rented housing to another organisation, usually a housing association specially set up for the purpose. Oddly enough, this form of privatisation was not initiated directly by the government, but by local authorities who found themselves unable to raise investment funds for their council housing by any other means. Since the Local Government and Housing Act, 1989 local authorities as landlords have been in a financial straitjacket. They cannot independently raise money for council housing from council tax payers, the City or anywhere else, and they can only recycle up to 25 per cent of their capital receipts from RTB sales. In coming to terms with this strait-jacket, local authorities in the suburbs and the shires realised that the capital values of their housing stocks far exceeded the outstanding debts attached to them. By transferring the stock to a new landlord they receive a large one-off capital receipt which pays off the debt and leaves a surplus for other uses. The new landlord is able to attract private investment funds to maintain the stock unconstrained by public spending controls. Most of the transfers so far have been implemented in small local authorities in the South of England outside the big conurbations. However a partial stock transfer is currently being implemented in Manchester. Research commissioned by the government suggests that LSVT has generally been a positive experience for both tenants and local authorities (Mullins, 1995) . However existing tenants at the point of transfer were given a rent guarantee for five years, while new tenants pay considerably higher assured rents, naturally generating some ill feeling. Some LSVT associations are having a tough time financially, particularly those which borrowed at high fixed interest rates in the late 1980s. West Kent is currently raising rents by 11 per cent and shedding 5 per cent of its staff (Weaver, 1996).

The government itself has been lukewarm about LSVTs because they entail increased public expenditure, particularly on housing benefit to tenants. Under the local authority regime, the rental income surpluses which occur in most suburban and shire areas contribute to the cost of housing benefit. Under LSVT, the Treasury has to bear the full cost of housing benefit, which in the case of by far the biggest LSVT so far in Bromley has cost it £7 million a year (Wilcox, 1993, p17). Hence the number and size of LSVTs has been closely regulated by the government and in April 1993 a transfer levy was introduced, which takes 20 per cent of the net transfer receipt (after the housing debt has been paid off). By March 1995 the levy had raised £77.5 million and up to 1993 would have raised a further £80 million if it had been levied from the start (Wilcox, 1993, p19). By the end of 1995, 40 local authorities had implemented LSVT, transferring

178,546 dwellings, generating gross receipts of over £1.6 billion. Private loans of over £2.6 billion have been raised by the new landlords from banks and building societies.

The White Paper does not introduce any major changes to LSVT, envisaging a continuation of the cautious rationing of LSVT proposals, bearing in mind the public spending implications. The White Paper acknowledges that LSVT is not appropriate for the transfer of poorer, urban housing where the debt burden often exceeds the current value. The White Paper expresses the hope that local authorities may be able to put together transfer packages of some of their stock 'which included some poorer housing but are still cost-effective and offer reasonable security for lenders' (DoE, 1995a, p29). This would be quite a delicate balancing act.

Local Housing Companies

Like LSVT, the concept of local housing companies (LHCs) emerged in the aftermath of the 1989 measures which ring-fenced the finance of local authority housing. It was advocated in the second report of the Inquiry into British Housing (1991) and at around the same time by Nick Raynsford, Labour's housing spokesperson, and by the Chartered Institute of Housing (see Wilcox, 1993, p6). As the Inquiry into British Housing put it:: 'it is not possible for local authorities to take spending decisions in a business-like fashion under the present arrangements ... they should have greater freedom to raise money and spend money' (1991, p70). The idea is that the housing landlord function of the local authority, including all assets, liabilities and staff, should be transferred to an independent, non-profit making body, a local housing company. The local authority however would participate in the management of the LHC alongside tenants, developers and other interested parties. In order to establish an LHC endorsement by a tenants' ballot would be required. LHCs would be registered with the Housing Corporation with access to social housing grant alongside housing associations. Essentially the concept is designed to be attractive to Labour metropolitan authorities who have fought shy of privatisation in the form of LSVTs which leave the local authorities with little influence over their former property. Wilcox (1993) has argued that LHCs are much less of a burden on public expenditure than LSVTs, particularly in the case of inner urban authorities with low value stocks and considerable housing debt. LHCs are quite common in the rest of Europe where deficit finance regulations for the public sector are much less stringent than PSBR restrictions here.

The White Paper is only lukewarm about CHCs and does not acknowledge Wilcox's elegant financial arguments. The only issue about LHCs on which the government has gone into any detail is the degree of local authority influence over them. In order to be private sector bodies the local authority cannot have a 'dominant influence', so that its management partners must be 'capable of acting independently and where necessary in concert' (DoE, 1995b, p17). The government suggests that property developers would be sufficiently independent but that 'it is likely to be more difficult where the partners are representatives of tenants and/or other local interests' (DoE, 1995b, p17). There would appear to be something of an impasse here between the Conservative government and Labour local authorities.

Extending the Right to Buy

The government is proposing a voluntary scheme under which those housing associations which are registered charities can help their tenants to buy their homes. Until now the considerable number of tenants of charitable housing associations have not had the right to buy (RTB) enjoyed since 1980 by other tenants in social rented housing. Cash grants of between £8000 and £16000 will be available depending on the valuation. The grants will eat into the Housing Corporation's cash limited funds, but the capital receipts will be have to be reinvested by the associations in replacement housing, unlike receipts from local authority RTB sales. In the future, tenants of all new houses and flats built with social housing grant or transferred from local authorities to new social landlords will have the right to a purchase grant. It is perhaps iniquitous that housing association tenants do not have the same RTB as council tenants. On the other hand this measure means that housing associations will lose some of their best stock. It also seems unlikely that such sales will 'help to build balanced and strong communities' as the White Paper (DoE, 1995a, p15) suggests. On the contrary, as with RTB generally, if anything it is a divisive and exclusionary measure, since the majority of housing association tenants can ill afford to exercise this right. From the government's point of view, the real benefit of this measure is surely its wider populist appeal, building on the undoubted popularity of RTB in the 1980s.

Conclusion

The year 1993 seemed to usher in a third stage in the Thatcher revolution in social policy with a renewed emphasis on marketisation and privatisation of social housing. However, the early ideological vigour seems to have seeped away to some extent in the face of reality. The policy of raising rents towards 'market' levels has come up against the realities of the rising cost of housing benefit and affordability/labour market constraints. Proposals to hold down demand for social rented housing by pushing homeless people into private renting have generated a lot of political resistance and are dependent on the so far somewhat fragile development of the private rented sector. Policies for privatising ownership of social rented housing have proved expensive in terms of housing benefit. The government may be reaching the limits of the extent to which private finance is able finance housing associations and maintain affordability. Local housing companies are regarded as politically suspicious by the present government. Tony Blair claimed recently that Labour is not only 'the party of social housing, but the party of private housing too', which translates into a fairly modest set of confidence-boosting proposals to help owner occupiers (Meikle, 1996). Mr. Blair also said that Labour would allow more of the capital receipts from council house sales to be reinvested in social rented housing. However it remains unclear whether Labour would change the rules on public expenditure to allow local housing companies to flourish and what its policies on rents and housing benefit might be. Strategic facilitation and development of the partnerships between local authorities, housing associations and private finance is surely needed.

Notes

1. The author acknowledges the invaluable assistance of Mary Carter in the preparation of this article, though responsibility for the content lies entirely with him.

References

AMA (1995) Fair and Seen to be Fair: Local Authority Housing Allocations Policies, London, Association of Metropolitan Authorities.

Butler, K., Carlisle, B. & Lloyd, R. (1994) Homelessness in the 1990s: Local Authority Practice, London, Shelter.

Campbell, R. (1995) 'Back to no future', Roof, September/October, p17.

Carter, M. & Ginsburg, N. (1994) 'New government housing policies', Critical Social Policy, no.41, pp100-108.

Coulter, J. (1996) 'Housing - cut, cut and cut again', Roof, January/February, p9.

CRE (1988) Homelessness and Discrimination, London, Commission for Racial Equality.

Curry, D. (1996) 'Need before morality' Roof, March/April, p9. Dean, H. (1994) 'Recreating the void: the November 1993 Budget', Critical Social Policy, no.41, pp109-116.

Dean, M. (1993) 'Will it be tax-man or axe-man?' The Guardian, September 11th, p23. DoE (1994) Access to Local Authority and Housing Association Tenancies, London, Department of the Environment, HMSO.

DoE (1995a) Our Future Homes, White Paper, London, Department of the Environment, HMSO.

DoE (1995b) More Choice in the Social Rented Sector: Consultation Paper, London, Department of the Environment.

DoE (1996) Allocation of Housing Accommodation by Local Authorities, Consultation Paper, London, Department of the Environment.

Ford, J. & Wilcox, S. (1994) Affordable Housing, Low Incomes and the Flexible Labour Market, London, National Federation of Housing Associations Research Report 22 London.

Hills, J. (1991) Unravelling Housing Finance, Oxford, Clarendon Press.

Hills, J. (1993) The Future of Welfare, York, Joseph Rowntree Foundation.

Holmes, C. (1995) 'Removing uncertainty for who?', Roof, November/December, p11. Inquiry into British Housing (1991) Second Report, June 1991, York, Joseph Rowntree Foundations.

Karn, V. (1993) 'Remodelling a HAT: the implementation of the Housing Action Trust legislation 1987-1992,' in P. Malpass, P. & R. Means, (eds) Implementing Housing Policy, Buckingham, Open University Press.

Malpass, P. (1996) 'The slippery slope to rent control', Roof, March/April, p13.

Meen, G. (1994) 'The impact of higher rents', Housing Research Findings, no.109, March 1994, York, Joseph Rowntree Foundation.

Meikle, J. (1996) 'Blair champions the home owner', The Guardian, March 6th, 1996, p4.

Mullins, D. (1995) Evaluating Large Scale Voluntary Transfers of Local Authority Housing, London, Department of the Environment, HMSO.

Newton, J. (1994) All in One Place: The British Housing Story 1973-1993, London, Catholic Housing Aid Society (CHAS).

Oppenheim, C. (1994) The Welfare State: Putting the Record Straight, London, Child Poverty Action Group.

Prescott-Clarke, P., Clemens, S. & Park, A. (1994) Routes into Local Authority Housing, London, Department of the Environment, HMSO.

Shelter (1995) Shelter's Response to the White Paper, London, Shelter.

Weaver, M. (1996) 'A desperate choice', Housing Associations Weekly, March 22nd, p10.

Wilcox, S. (1993) Local Housing Companies, York, Joseph Rowntree Foundation.

Wilcox, S. (1995) Housing Finance Review 1995/96, York, Joseph Rowntree Foundation.

9 From Stableboys to Jockeys? The Prospects for a Primary Care-led NHS

Roland Petchey

Introduction

'We're moving from being the stableboys of the NHS to being the jockeys. The question is, who's the owner?' (Anonymous GP, quoted in May and Robinson 1995, p24)

In October 1994 the government announced a major expansion of the General Practitioner Fundholding Scheme to take effect in April 1996 (NHS Executive, 1994). 'Standard' fundholding (ie. the current model with budgets covering staff, prescribing, and a range of hospital and community services) continues, but with the range of hospital services extended to include all but a few very costly elective procedures. The list-size requirement (which had been set at 10,000 in 1991) is further reduced from 7,000 to 5,000. In addition to the standard model, two new types of fund-holding are being introduced. 'Community' fundholding comes in as a means of allowing smaller (3,000+ patients) practices to participate in the scheme. Community fundholding budgets cover staffing, prescribing and community services, but exclude the hospital services element. 'Total purchasing' (where GPs in a locality purchase the full range of hospital and community services, including accident and emergency services and medical and psychiatric inpatient care) is to be rolled out from the existing four sites to a further 25 pilot schemes. Subsequently, the number of pilots has been increased to 51 and ultimately to 70 sites. In April 1995 an accountability framework for fundholding was published, clarifying lines of accountability and streamlining the reporting arrangements for fundholders (NHS Executive, 1995). These developments of fundholding are the culmination of a decade when what started as policy flirtation with primary care has matured into determined pursuit. Early overtures had included the Selected List prescribing initiative (1985) and Promoting Better Health (Department of Health, 1987). These were followed in 1990 by the New Contract for GPs (Department of Healthand the Welsh Office, 1989) and the NHS and Community Care Act and subsequently by The Health of the Nation and The Patient's Charter (Department of Health 1992a; 1992b). Their significance is that they are presented not simply as desirable ends in themselves but as:

> a significant step towards a primary care led NHS, in which decisions about the purchasing and provision of health care are taken as close to patients as possible (NHSE, 1994 para.1).

This announcement of a strategic objective for fundholding is significant for two reasons. First, it helps to resolve a persistent ambiguity about the role of fundholding in the NHS internal market. Although paternity of the scheme is disputed, forms of GP commissioning had been discussed in the early 1980s (Marinker, 1984; Maynard, 1986). Nevertheless, it is known to have been grafted onto the NHS reforms at a relatively late stage, and the absence of clear articulation between GP commissioning and health authority purchasing led to speculation that it might simply have been envisaged as a short-term expedient for kick-starting the internal market. Second, it signals an important shift in the evolution of purchasing in the NHS. The extension of fundholding and the policy transition from integration of primary and secondary care (NHS Management Executive, 1991) to a primary care-led NHS together suggest that fundholding is emerging as the government's preferred model of purchasing. It could foreshadow the most fundamental shift in the centre of gravity of the NHS in its history and the most radical revision of strategic direction for general practice since 1912.

This paper is in two parts. The first reviews research evidence on the operation of the fundholding scheme to date. The second attempts to locate the concept of a primary care led NHS in a broader health policy context (both cross-national and historical) and to evaluate the capacity of primary care (as currently constituted) to undertake the role now apparently envisaged for it.

Evaluating fundholding

Although the introduction of fundholding created deep divisions among GPs, the scheme has expanded rapidly in England and Wales.

Table 1: The growth of fundholding in England and Wales, 1991-5

Year	Number of funds
1991	303
1992	590
1993	1248
1994	1836
1995	2221

Source: Audit Commission (1995)

The Table understates the extent of GP involvement, since some funds consist of more than one practice. 'Linked practices' are a means of enabling smaller practices to reach the minimum list size. By 1994 roughly 650 practices had linked to form around 280 funds. In addition, at least 16 'multifunds' are in operation. These are created by practices pooling their management allowances to set up joint management arrangements. A handful of the larger multifunds cover upwards of 40 practices and 250,000 patients (the equivalent of a smaller district health authority before the current round of mergers). Finally, there are the total purchasing pilots already mentioned. As a result, fundholding actually involves 2603 practices out of 9,100 (28 per cent) and 10,401 GPs (39 per cent). In 1 994-5 their budgets totalled £2.8bn, or roughly 9 per cent of all NHS expenditure for that year. They were responsible for the care of 41 per cent of the population. However, the population coverage varied widely, ranging from 33 per cent (South and West) to 51 per cent (West Midlands) between regions. At district level variation was even wider, from 4 per cent (Camden and Islington) to 84 per cent (Derbyshire, Isle of Wight, Kingston & Richmond). Fundholding was generally more common in shires and suburbs than in inner city districts (Audit Commission, 1995).

By 1995, then, roughly half of the practices eligible for fund-holding on the basis of list size had been recruited to the scheme. The government has claimed this expansion as proof of success. Unfortunately, it is impossible to determine whether this official confidence is justified. In common with its other health service reforms, the government has consistently refused to commission a systematic evaluation of fundholding in England and Wales (although it did agree to evaluation of fundholders in Scotland during the 'shadow' year prior to full implementation). This refusal has been somewhat tempered by the recent announcement of a three year national evaluation of the total fundholding pilots coordinated by the King's Fund. Until those results are available, we are dependent on a number of small-scale studies conducted mainly in the Oxford, Grampian and Tayside regions. While they fall some way short of being a full scale evaluation, they do enable a somewhat approximate interim cost-benefit analysis of the scheme to date. Their findings are considered under four headings: prescribing, patient services, patient care, and operating costs.

Prescribing

By international standards British GPs remain conservative prescribers (Griffin and Griffin, 1993). Even so, in 1992-3 GP prescribing cost £3.6bn or 9.7 per cent of total NHS expenditure. At an average of £65.50 per head, it was the largest single item in the family health services budget. Between 1983 and 1993 it had increased by 80 per cent after adjustment for inflation (Central Statistical Office, 1994) and uncontrolled prescribing costs were specifically identified as a policy concern. One objective, therefore, of fundholding was to exert control over prescribing costs through the introduction of cash-limited prescribing budgets. This had been contemplated (but not enacted) as early as 1983 (Petchey, 1989a).

At national level there is evidence that fundholders have been more successful than non-fundholders in restraining the seemingly inexorable rise in prescribing costs. For example, in the sample of fundholders investigated by the Audit Office the cost of prescribing rose by 10 per cent, 8 per cent and 8 per cent per annum between 1991 and 1993; for non-fundholders the increases were 15 per cent, 13 per cent and 11 per cent (Audit Commission,

1995). It should be noted, however, that the differences were not statistically significant. The evidence from regional studies is much more equivocal. Earlier studies appeared to confirm that fund-holders were more successful than non-fundholders in restraining increases in prescribing costs, mainly through substitution of cheaper generic drugs (Bradlow and Coulter, 1993; Burr et al., 1992; Maxwell et al., 1993; Wilson et al., 1995).

However, a variety of methodological problems have been identified which mean that these findings must be interpreted with caution. First, the bulk of the evidence so far available derives form short-term observations in small samples of first wave fund-holders. These may not be generalisable. Second, in the Scottish study at least the non-fundholder controls themselves subsequent-ly became fundholders (Maxwell et al., 1993). Because the current method of budget setting exposes practices in the run up to fund-holding to perverse incentives to over-prescribe, their prescribing might not be representative of non-fundholders as a whole. Third, non-fundholders have claimed equally impressive reductions in prescribing costs. In Newcastle and North Tyneside 8.5 per cent and 6.6 per cent overspends have been turned into 2.6 per cent and 5.3 per cent underspends (Anon, 1995). Fourth, initiatives to encourage economical prescribing (largely informational and edu-cational) predate the introduction of fundholding. It is possible that innovative practices had begun to respond to these before they joined the fundholding scheme. Finally (and possibly most intriguingly), single-handed non-fundholding practices have been found to be as effective as fundholders in holding down prescrib-ing costs (Whynes et al., 1 995). The fact that such practices are not subject to budgetary restraint undermines the assumption of some commentators that there is a straightforward causal con-nection between fundholding and economical prescribing. It sug-gests that there is some intervening variable such as practice structure.

In addition more recent research into prescribing concludes that the optimistic conclusions drawn from earlier short term studies may have been premature. Over a three year study period differ-ences in prescribing costs between fundholders and non-fund-holders were found to be very small compared with the overall increase in prescribing costs. Inflationary pressures on prescribing costs (pharmacological innovation, marketing pressure, profes-sional initiatives such as health promotion clinics) were more pow-erful than the cost control influences (Brown et al., 1995)

Patient services

One of the rationales for fundholding was that the financial leverage it afforded GPs would galvanise service providers into increasing efficiency and improving the responsiveness and quality of their services. Budgetary flexibility would also stimulate innovation in the services provided by the practices themselves. Actual evidence on the effects of fundholding on hospital referrals is fragmentary and inconsistent. An early Oxford study (one of the few to have included non-fundholding controls) found striking similarity in the patterns of hospital referrals of fundholders and non-fundholders before and after the implementation of the reforms. There was no evidence that fundholding resulted in a shift from secondary to primary care or that referral was being influenced by budgetary pressures (Coulter and Bradlow, 1993). This pattern was found to persist by a follow-up study (Surender et al., 1995). By contrast, uncontrolled Scottish studies found reduced usage of hospital services and increased use of direct-access services such as physiotherapy and chiropody (Howie et al., 1993; Heaney et al., 1994).

Numerous studies report claims by fundholders that they have improved services (Newton et al., 1993; Glennerster et al., 1994; Corney, 1994; Bain, 1994; Audit Commission, 1995). The Audit Commission also reported that the hospitals it visited also attributed service improvements to pressure from fundholders. However, these claims too must be treated cautiously. First, few studies of fundholding have been designed in such a way as to allow them to measure such claims independently or to isolate the effects of fundholding from other health service changes. Thus, the Audit Commission notes that other initiatives (such as the Patient's Charter or the waiting list initiative) may have contributed to the reductions in waiting times claimed by fundholders. Similarly, Howie, et al., observe that: 'many of the positive features of the fundholding innovation we have described.... may be attributed to health service changes generally rather than to fundholding as the method of implementing them in particular' (1995b, p42).

Second, much of the research evidence refers to the early experience of the first wave of fundholders: it is debatable whether it can be generalised. Third, innovations and improvements are not necessarily the sole preserve of fundholders. Non-fundholders have also claimed to have improved the quality of in-patient care (Eve and Hodgkin, 1992; Graffy and Williams, 1994) and reduced waiting lists (Black et al., 1994). Finally, while they may be popular with patients and GPs, the value of many fundholder service innovations has been questioned. Some (such as direct access physiotherapy) are of unproven clinical value (Coulter, 1995), while others (such as the use of 'near-patient' diagnostic technology and outreach consultant clinics) are of dubious efficiency and cost effectiveness (Bailey, et al., 1994; Jones, 1995; Paton,1995). The cost per patient of an outreach ophthalmology service was three times greater than the hospital outpatient equivalent (£48.09 vs £15.70) because of lower throughput (Gillam et al., 1995). It has been suggested that, far from being evidence of increased efficiency, 'the proliferation of such clinics results from perverse incentives of the NHS internal market to extend inappropriate care' (Harris, 1994 p1053).

Patient care

Fundholders have claimed that their relationship with patients has not been affected by fundholding (Newton et al., 1993). Only one study has attempted to measure the actual (rather than claimed) effect of fundholding on patient care (Howie et al., 1995a). Taking length of consultation as a proxy for quality of care, they found that change to fundholding made little difference; mean consultation time was unchanged (7.5 minutes) between 1990 and 1992. However, the proportion of patients reporting satisfaction declined significantly (from 35 per cent to 30 per cent) even after adjustment for the increase in social problems over the study period. Patients with conditions attracting financial incentives (diabetes, chronic respiratory disease, cardiovascular disease) fared better than average (and were less likely to report social problems). Patients consulting with psychosocial problems did worse. They had shorter consultations and the proportion reporting satisfaction reduced significantly over the study period. These findings need to be interpreted cautiously, since this study was uncontrolled and was, therefore, unable to disentangle the effects of fundholding from other changes taking place at the time. In general, the study design deficiencies which have been identified mean that no reliable conclusions can be drawn about the impact of fundholding on patient care. By the same token, published studies of fundholding have found no evidence that patients have been denied treatment on financial grounds or that fundholders are discriminating against high cost patients.

Costs

The Financial Memorandum accompanying the NHS and Community Care Bill estimated fundholding would cost £15.6m per annum to implement - £14m for administration, £1.6m for computing (Secretaries of State, 1989). It was insistent that this additional expenditure would be more than recovered in efficiency savings. As early as 1992, however, it was becoming apparent that that figure was an underestimate (Petchey, 1993). In 1993-4, fundholders' budgets totalled £1,823m. In addition, they received: £38m in management allowances; £10m for preparation for fundholding; £18.6m for practice computing associated with fundholding (National Audit Office, 1994). Administration costs thus amounted to £66.6m or 3.5 per cent of total expenditure on fundholding. However, fundholding also imposes external costs. Health authorities have to meet the costs of setting and reconciling budgets, auditing accounts and monitoring the operation of the scheme, while providers' transaction costs are increased as a result of having to contract with an increasing number of small purchasers. One health authority calculated its fundholders' management costs at £31.5 thousand per practice for 1994-5 (this is broadly consistent with the Audit Commission's estimate). On top of that, it estimated its own costs at £5.3 thousand per practice and providers' costs at £14 thousand per practice. Inclusion of these indirect costs would substantially increase the total operating costs of the scheme.

Fundholding is claimed to compare unfavourably in terms of administration costs with other forms of commissioning (Ham and Shapiro, 1995). The typical health authority is estimated to spend less than 1.5 per cent of its budget on administration (Black et al., 1994). The Nottingham Total Commissioning Project, comprising 80 per cent of the city's 319 GPs, covering 630,000 patients and commissioning services jointly with the health authority, has estimated its annual operating costs at £1.3m as opposed to £2.4m if they were to become total fundholders (Pennington, 1995).

The implications of expansion

The developments that have been announced indicate that, at the least, the government is seeking significant expansion of fundholding. On its own, the relaxation of the list size criterion for standard fundholding will increase eligibility from 55 per cent to 71 per cent of practices. In combination, the proposals mean that as many as 90 per cent of practices could become eligible for fundholding in one or other form (Committee of Public Accounts, 1995). Even so, even after the anticipated increases in the numbers of fundholders of all kinds in April 1996, it is still worth noting that Health Authorities will remain responsible for an estimated 86 per cent of the hospital services budget (Audit Commission, 1995).

Considerable obstacles exist even to the simple expansion of the fundholding scheme. First, as the list size requirement is lowered, the relatively fixed management overhead will combine with the declining size of the fund to increase still further the proportion of costs spent on administration. In addition, the transaction costs of providers will rise again. On the evidence currently available it is impossible to be certain that this increased expenditure will be cost effective. Second, hitherto, the scheme has been voluntary for GPs. This will continue to be the case (formally at least). However, for health authorities, expansion of the scheme has been made a performance indicator, despite the fact that 65 per cent of small practices are opposed to fundholding. GPs have already voiced concern that health authorities might attempt to dragoon them into the scheme although this possibility has been strenuously denied (Daly, 1995a). If fundholding now becomes effectively compulsory for health authorities, they may be forced to abandon alternative models of commissioning and override the wishes of local GPs (Ham and Shapiro, 1995). Ministerial protestations that non-fundholding commissioning schemes are not being victimised ring somewhat hollow in light of the continuing refusal to fund them.[1] Third, fundholding imposes substantial additional workload (Corney, 1994; Daly, 1995b). Estimates vary widely, but GPs in two pilot sites for total fundholding reported having to work an extra 8-25 hours per week each (Andrews, 1995). The workload for standard fundholding is doubtless lower but unwilling recruits are unlikely to be prepared to sustain it. Finally, the majority of early fundholders achieved savings on their budgets. In 1993-4, 75 per cent of funds were underspent, 20 per cent of them by more than £100,000. The total underspend for the year was £64 million (roughly 3.5 per cent of the total budget). The cumulative underspend since the start of the scheme was £111 million, of which fundholders had spent only about 17 per cent by 1993-4. The precise origin of this underspending is unclear (Bowie and Spurgeon, 1994) but several contributory factors have been identified including historic cost funding, generous initial budget setting (Dixon et al., 1994) and lax financial accountability (National Audit Office, 1994). As budgets and accountability are tightened, the opportunities for savings will reduce and the cost-benefit balance for GPs will alter. The effect of this on the motivation of fundholders (both existing and prospective) is imponderable.

While costs are certain to rise with expansion, it is far from certain that the current level of performance will be maintained (as more recent research appears to indicate). Although the characteristics of fundholding practices have not been investigated, earlier research into GP responses to financial incentives revealed the existence of a stratum of better organised and better resourced 'innovator' practices (Bosanquet and Leese, 1989). Even if fundholders could be shown to be 'better' (however defined) than non-fundholders, it would still be necessary to demonstrate that they were better because they were fundholders rather than the other way round. It is known that for many early fundholders, fundholding was a logical next step ('the next mountain to climb') in a process of continuing professional and organisational development (Newton et al.,1993; Glennerster et al., 1994). Any apparent superiority might therefore be a product of their status as innovators or of some other (so far unidentified) pre-existing characteristic rather than of fundholding. Moreover, innovator practices were found to be better resourced and more likely to be located in more affluent areas with lower health needs. By selectively channelling additional resources and spending power into already advantaged practices, fundholding could aggravate the existing mismatch between the distributions of resources and needs.

Fundholding was introduced during a period of unprecedented turbulence for general practice and as a component of a complex programme of radical reform. Its introduction and implementation have not been subjected to proper evaluation, with the result that our understanding of its effects is rudimentary. The research that has been carried out is such that few reliable conclusions can be drawn about it and the debate about fundholding continues to be dominated by a priori arguments. Many key questions remain unanswered. What is the effect of of fundholding on the overall efficiency of resource utilisation? Are fundholders achieving equal or superior health gain per unit of resource to other purchasers and providers? How does fundholding impact on equity of resource distribution or on access? What are its effects on strategic planning? Or its consequences for the role of the doctor and the doctor-patient relationship? In addition, the emerging concept of a primary care-led NHS raises more fundamental questions about the capacity of primary care to perform the strategic role that now seems to be expected of it. It is to these questions that we now turn, following a brief discussion of the factors underlying primary care's rapid rise up the health policy agenda.

Towards a primary care-led NHS?

The supra-national policy context

It is not only in the UK that health policy in the 1980s has been shifting towards primary care. Three factors may be identified as contributing to this global awakening of interest in primary care: supra-national policy initiatives; health technology advances and health care cost inflation. The significance of each of these for UK primary care will be considered in turn.

Since the 1977 Alma Ata Declaration World Health Organisation member states have been formally committed to a policy of Health For All based on primary health care (PHC) (WHO, 1978). In WHO's conception, PHC was to be the foundation of, and point of entry to, a system of medical care of increasing complexity and sophistication depending on the individual's particular needs. However, its function would extend beyond medical care as traditionally defined, to incorporate a range of non-medical but health-related activities, such as water supply, sanitation, nutrition and the physical environment as well as health education. More importantly, it also embodied two further principles: multisectoral collaboration between agencies whose activities affect health, and community participation in health.

This global strategy was reformulated into a European Regional Strategy which was formally adopted by member states in 1980 (WHO, 1986). 38 regional targets were set against which progress would be monitored (WHO, 1985). They incorporate six themes: equity; health promotion; community participation; multi-sectoral cooperation; primary health care; and internation cooperation. So far, the most tangible expression of cooperation is the Healthy Cities Project involving (as of August 1995) 34 cities in 23 countries throughout Europe, including a number in central and eastern Europe and the newly independent states (Tsouros, 1995). However, in Britain at least, participation has been the product of initiatives at regional or municipal, rather than national, government level (Ashton et al., 1986). Perhaps more significantly, little involvement of GPs has been reported (Thomas, 1995).

Prima facie, then, the concept of a primary care-led NHS would appear to be entirely consistent with the broad thrust of global and regional health policy in the past two decades. However, doubts have been expressed about the extent to which UK primary care policy genuinely embodies the principles underlying the model of PHC advocated by the WHO. It has been argued that attempts to develop PHC in Europe generally (Vuori, 1984) and

in the UK specifically (Green, 1987) have been hindered by identification of primary health care with primary medical care, and
the equation of care with services. This reductionist tendency is
certainly visible in a number of recent cross-national comparisons
of primary care which (wittingly or unwittingly) redefine primary
health care as medical care (Starfield 1991, 1992, 1994; Fry and
Horder, 1994), or even as care delivered by GPs (Gervas et al.,
1994). In the case of the UK, Green claims that this reduction of
primary health care to general practitioner services has diverted
attention from health promotion to disease prevention and treatment, ignored community participation in health, and substituted
a narrow, biomedical model of illness and its causation for a
broader, multisectoral approach to health. Doubts have also been
expressed about the capacity and will of GPs to make the transition from conventional reactive, patient-focused biomedicine to
the proactive, multi-agency, population-based approach to health
advocated by WHO (Pratt, 1995).

One suggested solution to the problem of reconciling the two
perspectives is the notion of community-oriented primary care
(Gillam et al., 1994). Originally developed in Israel, community-
oriented primary care seeks to combine the traditional strengths
of British primary care (a community location, a registered population, accessibility, continuity of care) with health need assessment, strategic planning and coordination of services (Pollock and
Majeed, 1995). However, a pilot project identified a series of
problems. The first is variable access to GP services. Although
nationally more than 97 per cent of the population is registered
with a GP, in inner cities the proportion may be as low as 70 per
cent (London Health Care Planning Consortium, 1981). The
health needs of the homeless and other mobile or otherwise vulnerable sections of the population are likely to be excluded from
primary care-based health needs assessments. Even adolescents
have been found to be underserved (McFarlane and McPherson,
1995). Secondly, the relatively small size of practice populations
means that even common events are unusual. The special needs
of people with mental health problems or learning difficulties or
other disabilities may not register because of the small numbers
involved. A third problem is the lack of reliable routine information in general practice. Finally, attention has been drawn to GPs'
poor record in terms of community involvement (Neve and Taylor,
1995). Few of them have set out systematically to develop partnerships with community groups, to identify local people's own
health agenda, or incorporate their views into service development (Murray et al., 1994; Heritage 1994; Thomas, 1995).

Health technology advance is the second supranational development contributing to revision of the traditional boundaries between secondary and primary care. ('Health technology' is here used in its broadest meaning, to refer not only to hardware, in the sense of equipment and pharmaceuticals, but also to diagnostic and therapeutic techniques, treatment modalities and philosophies of care.) Stoeckle (1995) identifies five interrelated technical, clinical and organizational developments underlying the decline in hospital use. Although he refers to the US, his observations are equally applicable to the UK:

1. Decentralisation of dignostic-treatment technologies to out-of-hospital sites;
2. Substitution of rapid-result diagnostic testing of ambulatory patients for longer term diagnostic observation of hospitalized patients;
3. Reduced use of hospital bed-rest and increased use of exercise and activity for treatment, convalescence and rehabilitation;
4. Corporate reorganization of hospitals emphasizing process efficiency (reducing lengths of stay) to increase profits/reduce costs; and,
5. Group practice organization of primary care enabling more ambulatory diagnosis and treatment of patients who previously would have been admitted to hospital.

The final factor is health cost inflation, which throughout the 1980s was running at an annual compound rate of 0.8 per cent on average for OECD countries (Schieber et al., 1992). Primary care's rise up the policy agenda reflects a widespread presumption that primary care offers a solution to the cost problem, because it is cheaper. At a cross national level there is some evidence of an association between primary care on the one hand and lower costs and greater satisfaction on the other (Fry and Horder, 1994). However, this conclusion needs to be treated with extreme caution, not least because of doubts about the reliability and validity of primary care scores that are derived from meta-analysis of methodologically suspect, partial and often small-scale studies. For example, a key study of the primary-secondary interface in sixteen European countries relies on data from just sixteen GPs in each country (Crombie et al., 1990). Only one cross national survey of satisfaction has been conducted (Blendon et al., 1990) and the anomalous position of the UK (top-rated for strength of primary care, but third-from-bottom on satisfaction) raises questions about its reliability. Evidence of a correlation between strength of primary care and lower costs is somewhat more plentiful, although, even here, the data required intensive massaging to overcome the effect of outliers and exceptions. Finally, it remains to be pointed out that correlation does not imply causation, and that it is impossible to isolate the effects of primary care from other health system characteristics such as the method of financing which has also been found to correlate with cost containment. Such cavils have done little, however, to dent the optimism of those who see primary care as a panacea for whatever ails modern health care systems. In this regard, there are striking similarities between the hopes being pinned on primary care in the 1990s and expectations of community car e in the 1980s.

Domestic primary care policy

At the national level, the supra-national developments which we have been considering have been paralleled by more immediate domestic policy considerations. Prime among these was health care cost inflation, even though by the mid 1980s the British government was much more successful than comparator countries in restraining the increase in costs. This success was only partial, however. Following the imposition of cash-limited hospital budgets in 1976, spending on hospital and community services rose by only 4.5 per cent between 1978/9 and 1985/6. Over the same period spending on primary care rose six times as fast (27.8 per cent) (Bosanquet and Leese, 1 989). The cost of prescribing (the largest item of primary care expenditure after GP salaries) rose by 23.1 per cent between 1978 an d 1986, in part as a result of cost-shifting from cash limited hospital pharmacies to non-cash limited GPs. In the initial period, then, it seems probable that a main thrust of policy towards primary care was to extend into it the cost controls that had already been imposed on the hospital sector. The Binder Hamlyn inquiry of 1982, the Selected List Initiatives from 1985, and the cash-limited budgets of GP Fundholders may all be seen as expressions of this concern.

A second factor was growing awareness of widespread variations both in levels of activity within primary care and in practice development. At an aggregate level, much of the variation in outputs can be accounted for by population characteristics (such as standardised mortality ratios as a proxy for morbidity) or by practice characteristics (the number of GPs per unit of population, for instance), but (once again) the measures of both characteristics and outputs were crude and considerable variation remained unexplained (Baker and Klein, 1991). At practice or individual level, however, the picture is much more confused. There is considerable disagreement even over the scale of variation. At one extreme, referral rates have been argued to vary twenty five-fold (Acheson, 1985); at the other, it has been suggested that, due to the small scale of many of the studies, much of the variation observed could simply be random (Moore and Roland, 1992). Such academic niceties were ignored by the government. Variations in prescribing and referral rates were cited as prima facie evidence of inefficient use of resources both in Promoting Better Health (Department of Health, 1987) and Working for Patients (Secretary of State for Health, 1989).

Alongside evidence of variation in output, evidence was also accumulating of persisting geographical variations in the quality of general practice, despite the incentives for practice development available since the Family Doctor Charter of 1965. It made arange of financial inducements available to GPs: to reduce list sizes; to invest in premises; to employ support staff; to develop group practices; to engage in vocational training, and, to computerise. Although it helped raise standards overall, at local level the response to the Charter was extremely patchy (Royal College of General Practitioners, 1985). The Acheson report found that in inner London single-handed practices continued to predominate (elsewhere they formed a small and declining minority) and a higher proportion of GPs were elderly. Fewer practice staff were employed, there were few primary health care teams operating and many surgery premises were substandard (London Health Care Planning Consortium, 1981). A similar pattern was found in other major cities, both in t he UK and abroad (Maxwell, 1993). More recent research suggests that the situation in inner London is now more diverse than the uniformly gloomy picture painted by Acheson (Livingstone and Widgery, 1990), and that a simple inner/outer city dichotomy no longer applies (Powell, 1990). Nevertheless, substantial disparities persist. 45 per cent of premises remain below minimum standards (Tomlinson, 1992) while London practices still employ roughly 40 per cent fewer practice nurses and ancillary staff than the national average (Benzeval et al., 1991), and the number of recruits for general practice fell by 22 per cent between 1988 and 1993 (Harris et al., 1996).

Bosanquet and Leese (1989) have shown that these variations in development are related to the area in which a practice is located. Practices in more affluent urban or rural areas with stable or increasing populations have more margin available to invest in premises, staff and equipment. They have more (and younger) partners, employ more staff, are more likely to be computerised.

While their operating costs are higher, these are offset by higher practice incomes. In urban areas with declining or mobile populations practices face great disincentives to invest and have less margin available to take advantage of financial incentives.

In the policy response to these problems a number of themes can be discerned. One mechanism for levelling up the quality of general practice has been closer and more explicit linkage between GP remuneration and performance. The original 'good practice allowance' (Secretary of State for Social Services, 1986) payable on achievement of a set level of competence was dropped following opposition from the BMA. However, it was replaced by an equivalent system of payments for the achievement of targets for immunisations and cervical cytology. The 1990 Contract also offered financial incentives for performance of a range of other health promotion activities (Department of Health and the Welsh Office, 1990). The initial response appeared encouraging. By October 1990, 50 per cent of GPs were already achieving the higher target for immunisation, with the proportion rising to 80 per cent in some areas. More recently, though, doubts have been expressed over whether the strategy of increasing immunisation uptake overall is capable of reducing in equalities in uptake. Despite a substantial overall improvement in uptake, inequalities between affluent and deprived areas were found to remain unchanged or even to increase (Reading et al., 1994). Provision of health promotion clinics have also been found to be inversely related with health need (Gillam, 1992). These findings confirm the view that interventions applied across populations (even if they improve standards generally) may leave inequalities unchanged. This conclusion has been reached with respect to several ot her health promotion measures including cervical cancer, coronary heart disease and teenage pregnancy (Whitehead and Dahlgren, 1991).

Only two initiatives have sought to target resources selectively at practices in areas of high deprivation. The most important of these is the deprivation payment, introduced in 1990, under which GPs receive additional capitation for each patient who lives in an area defined as deprived by a complex formula (the so-called 'Jarman score'). While the principle of allocating additional resources to deprived areas is valid, the actual measure of deprivation has been severely criticised (Carr-Hill and Sheldon, 1991). The more recent initiative is the London Initiative Zone, set up in 1993 with funding of £35m over a four year period 'to concentrate attention and resources on developing primary care in the inner city' (Department of Health, 1993b). It has been allocated funding of £35m over a four year period. An educational incentives programme seeks to improve recruitment and enhance job satisfaction in general practice, while a workforce flexibility scheme will encourage singlehanded and two partner practices to work together, share resources and develop joint services. Pending evaluation of the LIZ initiative, it is too early to say whether it will prove successful or capable of application elsewhere. Its budget is substantially lower than two recent estimates which have costed the investment required in London primary care at £140m (Tomlinson, 1992) and £250m (King's Fund, 1992). Despite initiatives to counter them, it is clear that inequalities in development remain (Pringle et al., 1995) alongside inequalities in access to general practice (Benzeval et al., 1995).

A second theme is increased scrutiny and accountability. Again a variety of mechanisms to render general practice more transparent and accountable may be identified, although whether they add up to a coherent strategy is debatable. The first was increasing contractual explicitness. Under regulations associated with the 1990 contract, the task of the GP was defined in much greater detail than before. (Previously, their contracts had simply specified services 'of the type usually provided by general medical practitioners' - a form of contract described by Scott and Maynard (1991) as 'a 'John Wayne' contract - a GP's got to do what a GP's got to do'). Their review of the early evidence expressed doubts about the cost effectiveness of many of the new health promotion and disease prevention activities. Despite modifications to the contract which removed some of the least cost effective interventions and revised the structure of financial incentives, such doubts persist.

The second mechanism of accountability was increased managerial supervision. The process of extending the general management reforms from the hospital sector to the Family Practitioner Committees had been initiated in 1985, but the impetus of change was lost while The NHS Review switched the focus of attention back to the hospital system. The task of monitoring the new contracts was as signed to the new Family Health Services Authorities, the slimmed down and managerially enhanced successors to the old, professionally dominated and administration-oriented Family Practitioner Committees. At the same time, FHSAs themselves were incorporated into the Regional chain of command instead of being accountable directly to the Department of Health. Even though FHSAs and DHAs continued to operate in parallel, for the first time their chain of command was unified, opening the way to potential integration of primary care into national health policy and an end to the semi-detached status of general practice. However, attention was drawn to the limited powers of FHSAs to promote local priorities (Audit Commission, 1993) and, in any case, the new management arrangements for primary care had little opportunity to bed down. Almost from the beginning, FHSAs were destabilised by speculation about whether they should continue as separate organisations. More recently they have been distracted by the uncertainty arising from their formal merger (April 1996) with District Health Authorities. This merger obviously offers the potential for promoting the full integration of primary and secondary care, and eliminating duplication of functions such as local health need assessment which was required both of DHAs and FHSAs. Whether primary care will emerge as the lead partner, or whether FHSAs will simply be swallowed up by the unitary health commissions, it is, as yet, impossible to say. A third mechanism of accountability was consumerism, in the form of a series of initiatives aimed to make GPs more responsive to consumer preferences. Practices were required to provide information about their services; complaints procedures were simplified, as was the procedure for patients to change doctors; GPs' incomes were made more sensitive to list size by increasing capitation fees from 45 per cent to 60 per cent of income. More recently, patient's rights and service standards have been spelled out in Practice Charters. Despite these measures, there seems little reason to revise an earlier conclusion that there is no evidence to support the view that patients 'shop around' (Petchey, 1989b). Despite the simplified arrangements for transfer, the volume of inter-practice movement has been found to remain at a low level (1.6 per cent annually) (Thomas et al., 1995). It is worth noting, in passing, that if increased patient mobility had been achieved, it would have been at a cost to one o f the proclaimed traditional strengths of British primary care - namely, long term continuity of care (Taylor and Bloor, 1994).

The fourth mechanism of accountability was budgetary, principally in the form of the cash-limited budgets of GP fundholders, but also (potentially) in the shape of the Indicative Prescribing Amounts of non-fundholders. GP fundholding has already been discussed in some detail above. I wish here simply to observe that the introduction of fundholding, to a large degree, undercut the attempt to increase accountability through managerial supervision by FHSAs. While FHSAs were responsible for non-fundholders' finances, fundholders' budgets were allocated by Regions and they were accountable directly to Regions rather than locally. Fundholding thus offered an escape route from the perceived threat of increased external interference in GPs' activities, and there is evidence that some early fundholders were motivated at least in part by a desire to protect their traditional autonomy. These organisational anomalies have recently been clarified to some degree (NHS Executive, 1995) but creation of a unified chain of command and accountability so far remains elusive.

The third policy concern has been to shift the boundaries between secondary and primary care. A range of mechanisms and procedures are being introduced. Some, such as referral guidelines, are designed to reduce inappropriate admissions to hospital; others, such as shared care schemes for chronic disease management, are intended to prevent avoidable admissions by developing the clinical skills of the primary care team; hospital-at-home schemes have been developed to underpin day surgery and early discharge policies; outreach consultant clinics have been used as a basis for closer clinical partnerships between specialists and GPs; near patient testing and GP minor surgery are intended to reduce the workload of hospitals.

Listed in this way, these initiatives sound impressive. However, the vast majority are local schemes whose coverage may be limited, whose implementation may be poorly coordinated, whose funding may be insufficient. Moreover, hardly any of them have been properly evaluated in terms of their cost effectiveness relative to the service pattern they have replaced. Such evidence as there is suggests that, thus far, service developments in primary care may not have produced the desired effect of reducing demand on secondary care. For example, the 1990 contract introduced financial incentives for GPs to perform minor surgery in the expectation that this would reduce hospital out-patient workload. Although GPs estimated that 84 per cent of their minor surgery procedures represented referrals which had been avoided, it was found that minor surgery in general practice did not, in fact, substitute for hospital referrals. It was found superior in several respects (shorter waiting times, lower cost, greater patient satisfaction), but it increased the volume of minor surgery performed overall and therefore represented an increased cost to the NHS. There was no evidence that GP s had lowered their threshold to operate. Rather, it appeared that they were meeting previously unmet need (Lowy et al.,1993). Similarly, the introduction of near patient testing has also been found to increase rates of investigation and costs, rather than being used as a substitute for laboratory tests. Only one test (out of six) was found to be cost effective; otherwise, any saving per patient was lost overall because more patients were investigated (Rink et al., 1993).

Further food for thought comes from a study comparing integrated (GP-hospital) care for diabetes with conventional hospital out-patient care. Integrated care was found to be at least as effective and more acceptable to patients, but it cost substantially more (£101 per patient per year in a practice with a dedicated clinic, £78 in a practice without) than conventional care (£55). However, costs borne by patients showed the reverse pattern - lower for shared care (£1.70 per visit) than for conventional care (£8) (Diabetes Integrated Care Evaluation Team, 1994). It would be reasonable to anticipate that this pattern would be repeated for shared care in other conditions or, indeed, for any other initiative which involves decentralisation of care. Reduced throughput, loss of economies of scale, increased costs of coordination, increased time and travel and opportunity costs (eg. of consultants attending out reach clinics), are all likely to adversely affect the cost effectiveness of service provision overall. They may be offset (partially or wholly) by reductions in the currently invisible (to the NHS) costs (time, travel, inconvenience and other) borne by patients. In addition, by lowering barriers to access, they may well expose more of the hidden iceberg of concealed morbidity. For a variety of reason, it is probable that the costs to the NHS will rise.

Conclusion

Two conclusions emerge from this review: first, that the concept of a primary care-led NHS is characterised, so far, by imprecision and inconsistency; and, second, that the scale of change necessary has not been fully recognised. It does not simply imply a reversal of the priorities which have dominated British health policy since before the inception of the NHS. Making primary care the corner stone of the nation's health care strategy requires of it a level of homogeneity it has never possessed. It also presupposes a degree of strategic incorporation which stands in stark contrast with the semi-detached status it has occupied historically - and fought so determinedly to maintain (Honigsbaum, 1979). Substantial changes in the present organisation, operation and culture of primary care will be required before it is capable of assuming the role of lead agency in the commissioning and delivery of health care with the consistency and reliability that will be necessary.

   One final problem remains to be considered. Even if more radical concepts of primary health care are abandoned, the notion of a primary care-led NHS is certain to involve an increase both in GPs' workloads and in their role in care commissioning. This would indicate a need for an increase in the GP workforce. However, recent trends in the medical labour force are not encouraging[2]

Table 2: Consultant and general practice labour force (England), 1976-1991 (% change)

Year	1976	1985	1991
Consultants (w.t.e)	11,275	12,374 (+9.8)	14,502 (+17.2)
GPs (unrestricted principals)	20,551	24,035 (+17)	25,686 (+6.9)
GP trainees	763	1,758 (+130)	1,639 (-6.8)

Sources: Department of Health, 1987a (Tables 3.1, 3.4); Department of Health, 1993 (Tables 6.1, 6.5)

Between 1976 and 1985 (thanks to the temporary advantage it enjoyed due to its exemption from cash limits) general practice expanded at almost twice the rate of the consultant establishment. Since then, the situation has been more than reversed. Even more discouraging is evidence of falling recruitment to general practice, declining morale (McBride and Metcalfe, 1995) and rising rates of early retirement (General Medical Services Committee, 1995). To return to the horseracing metaphor with which we began; it appears that the potential jockeys, suspicious of the owner's intentions and the pedigree of the horse they are expected to ride, may be disinclined to enter the saddling enclosure.

Notes

1. Latterly (January 1996) there are indications that the government's intransigent opposition to non-fundholder commissioning may be softening. The National Association of Commissioning GPs (which represents 71 commissioning groups covering 7,753 GPs and 13.8m patients) reported receiving assurances from the Health Secretary that they would be recognised by the new health commissions (Kenny, 1996). 2. Analysis of trends in the GP labour force is complicated by lack of reliable historical data (particularly on recruitment) and the failure of the official statistics to distinguish less than full-time GPs. In 1990, 6 per cent of GPs were other than full time, but this proportion may have risen subsequently, not least because of the increasing reliance on women GPs (Allen, 1992).

References

Acheson, D. (1985). 'Variation in GP referral rates still unexplained', GP, 8 November p3.

Allen, I. (1992) Part-time Working in General Practice, London, Policy Studies Institute.

Andrews, J. (1995) 'GPs to abandon total funds trial', Doctor, 2 February p1.

Anon. (1995) 'Non-fund GPs cut costs', GP, 21 April p13.

Ashton, J. Grey, P.& Barnard, K. (1986) 'Healthy cities - WHO's new public health initiative', Health Promotion vol.1, no.3, pp319-3 23.

Audit Commission (1993) Practices Make Perfect: The Role of the Family Health Services Authority, London, HMSO.

Audit Commission (1995) Briefing on GP Fundholding, London, HMSO.

Bailey, J.J. Black, M.E. & Wilkin, D. (1994) 'Specialist outreach clinics in general practice', BMJ vol.308, pp1083-1086.

Bain, J. (1994) 'Fundholding: a two tier system?' BMJ vol.309, pp396-399.

Baker, D.& Klein, R. (1991) 'Explaining outputs of primary health care: population and practice characteristics', BMJ vol.303, pp225 -229.

Benzeval, M. Judge, K. & New, B. (1991) 'Health and health care in London', Public Money and Management, Spring, pp25-32.

Benzeval, M. Judge, K. & Whitehead, M. (1995) Tackling Inequalities in Health: An Agenda for Action, London, King's Fund.

Black, D.G. Birchall, A.D. & Trimble, I.M.G. (1994) 'Non-fundholding in Nottingham: a vision of the future', BMJ, vol.309, pp930-932.

Blendon, R.J. Leitman, R. Morrison, I. & Donellan, V. (1990) 'Satisfaction with health systems in ten nations', Health Affairs, pp18 5-192.

Bosanquet, N.& Leese, B. (1989) Family Doctors and Economic Incentives, Aldershot, Dartmouth Publishing.

Bowie, C.& Spurgeon, R. (1994) 'Commentary: better data needed for analysis', BMJ, vol.309, p34.

Bradlow, J. & Coulter, A. (1993) 'Effect of fundholding and indicative prescribing schemes on general practitioner prescribing costs ', BMJ, vol.307, pp1186-1189.

Burr, A.J. Walker, R. & Stent, S.J. (1992) 'Impact of fundholding on general practice prescribing patterns', Pharmaceutical Journal, 24 October p8.

Carr-Hill, R, Sheldon, T. (1991) 'Designing a deprivation payment for general practitioners: the UPA(8) wonderland', BMJ, vol.302, pp393-396.

Central Statistical Office (1994) Social Trends, London, HMSO.

Committee of Public Accounts (1995) General Practitioner Fundholding in England (House of Commons Paper 264-i, session 1994-5), London, HMSO.

Corney, R. (1994) 'Experiences of first wave general practice fundholders in South East Thames Regional Health Authority', British Journal of General Practice, vol.44, pp34-37.

Coulter, A. (1995) 'General practice fundholding: time for a cool appraisal' British Journal of General Practice, vol.45, pp119-120.

Coulter, A. & Bradlow, J. (1993) 'Effect of NHS reforms on general practitioners' referrals', BMJ, vol.306, pp433-436.

Crombie, D.L. van der See, J. & Backer, P. (1990) The Interface Study (Occasional Paper 48), London, RCGP.

Daly, N. (1995a) 'GPs warned on fund coercion', Doctor, 9 March p2.

Daly N.(1995b) 'Small practices dismiss budgets', Doctor, 9 March p2

Department of Health (1987a) Health and Social Service Statistics for England, London, HMSO.

Department of Health (1987b) Promoting Better Health, London, HMSO.

Department of Health (1992a). The Health of the Nation, London, HMSO.

Department of Health (1992b) The Patient's Charter, London,HMSO.

Department of Health (1993) Making London Better, London, HMSO.

Department of Health and the Welsh Office (1990) 'General Practice in the National Health Service: A New Contract, London, HMSO.

Diabetes Integrated Care Evaluation Team (1994) 'Integrated care for diabetes: clinical, psychsocial, and economic evaluation', BMJ, vol.308, pp1208-1212.

Dixon, J. et al. (1994) 'Distribution of NHS funds between fundholding and non-fundholding practices', BMJ, vol.309, pp30-34.

Eve, R. & Hodgkin, P. (1992) 'In praise of non-fundholding practices', in BMJ (ed) The Future of General Practice, London, BMJ.

Fry, J. (1993) General Practice: the Facts, Oxford, Radcliffe Medical Press.

Fry, J. & Horder, J. (1994) Primary Health Care in an International Context, London, Nuffield Hospitals Provincial Trust.

General Medical Services Committee (1995) Report of the GMSC Recruitment and Morale Task Group. London, GMSC.

Gervas, J. Fernandez, M.P. & Starfield, B. (1994) 'Primary care, financing and gatekeeping in Western Europe', Family Practice, vol. 11, no.3, pp307-317.

Gillam, S.J. (1992) 'Provision of health promotion clinics in relation to population need: another example of the inverse care law?' , British Journal of General Practice, vol.42, pp54-56.

Gillam, S.J. Ball, M. Prasad, M. Dunne, H. Cohen, S. & Vafidis, G. (1995) 'Investigation of benefits and costs of an ophthalmic outreach clinic in general practice', British Journal of General Practice, vol.45, pp649-652.

Gillam, S. Plamping, D. McLenahan, J. Harries, J. & Epstein, L. (1994) Community-oriented Primary Care. London, King's Fund.

Glennerster, H. Matsaganis, M. & Owens, P. (1994) Implementing GP Fundholding: Wild Card or Winning Hand?, Open University Press, Buckingham.

Graffy, J & Williams, J. (1994) 'Purchasing for all: an alternative to fundholding', BMJ; vol.308, pp391-394.

Green, A. (1987) 'Is there primary care in the UK?', Health Policy and Planning, vol.2, no.2, pp129-137.

Griffin, J.P. & Griffin, T.D. (1993) 'The economic consequences of therapeutic conservatism', Journal of the Royal College of Physicians, vol.27, no.2, pp121-126.

Ham, C. & Shapiro, J. (1995) 'The future of fundholding', BMJ, vol.310, pp1150-1151.

Harris, A. (1994) 'Specialist outreach clinics', BMJ, vol.308, pp1053.

Harris, T. Silver, T. Rink, E. & Hilton, S. (1996) 'Vocational training for general practice in inner London. Is there a dearth? And if so what's to be done?' BMJ, vol.312, pp97-101.

Heaney, D.J. Howie, J.G.R. & Maxwell, M. (1994) 'The referral component of fund-holding: can both quantity and quality be assessed on routine data?', Health Bulletin, no.52/4, July, pp285-286.

Heritage, Z. (ed) (1994) Community Participation in Primary Care, Occasional Paper 64, London, Royal College of General Practitioners.

Honigsbaum, F. (1979) The Division in British Medicine: a History of the Separation of General Practice from Hospital Care 1911-1968 , London, Kogan Page.

Howie, J.G.R. Heaney, D.J. & Maxwell, R. (1993) 'Evaluation of the Scottish shadow fund-holding project: first results', Health Bulletin, no.51/2, March, pp94-105.

Howie, J.G.R. Heaney, D.J. & Maxwell, R. (1995a) 'Evaluating care of patients with selected health problems in fundholding practices in Scotland in 1990 and 1992: needs, process and outcome', British Journal of General Practice, vol.45, pp121-126.

Howie, J.G.R. Heaney, D.J. & Maxwell, R. (1995b) General Practice Fundholding: Shadow Project - an Evaluation. Edinburgh, University of Edinburgh.

Jackson, C. (1995) 'European public heath policy', Eurohealth vol.1, no.2, pp11-14.

Jones, R. (1995) 'Endoscopy in general practice', BMJ, vol.310, pp816-817.

Kenny, C. (1996) 'Commissioning GPs win DoH backing', GP, 19 January, p3.

King's Fund Commission on the Future of London's Acute Health Services (1992) London Health Care 2010, London, King's Fund

Langham, S. Gillam, S. & Thorogood, M. (1995) 'The carrot, the stick and the general practitioner: how have changes in financial incentives affected health promotion activity in general practice?', British Journal of General Practice, vol.45, pp665-668.

Livingstone, A. & Widgery, D. (1990) 'The new general practice: the changing philosophies of primary care', BMJ, vol.301, pp708-710.

London Health Care Planning Consortium (1981) Primary Health Care in Inner London: Report of a Study Group, (Chairman: Prof. E.D. Acheson) London, DHSS.

Lowy, A., Brazier, J., Fall, M., Thomas, K., Jones, N. & Williams, B.T. (1993) 'Minor surgery by general practitioners under the 1990 contract: effects on hospital workload', BMJ, vol.307, pp413-417.

McBride, M. & Metcalfe, D. (1995) 'General practitioners' low morale: reasons and solutions', British Journal of General Practice, vol.45, pp227-229.

McFarlane, A. & McPherson, A. (1995) 'Primary health care and adolescence', BMJ, vol.311, pp825-826.

Marinker, M. (1984) 'Developments in primary care', in Office of Health Economics. A New NHS Act for 1996, London, Office of Health Economics.

Maxwell, M. Heaney, D.J. Howie, J.G.R & Noble, S. (1993) 'General practice fundholding: observations on prescribing patterns and costs using the defined daily dose method', BMJ, vol.307, pp1990-1994.

Maxwell, R. (1993) 'Other cities, same problems', BMJ, vol.306, pp199-201.

May, A. & Robinson, R. (1995) 'Mapping the course', Health Service Journal, 2 February, pp22-24.

Maynard, A. (1986) 'Performance incentives' in Teeling Smith, G (ed) Health Education and General Practice, London, Office of Health Economics.

Murray, S.A., Tapson, J., Turnbull, L., McCallum, J. & Little, A. 'Listening to local voices: adapting rapid appraisal to assess health and social needs in general practice', BMJ, vol.308, pp698-700.

National Audit Office (1994) General Practitioner Fundholding in England. London, HMSO.

NHS Executive (1994) Developing NHS Purchasing and GP Fundholding. Leeds, NHSE. (EL(94)79).

NHS Executive (1995) An Accountability Framework for GP Fundholding, Leeds, NHSE.

NHS Management Executive (1991) Integrating Primary and Secondary Care London, Department of Health.

Newton, J. Fraser, M. Robinson, J. & Wainwright, D. (1993) 'Fundholding in the Northern Region', BMJ, vol.306, pp375-378.

Neve, H. & Taylor, P. (1995) 'Working with the community', BMJ, vol.311, pp524-525.

Paton, C. (1995) 'Present dangers and future threats: some perverse incentives in the NHS reforms', BMJ, vol.310, pp1245-1248.

Pennington, S. (1995) 'GPs enter first total commissioning scheme', GP, 21 April, p28.

Petchey, R. (1989a) 'The NHS Review: the politics of destabilisation?', Critical Social Policy, vol.9, pp82-97.

Petchey R. (1989b). Primary health care: the way forward? in M Brenton & C Ungerson (eds) Social Policy Review 1988-9, London, Longman, pp.121-143.

Petchey R. (1993) 'NHS internal market 1991-2: towards a balance sheet', BMJ, vol.306, pp699-701.

Pollock, A.M, & Majeed, F.A. (1995) 'Community-oriented primary care', BMJ, vol.310 pp481-482.

Powell, M.A. (1990) 'Need for and provision of general practice in London', British Journal of General Practice, vol.40, pp372-375.

Pratt, J. (1995) Practitioners and Practices: A Conflict of Values?, Oxford, Radcliffe Medical Press.

Reading, R., Colver, A., Openshaw, S. & Jarvis, S. (1994) 'Do interventions that improve immunisation also reduce social inequalities in uptake?', BMJ, vol.308, pp1142-1144.

Rink, E., Hilton, S., Szczepura, A., Fletcher, J., Sibbald, B., Davies, C., Freeling, P, & Stilwell, J. (1993) 'Impact of introducing near patient testing for stanmdard investigations in general practice', BMJ, vol.307, pp775-778.

Roland, M. (1992) 'Measuring referral rates', in M. Roland & A. Coulter (eds) Hospital Referrals, Oxford, Oxford University Press

Royal College of General Practitioners (1985) Towards Quality in General Practice, London, RCGP.

Schieber, G.J., Pouillier, J.P. & Greenwald, L.M. (1992) 'OECD data', Health Care Financing Review, vol.13, pp1-71.

Scott,T. & Maynard, A. (1991) Will the New GP Contract Lead to Cost Effective Medical Practice?, Discussion Paper 82, York, Centre for Health Economics, University of York.

Secretaries of State for Health, Wales, Scotland and N Ireland (1989) NHS and Community Care Bill, London, HMSO.

Secretary of State for Health (1989) Working for Patients, London, HMSO.

Secretary of State for Social Services (1986) Primary Health Care: An Agenda for Discussion, London, HMSO.

Starfield, B. (1991) 'Primary care and health. A cross national comparison', JAMA, no.266, pp2268-2271.

Starfield, B. (1992). Primary Care: Concept, Evaluation and Policy, New York, Oxford University Press .

Starfield, B. (1994) 'Is primary care essential?', Lancet, no.344, pp1129-1133.

Stewart Brown, S., Surender, R., Bradlow, J., Coulter, A., & Doll, H. (1995) 'The effects of fundholding in general practice on prescribing habits three years after the introduction of the scheme', BMJ, vol.311, pp1543-1547.

Stoeckle, J.D. (1995) 'The citadel cannot hold: technologies go outside the hospital, patients and doctors too', Milbank Quarterly, vol.73, no.1, pp3-17.

Surender, R.S., Bradlow, J., Coulter, A., Doll, H. & Stewart Brown S. (1995) 'Prospective study of trends in referral patterns in fundholding ans non-fundholding oractices in the Oxford region1990-4', BMJ, vol.311, pp1205-1208.

Taylor, D. & Bloor, K. (1994) Health Care, Health Promotion and the Future General Practice, London, Royal Society of Medicine Press .

Thomas, K. Nicholl, J. & Coleman, P. (1995) 'Assessing the outcome of making it easier for patients to change general practitioner: practice characteristics associated with patient movements', British Journal of General Practice, vol.45, pp581-586.

Thomas, P. (1995) 'There is hope yet for the development of primary health care in deprived areas', British Journal of General Practice, vol.45, pp572-574.

Tomlinson, B. (1992) Report of the Inquiry into London's Health Service, Medical Education and Research, London, HMSO.

Tsouros, A. (1995) 'The WHO healthy cities project', Eurohealth; vol.1, no.2, pp15-18.

Vuori, H. (1984) 'Primary care in Europe - problems and solutions', Community Medicine, vol.6, pp221-231.

Whitehead, M. & Dahlgren, G. (1991) 'What can be done about inequalities in health?, Lancet, no.338, pp1059-1063.

Whynes, D. Baines, D. & Tolley, K. (1995) 'GP fundholding and the costs of prescribing', Journal of Public Health Medicine, vol.17, pp323-329.

Wilkin, D. (1992) 'Patterns of referral: explaining variation', in Roland, M. & Coulter, A. (eds) Hospital Referrals, Oxford, Oxford University Press, pp76-91.

Wilson, R.P.H. Buchan,I. & Walley,T. (1995) 'Alterations in prescribing by general practitioner fundholders: an observational study' , BMJ vol.311 pp1347-1350.

World Health Organisation (1978) Primary Health Care Geneva, WHO/UNICEF.

World Health Organisation (1985) Targets for Health For All. Geneva, WHO, Regional Office for Europe.

World Health Organisation (1986) Evaluation of the Strategy for Health for All by the Year 2000 Copenhagen, WHO, Regional Office for Europe.

10 Local Government Reorganisation in England and Wales: The Implications for Social Services

Lynda Bransbury

Introduction

Social Services Departments in England and Wales[1] over the years seem to have come in for more than their fair share of radical reorganisation of both structures and cultures. Some of this has been self-inflicted (Challis, 1990); but much has been imposed by central government. In the 1970s, they were reorganised twice in fairly quick succession. Children's and adult services were amalgamated in 1971. Then, as part of the overall reorganisation of local government in 1974, 116 Social Services Departments (SSDs) were created in England and Wales.

However, nothing could match the pace and scale of organisational and cultural change in the last decade. During a period when legislative reform has largely aimed to reduce local government's functions, influence and financial base, their work has been radically refocused and expanded. The 1989 Children Act, closely followed by the 1990 National Health Service and Community Care Act, required massive shifts in organisation and strategy within departments and in their relationships with users, carers and other organisations. Currently, many SSDs are once again in the midst of further upheavals due to local government reorganisation. Eight Welsh and three English counties were abolished on 31 March 1996 and their SSDs divided between smaller unitary councils. At the same time, the new City of York unitary council took over social services responsibilities within its boundaries from North Yorkshire County Council. As Appendix 1 shows, more councils are scheduled for reorganisation from April 1997. The government has decided to create a total of forty six new unitary councils in England, which will also involve a further twenty county councils facing some form of reorganisation.

The process leading up to reorganisation has diverted much time and energy from service considerations. In England, there have been almost five years of uncertainty which must have affected service developments and investment in interagency partnerships (Craig, 1993). In addition, widespread concern has been expressed about the capacity of the new and smaller unitaries to plan and manage social services functions effectively. It has also been predicted that many front line services may be disrupted or disappear in the process of disaggregation and transfer. The likely impact on community care services has been of particular concern (Page et al. , 1994; Craig, 1993). The tight timescales and budgets for the 1996 reorganisations can only have exacerbated these risks.

The successful transfer of social services is of critical importance to local government and the people it serves. We need social services at times of crisis, when we are extremely vulnerable. If libraries and swimming pools do not open, the public may be disappointed but no real hardship will occur. Breakdown of social services could literally be a life or death matter. In addition, social services account for over 15 per cent of all local government expenditure. It is the last major function over which local politicians can exercise any real control in terms of priority setting, charging policies or methods of delivery. Local management of schools, compulsory competitive tendering and ringfenced housing revenue accounts have effectively taken most decision making about other local government services out of their hands. There are some who have argued that the government intends the new councils should fail as social services authorities in order to justify taking responsibility for some or all of social services away from local government (Page et al., 1994). A smooth transfer is therefore not just significant for those who need social services, but may have implications for the future of local government as a whole.

Against this background of mounting concern, this chapter looks at some potential threats and challenges to social services delivery arising from local government reorganisation in England and Wales. Drawing on the author's research into the experience of some councils due for reorganisation on April 1st 1996, it first outlines attitudes towards and the wider debates over local government reorganisation.[2] It then considers the specific concerns and speculation about the likely impact on social services and suggests that certain factors may equip some new councils to manage social services more effectively than others. The chapter concludes by looking at those aspects of service delivery and inter-agency working that appear particularly vulnerable and which justify close monitoring following reorganisation.

Local government reorganisation: fit for the purpose?

> It is probably true that a single tier of government is more accountable and less confusing than two. But these unprovable benefits have clearly not been worth the effort (Local Government Chronicle, 5 January 1996 p9).

Michael Heseltine initiated the current round of reorganisation with the stated aim of promoting the unitary principle. He intended to abolish the two tier structure introduced in 1974 with a county council and several district councils covering one county and put smaller, unitary or all-purpose authorities in its place. The arguments initially put forward for this were that unitary councils would be less confusing and more responsive to public needs, services would be better co-ordinated and enhanced efficiency would be achieved. However, from the outset there was deep cynicism amongst local government professionals, academics and politicians about the justifications for major organisational change (Leach R, 1994; Leach S, 1994; Stevenson, 1994; Whitehead, 1994).

One important criticism was that neither government nor the Local Government Commission (the Commission) in England bothered to define the role and purpose of local government before deciding how to reorganise it. The Welsh Local Government Commission (Jones, 1986) and the Redcliffe Maud Royal Commission (1969) recommendations, which preceded the 1974 reorganisation, did at least consider how size and shape might need to vary according to function. But this time round, despite less consensus on the role of local government, little atten-tion was paid to these issues. Yet, as Boyne (1992, p49) points out the appropriate geographical or population size for one ser-vice may not be right for another. Particularly low priority appears to have been given to how social services might be affected. For instance, the Commission's proposals for Cleveland and Durham did not even mention that they were social services authorities. Indeed, worries about losing ceremonial trappings, and Lord Lieutenants in particular, seemed to have been more influential than service delivery considerations in determining the future of many areas.

Despite the government's starting point, the Commission's findings in England and the government's vacillating responses to it confirm how little popular or political consensus exists regard-ing the 'right' size or structure for local government. The lack of any continuity or consistency of approach on the question of size has been particularly evident in Wales. In terms of social services, the 1974 reorganisation created eight authorities out of thirteen existing councils, apparently accepting that larger councils would be better equipped to deliver such functions as social services (Jones, 1986). In April 1996, those eight social services departments were divided between twenty two new unitary authorities.

The process leading up to reorganisation has been fraught with acrimony and uncertainty. It may have been conducted in a more participative manner in England, but whether there is any more satisfaction with the outcomes or damage from the process than in Wales and Scotland is more debatable. Local authorities across the country have been pitted against one another, leading to soured political relations between counties and district councils. The legacy from this may have undermined and has certainly not contributed towards preparations for reorganisation in some areas.

The likely impact on social services

The creation of any new authority can disrupt existing services. The risks from dividing services run by one council between a number of smaller ones are much higher and widespread con-cerns have been raised about the likely impact of this reorganisa-tion on social services functions in Wales (Williams, 1995; Butler et al., 1995; Davidson & Bransbury, 1995; WRAC, 1995) and in England (ADSS, 1993 ; Page et al., 1994; Craig, 1993; Mitchell, 1993). In this respect, the disaggregating effects of abolishing the GLC, the ILEA and the Metropolitan Counties in 1986, while affecting different services are more relevant to the current reorganisation than the experience of the 1974 reforms. Partly based on the 1986 experiences (Riley, 1993), it has been suggested that:

Some services, for example, transport and other functions, such as payroll, appear particularly vulnerable to disruption from disaggregation and transfer;

Smaller authorities may have difficulty providing specialist support and services, such as planning, legal advice, training, child protection and services only required by a relatively small section of the population;

The viability of partnerships with other bodies may be threatened, both by the process of change and through having to work with a number of smaller authorities to cover the same area;

Loss of both strategic planning for the area and economies of scale may impede effective service delivery, hinder joint working and make it difficult to find enough representatives for joint committees, such as adoption or child protection panels; and,

Administrative and management costs will be higher. For example, when the ILEA was abolished, initially it cost four times as much - from £1.7m to £6.8m - to provide the top three tiers in the new Local Education Authorities as in the ILEA (Riley, 1993, p57).

In both England and Wales, as Appendix 2 shows, each wave of reorganisation will increase the number of SSDs and each new council will serve a much smaller population than the old county council did. But reorganisation in England will also result in a much more diverse range of social services authorities. This is because it was finally decided only to reorganise four English counties on the same model as Wales. Avon, Humberside and Cleveland, and eventually Berkshire, will have been divided between several new unitary councils. Most of other new English unitary councils, as Appendix 2 shows, will be towns and cities plucked out of the existing county. These urban centres will take over such services as education and social services from the county council, but with the existing two-tier structure continuing in the rest of the county.

Whatever our criticisms of how a blueprint was imposed on Wales, it has at least ensured a consistent system of local government. Reorganisation in England, however, will change the map of local government beyond recognition. Until April 1994, there were only three 'classes' of councils in England and Wales with responsibility for social services, County Councils, Metropolitan Districts and London Boroughs. Each 'class' had distinct characteristics and councils within them had much in common with each other. Reorganisation will blur these distinctions and create forms of English social services authorities that do not fit easily together. While metropolitan authorities and London boroughs remain unchanged, reorganisation will create several types of 'county councils'. Fifteen will be totally unaffected by reorganisation. But a further nineteen 'rump' county councils such as Hampshire, stripped of their main centres of population but responsible for social services in the rest of the two-tier county, will eventually emerge. How much these two groups of counties will still have in common remains to be seen.

The creation of some new unitary councils will muddy the county distinctions even further. Some, like the East Riding of Yorkshire and East Somerset, give the appearance of being mini 'shire' counties. But, as fairly rural councils, they will not fit easily into any of the existing groupings. Their economies, geography and populations may be closest to the county councils, but in terms of their functions and responsibilities they will have more in common with the metropolitan authorities. Then there will be the more urban unitary councils. The larger ones such as Bristol, Hull and Southampton, serving large cities and conurbations, will have most in common with their new cousins - the Metropolitan Districts and London Boroughs. But it is unclear whether smaller towns and new authorities, such as Windsor and Maidenhead or Thurrock, will have much in common with any of the other social services authorities.

This 'packet of allsorts' (Waddington, 1995 p4) has potentially profound implications for social services. First, the greater diversity may limit the comparisons that can be made across social services authorities. The Association of Directors of Social Services and a single Local Government Association may facilitate communication and information sharing. But English SSDs because of their diverse needs and situations may be disadvantaged in making the national case in, for example, responding to Department of Health proposals or in negotiations on how Standard Spending Assessments (SSAs) are calculated.

Secondly, there are particular implications from the removal of large towns or cities from the existing county. Unitary councils with a predominantly urban catchment appear, at least on paper, to have the best chance of making a fist of running social services.

They will be serving a relatively large population contained within a fairly compact area. However, whatever the new unitaries ' chances of success, concerns have been expressed about the capacity of the remaining 'rump' county to deliver social services adequately (Craig, 1993). These councils may face higher unit costs and a lower funding base once the urban centres go. In addition, there is some evidence, from the mapping done by the 1996 tranche, that existing social services provision is already clustered in the towns and cities. Reorganisation may therefore strip the county of much of its existing provision and establishments.

In addition to the impact of reorganisation itself, the process leading up to it has taken its toll on service delivery and development in every council which has been under the spotlight. Much senior officer time was diverted into making their authority's case. Experienced staff have left or taken early retirement. Care professionals have been unconvinced by the arguments for change and demoralised by the apparently low priority accorded to the potential impact on social services (Craig, 1993). Attitudes towards and the direct effects of the lead up to reorganisation may have weakened the quality and scope of provision leaving SSDs less fit to weather the traumas of being split up and transferred.

Factors which may aid or hinder transfer and service delivery

Experiences from earlier re-organisation and informed speculation suggest some councils may be better equipped than others to achieve a smooth transfer and maintain adequate social services after reorganisation. Several factors seem likely to influence a new authority's chances of success. The experience of some English and Welsh councils facing reorganisation in 1996 implies that each of the following may be influential: population size; early and accurate information on service audits and a disaggregated budget from the county; the state of the new council's budget; some continuity of strategy and leadership; attitudes towards reorganisation and the timing and quality of planning for change.

Optimum size?

Ever since it became clear that reorganisation would result in smaller councils, there has been much debate and little consensus over what constitutes the minimum, as well as the optimum, size for a social services authority (Mitchell, 1993). In practice the population of the new unitaries will vary enormously, ranging in Wales, for instance, from around 66,000 to 300,000. However, population size may not be the only factor to affect a new council's capacity to provide adequate social services. The logistics and costs of planning and providing services to a relatively compact urban population are quite different to those for a small population spread over a large rural area. Thus in Wales 60 per cent of the population is concentrated in 15 per cent of the land mass. This raises questions (Jones, 1986) about whether the same local government structure is appropriate for large urban areas, such as Cardiff and Swansea, and rural counties like Powys. Reorganisation in Wales appears not to have considered the financial and logistical problems of delivering social services in rural areas. Not only is Powys left virtually unchanged but several new counties, such as Merionethshire, have been created to serve similarly large and sparsely populated areas.

The income profile of a new council's population may also be significant. Those with a high proportion of low income residents may not only have a poor revenue base, but may also experience the greatest demands for social services. One advantage of a larger council spread over several population centres is the capacity to redistribute resources within its boundaries (Riley, 1993). This will be lost to most of the new authorities. On the question of size and transferred functions, a research study of five London authorities, after the abolition of the ILEA (Riley, 1993), offers useful pointers for social services reorganisation. This suggests that discrete and small scale tasks benefit from being run by a smaller authority and result in a more localised, responsive and efficient day to day service. However, these potential gains have to be balanced against greater problems with planning and providing a complex enough range of provision within the new boundaries. It will be a measure of each new unitary's success as a social services authority, if it can achieve a wide enough range of social services to meet local needs (including low incidence needs, such as drugs and alcohol counselling services) and promote better choices for consumers (Craig, 1993).

Accurate and early information from the county

Without accurate information about the services it will be inheriting and a disaggregated budget, a new authority will be seriously disadvantaged in preparing for transfer. The earlier this information is provided by the county, the better equipped a new council will be to start planning and identifying potential budgetary problems. For instance, getting a disaggregated budget from Avon County Council early in the transitional year allowed Bristol City Council to estimate a potential £33m shortfall, almost as soon as

the government published its notional amounts for the new unitary councils in August 1994. However, there were marked differences in when new authorities received such data from their
counties in 1995/96. At least one Welsh authority was still waiting for a disaggregated budget from its outgoing county as late as
December.

The state of the budget

Many new councils which came into existence in April 1996
faced serious fiscal problems and had to make considerable cuts
in order to balance their budgets before vesting day. There is no
doubt that many are very dissatisfied not only with the overall
financial settlement, but with the formulae used by the
Department of Environment and the Welsh Office to divide the
old county's SSA between them. Discontent over the financial settlement in Scotland may have received most publicity, but many
Welsh and some English authorities feel equally strongly. Bristol
was not the only council to consider their final settlement would
be well below what was needed to maintain the services it inherited. For instance, Monmouthshire reported a shortfall of £6.7m
(Municipal Journal, 8-14 March 1996,p 11) and North
Lincolnshire considered it was £10m down (Municipal Journal,
23-29 Feb. 1996, p7). Senior officers and members in those
councils facing a shortfall spent much time in the months leading
up to vesting day on budget balancing exercises, with each
department struggling to find savings. This may well have diverted too much attention away from planning for a smooth transfer.

At least councils, like Bristol, with early and reliable information from the outgoing county could identify their likely financial
position well before Christmas. There was more time for
Members to decide their priorities and strategy for managing the
cuts. In contrast, the realisation that they would have to make significant savings came very late in the day for some councils. This
meant decisions had to be taken hurriedly at the last minute.
Neither council staff nor groups funded by these councils had
much warning of the consequent job losses and cuts in grants.
The whole process in many areas has soured relationships and
may have undermined the new council's ability to gain the confidence and respect of its staff as well as the voluntary sector and
community groups.

In making cuts, many new councils tried to cushion the impact
on social services. For instance Monmouthshire and Bristol
imposed a smaller percentage cut on their social services budget
than on most other services. Similarly, Gwynedd's social services

budget was only cut by 0.75 per cent compared with a 1 per cent cut for all other budgets (Municipal Journal, 8-14 March, p11). But in some areas such protection was further constrained by the outgoing county's social services budgetary difficulties in 1995/96. Gwynedd County Council's SSD undoubtedly got the most publicity, but it was not alone in experiencing financial problems during the shadow year. Other counties were only able to avoid overspend on their community care budgets by imposing new and tighter eligibility criteria, setting higher charges or closing services such as day care centres. In these counties the new councils have taken over a greatly depleted service and inherited damaged relationships with users and carers which will prove difficult to rebuild.

Continuity of strategy and leadership

The Office of Public Management designed a simulation model, MOSAIC, which the Local Government Management Board (LGMB) used to help officers and members in some English counties work through the tasks involved in creating new unitary councils. An important message to emerge from these exercises was that the absence of a clear vision, identity and priority setting for the new authority hampers progress and hinders informed decision-making in the transitional period (LGMB, 1994c). It seems reasonable to assume that some continuity of senior management or lead councillors in social services will promote an early sense of direction and vision. The extent to which officers and members of the new authority come from a county council or social services background may also be significant.

For whatever reasons, there were considerable variations in the extent to which SSDs in the unitaries created in 1996 have achieved continuity in either senior management or political leadership. Middlesborough is looking like a mini Cleveland. Its social services management team is headed by Cleveland's ex-Director and its other three members have also come from broadly similar work in Cleveland. Similarly, although Bristol's Director comes from Wakefield, his management team are all ex-Avon social services managers. In contrast Stockton's Director is from Newcastle and only one member of the management team worked in the outgoing county.

In Bristol and Middlesborough, the Chair of Social Services of the outgoing county also became the Chair in the new authority. Three months before vesting day, officers in Bristol and Cleveland said that this had been a critical factor in generating a clear sense of direction and purpose from the first day of the transitional year.

Keeping the County Chair or having a new Chair with a strong background in social services may also determine how quickly the new council grasps the complexities of taking over these services and what priority it gives to this task.

Continuity of political leadership may be largely down to chance: there has to be an existing Chair or Vice Chair who lives in and is elected to serve in the new unitary area. But senior management appointments are firmly within the control of the new political groups. Who they appoint and how quickly they get them in post may determine how soon a clear sense of direction and planning begins. Despite the apparent benefits of continuity, several new unitaries appeared to opt deliberately for 'new blood'. In some, Chief Officer and other senior appointments appear to owe more to soured political relations between County and Districts, or to the new leadership wishing to make its mark or promote its friends, than to rational considerations of what might be best for the service . In places where very able and committed existing county staff were rejected, disillusion and demoralisation appeared not just to have affected these officers but spread down the service. This may well have undermined these officers' loyalty to their new management and their commitment in the run up to vesting day and may have encouraged them to leave the new authority, taking their experience and knowledge base with them.

A high degree of geographical mobility amongst senior management in the year leading up to vesting day, was inevitable and had several consequences. Managers new to the area faced an almost vertical learning curve and therefore it was vital to get them in post as early as possible. They had to decide whether to split themselves between their previous and future posts on a part-time basis, commuting long distances (Williams, 1995) or move full time to their new jobs. Towards the end of 1995 unfillable gaps appeared in many county hall's staffing complements, further constraining the smooth transfer of functions. Some senior staff with detailed knowledge or a strategic overview of existing policies and provision left; others found themselves covering as many as two or three vacant jobs in the run up to reorganisation.

Attitudes to reorganisation and planning for change

As this chapter has already demonstrated, officers and members in many areas were deeply cynical about the reasons for and process of reorganisation. These attitudes and the legacy of hostility between district and county council politicians may have undermined take-over planning in some areas. For instance where county hall staff did not believe the changes were necessary or likely to be beneficial, their investment in the change process is likely to have been impaired. As one officer put it 'county council staff want districts to work but are convinced that this reorganisation is a bad thing'. There was plenty of evidence of county council officers working hard to protect the services they cared about during 1995/96. But with such ambivalence, it would be surprising if a small part of each of them did not hold back and want to be proved right by the district's failure to deliver.

The outcomes from the MOSAIC simulation suggested planning this scale of change should begin as early as possible. They paint a fairly bleak picture of what can happen if all the work has to be condensed into a short period. In practice, therefore planning and auditing existing services and policies ought to start well before members for the new authority are elected and long before recruitment of Chief Officers begins. There is evidence that some outgoing counties started planning for transfer much earlier and more systematically than others. Cleveland and Avon SSDs provide good examples of counties investing heavily in the transfer process, providing high quality information to each new authority early in the transitional year about the range of provision in their area, the issues to be addressed in splitting up or transferring physical assets and county wide services, as well as county council policies and their implications for each new council. Social Services staff at all levels in Cleveland were similarly engaged in preparing for change. Starting from the premise that no one person could know about everything, officers in each section were asked to provide information about their responsibilities which was then included in briefings for the new authorities.

While these are examples of what can be done, it is essential not to overestimate how much a county council can contribute to the process of change. However much information or advice it is able to provide, it cannot pre-empt the new unitary's decisions. Indeed the more the county seeks to advise, the more officers and members in the new authorities may distrust its motives and reject proposals out of hand. They will want to show they are not going to have county solutions foisted on them. There can also be particular difficulties from having elected members in place several months before the Directors are appointed. For instance a Welsh SSD in consultation with members in each of the new shadow authorities, produced plans for maintaining the county wide training unit through joint arrangements in 1996/97. This proposal should have been agreed by each of the new social services committees in the autumn. However, by then the new Directors were in post and at least two decided participation was inappropriate for their department and the plan had to be abandoned.

Most front-line staff in counties due to be abolished in April 1996 remained largely unaffected by reorganisation until the end of 1995. In contrast strategic and county hall personnel experienced over 18 months of difficulties and uncertainty. Senior managers in some Welsh counties appeared to have more difficulty than others in beginning to prepare mentally for disaggregation. Long after parliament had approved the new boundaries, some appeared still operated as though the county would be there in perpetuity, planning county-wide provision well into the shadow year. In some of these authorities there came a point in about June, when middle management in some Welsh county halls gave the appearance of being on rudderless ships. A long gap between the election of councillors and the appointment of the chief officer, an absence of political direction from the new Social Services Chair and able second or third tier managers finding jobs elsewhere seemed most likely to result in this sense of drift. Those left behind had plenty to contribute to the process of change, but they clearly felt there was no one left in county hall to liaise with the new authorities.

District Councils taking over County functions

It is now clear that many of the new authorities will be continuations of existing district councils, taking over county council functions in addition to their existing responsibilities. Most are being reorganised on the existing district council boundaries. This should mean accurate population information is easily available, officers are conversant with existing county services within the borough and most front line staff will continue to work with the same people on the same patch. All of this should contribute to accurate auditing of county functions and reduce some risks at the point of transfer. However, attitudes and approaches in some district councils facing reorganisation, suggest that officers and councillors may have been too complacent about the planning necessary for a smooth transfer.

Though they were inundated with written briefings on managing the transition (Department of Health, 1995; ADC 1994; LGMBb, 1 994; Capita, 1994), members and officers, who have only worked in small district councils, have had great difficulties grasping the scale and complexity of their new social services responsibilities. In addition, councils being created in 1996 were forced to do so on impossibly short time scales. It was clear from their early thinking about priorities and their draft service plans that some had been more able than others to conceptualise the task facing them and give it due priority. Many of the apparently better prepared districts, not surprisingly, were those which had lost social services functions in 1974. Where shadow councils perceived education and social services as 'bolt on' extras, they may not have prepared adequately for transfer. Moreover the lack of personal commitment to these services by ex-district councillors may put the budgets at risk during financial crises. If Wales is at all representative, then the sheer size of the social services budget they inherited, compared with those they are used to for district council services, will exacerbate this tendency. Discussions with Welsh councillors suggest that some on the new councils simply cannot believe that so much expenditure is necessary. and are keen to redirect some of it to other services such as housing.

Better co-ordination of services?

One of the strongest arguments put forward for all-purpose councils is that they improve co-ordination between departments, one of the most cited examples being the lack of co-operation between housing and social services departments. However, anyone who has experience of metropolitan authorities or London Boroughs knows that having all local government services under one roof may create the conditions for co-ordination, but it certainly does not ensure that it happens. As Riley (1993 p59) observes: 'improved co-ordination depends on the relative strengths and attitudes of the departments, the effectiveness of corporate planning and the level of political expectation'. Clearly some problems between counties and districts will disappear as a result of unitary status (for instance the need for some SSDs to operate separate and conflicting agreements with each of their district council's housing departments for adaptations to disabled people's homes, Craig, 1993). Reorganisation will also overcome any problems due to the District and County Councils being under different political control.

But it would be naive to assume that having social services and housing in the same authority is in itself a recipe for joint working. Competition for budgets and political prestige are as likely to exacerbate conflicting philosophies and priorities between officers (as well as politicians) as to lead to greater co-operation. Inter-departmental co-operation tends to happen in an ad-hoc way between front-line staff in both two tier and unitary councils, what is more often lacking is real communication or formal arrangements between management in the different departments. Whether this can be achieved seems to depend less on whether the departments are within the same authority than the quality of historical relationships and the extent of risk-taking and investment on both sides to make it happen. It will thus be important to monitor how effective each new unitary council is at improving inter-department al collaboration.

Joint arrangements

As reported earlier in this chapter the viability of certain social services on transfer and following disaggregation has been
questioned. Joint arrangements between several new authorities
were suggested as one way to maintain some of these functions,
at least initially, and the LGMB (1994a) drew up guidelines to
assist new authorities identify, as early as possible, where joint
arrangements might be needed. By January 1996, it was apparent from draft service plans and discussions with officers that far
fewer joint arrangements were being proposed from April 1996
than had originally been considered. A mixture of political resistance and practical obstacles appear to have ruled out most of
them. Hospital and emergency social work cover emerge
amongst the few formal arrangements that have gone ahead.

Politicians in many of the new councils, wanting to prove they
could run everything themselves, were understandably hostile to
the principle of joint arrangements. Officers, however, saw a case
for some joint arrangements and persuaded their members to
consider them. But in practice it proved too difficult to find contract or cost-sharing terms which were viable and acceptable to
members in each new unitary. In addition, there were particular
social services functions such as child protection over which neither Chief Officers nor politicians thought it appropriate to relin-
quish operational control or political accountability. However, the
problems and risks which it was hoped joint arrangements could
mitigate will remain and councils will have had to invest heavily to
maintain the quality and range of some services or have any provision at all from vesting day. Very vulnerable clients depend on
many of the services which will be difficult to provide without joint
arrangements. Similarly, functions such as planning, legal advice
and staff training are essential for high quality provision. It is
therefore important to monitor what happens to these services
and functions in the coming year.

Networks and partnerships

It is not just local government that is being transformed by reorganisation. Redrawing geographical boundaries and transferring
functions have huge implications for the networks, partnerships,
contracts and other working arrangements which the old councils
had with a range of statutory and other bodies. In Wales for
instance, as Williams (1995) points out, while the contact between
front line staff remains relatively intact middle and senior management inter-agency relationships are now brand new, while

organisations that used to work within one county's borders now find themselves straddling two or more new unitaries. Effective joint working tends to result from how relationships have developed over time and a number of commentators have pointed to the risk of new authorities being too inward-looking in the shadow year to promote new patterns of joint working (Hambleton & Essex, 1995; LGMB, 1995c; Williams, 1995).

Reorganisation also has implications for the relationships between SSDs and health authorities. The simultaneous redrawing of health authority boundaries into larger units while local authorities were being downsized makes matters especially complicated in Wales. The five new health authorities now span two or more new unitary councils. Similarly in England the fairly recent gains in co-terminosity between county council and health authority in places like Cleveland, have been lost through reorganisation. Fears have also been expressed (Craig, 1993; Page et al., 1994) that the changes in organisational structures may also lead to an imbalance of power in community care between health authorities and SSDs, with the former driving the market. The future effectiveness of networks and partnerships will be an important measure of the extent to which social services successfully survive reorganisation.

Impact on the voluntary sector

There were early predictions that, if finances were tight, voluntary sector providers would fare badly, as a result of reorganisation (Mercer, 1995; Davidson & Bransbury, 1995). Voluntary organisations, through grant aid or contracts, now provide many essential children's and adult services. These may be services traditionally delivered by SSDs or where the voluntary sector has particular expertise or a distinct approach in providing highly specialist services. Many projects are small scale, relatively cheap to provide and work with small groups of very disadvantaged people (Davidson & Bransbury, 1995). They often depend on complex inter-agency agreements and funding (Williams, 1995) and were therefore held to be particularly vulnerable during the transition. There were also fears, particularly in Wales that the heavy investment since 1993 in developing links with voluntary organisations and organisations of users and carers and involving them in service planning would be jeopardised (Williams, 1995).

The Welsh experience to date tends to substantiate early concerns about the vulnerability of voluntary sector funding, although it is too soon to tell how many voluntary sector projects have been damaged or had to close. Voluntary sector umbrella groups lobbied the shadow authorities to confirm by December 1995 at least some interim guarantees on grant aid but this did not prove to be possible. Well into 1996, the new councils were unable to give any reassurances or firm commitments to projects about future funding . As has already been described, some then had to make substantial savings very close to vesting day, once they knew the full extent of their budgetary difficulties. The voluntary sector in places like Cardiff has undoubtedly fared badly as a result. In addition, dividing one county's social services budget between several smaller authorities had implications for grant aid. Each voluntary project's grant represented a much larger percentage of the new departments' grants budget than that of the outgoing county. For instance, the grant for one children's project in South Wales, previously funded by the county, would have consumed half the new social services committee's grants budget for the year.

Conclusions

To date, the debates on local government reorganisation have paid little attention to its impact on service delivery. It is too early to judge the impact on the first tranche of SSDs in the new authorities, similarly, we must wait to see whether the factors identified here prove to be significant in equipping some new unitaries to achieve a more successful transfer of functions than others. While major disruptions to existing services should be apparent by the end of May, it will take far longer to assess whether the small all-purpose councils have the capacity to: plan strategically; work effectively in partnership and provide a wide enough range of services and other functions such as staff training.

This chapter has identified a range of issues which deserve to be monitored closely during 1996/97, particularly as more than thirty three further English councils are scheduled for unitary status from April 1997 and twenty more county councils will be stripped of their urban centres. There will be valuable lessons for these councils from the current experience of SSDs in the new unitaries and North Yorkshire county council. But what is already clear is that a confused and unsatisfactory structure for English local government will emerge from these reforms. There was little firm evidence to justify the trauma of breaking up English and Welsh counties in the first place. It is essential before any government decides what to do next to monitor how competently small unitary councils can plan and deliver social services and whether they are indeed more responsive to local needs, better able to co-ordinate services and deliver them more efficiently.

Notes

1. Scotland is excluded as the chapter is based on monitoring by the Local Government Information Board (LGIU) of the likely impact on social services in its Welsh and English affiliates. LGIU is an independent unit funded by over one hundred local authorities and the main public sector unions. Four Welsh and nine of the fourteen English unitary councils created in 1996 are members, as were Cleveland and Avon.

2. Since 1994 LGIU has monitored attitudes towards reorganisation and the implications for social services through literature searches, a joint research project with the Welsh region of the National Local Government Forum Against Poverty, a series of workshops for officers, discussions with individual officers, members and voluntary organisations in affected areas, and analyses of the draft service plans for some Welsh shadow authorities. This chapter is based on this monitoring. The initial monitoring is to be followed up in June 1996 by questionnaires and structured interviews with officers and members in six new unitaries to identify the effects of transfer on social services and whether there are any lessons to be learnt for councils facing reorganisation.

References

ADSS (1993) The Review of Local Government and Personal Social Services, Northallerton, Association of Directors of Social Services Briefing.

ADC (1994) Local Government Reorganisation Implementation: Social Services Briefing Materials, London, Association of District Council's Implementation Circular 1994/578.

Boyne, G. A. (1992) 'The reform of local government in Wales: a critique of the case for unitary authorities', Public Money and Management, vol.12, no.4, pp49-52.

Butler, I., Davies, M. & Noyes, P. (1995) Planning for Children, Cardiff, NSPCC.

Capita (1994) Managing Social Services Through Transition, Making the Transition No. 7, London, Capita Management Consultancy.

Challis, L (1990) Organising Public Social Services, Harlow, Longmans.

Craig, G. (1993) Community Care Reforms and Local Government Change, Social Research Paper No. 1, Kingston on Hull, University of Humberside.

Davidson, J. and Bransbury, L.(1995) The Anti-poverty Implications of Local Government Reorganisation, London, Report from Local Government Information Unit and The National Local Government Forum Against Poverty.

Department of Health (1995) Local Government Reorganisation - Managing the Transition for Personal Social Services, London, Social Services Inspectorate.

Jones, B. (1986) Future Role and Organisation of Local Government, INLOGOV Study Paper No 2, Cardiff, University College Cardiff.

Hambleton, R. & Essex, S. (1995) Priorities for the Shadow Year, Occasional Paper in Planning Research no 3, Cardiff, University College Cardiff

Leach, R (1994) 'Restructuring local government', Local Government Studies, vol.20, no.3, pp345-360.

Leach, S. (1994) 'The Local Government Review: a critical appraisal', Public Money and Management, vol.14., no.1, pp11-16.

LGMB (1994a) Managing the Transition, Luton, Local Government Management Board.

LGMB (1994b) Introducing Social Services Managing Reorganisation Series, Luton, Local Government Management Board.

LGMB (1994c) Mosaic - Redesigning Local Government - Strengthening Responses to Change, Luton, Report from Local Government Management Board and the Office for Public Management.

Mercer, C (1995) 'The big freeze', Community Care, 19-25 October.

Mitchell, D. (1993) 'Bigger is better?', Community Care, 8 June.

Page, R., Shaw, J. & Silburn, R. (1994) 'Delivering social services at local level - will reorganisation matter?', Public Money and Management, vol.14, no.1, pp27-32.

Redcliffe-Maud (1969) Royal Commission on Local Government in England, Cmnd 4040, London, HMSO

Riley, K. A. (1993) 'The abolition of the ILEA: some implications for the restructuring of local government', Public Money and Management, vol.13, no.2, pp57-60.

Stevenson, B. (1994) 'Driven by misunderstanding', Municipal Journal, no.20, May, pp20-26.

Waddington, P. (1995) 'The local government review: a packet of all sorts', Public Money and Management, vol.13, no.2, pp94-99.

Whitehead, A. (1994) 'Redistributing the remains: a commentary on the 1993-4 local government review', Local Government Policy Making, vol.21, no.1, pp3-18.

Williams, C. (1995) 'The impact of Local Government Reorganisation in Wales', Children & Society, vol.9, no.4.

WRAC (1995) Poverty and Local Government in Wales, Cardiff, Welfare Rights Advisers Cymru.

Appendix 1

Councils with Responsibility for Social Services	April 1995	April 1996	April 1997	April 1998 or later
London boroughs	33	33	33	33
English Metropolitan Districts	36	36	36	36
English counties	38	35	35	34
New English unitaries	1	14	25	46
English totals:	108	118	129	149
Welsh counties	8			
Welsh unitaries		22	22	22
Totals:	116	140	151	171

Appendix 2 The State of Play in England at 20 March 1996

County	New Unitary	Start date	Abolition of county
Cleveland	Hartlepool, Middlesborough, Redcar & Cleveland Stockton on Tees	April 1996	Yes
Avon	Bath & N.E. Somerset East Somerset Bristol North West Somerset S.Gloucestershire		Yes
Humberside	Kingston on Hull East Riding of Yorkshire, North East Lincolnshire, North Lincolnshire		Yes No
North Yorkshire	York		No
Hampshire	Isle of Wight Southampton Portsmouth	April 1994 April 1997	

County	New Unitary	Start date	Abolition of county
Dorset	Bournemouth Poole	April 1997	No
E Sussex	Brighton & Hove		No
Buckinghamshire	Milton Keynes		No
Bedfordshire	Luton		No
Durham	Darlington		No
Staffordshire	Stoke		No
Wiltshire	Thamesdown		No
Derbyshire	Derby		No
Berkshire	Bracknell Forest Newbury Reading Slough Wokingham Windsor & Maidenhead	Date as yet unknown, possibly April 1998	Yes
Devon	Torbay, Plymouth		No
Essex	Southend, Thurrock		No
Hereford & Worcester	Herefordshire		No
Leicestershire	Leicester. Rutland		No
Nottinghamshire	Nottingham		No
Lancashire	Blackpool Blackburn		
Kent	Gillingham& Rochester		No
Cambridgeshire	Peterborough		No
Cheshire	Halton Warrington		No
Shropshire	The Wrekin		No

Sources: Secretary of State announcements December 1994
and 14 March 1996; Local Government Chronicle, 22 March 1996

11 Changing Patterns of Industrial Relations in the Public-Sector Welfare Services[1]

Sylvia Horton

This chapter describes and analyses the structures of industrial relations and the main changes which have taken place in the employment relationship in public-welfare services since 1979. It argues that there has been a movement away from an established pattern of industrial relations, characterised by a collectivise, pluralist tradition, with union recognition, high union membership, national collective bargaining and highly centralised, standardised and proceduralized practices, towards a new system which is management-led, more fragmented, decentralised, and dualist. The chapter concludes with an evaluation of these changes and some pointers to the future. It also contends that the model-employer tradition of the state is changing and now reflects a best-practice, private business model, rooted in new orthodox ideas of human resource management.

Context

During the last two decades the principles on which the welfare state was established in 1945 have all been challenged. The attack h as come from across the political spectrum with the 'New Right' challenging the 'welfare dependency culture' which, they argued, was the root cause of Britain's economic problems (Bacon & Eltis, 1976) and its moral decline (Thurow, 1983). The 'New Left', in contrast, questioned whether welfarist principles were ever seriously applied and sought to rid the system of its professional domination and bureaucratic centralism in favour of more democratic, responsive and accountable structures (Gyford, 1984). The Conservative Government, elected in 1979, reflected New Right thinking and was committed ideologically to many of its basic tenets. These included transforming and reducing the role of the state; making those parts that remained more efficient; moving society to an enterprise culture in which the state would have an enabling rather than a provider role; breaking the power of the trade unions and the professions, particularly in the public sector; and using markets as a means of making the most effective use of resources, giving people more choice and releasing the creative and entrepreneurial potential within society (Farnham & Horton, 1996a).

Although many of the Conservative governments' policies proved popular and the electorate returned four consecutive governments in 1979, 1983, 1987 and 1992, weaning society away from the welfarist tradition has proved more difficult. There is widespread public support for the welfare services as shown in the Social Attitude Surveys (SCPR, 1981 to 1995) and this has constrained what governments could do. Not until 1988 did a third conservative government embark upon radical reforms of the Welfare State. These involved organisational restructuring, decentralisation of decision making, the introduction of pseudo-markets and increased consumerism (LeGrand & Bartlett, 1993). The outcome has been the emergence of a new system of 'welfare pluralism' in which the state no longer has a monopoly of welfare service provision. Both the private commercial sector and the non-profit voluntary sector now play an important part in both provision and funding, although this varies amongst the services.

These changes have had effects upon both service users and providers. Those who deliver the services have been greatly affected by the structural and managerial reforms. Although the numbers employed in the welfare services overall have not fallen as much as in other parts of the public sector, there have been significant changes in the composition of the labour force, their employment status, conditions of employment and in relationships between employers and employees, as new cadres of managers have been appointed to direct and control the implementation of government policy.

The employment structure of the welfare services

It has always been difficult to draw boundaries around the public welfare services and to decide what constitutes the welfare state (Mishra, 1984). This paper adopts a narrow definition and focuses on the major social services including education, health, social security and income maintenance, housing and personal social services for children and families, the elderly and the physically and mentally disabled which are provided by central and local government and funded from general taxation.

Size of the workforce

The numbers employed in the public sector fell from 7.4 million to 5.2 million between 1979 and 1994. Table 1 shows the contraction has not been evenly distributed. The major reduction has been in the public corporations where over eighty public enterprises have been sold to the private sector resulting in a fall of nearly one million public employees.

Table 1: Public Sector Employment by Headcount, 1979 and 1994

	1979	1994
Total public sector	7449	5290
Public corporations	2065	1433
NHS Trusts		966
Other	2065	467
Central Government	2387	1215
HM Forces	314	250
NHS	1152	205
Civil Service	738	555
Other	197	205
Local Authorities	2997	2642
Education	1539	1176
Social services	344	408
Police	176	207
Construction	156	87
Other	782	764

Source: Derived from Central Statistical Office 1979 and 1994

In education the loss of 400,000 staff between 1979 and 1994 is also accounted for in part by transfers from the public to the private sector. In 1989 the former Polytechnics and Colleges of Higher Education (39,000) were transferred from local authority control to Higher Education Corporations (HECS) and schools, choosing to adopt Grant Maintained status (23,000), were also transferred to the private sector. In 1993 all further education and sixth-form colleges (119,000) became Further Education Corporations (FECS) also with independent status. The reduction in employment, therefore, is more apparent than real, since all the education corporations are still controlled and funded by the state.

Employment in the NHS has remained around the million level, although most employees are now employed by nearly 500 independent NHS Trusts, which have the status of public corporations. Although there has been only a small fall, of around 5 per cent, in the NHS since 1979, there have been significant changes in the composition of the workforce. The numbers of ancillary workers declined by over 50 per cent, due to competitive tendering and contracting out, whilst the numbers of managerial staff increased by 400 per cent between 1989 and 1994, following the introduction of the internal market (Mihill, 1996). A new category of health care assistants has also been a growth area.

Table 1 shows a fall of 200,000 civil servants since 1979 but the numbers in social security have actually increased. The Department of Social Security (DSS) is responsible for the social security system but the Department for Education and Employment acts as an agent for paying unemployment benefit. 95 per cent of all staff involved in social security are now in agencies, leaving only a small core of around two thousand in the central departments.[2] There were nearly 90,000 employed in the Social Security Agencies in 1995 and most were in the Benefits Agency (67, 000). A further 40,000 were in the Employment Service. Other areas which show a major growth in employment are housing and personal social services, within local government. Social services rose from 344,000 in 1979 to over 408,000 in 1994, whilst the corresponding figures in housing were 56,000 and 77,000. These increases are due to new policies, rising demand for services and transfer of responsibilities from central to local government.

Gender and employment

A significant characteristic of employment in the public sector in general and the welfare services in particular is the large number of women workers. Women account for 56 per cent of the public sector workforce but 89 per cent of the part-time workforce which, in turn, is 31 per cent of the total (Hughes, 1995). They are concentrated in the welfare services and in clerical and administrative work. In 1994 female part-time and full-time workers represented 47 and 32 per cent respectively of the education workforce. In the NHS, 74 per cent of employees were women and of those 38 per cent were full-time and 36 per cent part-time. In social services, 34 per cent of employees were women full-time and 52 per cent were women part-time workers. In housing and social security the majority of employees again are women but the proportions in part-time employment are lower, although their numbers are rising. This pattern of part-time employment in state welfare is a distinct form of employment which is gender specific and central to the labour process changes occurring throughout the welfare services (Hallett, 1989).

There are other forms of vertical and horizontal gender segregation throughout the welfare services. Most senior posts are held by men, with women managers concentrated in the lower supervisory or middle management posts (Eley, 1989; Corby, 1995; Horton, 1996). Men tend to hold management posts in finance, IT and planning while women are concentrated in personnel management and public relations (Davidson & Cooper, 1992; Coyle & Skinner, 1988).

The parties and institutions of industrial relations

There are a multiplicity of union, professional and employer organisations in the welfare services, where collective bargaining has traditionally been the dominant form of industrial relations. The recognition of employee bodies to promote 'good' industrial relations jointly with employers has not been a contentious issue since the publication of the Whitley reports in 1917-18. Both collective bargaining and joint consultative arrangements exist at national and local levels within all the services and more recently pay review bodies have been created for particular groups of welfare-service staff.

Education

Both the school and the post-school sectors are characterised by a large number of employers. There are over 30,000 maintained and 820 grant maintained schools, over 350 further education and sixth-form colleges and 104 public universities. Schools have always been highly unionised with union density currently at around 80 per cent (Beatson & Beaty, 1993). The teaching profession is the most highly unionised of all the qualified professions, along with nursing. There are six major teaching unions, covering schools, the largest of which are the National Union of Teachers (NUT) and the National Association of Schoolmasters and Union of Women Teachers (NAS/UWT) . Both of these are TUC affiliates but the other four unions are not (Ironside & Seifert, 1995). There are also three general unions representing non-teaching staff.

The composition of the workforce in further and higher education (FE and HE) is diverse with academic, research, technical, managerial, administrative, clerical and ancillary groups. Union membership across all these is high especially in the FE sector. There are five unions to which lecturers can belong. The largest are the Association of University Teachers (AUT), which represents academics and non-academics in the old universities, and the National Association of Teachers in Further and Higher Education (NATFHE) whose membership comes from the FE sector and the new universities. Non-teaching staff belong to general unions including UNISON, the Manufacturing Science and Finance Union (MSF), Transport and General Workers Union (TGWU) and the GMB.

From 1919 until 1987 industrial relations in school education was conducted within a Whitley system. Union representatives met with employers (LEAS) to negotiate on pay and other conditions. The teacher's negotiating forum in England and Wales was the Burnham Committee, whilst non-teaching staff came under local authority National Joint Councils. The national agreements, determined for primary and secondary education, were legally binding on LEAs with little scope for local variations. During the 1980s it became increasingly difficult to reach settlements and in 1987 Burnham was abolished, although the NJCs remain. A Pay Review Body was set up to determine teachers' pay, but recommendations of the Statutory Teachers Review Body (STRB) are not legally binding on government or employers.

Industrial relations are more complex in FE and HE for historical reasons. There is national pay bargaining for most staff, except senior staff in the university sector, and there are a multiplicity of bodies involved. These include negotiating bodies for teaching and non-teaching staff in FECs where employers are represented by the Colleges Employer's Forum (CEF), and three major unions - NATFHE, the Association of Teachers and Lecturers (ATL) and UNISON, represent staff. In HE, where the system is currently under review, there are still separate systems for the new and old universities. In the new universities there is a Lecturer's National Negotiating Committee which determines salaries of all academic staff up to principal lecturer level. There is also an administrative, technical, professional and clerical (ATP&C) National Negotiating Committee and a Manual National Negotiating Committee for non-academics. Employers are represented by the Universities and Colleges Employers Association (UCEA), and six unions represent staff including NATFHE, the Association of University and College Lecturers (AUCL), UNISON, GMB and TGWU. The arrangements for senior academic and managerial staff vary between institutions, with some having abandoned any form of collective bargaining in favour of individual negotiation (Farnham & Giles, 1996). In the old universities a separate system operates. A National Council consisting of representatives of AUT and the UCEA negotiate on pay, whilst conditions of service are determined in each university. Non-academic staff have their pay and conditions determined within four JNCS, although not all universities adopt their recommendations.

The NHS

The NHS is characterised by a diversity of professional and occupational groups including nurses, midwives, doctors, radiographers, physiotherapists, pharmacists, opticians, biochemists, clerical and ancillary workers. This is reflected in the multiplicity of trade unions and professional associations that represent them. In the early 1980s there were over thirty professional associations and nine major trade unions (Riseborough & Walter, 1988). Two-thirds of NHS employees belonged to trade unions and 80 per cent of those were members of three major trade unions, the Confederation of Health Service Employees, National and Local Government Officer's Association and National Union of Public Employees. In 1993, these bodies merged to form the largest white-collar union in Britain, UNISON. The largest professional associations then and now are the Royal College of Nursing (RCN) and the British Medical Association (BMA), both of which are certified unions but not members of the Trade Unions Council.

The system of industrial relations in the NHS is again based on the Whitley model of joint regulation. A General Whitley Council, with a remit to cover matters of general application, covers the whole service and functional Whitley Councils determine pay and/or other conditions for the separate occupational and professional groupings. The composition of the councils is extremely complex because of the number of recognised staff associations. In 1990 thirty eight organisations representing staff had at least one seat on the Whitley Councils (Bryson et al., 1995). Although a large number of unions and staff associations is common throughout the public sector, 'the multiplicity of bodies representing the NHS staff, with their overlapping jurisdictions, is unique' (Corby, 1996, p172). This complexity has often made it difficult to get agreements and added weight to the demands for simplification and reform of industrial relations in the NHS. One response has been to move to pay review bodies. There are three NHS pay review bodies. The first, introduced in 1963, covers the remuneration of doctors and dentists and the other two, created in 1983, cover Nurses and Midwives and Professions Allied to Medicine. Since 1983 more than 50 per cent of NHS staff have had their salary levels decided by review bodies rather than by negotiation. However, in both cases Whitley Councils continue to deal with conditions of service.

Social security

Industrial relations in the civil service have also been dominated by Whitleyism since 1919. Trade union membership has been traditionally high, extending from the top to the lowest grades and covering all occupational groups. There are seven unions, the largest of which is the Civil and Public Services Association (CPSA), which covers clerical, secretarial and typing grades. The other major general unions are the National Union of Civil and Public Servants (NUCPS), which represents executive and middle management staff, t he Institution of Professionals, Managers and Specialists (IPMS) and the First Division Association representing the Senior Civil Service. The unions are organised into a federation, the Council of Civil Service Unions, which co-ordinates union policy. At national level the Treasury, representing the employer or management side, has traditionally met with the unions to determine pay and a wide range of other conditions of service. Every government department has its own Whitley Committee and some have local committees involved in joint consultation. Top civil servants have their pay determined by a pay review body. Most non-industrial staff in the Social Security and Employment services are represented by either CPSA or NUCPS with senior staff joining FDA. Up to 1994 their pay and conditions were determined through national Whitley Councils along with all other departments and agencies. Since then the two agencies have been independent and determine their own pay, although still through Whitley structures and procedures.

Housing and personal social services

Both housing and personal social services come under local government which has been characterised by national collective bargaining for over fifty years, although 'the national system of industrial relations has always had a fragile base' (Kessler 1991, p7). With some 500 separate local authority employers many issues have always been decided locally. But pay and major conditions of service have been determined nationally through fifteen negotiating groups (Fowler, 1988). Professionals and administrative staff within housing and social services are represented in the 'APT&C' group which covers 735,000 employees, whilst manual and ancillary staff are covered by the NJC for manual workers. Provincial or regional councils, negotiate and conclude agreements on pay and conditions which are supplementary to national agreements, as well as acting as appeal bodies to consider disputes between individual local authorities and their unions. The employers are represented by the Local Government Management Board (LGMB) which in turn represents the Association of County Councils, Association of Metropolitan Authorities and Association of District Councils in England and Wales. There are a large number of trade unions but the main one to which housing and social services staff belong is UNISON which, with over 1 .6 million members, is by far the largest. Two smaller trade unions representing senior management are the Society of Local Authority Chief Officers (SOLACE) and Managerial and Professional Officers (MPO).

The new industrial relations?

The strategy of the government since 1979 has clearly been to steer public employers towards a 'new' industrial relations, which brings the public services closer to private-sector practices (Farnham & Horton, 1996b). Wedded to the market and antagonistic to both trade unionism and collective bargaining, successive Conservative governments used legislation to strengthen the right to manage, weaken collectivism and the role of the unions, regulate and reduce union power and influence in the labour market and depoliticize trade unions and industrial relations (Farnham, 1993). Seven major pieces of trade union and industrial relations legislation removed many of the immunities of trade unions, limited their opportunities for collective action, increased the control over internal union rules and weakened the solidarity of unions by giving individual members rights to challenge union decisions. This has clearly made life more difficult for unions, but it has been labour market conditions and the policies of the government which have had the greatest impact. However, the strong tradition of unionism in the public sector, good organisation and the ability to work together, especially in the civil service, has enabled unions to generally hold membership levels better than unions in the private sector (Milward et al., 1994).

Managerialisrn, human resources management and flexibility

Government has used its power as an employer to set an example of strong management for other public organisations and the private sector to follow. Its reforms of education, the NHS, the civil service and local government not only redefined the nature and role of the state but also showed how radical policies could be implemented by resolute government and assertive and persistent management. It also showed how trade union pressures could be successfully overcome by standing firm. Industrial disputes in the civil service (1981), health service and railways (1982), electricity, gas and water (1983) and the coal industry (1984-85) were all successfully defeated by the government. This has resulted in a reluctance, since the mid 1980s, by public-sector unions and their members to take strike action against employers, although there are instances of working to rule, non-co-operation with management (such as teachers over pupil assessment in 1994) and seeking public support for actions taken by groups such as ambulance personnel in 1989. Although unions have been more subdued there have still been more industrial disputes within the public than the private sector (Milward et al., 1994).

The government has systematically introduced managerialism into the public services to increase efficiency, subordinate the professions and facilitate major reforms. In addition to imposing structures of general management, governments have changed the culture of the services. They have imposed a 'business paradigm'. The welfare services have been encouraged to see themselves as enterprises', committed to raising productivity and using resources as economically, efficiently and effectively as possible. During the 1990s the emphasis has turned increasingly to consumerism, quality and excellence, reflecting the dominant concerns of the 'business' sector. This has resulted in significant changes in personnel and industrial relations practices (Clarke et al 1994; Farnham & Horton, 1996a) and a move away from traditional personnel management towards a 'hybrid' form of Human Resource Management (HRM) (Farnham & Horton, 1993; Farnham & Horton 1996c).

HRM has been identified with four main features (Storey, 1989). Employees are viewed as resources who need to be - proactively managed to ensure that they achieve organisational objectives; commitment rather compliance of employees is sought; line managers have the major responsibility for managing people and finally individualistic rather than collectivise means of accommodating the workforce are preferred. The central focus of HRM is on employee performance and ways of ensuring that management get the best people to do the job, retain them with good rewards and develop them to utilise their full potential.

There is clear evidence that this HRM approach is being practised to some extent throughout the welfare services, although it is more comprehensive and extensive in some organisations than in others. It has gone furthest in the civil service where managers are utilising performance management, staff appraisal, performance related pay (PRP), new and more flexible modes of employment and, increasingly, personal contracts of employment. HRM can also be found in the NHS (Corby, 1996) and education (McVicar, 1996; Farnham & Giles, 1996). Further, whilst there is wider variation in local government, there is clear evidence of HRM in most Social Services and Housing departments.

There is a move in all these services towards greater flexibility and a distinction is emerging between a core of employees benefiting from the more positive aspects of the new managerialism and a peripheral workforce of part-time, temporary and contract staff. An increasingly wide range of working patterns is now evident across all the public welfare services (Mueller, 1987; Fowler, 1993; Corby, 1996). In addition to this numerical flexibility, which particularly affects women who make up most of the peripheral workforce, there is evidence of what Atkinson (1986) calls functional flexibility. Job descriptions are increasingly broad and there is more mixed skilling with greater use of lower skilled workers such as care assistants, nursing aides and auxiliaries. Mixed modes of employment and mixed skilling both facilitate more financial flexibility over labour costs and tend to lead to wider differentials in income between core and periphery workers.

Devolved bargaining and single table bargaining

In addition to battling against restrictive legislation, falling membership and increasing exclusion from areas of decision-making previously subject to collective bargaining (Smith & Morten, 1994), trade unions and staff associations are no longer as actively encouraged by public employers as they were in the past. Although there has been no large-scale, public-service union derecognition, employers are shifting away from the traditional patterns of national collective bargaining and multi-employer, 'many'-union bargaining.

Throughout the 1980s the government sought to break up national pay bargaining and devolve pay and grading arrangements to individual departments. It encouraged health trusts, local authorities and agencies in the civil service to determine their own systems of industrial relations and not be bound by those they inherited on their creation. Management throughout the public sector now has wide discretion to vary pay and conditions. The major exception is further and higher education where national bargaining is holding up, except for staff above the principal lecturer grade in FE and HE who have been taken out of the system. Some universities and colleges have introduced elements of local bargaining for these groups but not all (Farnham, 1996).

In the NHS, national agreements are still the norm but the move towards devolved bargaining is evident. Trusts are not bound to the national system of collective bargaining nor to accept the recommendations of the pay review bodies. This was spelt out by the government in 1994 (Langlands, 1994) and tested out in the 1995 nurses' pay award, when government agreed to fund a 1 per cent rise but gave trusts the discretion to award a further 2 per cent. The government did the same in 1996 when they accepted the Pay Review Body's recommended 4 per cent rise for nurses but only agreed to fund 2 per cent leaving the trusts, if they wished, to find the other two per cent from efficiency savings. A further impetus to devolved bargaining in the NHS derives from managerial responses to the pressures of contractorization and underfunding (Huddart, 1994; Corby, 1996). Radical new pay-setting arrangements were agreed by NHS employers and some unions in 1995. Local bargaining is likely to increase greatly in importance in the future.

Research findings by Bryson et al. (1995) illustrates the varying responses of trust managements to opportunities for redesigning industrial relations. Unions are generally maintaining as much influence in the emerging decentralised systems as they have traditionally had at the national level. The larger unions with higher density are benefiting the most with smaller unions being squeezed out through lack of recognition. However the research points to the beginnings of mechanisms which may lead to the weakening of union positions in the future, such as the use of joint consultation substituting for collective bargaining, the use of PRP which is determined unilaterally by management and the exclusion of non-trust full-time lay officials from the bargaining and consultation process.

Nearly eighty years of national (central) pay bargaining in the civil service ended in 1995, when all departments and most agencies became responsible for determining their own pay and conditions except for the new Senior Civil Service (grade five and above). This movement from multi-employer to 'corporate' bargaining still operates within a Whitley structure but around one hundred 'local' agreements are now negotiated. The Benefits and Employment agencies have both agreed new pay structures based on single spines with every job placed on an appropriate salary band using in-house job evaluation schemes.

Local government is still dominated by national collective bargaining, although national agreements have always been locally modified, with many councils paying basic rates above national levels (Ingham, 1985). During the 1980s, however, local authorities introduced 'pay supplements' for selected groups of employees who were difficult to recruit or retain and some local authorities opted out of national bargaining for certain groups of staff (Bryson et al., 1993). CCT was a major catalyst in these opt-outs for manual workers but only 34 councils had opted out of the national agreement covering APT&C grades in 1994 (White & Hutchinson, 1996). However in 1994 'the most radical set of changes in local government industrial relations since Whitleyism first emerged at the end of the First World War' (LGMB, 1995) were agreed with the unions. From 1996 all national agreements will become frameworks, within which local authorities will negotiate locally. This gives the opening for more devolved bargaining and local variations in both pay an d conditions in the future.

A much stronger trend throughout the public services is towards single table bargaining (STB) and 'prime union' deals. The advantage of STB is that it simplifies negotiation, facilitates the introduction of new employment practices and encourages a move to wards harmonisation. Both the Benefits Agency and the Employment Service have adopted STB. In 1994 local government unions agreed to a 'mould breaking' deal committing them to STB, covering manual and APT&C staff, from April 1996 at both national and local levels. Many NHS trusts are also turning to STB to help them adapt to negotiating pay and conditions at local level. A system of 'prime union deals' also enables trusts to continue recognising a multiplicity of unions and staff associations locally, whilst only consulting and negotiating with a selected number of them (Bryson et al., 1995). STB is currently under review in the universities. The employers body, the UCEA, has consulted its members on whether to opt for a STB covering all employees across the old and new universities or two bargaining tables for academic and non-academic staff. The AUT is lobbying hard against a single STB, whilst the other unions are divided. This debate is unlikely to be resolved in the short term.

Pay review bodies

Although pay review bodies (PRBS) have been in existence since the 1960s, they have been used since the 1980s to break up national collective bargaining. First nurses, midwives and professions allied to medicine (PAMS) and then teachers in schools in England and Wales were taken out of collective bargaining for pay purposes in 1983 and 1987 respectively. The effect of these changes was to remove over 800,000 public employees from national collective bargaining, making a total of 1.3-million public sector employees covered by PRBS. Trade unions and staff associations are still able to present evidence to the PRBs but they are excluded from any direct negotiation or bargaining.

The move to PRBs has been partly to take pay issues out of the power context of collective bargaining and to curb possible industrial action. In return, PRBs allegedly adopt a more rational approach to pay determination weighing up the information and advice of a large number of organisations. It is expected that they will provide higher than average pay increases for the group, especially in times of adverse labour market conditions although this is questioned by some observers.

From the government's point of view, PRBs provide a semblance of centralised control over the size of pay budgets as it decides whether to accept the recommendations and when to implement them. Although there are no examples of total rejection, government has resorted to phasing in pay increases, effectively reducing the pay award. On other occasions it has accepted the awards but failed to provide extra funds, expecting employers to find the additional money from efficiency savings. These practices have been extensively used since 1993. For example, after the review body recommendations in February 1996 the government decided to withhold 1 per cent of the recommended pay rises for teachers, civil servants and doctors for eight months, until December, effectively saving £330 million.

They also agreed to fund only a 1 per cent pay rise for nurses leaving NHS trusts to negotiate further increases locally.

Trade unions and professional associations are ambivalent about PRBS. The RCN, RCM, BMA and other professional associations supported the NHS PRBs when they were created but union support for the teachers PRB was more divided, along the lines largely of TUC and non-affiliated bodies. Attitudes depend now more on the evidence that PRBs are able to deliver higher than average pay increases. Generally PRBs are keeping pay in line with inflation but less in line with the private sector. Nurses and paramedics, however, are becoming increasingly alienated as their PRB is steering the trusts towards local bargaining, thus providing the basis for the replacement of national contracts with local trust contracts. This is strongly opposed by the RCN, which still supports national pay determination.

Personal contracts

There is an emerging fission within the public services between the ways that employers deal with managerial staff and non-managers. Managerial staff increasingly have personal, fixed term contracts, separately and individually negotiated, with PRP. Employers set the parameters within which contracts are determined and the content of individual contracts is related to the market and what employers have to pay to get the managers they want. These practices effectively derecognize trade unions for these staff, even though they may remain individual members (Farnham & Giles, 1996; Claydon, 1989).

The strategy is more evident in education, health and the civil service than in local government, although some chief executives have personal contracts. New managerial elites on fixed or renewable contracts have been appointed to head the FE and HE corporations. Research by Farnham (1996) shows that in many of the new universities all senior management and professors have been taken out of national collective bargaining, although some form of local bargaining is still practised in the majority of them. In the NHS, all chief executives and managers of trusts are appointed on individual contracts, usually with elements of PRP attached and this practice is spreading to all senior and middle managers. Salaries vary with the highest of £109,000 being paid to the Chief Executive of the Addenbrooke Hospital Trust in 1996. In addition to basic salary there are generous fringe benefits and bonuses which widen relativities between top and bottom incomes. Contracts are renewable but this depends on the performance of the trust in meeting its business plan objectives.

Within the civil service, all chief executives of agencies, including the Benefits Agencies and the Employment Service, are on personal contracts with salaries depending upon their size, grade equivalent to senior civil service posts and whether incumbents are recruited internally or externally. Where posts are filled by external candidates they tend to be paid higher salaries than internal civil servant appointees and also more generous bonuses (Horton, 1996). The insecurity of these posts is exemplified by the replacement of Rose Hepplewhite by Ann Chant at the Child Support Agency after the political outcry over the agency's role in 1996.

Senior managers in local government, including housing and personal social services, still tend to be drawn from professionals. Although new types of fringe benefits, private health insurance and company cars have been introduced to attract and retain senior staff, most salaries are still determined through national NJCs and are linked to the size of the local authority. Only about a quarter of local authorities have introduced PRP and it is confined largely to senior staff (LGMB, 1994).

Discussion

The restructuring of government organisations and the introduction of devolved and decentralised management systems since 1979 have provided the context for greater variation in people management and industrial relations, although these should not be exaggerated. The monolithic structures which characterised traditional people management, with policies set down centrally and implemented locally and with pay and conditions negotiated through national collective bargaining and adopted locally, are being replaced by a multiplicity of practices. Hundreds of separate employers, including FE and HE corporations, NHS trusts, local authorities and civil service agencies, are evolving their own people management systems which are characterised by 'dualism' in both personnel policies and industrial relations.

The public welfare services are no longer production oriented but market and consumer oriented and public managers are no longer managing stability but constant change. That change is largely politically directed, although demographic and economic pressures are also important. Managers are increasingly driven by the need to get results and deliver efficiency savings. There is therefore a tension between resorting to means which reduce costs, especially labour costs, and those which raise the quality of employee performance and their commitment to the organisation. This tension is reflected in different personnel policies for core staff and a gr owing number of peripheral staff on part-time, temporary or short term contracts. A HRM or 'new managerialist approach' is matched by a more traditional scientific management control strategy for the majority of employees (Clarke et al., 1994).

There is also an emerging dualism in the new industrial relations. Managerial staff are increasingly employed on personal contracts which are negotiated individually. Their salaries are performance related and their tenure depends on their ability to do the job and to get results. Non-managerial staff remain subject to collectively negotiated pay and conditions agreements which are increasingly determined wholly or in part at local level.

Although up to 1995 there is little evidence of wide divergences in pay increases between different public bodies, the move to greater decentralisation and increased devolved bargaining is likely to produce greater variations in the future. Pay is currently constrained by the government's public pay policy which has been to keep pay in line with inflation or below and to use pay policy as a way of increasing efficiency and reducing the numbers employed in the public services. Until that policy is lifted there is little scope for any major improvements in relative or absolute pay. A great deal will depend on the reaction of the unions to devolved bargaining. If they break ranks and negotiate independently at local level, wider variations are likely to appear than if they close ranks and keep to nationally recommended awards.

However, there is more scope for changes in other terms and conditions. An analysis of the developments in the civil service during 1994 indicates that whilst there were a number of broad common themes there was considerable diversity in the agreements made by individual agencies (IRS, 1995). Pay structures varied widely reflecting the different compositions of the agencies, the duration of settlements differed, whilst some agencies used individual merit pay and others corporate bonus schemes. The Benefits Agency also changed the terms of its sick pay scheme to exclude employees with less than twelve months' service. Similar variations are also in evidence in local authorities and trusts which have opted out of national agreements. Bryson et al (1995) found changes to terms and conditions within the nineteen trusts that they surveyed being driven by management goals of rationalisation and harmonisation. They pointed to the potential for most profound changes in the movement to 'skill mix' or workforce reprofiling being initiated by management and largely excluding the involvement of unions.

Those groups of employees increasingly exposed to market and competitive conditions, in whatever public service, are likely to see a deterioration in their terms and conditions. CCT has generally resulted not only in job losses but also a reduction in holidays, sick pay and bonus schemes to levels closer to those of private contractors, even though base rates of pay have usually remained the nationally recommended ones (White & Hutchinson, 1996).

It is possible that rather than more decentralisation and local bargaining there will be further extensions of PRBS, especially if there is a change of government. Areas which might be covered are the non-medical sections of the NHS and teachers in FE and HE. Those advocating more PRBs see them as a way of maintaining national standards, ensuring some degree of comparability with the private sector and keeping pay at least in line with inflation. The return of another Conservative government, however, with a strengthened commitment to devolved bargaining and allowing local labour market conditions to determine pay is more likely to lead to the abolition of PRBs once local bargaining structures and practices are more firmly in place.

The future of the welfare services is unclear but it is certain that they will not go back to the way they were. New people management policies and practices will evolve. But there is a legacy which constrains the speed of change and fashions the options which are available. That legacy in the welfare services is one of recognition of the rights of employees to join unions to protect and further their interests, of a preference for joint regulation and consultation, and a view that public welfare services are about the welfare of workers as well as customers. That legacy is likely to limit very radical as opposed to pragmatic, incremental change in the foreseeable future.

To conclude, what of the state's traditional role as a 'model employer'? In the past, the model employer was associated with setting standards of good employment practice which the private sector would be encouraged to follow. Today the state increasingly is setting standards which deviate from past practice and tend to reflect private-sector experience. Public employers no longer offer job security and jobs-for-life. Pay is no longer based upon fair comparability but what the market will bear, whilst a proportion of pay rewards for 'senior staff' are increasingly based on performance rather than length of service (Farnham & Horton, 1993). In the civil service all staff have been on PRP since 1992. As one local government manager has suggested, the model 'good employer' is incompatible with 'free market principles' (Griffiths, 1993, p45). The traditional philosophy of the model employer is being eroded as the employment function of state organisations is being subordinated to its business function of delivering services as economically as possible. The state has moved from a paternalist style of management to an instrumental one, aimed at maximising the productivity of its workforce and increasing efficiency.

It is difficult to sustain a 'model employer' approach and at the same time pursue policies of CCT, market testing, delayering, structural re-engineering and permanent economy drives. Even where there has been an increase in the numbers employed in the welfare services, there is evidence of job deskilling, work intensification and job insecurity. In other areas of contraction, job losses also lead to increased work-loads and a feeling of insecurity amongst those who are still employed. Throughout the public services there is evidence of low morale as further cuts in the civil service, the NHS, education and local government are imminent. The announcement in February 1996 that some 20,000 jobs will go over the next three years in the Benefits Office may well incite industrial action. Similar cuts are likely in the Employment Service as the departmental reviews, instigated in 1995, are delivering the delayering of senior management and the 20 per cent cuts in running costs required by the Treasury.

In the NHS the first redundancies of middle managers were recorded in 1995 as Trusts facing budget overspends are having to find cuts. Losses of contracts are also resulting in shedding of staff. Universities and colleges, also affected by swinging budget cuts, are trawling for voluntary redundancies but may well have to enforce job losses. In many cases, permanent staff are being replaced by ten month temporary and contract staff to ease pressure on costs. It is becoming evident that there are now far fewer distinctions between the public and private sectors in terms of career prospects and job security, compared with the past. The mixed economy of welfare service employment is now the norm.

Notes

1. Thanks are due to Professor David Farnham for comments on an earlier draft of this chapter.

2. There are seven agencies in the DSS - These are: The Social Security Agency (Northern Ireland); Social Security Benefits Agency; Social Security Child Support Agency; Social Security Contributions Agency; Social Security Information Technology Services Agency; Social Security Resettlement Agency; Social Security War Pensions Agency

References

Atkinson, J. (1986) Changing Work Patterns: How Companies Achieve Flexibility to Meet New Needs, London, National Economic Development Office.

Bacon, R. & Eltis, W. (1976) Britain's Economic Problem: Too Few Producers, London, Macmillan.

Beatson, M. & Beatty, S. (1993) 'Union density across the employed workforce', Employment Gazette, January.

Bryson, C. Gallagher, J. Jackson, M. Leopold, J. & Tuck, K. (1993) 'Decentralization of collective bargaining : local authority opt outs', Local Government Studies, vol.19, no.4, pp558-583.

Bryson, C. Jackson. M. & Leopold, J. (1995) 'The impact of self governing trusts and staff associations in the NHS', Industrial Relations Journal, vol.26, no.2, pp120-133.

Clarke, J. Cochrane, A. & McLaughlin, E. (1994) Managing Social Policy, London, Sage.

Claydon, T. (1989) 'Union derecognition in Britain in the 1980s', British Journal of Industrial Relations, vol.27, no.2, pp214-24.

Corby, S. (1995) 'Opportunity 2000 in the NHS: a missed opportunity for women', Employee Relations, vol.17, no.6 pp23-37.

Corby, S. (1996) 'The National Health Service', in D. Farnham & S. Horton (eds) Managing People in the Public Services, London, Macmillan.

Coyle, A & Skinner, J. (eds) (1988) Women and Work: Positive Action for Change, London, Macmillan.

Davidson, M. & Cooper, C. (eds) (1992) Shattering the Glass Ceiling: The Woman Manager, London, Paul Chapman.

Eley, R. (1989) 'Women in management in social services departments', in Hallett, C. (ed) Women and Social Services Departments, London, Harvester Wheatsheaf.

Farnham, D. (1993) Employee Relations, London, Institute of Personnel Management.

Farnham, D. (1996) 'Pay and conditions of professors and heads in the new universities', Higher Education Review, vol.27, no.3, pp20 -33.

Farnham, D. & Giles, L. (1996) 'Education' in D. Farnham & S. Horton (eds) Managing People in the Public Services, London, Macmillan .

Farnham, D. & Horton, S. (1993) 'Human resource management in the new public services: leading or following private sector practice? ', Public Policy and Administration, vol.7, no.3, pp42-55.

Farnham, D. & Horton, S. (eds) (1996a) Managing the New Public Services, second edition, London, Macmillan.

Farnham, D. & Horton, S. (1996b) The New People Managment in the UK's Public Services: A Silent Revolution? Paper given to International Colloquium on Contemporary Developments in HRII, Ecole Superieure de Commerce, Montpellier, October

Farnham, D. & Horton, S. (1996c) 'Towards a new people management' in D. Farnham & S. Horton (eds) Managing the New Public Services, second edition, London, Macmillan.

Fowler, A. (1988) Human Resource Management in Local Government, London, Longman.

Fowler, A. (1993) Taking Charge, London, Institute of Personnel Management.

Griffiths, W. (1993) 'Facing the Future' in G. Armstrong (ed) View from the Bridge, London, IPM.

Gyford, J. (1984) The Politics of Local Socialism, London, Allen and Unwin.

Hallett, C. (ed) (1989) Women and Social Services Departments, Hemel Hempstead, Harvester Wheatsheaf.

Horton, S. (1996) 'Civil service' in D. Farnham & S. Horton, (eds) Managing People in the Public Services, London, Macmillan

Huddart, G. (1994) 'NHS Pushes on Local Pay', Personnel Today, 11 October, p1.

Hughes, A. (1995) 'Employment in the public and private sectors', Economic Trends, no.495 pp14-22.

Industrial Relations Services (1995) Agencies Wrestle with Delegated Pay in 1994, IRS, March no.579.

Ingham, M. (1985) 'Industrial relations in British local government', Industrial Relations Journal, vol.16, no.1, pp6-15.

Ironside, M. & Seifert, R. (1995) Industrial Relations in Schools, London, Routledge.

Kessler, I. (1991) 'Workplace industrial relations in local government', Employee Relations, vol.13, no.2, pp2-31.

Langlands, A. (1994), 'Local pay determination' Letter to Chief Executives of NHS Trusts, 6 June, Leeds, NHS Executive.

LeGrand, J. & Bartlett, W. (1993) Quasi-Markets and Social Policy, London, Macmillan.

Local Government Management Board (1994) Performance Management and Performance Related Pay Survey, Luton, LGMB.

Local Goverment Management Board (1995a) Joint Staffing Watch, Luton, LGMB

Local Government Management Board (1995b) Framework and Flexibility, Luton, LGMB.

McVicar, M. (1996) 'Education' in D. Farnham & S. Horton (eds) Managing the New Public Services, second edition, London, Macmillan.

Mihill, C. (1996) 'NHS managers 'up 400 per cent on 1989', The Guardian 18 January.

Milward, N. Stevens, M. Smart, D. & Howe, A. (1992) Workplace Industrial Relations in Transition, Aldershot, Dartmouth.

Mishra, R.(1984) The Welfare State in Crisis, London, Harvester Press.

Mueller, A. (1987) Flexible Working Patterns, London, Cabinet Office.

Riseborough, P. & Walter, M. (1988) Management in Health Care, London, Wright.

Smith, P. & Morton, G. (1994) 'Union exclusion -Next Steps', Industrial Relations Journal, vol.25. no.1 pp3-14.

Social Community Planning Research (1981 to 1985) British Social Attitudes, Aldershot, SCPR.

Storey, J. (1989) 'Human resource management in the public sector', Public Management and Money, Autumn, pp19-24.

Thurow, L. (1983) Dangerous Currents: The State of Economics, New York, Vintage

White, J. & Hutchinson, B. (1996) 'Local government' in D. Farnham & S. Horton (eds) People Management in the Public Services, London, Macmillan.

12 Reforming the Probation Service

David Smith

The focus of this chapter is on the efforts since the mid-1980s of the government, and specifically of the Home Office, to bring about changes in the probation service in England and Wales. These efforts can be grouped into two distinct phases. The first, from 1984 to 1992, consisted of a number of linked initiatives whose broad aim can be understood as the modernisation of the service in ways which would make it fit to play the part the Home Office envisaged for it in a modernised criminal justice system (Smith, 1994). The second phase, which may prove shorter-lived, can be dated from early in 1993, when the then Home Secretary, Kenneth Clarke, announced that important sections of the 1991 Criminal Justice Act, implemented only a few months previously, were to be drastically amended; and in the harsher penal climate which has persisted during Michael Howard's time at the Home Office, this phase is clearly still very much with us. The kind of reform associated with it is very different from what was aimed at in the earlier period.

The prehistory of probation reform

Although the pace and intensity of efforts to reform the probation service have been far greater since 1984 than in any previous period, it would not be true to say that until then the service had been entirely left to its own devices. Both the Streatfeild (Home Office, 1961) and the Morison (Home Office, 1962) Reports considered the function of the service, the former in the context of reviewing the overall workings of the criminal courts, the latter solely concerned with probation. As May (1994, pp863-4) has noted, the Morison Report was in line with the expert consensus of the time in its support for non-custodial penalties which allowed for 'rehabilitative casework', but it would never have appeared if there had not been, then as now, a sense of public anxiety about rising crime, and a perception of the probation order as a 'soft option'. The Morison Committee was in general more cautious than Streatfeild about the value of the expert knowledge which probation officers could offer to courts and use in their work with offenders, and it reminded the service of its duty 'to protect society and ensure the good conduct of the probationer' (May, 1994, p864). Nevertheless, the Report was a product of its time - a time in which it was widely believed that something would soon be shown to work in the 'treatment' of offenders, and that the probation service had the potential to deliver it (Raynor et al., 1994).

The Criminal Justice Acts of 1967 and 1972 both contained new measures which depended on the probation service for their implementation, and which required its officers to work in new ways and with offenders who had not historically formed a significant part of their caseload. A main aim of both Acts was the reduction of the prison population, which the 1967 Act sought through the introduction of parole and suspended sentences, and the 1972 Act through new 'alternatives to custody', in the form of community service orders and a new type of condition which could be included in a probation order, a requirement to attend a 'day training centre'. Supervision of prisoners released on parole meant that probation officers had to work with offenders who had been convicted more often, and in many cases of more serious crimes, than they had been used to; and with this came the expectation that parolees should be supervised more intensively, in the interests of public protection, than had been usual in probation practice. It seems that at least in the early years of parole probation officers in fact worked with this higher-risk group of offenders in much the same way as they had always worked (Morris & Beverly, 1975), but the official position was plainly that in work with parolees the purely supervisory and monitoring elements should be emphasised, at the expense of the traditional commitment to trying to help.

Such a shift was inevitable: when the probation service, often reluctantly and hesitantly, accepted its role as the agency through which the prison population could be reduced, it was also accepting that the surveillance elements of its work would become more important, and beginning the process which led to what came to be called 'punishment in the community'. The process was recognised early on by practitioners and academics, and formed the theme of the 1975 Cropwood Conference of the Cambridge Institute of Criminology - Control without Custody? (King, 1976). Community service provided a particularly clear example. The new measure, introduced on a local and supposedly experimental basis, quickly became popular with sentencers, and pressure was put on the Home Office researchers who were evaluating it to produce a positive report, preferably to coincide with the announcement of the extension of community service to the country as a whole (Pease, 1983). Community service, whose 'philosophy' was deliberately defined in various different ways so as to appeal to a wide and disparate audience (Advisory Council on the Penal System, 1970), had a number of features which probation lacked, and which were taken to explain its attractiveness to sentencers. It contained a clear punitive element, in depriving offenders of their leisure time; its reparative aspect - repaying a debt to the community - had a common-sensical appeal; its content was known and predictable; and sentencers could decide its duration precisely. Perhaps most importantly, it appeared to give sentencers stronger guarantees than had ever been given for probation orders, where professional discretion was stronger, that offenders who breached the conditions of the order would be brought back to court. During the 1980s, the sheer volume of orders meant that the work available tended to become exclusively unskilled manual labour, a trend born of necessity which became a positive virtue when in 1988 community service was the first aspect of probation work to be made subject to a 'national standard', which stressed the punitive value of hard physical work and the need for clear and rigorous action in the event of a breach of the order (Blagg & Smith, 1989).

The day training centres which were the other main alternative to custody under the 1972 Act took longer to achieve a general influence on probation and sentencing practice. Research on the four centres set up following the Act was never completed or published (Vanstone, 1993), and the government displayed none of the enthusiasm for them which it showed for community service. By the late 1970s, however, probation managers were beginning to worry about the apparently declining credibility of probation, when compared with community service. As May (1991) has shown, one line of thinking which developed stressed the need for organisational accountability on the part of individual officers, traditionally attached to an ideal of professional autonomy; this foreshadowed the 'managerialism' which was to be much talked about and criticised in the 1990s. Another strand of thought suggested that probation lacked credibility because it lacked the features of community service described above; the answer, therefore, was to make probation more like community service - more punitive and controlling, with a clear commitment that offenders in breach of the conditions of their orders would be returned to court. In response, a number of services began to encourage courts to include in probation orders conditions similar to those for the day training centres, requiring attendance at a 'day centre' for up to 60 days. In Kent, famously, the service established a 'Probation Control Unit' which gave credibility to Jordan's (1983) claim that the aim was to make probation a modified form of imprisonment rather than what it had been - a modified form of liberty. Unfortunately from the point of view of these pioneers and of the Home Office, these developments were judged to be illegal by the Court of Appeal in 1981 (Raynor, 1985) - a position which the Home Office hastened to remedy in Schedule XI of the 1982 Criminal Justice Act.

The White Paper which preceded this Act (Home Office, 1980) had not been primarily concerned with the probation service; its focus was on young offenders, and much of the rhetoric surrounding it was derived from criticism of the supposed leniency of the existing legislation on juvenile offenders, principally the 1969 Children and Young Persons Act. Despite the contemporary talk of 'short, sharp shocks' and the commitment to increase the power of sentencers at the expense of that of social workers, however, the White Paper also encouraged the diversion of juveniles from prosecution and promised a wider range of non-custodial measures. The 1982 Act was a similar compromise between a by now traditional Conservative hard line on law and order and a pragmatic interest within the Home Office in reducing the prison population. As well as reforming youth custody in ways which initially seemed likely to promote an increase in its use (Burney, 1985), it both broadened the range of conditions which could be included in probation and supervision orders and sought to make it more difficult for courts to send young (under 21) offenders to custody, by establishing criteria which had to be satisfied before a custodial sentence could be justified. This provision was one of several factors which contributed to a dramatic decline in the juvenile (and to a lesser extent the young adult) prison population by the end of the decade. By this time the contribution of social work agencies to juvenile justice was being recognised in the Home Office, and one theme of the policy documents of the late 1980s was that the probation service ought to learn from the practice of voluntary organisations in particular, and swallow its qualms about drifting into a more controlling style of work, if it was to be taken seriously as the agency which could reduce the adult prison population (Raynor et al., 1994). Thus one source of ideas about reforming the probation service was the 1980s' experience of juvenile justice, a point to be explored in its chronological place in the next section.

To summarise the argument so far, by 1984 the probation service had been through some years of pressure to demonstrate that it was capable of supervising offenders in the community in ways which provided some guarantee of public protection, and were credible with sentencers as valid options in cases where they might have considered a custodial sentence. This was taken to mean that they must achieve an adequate level of intensity, be reasonably fixed and predictable in content, and provide some guarantees that offenders who breached the conditions of orders would be returned to court. At the same time, the rapid expansion of the service since the late 1960s and the diversification of its tasks were said to require a new organisational structure more capable of ensuring accountability to courts, the public and the Home Office (May, 1991). Although the rhetoric of the 1982 Act meant that it was greeted with initial suspicion by probation officers, the parts of it which affected the service most specifically - the day centre and other new conditions of probation orders in Schedule XI - merely empowered officers to do what many of them had already shown themselves perfectly willing to do without a legal mandate. And it was difficult to argue, although some tried, that the administration of measures with a punitive element was inherently alien to the service's philosophy or traditions when community service had been accepted without serious opposition. The 1982 Act (in this and other respects like its successor, the 1991 Criminal Justice Act) was more strongly based on probation practice over the previous few years than was generally recognised at the time, even if, so to speak, this practice was now returned from the Home Office in an alienated and unwelcome form. Importantly, too, the practice which was beginning to emerge in the main sites of contention, probation day centres, was that which was closest to the work in juvenile justice being developed at the same time, and was arguably the most creative, innovative and potentially effective probation practice of the time (Vanstone, 1993).

1984 and all that

Near the start of a chapter summarising recent developments in the probation service, Mair (1996, p25) writes that he chose 1984 as his starting date 'somewhat arbitrarily'; but, given that all such decisions have an arbitrary element, the ominous date marks a real shift in the relationship between the Home Office and the probation service, as Mair's own discussion shows. This was the year of the Statement of National Objectives and Priorities (known, not always affectionately, as SNOP) (Home Office, 1984), which, as Mair says (p25), 'sent shock-waves through the probation service' at the time, though in comparison with what was to come its proposals were modest and limited.The explosive character of its six typed pages came firstly from the fact that it existed at all: it announced that the Home Office was going to take a much closer interest in the doings of the probation service than the service had been used to. Diversity between services, which internally had usually been regarded as a virtue, would now, if tolerated at all, have to be constrained within prioritised objectives with a national application. There were clear implications for the management of the service: its managers were to be responsible for ensuring that local practice was in line with the national statement; and this had implications for the cherished ideals of autonomy and discretion at the level of the individual officer. In response to SNOP, areas were expected to produce SLOPs, local statements showing how the national guidance was to be implemented locally; some areas apparently did not do so (Mair, 1996), and those which were produced were a very diverse set of documents (among other things, the amount of effort put into them appears to have varied widely) (Lloyd, 1986). Given this continued evidence of local variations and possible recal citrance, it is not surprising that the kind of thinking represented by SNOP should have been maintained in subsequent Home Office initiatives, notably in the two versions of National Standards for the service (Home Office, 1992; 1995a) and the series of three year plans - the latest available being that for 1996-1999 (Home Office, 1996).

Secondly, SNOP took a particular view of what the service's priorities and objectives should be which marks it, like the Streatfeild and Morison Reports of twenty years before, as a product of its time. The main priority was to persuade courts to make more use of non-custodial sentences, and social inquiry (later to be called pre-sentence) reports were the means by which this was to be achieved. Effort in the preparation of reports should therefore be concentrated on cases where there was a risk of custody, and the service needed to establish and maintain resources for community supervision which were sufficiently rigorous to gain credibility with sentencers. Other aspects of probation work (through-care and after-care of prisoners, civil work and the vaguely defined 'wider work in the community') were to be subordinated, in terms of resources and organisational effort, to the main tasks of diversion from custody and the provision of suitably stringent community-based measures. SNOP thus reinforced an emerging distinction between 'core' tasks, defined as offence-focused work within statutory orders and the supply of information to the courts, and other tasks which were seen as more peripheral because not directly concerned with diversion or with reducing offending, such as the 'welfare' work the service had traditionally undertaken with the female partners of prisoners (Peelo et al., 1991). This criminologically dubious separation of 'offending behaviour' from its social, economic and personal context came to be criticised for encouraging a narrow behaviourism and promoting a naive and over-simple view of the factors which might be relevant to helping people stop offending (e.g. Stewart et al., 1994).

SNOP did, then, espouse a particular view of what kind of work with offenders was most appropriate, but this preference was based more on considerations of credibility with sentencers than on any faith that probation officers could help offenders change. The priority it set for the service was one of changing the system, towards a reduced use of custody, not of changing individuals. In this it reflected the contemporary consensus that 'nothing worked': that there was no evidence that any form of programme or style of intervention was more effective than any other in reducing the risk of reoffending. Though this belief was in fact ill-founded (McIvor, 1990), it was based on the interpretation placed on a series of research reports from north America and Britain in the 1970s, of which the most damaging to probation service optimism was probably the report on the IMPACT experiment (Folkard et al., 1976). The sense that if it really were true that nothing worked any better than anything else the probation service needed a new rationale for its existence, and that diversion from custody was likely to be an important element in this, had already informed the most sophisticated attempt to provide one, the 'non-treatment paradigm' of Bottoms and McWilliams (1979). Even this, though, was not entirely consistent in its pessimism about rehabilitation (Raynor & Vanstone, 1994), and although the dominant gloom had permeated the probation service during the 1980s (Humphrey & Pease, 1992), it is likely that in practice most probation officers continued to behave as if something might work. This intuitive hopefulness, however, was no basis for the rational justification for the probation service's existence which the Home Office was seeking; the question of whether there are now more than intuitive grounds for hope will be considered towards the end of the chapter.

Punishment in the community

SNOP's pessimism about the feasibility of individual change as an aim for the probation service continued to inform Home Office statements to the end of the 1980s.The Green Paper Punishment, Custody and the Community (Home Office, 1988a) made explicit the expectation that the community-based measures which it sought to encourage should have a punitive element. It also made clear that if the probation service was not prepared to accept this role the government could find other organisations which would. By this stage the Home Office was influenced by the success of voluntary organisations in providing what at least looked like tough-minded, rigorous ad offence-focused programmes of community supervision for juvenile offenders, and the resulting reduction in their use of custody, and the message to the probation service was that it should adopt the same approach in its work with adults. An 'Action Plan' (Home Office, 1988b) followed the Green Paper, and urged the service to concentrate on 'tackling offending' with the young adult offenders (aged seventeen to twenty-four) who contributed a disproportionate amount to the total volume of crime. This paper, which included suggestions on how supervision could be made deliberately burdensome and unpleasant (to the supervisee) was circulated not only to probation areas and to other criminal justice agencies but to the voluntary organisations which had been most active in developing services for juveniles and were now expressing interest in moving into the young adult field (Blagg & Smith, 1989). This was a clear hint , reiterated by the Audit Commission (1989) in its report on value for money in the probation service, that parts of the service's work might be hived off to the voluntary sector, if not literally privatised, if the service failed to come into line with what was being demanded.

Very largely, the service came into line, or at least convinced the Home Office, for the time being, that it had done so. The Action Plan after all contained ideas with which the service could feel reasonably at home, and which, as the 1982 Act had done, reflected developments in practice, such as the suggestion that we should stop thinking of community-based measures as 'alternatives' to custody, since this implied that custody was the norm. Enough of it was acceptable to enough members of the service for a move in the direction it encouraged to be made. The next important policy statements, the White and Green Papers of 1990 (Home Office, 1990a; 1990b), showed little interest in hiving off core tasks such as the delivery of 'punishment in the community'; the emphasis was rather on the need for these to be performed by statutory agencies which could be held directly accountable for the implementation of policy.

The White Paper set out the framework for the parts of the 1991 Criminal Justice Act which dealt with sentencing. Despite the difficulties which the Act encountered shortly after its full implementation in October 1992, these represented a coherent and logical development of the principles which had underpinned the 1982 Act, and had been reinforced by a further Criminal Justice Act in 1988. The main aim of sentencing was conceived as punishment, which was defined as restriction of liberty. The primary basis for sentencing was to be the seriousness of the offence. This would determine the appropriate degree of restriction of liberty, with imprisonment at one end of the scale and monetary penalties and discharges at the other. Community sentences (and probation was to become a sentence, rather than, as it had been, an alternative to a sentence which allowed the offender to 'prove' him or herself) were in the middle band. Within each band, restriction of liberty could be calibrated according to the seriousness of the offence. The concept of 'suitability' for one sentence or another was introduced to dilute the 'just deserts' approach of the Act and allow sentencing discretion; for example, a community service order of a given length might notionally restrict liberty as much as a probation order of a given length and with certain conditions; it would then be relevant to consider the offender's individual situation in deciding which order was appropriate. Although imbued with the language of punishment the White Paper was strongly anti-custodial: imprison ment was to be reserved for the most serious offences, particularly those of sex and violence. This element was expressed in those parts of the 1991 Act which directly sought to reduce sentencers' freedom to send people to prison, by restricting to two the number of offences of a particular type which could be aggregated to produce a total 'seriousness weighting', and discouraging attention to previous convictions as an aggravating factor in the current offence. It was these parts of the Act, along with the introduction of unit fines, which aroused the fiercest criticism, and which were in effect removed when the Act was amended with unusual haste in 1993 (for an ex-insider's view of these developments see Faulkner, 1993).

It was not to be expected that an Act which stressed just deserts as the basis for sentencing and conceived of probation, community service and the new combination orders as 'community penalties' would be greeted with unalloyed enthusiasm by the probation service, although (as before) it contained more influences from practice and from related academic work (e.g.

Bottoms, 1989) than most officers were willing to acknowledge. It also put into legislation the 'anti-custodialism' which Nellis (1995a) argues should be one of the central values of probation, and which has certainly been a major part of the motivation of many officers over the years. In the language of the time, the Act gave the service an opportunity to 'move centre stage', since its modified version of just deserts sentencing allowed room for individualisation on the basis of suitability as well as of aggravating and mitigating features of the offence. It enhanced the importance of pre-sentence reports, and, in the sections which introduced a new system of conditional supervised release to replace parole, it both increased the service's workload in through-care and after-care and, potentially, gave the service a new role in 'sentence planning'. Resources were made available for officers to be trained in the Act's provisions and their implications for practice, particularly in the preparation of pre-sentence reports, which were expected (again in a practice-led development) to be much more offence-focused and much less like social histories than they had been (Smith, 1996). Despite the criticisms which accompanied its implementation, the Act was preceded by an unparalleled investment in training and consultation, and the probation service gained resources from it, in recognition of its increased workload and its centrality to the successful achievement of the Act's intentions. Just how compatible the Act was with probation values and interests perhaps only became apparent after its sentencing framework had been dismantled, in the new political context which will be discussed towards the end of this chapter .

It is possible that the service was distracted from giving the Act and the thinking behind it the appreciative attention they deserved by a number of other initiatives which showed how interested the Home Office had become in probation affairs. There is no space to deal with them in detail here (some are discussed in Mair, 1996), but it is worth noting that in the same year as the White and Green Papers appeared (1990), the Home Office also produced, at least, a review of the service's management structure and papers on partnerships with the 'independent sector' and in crime prevention (Raynor et al., 1994). In the following year it produced a paper on possible amalgamations of probation areas, which have yet to materialise, and on a new structure for probation committees, on which there has as yet been no legislation, although the new system is largely in place. The initiative on partnerships with the independent sector was, however, developed through a 'decision document' in 1992, and probation areas will soon be required to devote at least 5 per cent of their budgets (cash-limited since 1992) to partner organisations for the provision of specialist services. Arguably, this is another instance in which practice preceded policy (Smith et al., 1993; James & Bottomley, 1994), since probation services already had well-established if relatively informal partnerships, particularly in the field of offender accommodation. It is also possible that in this initiative two policy aims of the government have come into conflict: the diversification of services which partnership entails fits awkwardly with the demand for accountability and close managerial control. It is with issues of management that the next section is concerned.

Management and managerialism

Concurrently with these developments, the probation service, like other public sector agencies, has been required to develop management systems to ensure that its work is performed with maximum economy, efficiency and effectiveness, and to be able to demonstrate that it is achieving specified goals. In addition, the service has been exposed to the specific pressures described above, which in the sphere of its internal management imply greater control and standardisation, and reduced scope for professional discretion. There are critical discussions of the trend towards 'managerialism' in Beaumont (1995) and Nellis (1995a), who is brave enough to note th at pressures towards conformity have come not only from the Home Office but from the probation officers' own trade union, NAPO, and the Central Council for Education and Training in Social Work; and Statham and Whitehead (1992) provide a number of discussions, mainly from the perspective of managers, of what management in the probation service means and how it may develop. Despite the benign tone of most of these contributions - what Nellis (1995a, p180) calls their 'benevolent corporatism' - it is difficult to disagree with his argument that the effect of the stress on managerial imperatives is to encourage obedience and uncritical conformity, even if the results may not be as apocalyptic as he fears. The intention here is not to provide an account or critique of managerialism as a whole, but to identify some of the most important specific developments which have impinged on probation managers at all levels, a nd, insofar as the managers succeed in managing, on practitioners too. Although it is not the first chronologically, it will be convenient to begin with the development of national standards, because of their inherent importance and because they were closely linked, in their original form, with the implementation of the 1991 Act.

It was mentioned above that national standards for community service were introduced in the late 1980s, with the aim of
ensuring greater uniformity of practice, and providing guarantees
both that the work would be suitably demanding and that brisk
and predictable action would be taken when orders were
breached. That there was a case for greater uniformity in other
aspects of practice w as suggested by, for example, Mair's (1988)
work on probation day centres, which found wide variations in
what was actually meant by day centre attendance, as well as in
effectiveness. Such variations are arguably unjust as well as liable
to undermine the confidence of sentencers, and were held to support the case for introducing standards which services should aim
to achieve across the range of probation activities. The first draft
of these was mainly concerned with procedures rather than with
the content of work, and mad e assumptions - for example about
the length of time between the making of a probation order and
its delivery to the offender - which were not solely within the gift
of the probation service (in this instance, because the service cannot guarantee that the court office will send the order out in good
time). The Home Office responded to such criticisms before publishing the final version in October 1992, to coincide with the
implementation of the 1991 Act. As a result, the standards were
seen as broadly acceptable, despite fears of loss of professional
autonomy: as well as more achievable procedural requirements,
on frequency of contact at different stages of orders, and the like,
they contained suggestions on the content and organisation of
work which (once again) more or less reflected the best of existing practice.

Here it is necessary briefly to anticipate the final (post-1992)
phase of probation reform. It was perhaps inevitable that a new
Home Secretary who, in flat contradiction of the policies of his
predecessors, believed that prison worked, and had correspondingly little interest or faith in the probation service, should have
seen the national standards as a prime target for revision in th e
direction of greater rigour and punitiveness. Revised national
standards (Home Office, 1995a) appeared less than three years
after the first version. The most obvious change at first glance is
that the new standards make for a much slimmer volume. This
economy was achieved by the removal of much of the material
which gave suggestions on good practice; what remains by way of
content and methods of work is either highly prescriptive or
bound to strike any moderately experienced practitioner as obvious, although an interest ing new element in the sections on probation orders and supervision orders says, with emphasis, that if
physical activities are included in the work they 'should be care-

fully assessed to ensure that their location or nature could not give the impression of providing a reward for offending' (Home Office, 1995a, pp. 20, 28). Whatever is done, offenders must not enjoy it. It is not surprising that the reaction of many practitioners and managers has been that the new standards are both insulting and (because of their procedural rigidity, which has introduced new requirements at a time when resources have been reduced) large-ly impractical.

Two other important, and linked, developments which have changed the nature of management in the probation service are management information systems and performance indicators. The Home Office Research and Planning Unit produced a com-puterised information system for probation (PROBIS) which was being widely used by the late 1980s (Mair, 1996), and it was pos-sible to derive performance indicators and targets from it. It is now being replaced by a Case Record Administration and Management System (CRAMS), developed in collaboration with the private sector. The considerable costs of this ambitious pro-gramme will, it is hoped, be met by cuts in clerical and adminis-trative staff, since much of the work they have done will in future be done by newly computer-literate probation officers. The Home Office (1994) planned for installation of the system to start in January 1995 and to be complete by the end of 1999 ; the first date has already proved over-optimistic, partly because of cuts in probation budgets.

Again according to the Home Office (1994, p20) in the third of its three year plans, 'RMIS has been installed in all areas a nd has begun to deliver KPI 4 data'. This rather cryptic statement means that a Resource Management Information System has begun to produce figures relevant to Key Performance Indicator 4, which relates to the unit costs of different probation activities (cost per pre-sentence report, annual costs of community sen-tences, etc.). RMIS started off as a part of the government's Financial Management Initiative, launched in 1982 and applied to the probation service in 1986, when a team of consultants from an international accountancy firm was employed following the failure of the Probation Inspectorate to overcome the first prob-lem of defining what the work of probation officers actually was (Humphrey, 1991 pp4-5). Humphrey, an academic accountant who researched the early development of RMIS, writes of the 'appealing rationality' of the initiative's 'emphasis on objective setting, performance measurement, delegated resource manage-ment responsibilities and critical scrutinies of the value for money of service provision' (Humphrey, 1991 p1). His general scepti-cism about whether it is either feasible or desirable to apply the principles of accountancy to the probation service seems, however, to have been justified, in view of the length of time it took for the system to begin to produce information which would allow value for money conclusions to be drawn.

The latest three year plan (Home Office, 1994; 1996) contains nine key performance indicators (KPIs) which relate to three goals, rather confusingly reduced from eleven in the previous plan. In addition to costs, the KPIs cover the proportion of orders and licences completed satisfactorily, the time taken to produce court reports, occupancy of hostels, numbers of hostel residents, and court satisfaction with what the probation service provides. Perhaps most interestingly and innovatively, KPI 1 is 'to maintain actual reconviction at a rate lower than predicted' (Home Office, 1994, p41). This is oddly expressed, since the data provided on reconvictions following various sentences do not show an actual rate of reconviction following community sentences which is significantly lower than that predicted. The new KPI has been made possible by the development of a reconviction predictor (Lloyd et al., 1994; Co pas, 1995) which, in the Home Office's view, can be used as measure of probation effectiveness (although this view is not shared by the predictor's designer, John Copas, who conceived it as a tool which probation officers could use in risk assessment when preparing pre-sentence reports). The presence of this KPI suggests that the Home Office has quietly shifted from the 'nothing works' position, and now - perhaps alarmingly for probation officers - expects evidence that something works, and believes that the probation service knows what it is.

In summary, the story so far has had a relatively coherent and predictable narrative. Most of the important efforts to reform the probation service between 1984 and 1992 were consistent with SNOP's emphasis on diversion from custody and the development of well-focused and credible non-custodial measures. The growing stress on the importance of firm and well informed management which paralleled legislative and policy changes was consistent both with the government's overall approach to the public sector and with its aims for the probation service. Probation staff at all levels may often have felt vulnerable and exposed to too much scrutiny, but generally during this period they could be fairly confident that the Home Office saw the point of having a probation service and that, given reasonable efforts to comply with its demands, it would continue to support their work. Early in 1993, the penal climate changed suddenly and dramatically.

Deforming the probation service?

As mentioned above, the 1991 Criminal Justice Act was subjected to a barrage of criticism just as it was being implemented, and
in the face of this the government moved quickly to amend its
most objectionable features. The Act, which had been supposed
to establish an enduring framework for sentencing, based on
coherent and logical principles, was effectively dismantled by the
1993 Criminal Justice Act, which removed the main restraints on
custodial sentencing and abolished the system of unit fines. The
1994 Criminal Justice and Public Order Act removed the requirement to obtain a pre-sentence report in all but exceptional cases,
introduced Secure Train ing Centres for twelve to fourteen year-
old persistent offenders (with an undemanding criterion of persistence), and criminalised whole groups of travellers, ravers, squat-
ters and environmental protesters. Probation budgets were cut,
leading first to the closure of hostels and, in 1995, to the strong
possibility of compulsory redundancies among probation officers.
New and more restrictive guidelines on cautioning were issued.
The prison population increased at a probably unprecedented
rate, from just over 42,000 at the beginning of 1993 to a current
total of about 52,000. This trend began when it first became clear
that the government was not committed to defending the 1991
Act, and was certainly encouraged by Howard's declaration to the
1993 Conservative Party Conference that 'prison works'. All of
this amounted to 'a moral (and political) panic...which threatened
the reforms of the previous decade, and seemed likely to place
social work once again on the defensive' (Smith, 1995, p85).

One sign of the changed penal climate was the way in which
the press treated the publication of the first results of the comparisons of reconviction rates following different sentences, using
the reconviction predictor. In The Times, for example, Ford
(1995) wrote under the headline 'Probation is no better than jail
at curbing crime' that 'the figures will disconcert the penal reform
lobby' and undermined its criticisms of imprisonment. In fact, the
figures as reported were meaningless, since they did not give the
predicted rates of reconviction compared with the actual rates; but
the main point is that had the figures appeared even three years
previously the headline would probably have read 'Prison is no
better than probation at curbing crime', in line with the long-stand
ing consensus that non-custodial measures have advantages in
economy and humanity which make them preferable to imprisonment except for the most serious offences provided that they
do not lead to an increase in the victimisation risk (Raynor, 1985).
The figures did not suggest that prison worked except in the sense

of temporarily incapacitating offenders, and indeed Lloyd et al. (1994, p53), while cautious about inferring anything from small variations between actual and predicted rates, had suggested that over a longer follow-up period than the two years used in their study the balance might tilt against prison and in favour of community penalties.

In 1994 Howard announced a review of probation officers' qualifying training, the findings of which appeared in September and became known as 'the Dews Report,' (actually Dews and Watts,1994). This document gave the strong impression that its conclusions were determined in advance: the Home Secretary had let it be known that he considered a university qualification unnecessary for probation officers, and that he felt that the statutory requirement that they should hold a social work qualification was blocking the recruitment of suitable people, notably ex-servicemen (with a stress on 'men') made redundant as a result of defence cuts. The report, while finding that existing training arrangements were effective and gave good value for money, and that there was very little informed support for the changes proposed, nevertheless concluded that with the exception of a few 'high-fliers' who would be the service's future managers, and for whom an MA route should be available, the probation officers of the future should receive mainly 'on-the-job' training once they had demonstrated their basic competence and suitability for employment. The recent tendencies to recruit more women than men, and a higher proportion of black people than in the population as a whole, were regarded as signs that current patterns of recruitment were the wrong ones, as was the (barely perceptible) trend towards recruiting younger people. On the basis of the report, the Home Office invited comments in a discussion paper issued in early 1995, and received almost 500 replies (Home Office, 1995b) in the three months' consultation period. Although very few of these supported the proposals, the decision document which appeared in October 1995 announced the effective removal of probation training from higher education. In future officers' competence was to be recognised by the award (by the service) of QPOS (qualified probation officer status) and 'an appropriate level NVQ' (Home Office, 1995b, p5).

There were a number of ironies in the situation. Firstly, even if (improbably) there does exist a large pool of potential probation officers among about-to-be ex-servicemen, it is most unlikely, judging by men and women with an armed services background whom the probation service has always recruited, that they would have the attitudes towards offenders that Michael Howard would wish . There are better organisations to join if you want to be nasty to young thugs. Secondly, the budget cuts which probation services suffered in 1995-6 meant that in many areas the number of new recruits was zero. Thirdly, these proposals for the drastic deprofessionalisation of the service succeeded, perhaps uniquely, in uniting probation employers, chief officers and NAPO in opposition, which was mobilised effectively enough for the government to be defeated in the House of Lords in December 1995 (Travis, 1995). Fourthly, the lower esteem in which the probation service was now evidently held by the Home Office came at a time when research findings were beginning to encourage cautious optimism about the service's capacity to help offenders offend less (e.g. Raynor & Vanstone, 1994) . Finally, there were some signs in 1995 that the Home Office (civil servants rather than ministers) was beginning to be concerned about the rise in the prison population and was looking for ways to reverse it. A Green Paper issued in March (Home Office, 1995c) explored the possibility of creating a single community sentence whose components (bits of probation, of community service, perhaps of attendance centres) would be decided (on probation advice) by sentencers. Cavadino (1995) predicted that this 'pick and mix' approach, if implemented, would tend to increase the use of prison because courts would in effect lose sentencing options with a single community sentence; and they might well be tempted to 'lay down excessively detailed and rigid requirements', increasing the risk that one of them would be breached. The Home Office conducted a sentencing exercise with magistrates with this second possibility in mind, which apparently confirmed Cavadino's prediction. The fate of the proposals remains uncertain.

According to Christie (1993), what happens in America sooner or later happens in Europe. In California, Christie writes (pp112-13), 'probation officers had to choose sides - between being social workers without jobs or crime-controllers with both jobs and guns. They chose the latter alternative...'. And Christie quotes an article by one of these probation officers: they chose 'the Smith & Wesson 64 .38 calibre revolver' and 'ammunition that had the maximum stopping power without fragmenting'. Even with an influx of redundant sergeant-majors, the probation service in England and Wales is unlikely to be faced with quite this choice in the near future; but the fact that it happened anywhere suggests the need for clarity within the service about what its values and purposes are (Nellis, 1995a, 1995b; James, 1995; Spencer, 1995), if it is to survive the present punitive climate in a recognisable form.

References

Advisory Council on the Penal System (1970) Non-Custodial and Semi-Custodial Penalties, London, HMSO.

Audit Commission (1989) The Probation Service: Promoting Value for Money, London, HMSO.

Beaumont, B. (1995) 'Managerialism and the probation service', in B. Williams (ed.) Probation Values, Birmingham, Venture Press.

Blagg, H. & Smith, D. (1989) Crime, Penal Policy and Social Work, Harlow, Longman.

Bottoms, A.E. (1989) 'The concept of intermediate sanctions and its relevance for the probation service', in R. Shaw & K. Haines (ed s) The Criminal Justice System: A Central Role for the Probation Service, Cambridge, Cambridge Institute of Criminology.

Bottoms, A.E. and McWilliams, W. 'A non-treatment paradigm for probation practice', British Journal of Social Work, vol. 9, pp159-20 2.

Burney, E. (1985) Sentencing Young People, Aldershot, Gower.

Cavadino, P. (1995) 'Getting lost on Howard's way', The Guardian, 22 March.

Christie, N. (1993) Crime Control as Industry: Towards GULAGS, Western-Style?, London, Routledge.

Copas, J. (1995) 'On using crime statistics for prediction', in M. Walker (ed) Interpreting Crime Statistics, Oxford, Clarendon Press.

Dews, V. & Watts, J. (1994) Review of Probation Officer Recruitment and Qualifying Training, London, Home Office.

Faulkner, D.E.R. (1993) 'All flaws and disorder', The Guardian, 11 November.

Folkard, M.S., Smith, D.E. and Smith, D.D. (1976) IMPACT Vol. II: The Results of the Experiment, London, HMSO.

Ford, R. (1995) 'Probation is no better than jail at curbing crime', The Times, 9 February.

Home Office (1961) Report of the Inter-Departmental Committee on the Business of the Criminal Courts (the Streatfeild Report) (Cmnd. 1289), London, HMSO.

Home Office (1962) Report of the Departmental Committee on the Probation Service (the Morison Report), London, HMSO.

Home Office (1980) Young Offenders (Cmnd 8045), London, HMSO.

Home Office (1988a) Punishment, Custody and the Community (Cmnd 424), London, HMSO.

Home Office (1988b) Tackling Offending: An Action Plan, London,

Home Office. Home Office (1990a) Crime, Justice and Protecting the Public (Cmnd 965), London, HMSO.

Home Office (1990b) Supervision and Punishment in the Community (Cmnd 966), London, HMSO.

Home Office (1992) National Standards for the Supervision of Offenders in the Community, London,

Home Office. Home Office (1994) Three Year Plan for the Probation Service 1995-1998, London, Home Office.

Home Office (1995a) National Standards for the Supervision of Offenders in the Community, London, Home Office (with Department of Health and Welsh Office).

Home Office (1995b) New Arrangements for the Recruitment and Qualifying Training of Probation Officers: Decision Paper by the Home Office, London, Home Office.

Home Office (1995c) Strengthening Punishment in the Community: A Consultation Document, London, Home Office.

Humphrey, C. (1991) 'Calling on the experts: the financial management initiative (FMI), private sector management consultants and th e probation service', Howard Journal of Criminal Justice, vol. 30, pp1-18.

Humphrey, C. & Pease, K. (1992) 'Effectiveness measurement in the probation service: a view from the troops', Howard Journal of Criminal Justice, vol. 31, pp31-52.

James, A.L. (1995) 'Probation values for the 1990s - and beyond?', Howard Journal of Criminal Justice, vol. 34, pp326-43.

James, A. L. & Bottomley, A. K. (1994) 'Probation partnerships revisited', Howard Journal of Criminal Justice, vol. 33, pp. 158-68.

Jordan, B. (1983) 'Criminal justice and probation in the 1980s', Probation Journal, vol. 30, pp83-88.

King, J.F.S. (ed.) (1976) Control without Custody?, Cambridge, Cambridge Institute of Criminology.

Lloyd, C. (1986) Response to SNOP, Cambridge, Cambridge Institute of Criminology.

Lloyd, C., Mair, G. and Hough, M. (1994) Explaining Reconviction Rates: A Critical Analysis (Home Office Research Study 136), London , HMSO.

Mair, G. (1988) Probation Day Centres (Home Office Research Study 100), London, HMSO.

Mair, G. (1996) 'Developments in probation in England and Wales 1984-1993', in G. McIvor (ed) Working with Offenders (Research Highlights in Social Work 26), London, Jessica Kingsley.

May, T. (1991) Probation: Politics, Policy and Practice, Buckingham, Open University Press.

May, T. (1994) 'Probation and community sanctions', in M. Maguire, R. Morgan and R. Reiner (eds.) The Oxford Handbook of Criminology , Oxford, Clarendon Press.

McIvor, G. (1990) Sanctions for Serious or Persistent Offenders: A Review of the Literature, Stirling, Social Work Research Centre, University of Stirling.

Morris, P. & Beverly, F. (1975) On Licence: A Study of Parole, London, Wiley.

Nellis, M. (1995a) 'Probation values for the 1990s', Howard Journal of Criminal Justice, vol. 34, pp19-44.

Nellis, M. (1995b) 'The 'third way' for probation: a reply to Spencer and James', Howard Journal of Criminal Justice, vol. 34, pp350 -53.

Pease, K. (1983) 'Penal innovations', in J. Lishman (ed.) Social Work with adult Offenders (Research Highlights on Social Work 5), Aberdeen, University of Aberdeen Press.

Peelo, M., Stewart, J., Stewart, G. & Prior, A. (1991) 'Women partners of prisoners', Howard Journal of Criminal Justice, vol. 30, p p311-27.

Raynor, P. (1985) Social Work, Justice and Control, Oxford, Blackwell.

Raynor, P., Smith, D., & Vanstone, M. (1994) Effective Probation Practice, Basingstoke, Macmillan.

Raynor, P. & Vanstone, M. (1994) 'Probation practice, effectiveness, and the non-treatment paradigm', British Journal of Social Work , vol.24, pp387-410.

Smith, D. (1994) The Home Office Regional Criminal Justice Conferences 1990-1993, Liverpool, Home Office Special Conferences Unit.

Smith, D. (1995) Criminology for Social Work, Basingstoke, Macmillan.
Smith, D. (1996) 'Pre-sentence reports', in T. May & A.A. Vass (eds.) Working with Offenders: Issues, Contexts and Outcomes, London, Sage.

Smith, D., Paylor, I. & Mitchell, P. (1993) 'Partnerships between the independent sector and the probation service', Howard Journal of Criminal Justice, vol.32, pp25-39.

Spencer, J. (1995) 'A response to Mike Nellis: probation values for the 1990s', Howard Journal of Criminal Justice, vol.34, pp344-49 .

Statham, R. & Whitehead, P. (1992) (eds) Managing the Probation Service: Issues for the 1990s, Harlow, Longman.

Stewart, J., Smith, D. & Stewart, G. (1994) Understanding Offending Behaviour, Harlow, Longman.

Travis, A. (1995) 'Lords defeat for Howard', The Guardian, 6 December.

Vanstone, M. (1993) 'A missed opportunity reassessed: the influence of the Day Training Centre experiment on the criminal justice system and probation practice', British Journal of Social Work, vol. 23, pp213-29.

13 Putting Transport on the Social Policy Agenda

Linda Jones

Introduction

Transport policy has not generally been seen as part of the social welfare agenda but it is time for this to be reassessed. Transport is such a significant instrument of social division in contemporary UK society and connects to so many aspects of health, welfare and community care that a systematic review of its social impact would enrich social policy. There is long standing evidence of social class and age gradients in road accidents, in respiratory disease and in falls (Townsend et al., 1988). The deliberate nurturing of a motorised society from which some social groups, such as young people, children, women and elderly people, are largely excluded has been an increasing feature of the post-war period, exacerbated by the de-regulation and privatisation policies of the 1980s. At the same time, the marginalisation of transport as a 'technical' issue has limited serious discussion of its social impact.

In the wider public policy arena there is an emerging understanding of some key connections: between transport and land use planning (Sherlock, 1991; Goodwin, 1994), transport and the environment (United Nations, 1992a; DoEa, 1994), health and transport (THSG, 199 1; Jones, 1994; DoH, 1995) and the social impact of transport policies (Hillman et al., 1990; THSG, 1994). In 1995 Brian Mawhinney, as Secretary of State for Transport, launched a 'great debate' in a series of major speeches which posed questions about target setting, limiting traffic growth and encouragement for public transport, walking and cycling. Public concern about the social and environmental effects of road-building has been translated into a new social phenomenon: socially inclusive 'rainbow' coalitions of anti-road campaigners, many of whom are prepared to take direct action. The Royal Commission on Environmental Pollution report (DoE, 1994b), which included over a 100 policy recommendations, captured some of this concern, commenting that 'there is now general recognition that a continuing upward trend in road traffic would not be environmentally or socially acceptable'. It called for 'a fundamentally different approach to transport policy' which would avoid serious environmental damage and preserve reasonable access for work and leisure (DoEb, 1994, para. 14.1).

But most of the key questions about transport still to be asked or answered relate to social policy. How widespread is 'transport poverty' and relative deprivation and what do these mean when translated into journeys foregone, access prevented and wider social participation denied? To what extent does transport poverty reinforce or extend other types of poverty? What evidence is there of how gender, age, class and disability map onto transport disbenefits? Does transport parallel other social services, such as education, where the major contributors through taxation to the costs of services reap least benefit from them? How critical a factor is transport in the development of effective community care strategies? What links can be demonstrated between traffic restraint, levels of social interaction and 'neighbourliness'? What evidence is there of a link between city centre and inner suburb decline, fuelled by outer ring development, and social unrest in inner areas? Social policy can help to provide answers to these questions but as yet we have barely begun to ask them.

Welfare or market?

It may be argued that some aspects of transport provision have had a decidedly 'welfarist' element. For example, the municipalisation of the tramways systems in major cities in the early twentieth century was driven by a mixture of economic and utilitarian arguments which included the call for a cheap workman's fare to facilitate travel between city suburbs and inner area workplaces (Jones, 1995). The nationalisation of the railways, although not achieved until 1948, was advocated by Gladstone on the grounds that they formed 'a natural monopoly' (Morley, 1903). Part of the justification for nationalisation was to create a national rail system which, through long term investment, could provide efficient passenger as well as freight handling services. More recently, in the South York shire County Council area between 1974 and 1985 and in the Greater London Council area in the early 1980s, public transport fares were held down through rate subsidies until government legislation or court rulings forced a change of policy (Hamilton & Potter, 1985).

Local authorities have always subsidised some transport services, by cross-subsidisation from profitable to unprofitable routes before 1986, and through limited central and local government support through the Passenger Transport Executives since then. In 1994, 80 per cent of services in rural Shropshire operated by means of subsidies (Rust, 1994). Since the mid-1980s local authorities have also supported the development of Ring-and-Ride type services for people with disabilities and have subsidised Community Transport initiatives in many parts of the UK. These have enhanced access for disabled people and have mitigated some of the negative effects of the 1986 de-regulation of the bus industry, which resulted in the withdrawal of services from many less profitable routes. In some parts of the country pensioners' travel is directly subsidised, but this varies considerably. In Birmingham, for example, pensioners have free off-peak travel whereas in Taunton (which has a disproportionately high number of retired people) there are no such concessions.

Some enterprising local authorities have initiated policy reviews which recognise the central role of transport in the social life of cities and have pursued policies with a decidedly 'welfarist' character. Tyneside Passenger Transport Executive, for example, used its planning powers to create an integrated transport system based on the Tyne and Wear Metro completed in 1984. Bus services feed and complement the Metro and park-and-ride schemes control traffic density in the city centre. York, Oxford and other medium sized cities have extended pedestrianisation, introduced extensive bus lanes, cycle lanes, Park-and-Ride and restricted city centre parking . Sheffield and Manchester have introduced the metro in a bid to increase public transport ridership and cut pollution. Even the great conurbations such as Birmingham are now initiating policies which explicitly attempt to achieve a more equal balance between the demands of commuters and those of local residents, pedestrians and cyclists (MVA, 1992; Birmingham City Council, 1994). Some of the shifts in central government funding for public transport initiatives have been achieved because of the growing pressure from local authorities exerted through their annual transportation policy and planning bids. The West Midlands group of local authorities, for example, developed a 'balanced package' approach in which public transport support measures were projected as an essential part of the transport strategy.

The crisis in transport policy

The most significant change has come at central government level. Over the last fifty years all major political parties have embraced the vision of a 'motorised society'. Admittedly the 'Beeching axe' of the 1960s, which closed down one-third of the rail network, and the privatisation policies of the 1980s were carried through by a Conservative government while the Labour Party's links to trade unions have made it more sympathetic to public transport. But the pivotal role of the West Midlands in British elections has resulted in support by all sides for a strong motor industry, for road building and for the view that roads are essential to economic development and prosperity.

Transport policy has often been cast as 'technical' and as the domain of the (neutral) expert, such that Barbara Castle when she became Minister of Transport in the Wilson government was criticised on the grounds that as a non-car driver she would be biased against road development (Hamer, 1974). Those who identified some central dilemmas about equity and access in energy and transport policy (Hillman, 1975; Illich, 1974) were dismissed as visionaries and, worse still, 'idealists' (Buchanan, 1975). The marginalisation of public transport, particularly in the 1980s, may have some parallels with the decline of public sector housing. In both cases energetically pursued policies - of council house sales and restriction of local authority freedom to invest in public housing and of major roadbuilding plans (Roads For Prosperity as they were characterised), de-regulation and de-investment in railways - signalled a rejection of cautious social planning in favour of 'market forces'.

Government expenditure on transport policy and investment in transport infrastructure since the 1950s has been directed increasingly towards roadbuilding and repair, in particular the creation of a motorway network, whereas public transport has been viewed as parasitic and inefficient. In 1992-3 £4.2 billion was invested in roads whereas less than £1.8 billion went to rail, of which 35 per cent was private investment from Eurotunnel Plc (Social Trends, 1994). The taxes on vehicles and petrol, which total around £18 billion a year, must be set against the full cost of roadbuilding, including accidents, landtake, pollution and congestion. The cost of accidents, for example, (which is currently borne by the health services) was calculated in 1990 at £6.77 billion (DoT, 1992). The main beneficiaries of public roadbuilding programmes have been private car owners and private haulage companies. It is an open question whether manufacturers and retailers have gained more through roadbuilding than they have lost through congestion (estimated at £200 million per year) and the rundown of the rail system.

The result of deregulation and the growth of the road building programme in the 1980s was a fall in public transport patronage and spiralling car ownership. In cities where car growth had been restrained by subsidising public transport, car ownership and use rose steeply. In Sheffield, city council monitoring of the impact of deregulation demonstrated that people on low incomes made fewer journeys, support for voluntary organisations and youth clubs fell, families found it more difficult to support sick relatives and demand for statutory services increased (Hamilton & Gregory, 1989). The amount of bus miles travelled rose after deregulation but much of this was due to competition between bus companies for passengers on the busy major roads in peak hours. On less profitable routes a nd in off-peak hours services have been cut back and in rural areas many have been withdrawn altogether (Savage, 1985; Rust, 1994).

It is only in the mid-1990s that the assumptions about roads and economic prosperity, unlimited car growth and the desirability of 100 per cent car ownership have been seriously questioned. A spate of reports on environmental and health issues have cast a spotlight on the cumulative adverse social (and economic) effects of transport policies. The Department of the Environment's Planning Policy Guidance paper 13 (1994a) acknowledged the destructive effects of outer ring development on city centres and advised local authorities not to approve new out-of-town superstores and other facilities which drew car owners onto the roads and undermined city centre shops. The Royal Commission Report, Transport and the Environment (DoE, 1994b), as we noted, highlighted the rising level of pollution from motor vehicles and called for curbs on car use, such as road pricing. SACTRA, the government's Standing Advisory Committee on Trunk Road Assessment, reported late in 1994 that under some circumstances new roadbuilding, which had always been defended as the cure for congestion, actually generated traffic by encouraging new drivers onto the new roads. The government task force on physical activity, set up under the Health of the Nation strategic initiative (1992), reported in June 1995, identifying lack of physical activity as a major health problem in contemporary society and acknowledging that walking and cycling could play a significant part in reversing this trend (DoH, 1995). The 1995 Environment Act requires local councils to act in areas where pollution is high by establishing air quality management areas to monitor and reduce emissions. The emerging message from central government in the later 1990s is about 'making best use of the highway network we have'. Together, these policies and initiatives demonstrate how transport policy is moving from the periphery into the mainstream of social welfare debate, connecting to environmental, health and broader planning issues. They do not, of themselves, justify the inclusion of transport on the social policy agenda but when reinforced by evidence about inequity and inequality a powerful case can be made.

Transport and social divisions

Transport policy provides a timely illustration of the allocation of values in social welfare. It has developed through processes in which greater value is attached to the needs of some groups - car drivers, road based commuters, adult men, middle and higher income groups - than to the needs of others, such as children and teenagers, poorer people (especially those who are female or old), informal carers and those who are unemployed.

Two examples illustrate this point. Until the 1990s Department of Transport statistics did not classify walking as a mode of transport and its central importance for lower income groups, young and retired people and mothers with young children has consequently been overlooked in transport planning (Hillman & Whalley, 1979; Sherlock, 1991). Consumer Council and MORI surveys in the late 1980s demonstrated that between 35 and 45 per cent of all journeys were by walking. Yet the maintenance of pavements has been an increasingly neglected and underfunded aspect of transport policy - leading to an estimated 450,000 falls each year on damaged pavements of which 10 per cent require medical treatment (Consumer Council, 1987). The needs of pedestrians are now beginning to be seen as an essential part of city centre planning but pedestrian friendly schemes in suburban areas are rarely attempted.

A similar set of judgements about relative value pervades the cost-benefit analysis of road development. The Department of Transport puts a much higher value on time savings to motorists than to bus travellers when determining the costs and benefits of building a new road. In calculating the benefits to the community of a speedier 'journey to work', bus travellers are characterised as enjoying low value 'leisure time' whereas car drivers are said to be 'working' and thus saving their time is worth considerably more

(Walker , 1992). The other major element in the calculation of the potential benefits of a new road is reduction in accidents. The bigger dual carriageway developments demonstrably 'save' more lives and can be justified accordingly but the saving of lives actually comes about because of the increased danger of such roads. Pedestrians wisely do not (and sometimes may not) cross major roads because of the high speed of traffic on them (Hillman, 1993).

Transport and poverty

The importance of transport in reinforcing deprivation and social inequality have been noted in passing by researchers. Townsend (1979) reported that households experiencing high levels of material deprivation were isolated and unable to travel or make much use of public transport. An essential part of 'participating in the activities...which are customary..in the societies to which they belong' would be for people to be able to afford the bus or train fare for an evening out or a few days holiday. The decline of public transport services and the increasing dominance of private transport 'can only be at greater real cost per family' (p.51). Earlier research by Rowntree (1901) and later work by Mack and Lansley (1991) also noted that travel costs were significant elements that poor households could not afford. Rowntree commented of his prescription for subsistence living in York in 1900 that 'a family living upon the scale allowed for in this estimate must never spend a penny on railway fares or omnibus. They must never go into the countryside unless they walk' (Rowntree, 1901, p49) .

Today, transport poverty, like fuel and water poverty, is a growing problem. Low income groups who depend on public transport have experienced increasing fares and decreasing services in many areas since the 1970s. Government statisticians reported in 1994 that rail, bus and coach fares had increased by over 130 per cent whereas motoring costs rose by just over 80 per cent. An analysis of local bus fares shows that between 1982 and 1992-3 there were marked regional differences in fare increases. In Scotland, for example, fares rose by 50 per cent but in the English Metropolitan areas they more than doubled (Social Trends, 1994). On outer ring estates bus penetration is poor and as shops and other facilities (such as health centres) have been withdrawn so households have become more dependent on expensive local shops which cannot offer the same choices as larger stores. One study of women's health noted that 'th e cost of public transport, and the problems it presents for travellers with children, lead many women to prefer to walk. As a result women with children, like pensioners, become heavily reliant on local facilities' (Graham, 1984, p145).

In fact, there is a much greater dependence on walking in all low income groups. Studies in Glasgow (SAPT, 1985; Bradley & Thompson, 1981) indicate that all age groups in working class areas, in particular young people, used walking as a main means of transport. Teenagers in middle class areas of Glasgow made 50 per cent more journeys than working class teenagers, either ferried around by parents or on buses whereas teenagers in working class areas walked. In rural areas such as parts of Northamptonshire this translates into a grosser disparity, since distances to amenities are much greater and bus services very poor especially in the evenings. Only those with access to private cars could visit nearby towns for shopping or the cinema (Open University, 1992).

Transport and 'race'

Transport has a 'race' dimension too, though there is very little research into minority ethnic use of transport services. Many of the highest rates of unemployment in UK cities are experienced by these groups; for example, 44.2 per cent of minority ethnic young men under twenty five in Moss Side, Manchester, were unemployed in December 1995 (The Guardian, 13 January 1996) and such groups are unable to afford public transport. Historically public transport has depended on a minority ethnic workforce and in the 1980s and 1990s, as services have been deregulated, conditions have deteriorated. The report of the Women and Transport Conference (1993) noted that black women 'often work in the poorest paid and least influential levels of public transport' (p9), experiencing overt and covert racism and excluded from higher levels of employment.

Women and transport

Women face particular problems in using public transport, with a 'self-imposed curfew' limiting their use of buses and trains after dark and declining public provision reinforcing their transport deprivation (Hamilton and Gregory,1989). There are also public concerns expressed by women about the safety of private motoring. This links to an important debate about the relative merits of more widespread car use, safer public transport or more localised services and employment (Beuret, 1991; Open University, 1992). Beuret's discussion of the hidden needs of women highlighted how the forms of transport on which they most depend, such as walking and public transport, were least funded and developed. In particular, the lack of transport had a significant impact on women's ability to make use of services and take up employment. The 1991 conference report on women and transport highlighted the predominance of male, able-bodied and car-focused assumptions in road and public service vehicle design and the lack of consultation with women as users. Women's groups and women's committees in local government have been active in campaigning for safety and public transport measures to improve city streets. One survey in Birmingham reported that 'women's perceptions of the city were constantly dominated by traffic' and they felt nervous about moving round the city even in daytime (BFPWG, 1992).

Disabled people and transport

Over the last decade there has been a significant increase in special community-based provision for people with physical disabilities, as we noted earlier. Ring and Ride services supported by local authorities have enabled disabled people to book door-to-door transport to leisure facilities and social engagements and to supplement hospital and social services transport to support treatment and care. Pavement and building design, pushed on by legislation, has made wheel chair access easier. New options, such as specially adapted taxis, have given some disabled people much greater freedom of movement. There has been a small, but significant increase in t he numbers of low floor buses in the UK and, like the Metro systems in cities such as Manchester and Sheffield, these give easy access to wheelchairs. On the other hand, progress on accessible transport has been much slower than in many other European countries. Government responses have been influenced by European Commission initiatives but there is no legislative encouragement to build low floor buses or retro-fit existing bus stock. Claims from the Disability Unit of the Department of Transport that by the mid-1990s existing vehicles would be retro-fitted under a voluntary code (Frye, 1990) have proved to be groundless. Deregulation of buses has resulted in an ageing bus stock and only the larger companies are investing in a few low floor buses.

There are several issues for social policy here. First, whatever the immediate benefits of special transport are, it both underlines the segregation experienced by disabled people and helps to justify the marginalisation of them from 'normal' services. It was this frustration with government inaction over transport that led to the development of groups such as the Campaign for Accessible

Transport which adopted a direct action approach. Ruth Bashall, one of the London organisers, has argued that the needs of disabled people are easily overlooked; direct action, which has included chaining wheelchairs together across the centre of Oxford Street, can have an immediate effect on public opinion (Open University, 1992).

Second, making public transport more accessible brings benefits not only for wheelchair users but a much broader group of regular public transport users: for example, older people, who often find ordinary buses difficult to use, and parents (especially women) with young children. The rising fares and increasingly patchy and unreliable character of bus services (on average around 150 changes to services are announced every quarter to the Birmingham Transport Users Advisory Committee) have led to falling patronage, a nd have arguably increased the isolation of the less able-bodied who do not meet the criteria for disabled transport. There is greater penetration of buses into some residential areas of larger cities, which may have helped to meet their needs, but in suburban and rural areas bus mileage has fallen significantly and bus timetables and information are poor (Cahm, 1990).

Social class gradients

The 'social class' gradient in transport is still marked. Averaged across the UK around 70 per cent of households own a car but in m any poorer areas car ownership is much lower. In Birmingham, for example, only 55 per cent of households own a car. 95 per cent of the 3.3 million 'employer and manager' households in Great Britain own a car, and 55 per cent own two or more cars, whereas only 43 per cent of 'unskilled' worker households and 45 per cent of the 5.5 million households classified as 'retired' own a car (DoT, 1993) . Poor families, who depend on public transport, spend a larger proportion of their income on transport to work than those in social classes I and II, whose travel costs are often borne by their employers. In parallel with some other social services such as education (Le Grand, 1982), it is likely that the costs of transport policy are borne disproportionately by lower socio-economic groups whereas the benefits are reaped by higher income groups.

The social class gradient is also apparent in accidents. Child pedestrians in social class 5 are over four times as likely to die on the roads each year as those in social class 1 (Townsend et al., 1988). While child safety literature has largely targeted parents and blamed accidents on lack of supervision and proper training, the evidence about environmental hazards has been viewed with suspicion (Davis & Jones, 1996). In one study (Hillman et al., 1990) the police blamed children for 90 per cent of accidents and over half the children held themselves responsible. Yet as studies of traffic injuries sustained by young pedestrians have shown, nearly half the motorists involved in fatal pedestrian accidents were exceeding the speed limit (Lawson, 1990; Pitt et al., 1990).

Such gradients are also present for a broader range of transport related health problems. For example, it is the lower income groups who are most likely to live alongside major arterial roads or in heavily trafficked streets. Noise and atmospheric pollution from motor vehicle exhausts are therefore disproportionately experienced by poorer households - those who are least likely contributors because they are not so likely to own a car. Severance of streets and communities by traffic and road building, bringing quantifiable accidents but also less detectable social isolation and mental health effects, are also most likely to affect lower income groups. There are claims that households living along heavily trafficked streets are more likely to suffer colds, flu like symptoms and coughs (Whitelegg et al., 1993). Certainly there is increasingly strong evidence that asthma sufferers and those with respiratory diseases (especially older people and children) who live beside major roads and therefore experience peak pollution from vehicle emissions suffer more hospital episodes than other sufferers. It has been demonstrated that there is a clear relationship between peak pollution levels and hospital admission rates (Walters, 1994).

Transport, access and community care

In an increasingly motorised society the position of those without access to a car has become more difficult. It is not simply that significant numbers of households do not own a car but that within car owning families some members may not have access. Interviews with mothers with young children in rural Northamptonshire in 1991 revealed that the decline in public transport resulted in men using the family car for the journey to work, leaving women and children trapped in villages with no amenities or prospects of part-time work (Open University, 1992). Their isolation had become designated as a 'health' problem by public health professionals and WEA classes and a creche had been started to bring women together. Older people in the area found travel outside the area, in particular to hospital appointments, very difficult and time consuming. A voluntary scheme in which car drivers were paid expenses to take their neighbours to hospital was also being supported as a 'health' initiative.

Community care

In Shropshire access to health facilities, though not originally viewed as of major concern in establishing community care, has proved to be of the utmost importance (Rust, 1994). The decline of public transport in rural areas has left those being cared for in the community isolated and at risk. Gaining adequate support to enable people to get to day centres, special schools, respite care, clinics and hospitals has required the use of a range of community transport and voluntary car driver schemes. The local authority had been forced to weave together an elaborate web of social services, education, ambulance, and voluntary transport services to support its community care strategy. This includes acting as an information broker and encouraging the development of transport 'webs' which co-ordinate the mixed provision. The Oswestry Community Transport Initiative is the first of such schemes to emerge.

Research by the Accessible Transport Unit in London has also identified a need for some co-ordination of community care related transport. A report on two outer London boroughs indicated that subsidies are uncoordinated and not always effective, that unrealistic demands are being placed on the voluntary sector and that the demand for flexible transport for community care would go on growing (Worsley, 1994). The report highlighted the fragmentation of services and poor co-ordination between different providers. It called for the co-ordination of demand through the creation of one operational centre which could bring together all demands for accessible transport purchased by not-for-profit agencies. The centre could pool transport expertise, ensure competitive contract rates, optimise scheduling and provide accurate data for planning mainstream transport.

There is long-standing evidence that social interaction on city streets falls as traffic levels rise (Appleyard & Lintell, 1972). This has implications for community care policies in an era when 'care by the community' is a major emphasis in government policy. Community severance by traffic and road building means that people are less likely to know their neighbours or feel a sense of responsibility for them. Yet social network analysis suggests that involvement in social interaction is protective of health and that people with restricted or non-existent social networks suffer higher levels of morbidity and mortality (Berkman & Syme, 1979).

Access

The lack of access of poorer households to shops and other amenities has already been noted but during the last two decades spatial divisions have become more marked. As private car ownership has risen, both fuelled by and fuelling roadbuilding, it has encouraged the relocation of essential facilities beyond the easy reach of non-car users (Sherlock, 1991). The 'doughnut effect', that is the intense outer ring activity in cities compared with the decline in city centre use, has been a major factor in shifting local authority and central government views about transport policy. A range of essential services from supermarkets to hospitals have become increasingly remote.

Arguably, it is not hospital closures alone which have caused resentment but the closure of city centre hospitals in favour of outer-ring hospitals. These are often more modern, better equipped, more easily accessible by car and with extensive car parking facilities but travel costs are higher (in time and cost) for inner city households. In Birmingham, for example, the closure of a local maternity hospital adjoining an inner suburb with a high concentration of British Asian households resulted in much longer and more complex journeys and higher costs for some women. The other effect has been the rapid growth of demand for car parking at the peripheral hospital site, congestion, charging and car park extensions. The increasing transfer of travel costs to patients, as hospitals close and tertiary care provision is clarified, has been a marked feature of the last decade (Jones, 1994).

Children's access and independence

Children have largely been treated as objects in road safety and related research, with assumptions that their behaviour can be manipulated to conform to adult requirements.

> While acknowledging that children see the world differently - not recognising danger from traffic or judging distance accurately - transport researchers conclude not that motor vehicles should be strictly controlled but that children should be. The result is a set of policies which serve the economic interests of [some] adults... and marginalise those of children' (Davis & Jones, 1996a).

Children rarely have any voice in the planning process and in the political and economic decision making processes of the city. They are conceptualised as less than competent and in need of protection and restriction; their problem solving capacities, entitlements and personal and peer experiences are seldom seen as relevant. Yet children make greater use than most adults of walking and cycling and significantly different use of their local environments, for journeys to school, leisure pursuits, exercise and seeing friends . Relatively little is known about how children use - and would like to use - their local areas, what they see as major hazards, what factors they perceive as improving their quality of life and whether they link together health issues and transport. One path breaking study in the 1970s, repeated in 1990, demonstrated that parents had grown much more cautious about giving their children 'licenses' to cross roads alone, use buses and go to leisure places alone (Hillman et al., 1990). In most cases parents cited traffic danger as the main reason for their response.

Current research into children's views about transport, access and health illustrates from a different angle some of the arguments sketched out in earlier sections for putting transport on the social policy agenda. It is beginning to identify barriers to independent mobility which arise from the interplay of high traffic volume, speeding and unsafe driving on the one hand and 'stranger danger' , declining social interaction and environmental decay on the other - a situation compounded by increasing car use (Davis & Jones, 1 996b). It records ten, eleven and fourteen year old childrens' accounts of life in working class neighbourhoods in the inner city an d the outer suburbs, in particular the inadequacy and danger of public facilities deliberately provided for children, such as parks and open spaces. Attempts to slot young teenagers into specific safe spaces are shown by their reports to be unrealistic. Football is played in the pub car park because it is safer; the response to stranger danger is to go round in a gang and create convincing stories for anxious parents; hanging around with friends is inevitable because there are so few facilities for young people.

Children presented very clear ideas about how they would like their areas to be: clean, friendly, safe, traffic-free or traffic safe , with local amenities they could use and safe parks and open spaces. Most of the children we interviewed would like to travel round their local area by foot or bike. They are well aware of current health messages about the importance of a healthy diet and exercise and they accept the warnings about road safety and their personal responsibility. But they also point out the contradictions: motorists are often to blame for accidents, junk foods are fun, exercise requires safe streets and parks or fitness clubs which young people can use. As one fourteen year old girl replied 'how can we be healthy when there is nothing to do?'

Conclusion

Transport policy, therefore, clearly connects to a wide range of social policy debates, such as those about health, community care, poverty and area deprivation. While this has been briefly acknowledged in research into poverty and health, transport has not yet found its way onto the social policy agenda. Yet transport reflects and fuels social divisions in contemporary society: lack of access, severance, pollution, accidents are all differentially distributed. The UK has the highest rate of road casualties among child pedestrians in Western Europe and, as we noted above, children in social class 5 are most at risk. In total, over 50,000 people are killed or seriously injured each year on UK roads. The values that have shaped transport policy have led us to accept such outcomes as the unavoidable consequence of a motorised society.

The crisis in transport policy, brought on by economic and environmental concerns, provides a significant opportunity for social policy analysts to influence the policy debate. Already transport researchers are investigating the social effects of different types of policies but an analysis of transport within a broader framework of social welfare debate, in which divisions around class , 'race', gender, age and disability are systematically drawn out, would create a much richer account. There is some evidence that transport deprivation is a significant factor for poorer families but we need to know a great deal more about the extent of transport poverty and how this interacts with age, gender, disability and 'race' and with changing levels of public transport provision. If transport does serve to reinforce other types of poverty, as seems likely, then it is important to understand how this happens and what the economic and social consequences might be.

In particular, the transport needs and choices of older people and children are in need of investigation. The impact on children's quality of life of affordable and accessible local transport, safe pavements and accessible local environments looks to be considerable (Davis & Jones, 1996a). Discussion of the impact of changing health and community care policies needs to incorporate a systematic understanding of how transport influences mobility and access among older people. What evidence we have suggests that there are links between traffic restraint and levels of social interaction and that these may impact upon the ability of the community to care. The privatisation of health costs, through transferring or increasing travel costs to individuals and families as hospital facilities are centralised and tertiary specialisation increases, is one aspect of this. A more complex issue to tease out is the extent to which transport is failing to meet community care 'needs', both because this inevitably depends on who defines those needs and how broadly they are framed. Needs for transport to day centres and hospital appointments are quantifiable but it is more difficult to measure journeys foregone, access prevented and wider social participation denied. Social policy has a central role to play in linking investigations of transport services to broader issues about equity and social justice.

References

Appleyard, D. & Lintell, M. (1972) 'The environmental quality of city streets: The residents' viewpoint', American Institute of Planners Journal, vol.38, pp 84-101.

Berkman, L.F. & Syme, S.L.(1979) 'Social networks, host resistance and mortality: A nine year follow-up study of Alameda County residents', American Journal of Epidemiology, vol.109, pp186-204.

Beuret, K. (1991) 'Women and transport', in M. Maclean & D. Groves (eds) Women's Issues in Social Policy, London, Routledge.

Birmingham City Council (1994) Transport For a Better Birmingham, Summary Report of Transport for a Better Birmingham Conference, Birmingham, Birmingham City Council.

Birmingham For People Women's Group (BFPWG) (1992) Women in the Centre, Birmingham, Birmingham For People.

Bradley, M. & Thompson, S. (1981) A Survey of Teenagers and Young Women in Glasgow, Glasgow, Consumers Association.

Buchanan, C. (1975) Response to Mayer Hillman's paper, London, Proceedings of the Conference of the Institute of Civil Engineers, pp 20-22.

Cahill, M. (1994) The New Social Policy, Oxford, Blackwell.

Cahm, C. (1990) Have the Buses Caught Up? A Review of Passenger Information Since Deregulation, London, National Consumer Council/Buswatch.

Consumer Council (1987) What's Wrong with Walking? London, Consumer Council.

Davis, A. & Jones L.J. (1996a) 'Children in the urban environment: an issue for the new public health', Journal of Health and Place, vol.2 (forthcoming).

Davis, A. & Jones L.J. (1996b) 'Transport and the health of urban children', Journal of Town and Country Planning (forthcoming).

Department of the Environment (1994a) Policy and Planning Guidance Note 13, London, HMSO.

Department of the Environment (1994b) Royal Commission on Environmental Pollution, Report on Transport and the Environment, London, HMSO.

Department of Health (1992) Health of the Nation, London, HMSO.

Department of Health (1995) More People, More Active, More Often, Physical Activity Taskforce Consultation Paper London, HMSO.

Department of Transport (1992) Transport Statistics, London, DoT.

Department of Transport (1993) Transport Statistics, London, DoT.

Frye, A. (1990) Consumer Council Conference Speech, 5 Nov., cited in Open University (1992) K258 Health and Well-being, Workbook 3, Part 2, p64.

Goodwin, P. (1994) Transport Policies, Linacre Lecture, Oxford University.

Graham, H. (1984) Women, Health and the Family, Brighton, Harvester.

Hamer, M. (1974) Wheels within Wheels, London, Routledge & Kegan Paul.

Hamilton, K. & Potter, S. (1985) Losing Track, London, Routledge & Kegan Paul/Channel 4.

Hamilton, K. & Gregory, A. (1989) Women and Transport in West Yorkshire, Phase 2: The Post Deregulation Study, WYCROW.

Hillman, M. (1975) 'Social goals for transport policy', London, Proceedings of the Conference of the Institute of Civil Engineers, p p13-20.

Hillman, M. & Whalley, A. (1979) Walking is Transport, London, Policy Studies Institute.

Hillman, M, Adams, J. & Whitelegg, J.(1990) One False Move. London, Policy Studies Institute.

Hillman, M. (1993) 'Social goals for transport: a retrospective commentary', in A. Beattie, M.Gott, L. Jones & M. Sidell (eds) Health and Well-being: A Reader, Basingstoke, Macmillan, pp246-7.

Illich, I. (1974) Energy and Equity, London, Marion Boyars.

Jones, L.J. (1994) Transport and Health: the Next Move. London, Association of Public Health (reprinted/redated in 1995).

Jones, L.J. (1995) 'Business interests and public policy making', in H. Jones & J. Lansley (eds) Social Policy and the City, London, Avebury.

Lawson, S. (1990) Accidents to Young Pedestrians: Distributions, Circumstances, Consequences and Scope for Countermeasures, London, Automobile Association Foundation for Road Safety Research.

Le Grand, J. (1982) The Strategy of Equality, London, Allen & Unwin.

Mack, J. & Lansley, S. (1991) Poor Britain, London, Harper Collins.

Morley, J. (1903) Life of Gladstone, London, Macmillan.

MVA Consultancy (1992) SOBETMA South Birmingham Environmental Traffic Management Study, Woking, MVA House.

Open University Course (1992) K258 Health and Well-being, Milton Keynes, Open University, Workbook 3, Part 2, pp41-68.

Pitt, R., Guyer, B., Hsieh, C. & Malek, M. (1990) 'The severity of pedestrian injuries in children: analysis of the pedestrian injury causation study', Accident Analysis and Prevention, vol.22, no.6, pp549-559.

Rowntree, S. (1901) Poverty: A Study of Town Life, London, Macmillan.

Rust, A. (1994) 'Rural transport and community care: a case study of Shropshire', paper delivered at Community Care or Community Severance Conference, London.

Savage, I. (1985) The Deregulation of Bus Services, London, Routledge.

Scottish Association for Public Transport (SAPT) (1985) Getting There, Glasgow, SAPT.

Sherlock, H. (1991) Cities are Good for Us, London, Paladin.

Social Trends 24 (1994) London, HMSO.

Townsend, P. (1979) Poverty in the UK, London, Penguin.

Townsend, P., Davidson, N. & Whitehead, M. (1988) Inequalities in Health: The Black Report and The Health Divide, London, Penguin.

Transport and Health Study Group (THSG) (1991) Health on the Move, Birmingham, Public Health Alliance.

Transport and Health Study Group (1994) Community Care or Community Severance: How Can Transport Help Build Healthy Communities? London, THSG.

United Nations (1992) Agenda 21: Programme of Action for Sustainable Development, Rio de Janiero, United Nations Conference.

Walker, M. (1992) 'Buses in the COBA maze', Transport Retort, vol.15 no.1, pp8-9.

Walters, S. (1994) 'What are the respiratory effects of vehicle pollution?', in C. Read (ed) How Vehicle Pollution Affects our Health, London, Ashden Trust, pp 9-11.

Whitelegg, J., Gatrell, A. & Naumann, P. (1993) Traffic and Health, A report for Greenpeace Environmental Trust, University of Lancaster, Environmental Epidemiology Unit.

Women and Transport Conference Report (1993) Moving On, Manchester, Transport Resource Centre.

Worsley, L. (1994) The Co-ordination of Transport in the Context of Community Care in London, London, Accessible Transport Unit.

14 From Safety Nets to Springboards? Social Assistance and Work Incentives in the OECD Countries

Tony Eardley

Introduction

The term 'safety net', alluding to the protection offered to circus performers, is widely used to describe the basic social protection provided by the state to people lacking sufficient financial support from market or other private resources. Safety nets can take many forms, but they are generally conceived of as cash transfers, or benefits in kind, targeted to those with minimal resources of their own, via an income or means test. Such provision is also commonly described as social assistance.

   Most of the industrialised countries which are members of the Organisation for Economic Cooperation and Development

(OECD) have social assistance schemes of some kind. These commonly grew out of earlier Poor Law provision and were generally intended to offer last resort assistance to small numbers of people who fell outside more mainstream forms of provision. In some countries this residual role has persisted, but in recent years many assistance schemes have assumed an increasing significance within social security as a whole. The extent to which this has been a result of persistent unemployment, growth in lone parenthood, or weaknesses in social insurance protection has varied according to the circumstances of different countries. Yet there is little doubt that demand has grown in virtually every OECD country, whether social protection systems have been primarily insurance based, as in most continental European countries, or almost entirely assistance based, as in Australasia.

With assistance schemes taking on the role of large-scale (and sometimes long-term) income maintenance, there has been pressure to ensure that payments are sufficient for a reasonable minimum standard of living. But payments approaching adequacy level may end up close to insurance benefit levels or to the wages of people in lower paid employment - especially where there are dependent children. This in turn tends to raise questions about disincentives to seek work and of 'welfare dependency'. Even where it is widely accepted that assistance benefits are not suficient to keep people out of poverty, as in the USA, the existence of a large identifiable group of welfare recipients is sufficient to fuel debate about welfare dependency and its supposedly corrosive moral and social consequences.

In the UK, in spite of considerable empirical evidence that unemployed people and other assistance recipients would prefer to work if jobs were available and that most share the values of mainstream society (see, for example, Dean and Taylor Gooby, 1993), welfare dependency among a potential 'underclass' has been a recurrent theme in right-wing political discourse. It is not only the ideological Right, however, which has viewed the growth of reliance on means-tested benefits with concern. Arguments have also been made from a 'social justice' perspective that it does claimants no service to trap them in unemployment and on inadequate incomes through the structure of benefit systems. This was a central theme of the report of the Commission on Social Justice (1994) in the UK and has been vigorously pursued (from a somewhat idiosyncratic perspective) by the Labour chair of the parliamentary Social Security Select Committee, Frank Field (1995) and by the new Labour Party more generally. At an international level, bodies such as the OECD have been arguing that social policy structures inherited from the post-war period are outdated and should be moving beyond the simple allocation of welfare resources to a closer integration of public and private responsibility (OECD, 1988; 1994a).

It is possible, therefore, to observe that the dominant discourse on social protection has, to extend the circus metaphor, shifted from the provision of 'safety nets' to one of 'springboards' to independence - certainly in the English-speaking world. In theory, the expressed aims of all social assistance schemes include the promotion of self-sufficiency and independence, but what is less clear is how far and in what ways actual policy approaches have moved beyond the rhetoric.This chapter attempts to provide some preliminary answers to this question, with a comparative discussion of the main work incentive features of assistance schemes, drawing on a study of social assistance in the member countries of the OECD (Eardley et al., 1996).[1] It begins by briefly outlining what is meant by social assistance and discussing trends in expenditure and in the numbers of people receiving benefits. Some key aspects of work incentive policies are then examined. The chapter concludes by attempting to locate these policies within the broader framework of social security in different types of country.

Social assistance schemes in the OECD countries

There is no clear cut definition of 'social assistance'. In some countries, particularly those of the Nordic group, it is a concept associated not only with income maintenance but also with social work services. In others it is understood as referring mainly to discretionary supplementary schemes which are subsidiary to the primary minimum income benefit. For the purposes of the study reported here, the key distinguishing element was the presence of a means test. Thus social assistance was defined broadly as the range of benefits available to guarantee a minimum (however defined) level of subsistence to people in need, based on a test of resources, tho ugh even this fairly inclusive approach is not without its problems (for a discussion of the difficulties of defining social assistance readers are referred to Eardley et al., 1996).

In spite of the growing importance of assistance schemes it is evident that they continue to perform very different functions in different countries. This is illustrated in Table 1, which gives summary data on estimated expenditure on social assistance and numbers of beneficiaries. Comparable data on social assistance expenditure and recipients are not easily obtainable. Making sense of them is rather like assembling a jigsaw puzzle of which many pieces are missing and some are from the wrong box. Table 1. therefore needs to be read with a number of caveats (which are discussed in more detail in the research report).

Table 1. Estimated expenditure on social assistance and numbers of recipients, OECD countries 1980-1992

Country	Total social assistance expenditure as a % of GDP, 1992	Total social assistance expenditure as a % of social security, 1992	Change in SA spending as % of social security Index 1980/1992[1] 1980 = 100	Individual beneficiaries of social assistance[2] as a % of national population 1992	Change in SA beneficiaries as % of population Index 1980/1992[1] 1980 = 100
Australia	6.8	90.3	134[3]	17.8	131
Austria	1.2	6.7	117	4.8	92
Belgium	0.7	3.0	129	3.6[4]	189
Canada	2.5	18.9	96	15.1[4]	135
Denmark	1.4	7.8	-	8.3	-
Finland	0.4	2.1[4]	240	9.2	265
France	2.0	6.4	184	2.3	296
Germany	2.0	11.9[5]	167	6.8	172
Greece	0.1[5]	0.9[5]	-	0.7	-
Iceland	0.2	1.2	-	3.7	-
Ireland	5.1	41.2[4]	133	12.4	142
Italy	3.3	9.1	100	4.6	135
Japan	0.3	3.7	51	0.7	59
Luxembourg	0.5	1.4	-	2.7	-
Netherlands	2.2	10.9	131	3.7	143
New Zealand	13.0	100.0	137	25.0	82
Norway	0.9	4.8	191[3]	4.0	271
Portugal	0.4	3.8	167	2.1	241
Spain	1.1	8.4	403[3]	2.7	-
Sweden	1.5	6.7	146	6.8	164
Switzerland	0.8	1.8	-	2.4	130
Turkey	0.5	-	-	-	-
United Kingdom	4.1	33.0	151	15.3	177
United States	3.7	39.8	136	17.5	117

Notes:
- Indicates that information is not available.
1. Increase to 1991 or 1990 where no data for 1992
2. Excluding housing assistance
3. 1982-1992
4. 1991
5. 1990

Source: Eardley *et al.* 1996, Chapter 2, derived from data supplied by national official or academic respondents. Denominators are from the OECD Household Transfer Database, except for Australia, Iceland, Luxembourg and Portugal (1990 onwards), Belgium (1985 onwards) - where national government calculations of social security expenditure used. These different denominators can affect the percentages shown.

The share of total social security expenditure devoted to social assistance in 1992 was less than 10 per cent in two-thirds of the countries, and under 5 per cent in several countries. The latter include Greece and Portugal, where provision is non-existent or minimal, Japan and Luxembourg, where nationally regulated schemes exist but are overshadowed by other social programmes, and Switzerland, where assistance is highly localised and discretionary. By contrast, the English-speaking countries (including bilingual Canada) led the field in spending, both in terms of GDP and as a proportion of overall social security expenditure, and also had the highest percentages of their populations in receipt of assistance. Australia and New Zealand are clearly suigeneris: since they have no social insurance benefits their means tested systems serve both poverty alleviation and more general redistributive objectives. The group of high spenders on social assistance is similar to those to whom Esping-Andersen (1990), in his well-known typology of welfare state regimes, awards low 'decommodification' scores. It maps less easily, however, onto his clustering of 'liberal' regimes, since this includes both Japan and Switzerland, who are among the lowest spenders on assistance.

If we look at proportionate increases in spending over the 1980s a somewhat different picture emerges. It was in Spain, Norway and Finland that the biggest relative increases took place. In Spain this was partly the result of the introduction of the Ingreso Minimo in its various forms in most of the autonomous regions during the period. In the Nordic countries, however, it was a more direct reflection of recession and unemployment. Finland, in particular has suffered a major recession since 1989, aggravated by loss of trade with the former Soviet Union.

Growth in the numbers of recipients over the 1980s followed a similar pattern, though with France and Belgium also among the leaders. In France this reflected the introduction in 1989 of the Revenu Minimum d'Insertion (RMI), while in Belgium there were substantial increases across all their assistance benefits, including those for disabled people and the aged. Although Sweden was not amongst those exhibiting the highest growth up to 1992, unemployment has risen rapidly since then and by 1994 just over 8 per cent of the population were in receipt of some social assistance. After Australia and New Zealand the highest proportion in receipt of social assistance was in the United Kingdom, where one person in six in the population was covered by Income Support.

However, more relevant in looking at welfare-to-work policies than the salience of social assistance generally is its importance for those people of workforce age who would normally be expected to be active in the labour market. How many of these are among assistance recipients is clearly influenced not only by variation in the levels of unemployment in general and long-term unemployment in particular, but also by the coverage and level of social insurance benefits for the unemployed. Table 2 gives some background data on unemployment and briefly outlines the conditions of duration for unemployment insurance in the OECD countries.

It is not immediately obvious from inspection of the table that there is a close relationship between the availability of unemployment insurance benefits and the long-term unemployment rate. There are several countries, for example where around with one-third of all those unemployed have been out of work for a year or more, including Australia, France, the Netherlands and New Zealand, but the availability and duration of unemployment insurance varies substantially between them. Also, in Scandinavia, Sweden, which has experienced a substantial increase in unemployment and has fairly extensive unemployment insurance has still managed to keep long -term unemployment relatively low, whereas the proportion of long-term unemployed in Finland has climbed rapidly from only around 9 per cent in 1991. Clearly the availability of unemployment insurance is only one element among many which could be influencing levels of unemployment.

Information is sparse on the proportion of assistance recipients in different countries who are classified as unemployed. Among those for which data were available, this appeared to vary in 1992 from relatively few in Luxembourg and Portugal to about one-third in the UK, half in Canada and Ireland, two-thirds in the Netherlands and nearly all in Sweden. The types of unemployed recipients of social assistance also differ: about two-thirds of social assistance recipients in the Nordic countries, for example, are young single persons who have not established entitlement to insurance benefits. By contrast, in the UK, couples with children are the largest group of unemployed recipients of social assistance.

As the chapter discusses later, countries vary in the extent to which (in the Canadian parlance) they regard lone parents as 'employables'. In 1992, lone parents formed a relatively large group of assistance beneficiaries in the USA, Canada, the UK and New Zealand, reflecting in part their incidence in the populations, and were significant also in Australia and Finland. Elsewhere they made fewer demands on social assistance, for reasons which vary according to the country, but include low numbers, their rate of labour market participation and the relative success of other income maintenance systems in supporting separated parents

Table 2. Unemployment and unemployment insurance in the OECD countries

	Unemployment rate[1] 1994 %	Long-term unemployment rate[2] 1993 %	Duration of unemployment insurance 1994
Australia	9.7	36.5	No unemployment insurance
Austria	4.4	-	5-12 months, then unemployment assistance
Belgium	12.9	52.9	15 months, plus 3 months per year of employment. Unlimited for those who worked 20 years or more, or one-third incapacitated
Canada	10.4	11.4	Maximum of 50 weeks, according to previous employment and local unemployment rate
Denmark	12.1	25.2	Up to 2.5 years
Finland	18.4	30.6	2 years. Indefinite flat-rate benefit thereafter, but lower than social assistance
France	12.2	34.2	Maximum of 60 months
Germany	9.6	40.3	17-52 weeks depending on contributions, or 104 weeks for older workers. Unemployment assistance unlimited in principle
Greece	9.6	50.9	Maximum of 12 months
Iceland	4.7	-	Up to 180 days in a 12 month period. Entitlement based on having worked 425 hours in the previous 12 months
Ireland	14.2	59.1	Maximum of 15 months
Italy	11.3	57.7	If redundant, up to 270 days. Otherwise up to 6 months
Japan	2.9	17.2	90-300 days, depending on contributions
Luxembourg	3.0	32.4	365 days in a 24 month period. Further 6-12 months for those aged over 50
Netherlands	7.6	52.3	6 months if covered for 26 out of previous 52 weeks, or up to 4.5 years if employed for 3 out of 5 previous years
New Zealand	8.1	33.2	No insurance
Norway	5.4	27.2	Up to 186 weeks, depending on contributions
Portugal	6.9	43.4	10-30 months, depending on age
Spain	24.2	50.1	Maximum of 24 months
Sweden	8.0	10.9	300 days maximum, or up to 450 days for those aged 55-65
Switzerland	4.7	20.2	Maximum of 250 days if contribution paid for 1.5 years
Turkey	10.9	-	Termination benefit available for a short time on redundancy
UK	9.2	42.5	12 months. From 1996 insurance element of Jobseekers Allowance only available for 6 months
USA	6.1	11.7	Up to 26 weeks, extended in some states and depending on unemployment rate, to up to 1 year

Notes:

1. Commonly used definitions: percentage of total workforce
2. Unemployed for more than 12 months, percentage of total unemployed
3. 1991

Sources: OECD (1994b, 1995a, 1995b); Eardley *et al.*, 1996

with children. Nevertheless, they made up a significant proportion
of all assistance claimants in a number of countries. In the
Netherlands they made up nearly half of all those receiving
General Assistance (ABW) and around 4 per cent of
Unemployment Assistance (RWW) recipients . Other countries
with substantial assistance receipt by lone parents included
Canada (around 27 per cent), Denmark (22 per cent), Austria
(around 20 per cent) and Belgium, Germany and the UK (all
around 18 per cent). In the USA, recipients of Aid to Families
with Dependent Children (AFDC), most of whom are lone parents, made up about 30 per cent of all assistance programme
recipients.

Variation in the composition of assistance populations may be
both an influence on and a consequence of work incentive policies. We now move on to discuss how different countries build in
these incentive structures into their social assistance arrangements

Incentive structures in social assistance

There are four main features of income support programmes that
are typically used to encourage independence through the labour
market, representing both 'carrot' and 'stick' approaches: Job
search tests: recipients may be required to be available for or
actively seek employment, with possible sanctions for non-compli
ance. Financial incentives: payments and taper rates may be
designed to ensure that full (or in some cases part) time employment is more financially attractive than income support. Policies
here may include back-to-work bonuses to help with the costs of
taking up work, and earnings credits. Labour market assistance:
recipients may be offered voluntary or compulsory training or
work experience. Support services: recipients with dependent
children may have access to free or subsidised child care services
to enable them to take paid work.

There are, of course, many other aspects of benefit rules
which can affect workforce participation. It is a well-known feature of means-tested systems, for example, that among couples
the labour force behaviour of partners may be affected by the substitution effects of the benefit withdrawal rate - the 'perverse additional worker effect' (Scherer, 1978; Bradbury, 1993). Thus,
recent reforms to the Australian income support scheme include
a partial individualisation of the family means test, in order to
improve work force incentives for second earners in couples
(Saunders, 1995). All the other OECD countries continue to base
their income tests on the earnings of both partners in a couple,
even where, as in countries such as Sweden, eligibility is

notionally based on the individual. Other factors such as whether universal child benefits are counted in the means tests, the way benefits are administered and the ease by which claimants are transferred from out-of-work benefits to in-work benefits can all also influence the willingness of recipients to move into work. Here, however, the focus is on the key incentive policies outlined above, and in particular the first two - job search requirements and financial incentives.

Job search requirements

How far do different countries insist that recipients of means-tested social assistance must seek work, and to whom and under what conditions do these rules apply? First, it appears that the great majority of countries have some form of requirement that recipients register as unemployed and establish that they are actively looking for work, although people may be exempted on grounds of age or lone parenthood. In Canada a strong distinction is made between the 'employable' and the 'unemployable', to whom different rules apply, while in several states of the USA, General Assistance is simply not available to able-bodied single people or couples without children - surely the strongest possible expression of the requirement to be actively seeking work. In Japan, in Iceland outside Reykjavik and in Switzerland it appears that the requirement to seek work is not a formal rule, but there are strong expectations that individuals will make full use of their capacities. The extent of exemptions from the work test is another reason why in some countries very few assistance recipients are 'employables': in Luxembourg, for example less than 10 per cent of the already small number of social assistance recipients are required to be available for work.

Although the presence of activity tests within social assistance is widespread, it is difficult to determine how vigorously they are enforced. In the UK, there has been increasing policy emphasis on enforcing job-search activity in recent years (Bryson and Jacobs, 1992), while in Australia too the Working Nation reforms have involved more intensive case management of unemployed people as part of the 'job compact'. In some continental European countries, on the other hand, in spite of the introduction of 'insertion' programmes aimed particularly at young people, it appears that monitoring of job-seeking activity has moved little beyond the routine. Most social assistance schemes have some form of sanctions if claimants do not fulfil the work test, generally involving full or partial loss of benefits for defined periods. There is very little information available, however, from most countries about how of ten these sanctions are applied or how effective they are judged to be.

For lone parents, exposure to work or activity tests mainly depends on the age of their youngest child. The most liberal pro visions apply in Ireland, the United Kingdom, Australia and New Zealand, where lone parents are not required to seek work until their youngest child is sixteen or over. Requirements vary across provinces of Canada, from the most restrictive (six months) to the more generous (twelve years). Germany is also relatively liberal in this respect, as lone parents must normally seek part-time work when their youngest child is at school, and full-time work when the child is fourteen or over. Several countries expect lone parents to be available for work once the youngest child reaches either school or pre-school age. Thus in the Netherlands the qualifying is five years, while in Austria and Finland it is three. Sweden and Denmark - two of the countries where women's overall labour market participation is particularly high - make little distinction between lone parents and other assistance recipients in terms of activity testing. In both countries, however, municipalities are required to provide child care for lone parents looking for work, and rules can be applied with discretion to suit individual circum-stances. In France too, the extent to which lone parents receiving the RMI would be expected to engage in insertion activities varies both by departements and according to individual circumstances.

Income tests and tapers

Table 3 outlines the key features of the income tests for unem-ployed people and lone parents in social assistance schemes. Nearly half the countries do not apply a direct disregard to earn-ings, or only do this on a discretionary basis - mainly the Scandinavian countries and others where assistance is or has been residual. Where levels are stated clearly, disregards appear to be lowest in the United States (other than for Food Stamps), followed by Belgium and the United Kingdom. Disregards seem to be most extensive in Ireland, Australia and New Zealand.

Virtually all social assistance schemes operate an income test with a withdrawal rate of 100 per cent for the unemployed and lone parents. The exceptions are Australia, New Zealand, Ireland for lone parents since July 1994, and the United States, where lower withdrawal rates operate on earnings, and Food Stamps are reduced by only 30 per cent of net income. Arrangements in Australia and New Zealand appear to be the most liberal, although this reflects the absence of social insurance benefits. Also, in these countries, unlike most, income is counted gross

Table 3. Incentive structures in social assistance income tests, 1994*

	Earnings disregards	Benefit withdrawal rate
Australia	For unemployment payments, basic free area of £14pw, plus earnings disregard of £14pw for singles and £12pw for each member of a couple. Earnings credit of £240. From 1995, free area to be reduced to £14 - but see changes to withdrawal rate. Also partial individualisation of structure. Based on gross income	For unemployed, 50% for first £19 per week, and then 100%. From 1995, 50% between £14 and £33 per week, and then 30%
Austria	Work expenses can be deducted, but no specific income disregard	100%
Belgium	Minimex: general disregard of £17pm for families with children, £8pm for couples without children, £14pm for singles. Additional earnings disregard of £106pm for first year of claiming, reducing over time	100%
Canada	Partial exemption of earned income (variable)	100%
Denmark	Discretionary guideline of up to £136 per month, but rarely applied. Based on gross income from 1994	100%
Finland	Local and rarely applied directives - £30-£50 per month of net income	100%
France	RMI: Earnings disregard of 50% of net wage	100%
Germany	30-50% of scale rate for head of household (£45-75 per month net)	100%
Iceland	No earnings disregards	100%
Ireland	Daily rate of Unemployment Assistance, plus £15 per day worked. £31 per week for lone parents	Normally 100%. 50% for lone parents from July 1994
Italy	Discretionary	100%
Japan	£27-80 net per month depending on family type	100%
Luxembourg	Up to 20% of household benefit rate - £88 per month for single person	100%
Netherlands	25% of net earnings up to 15% of benefit rate. Extra 15% for lone parents	100%
New Zealand	£20 net per week or £24 pw with children. Extra £8pw for lone parents with child care costs	30% between disregard and £33 pw, then 70%
Norway	Earnings disregard on Transitional Allowance only. None for Social Economic Assistance	100%
Portugal	No earnings disregards	100%
Spain	No earnings disregards	100%
Sweden	No earnings disregards	100%
Switzerland	No formal earnings disregards (though local rules may apply)	100%
Turkey	No earnings disregards	100%
United Kingdom	£5 per week for singles and each member of couple; £15pw for lone parents, couples under 60 on Income Support for two or more years, carers, and people receiving disability premium. Special rules for childminders, and income from subtenants and lodgers. Other disregards for lone parents under Family Credit	100%
United States	AFDC: £19 per month, plus any Earned Income Tax Credit received. Food Stamps: £80pm, plus 20% of household earnings, EITC	AFDC: 66.7% for

* Monetary units expressed in rounded sterling purchasing power parities.

rather than net of tax, so that the effective withdrawal rate is increased over income ranges where there is also a tax liability. The change to unemployment assistance arrangements in Australia from 1995 has substantially lowered the withdrawal rate at higher levels of earnings, although disregards have been reduced at the same time.

Benefit replacement rates

So far, this chapter has concentrated on the rules of social assistance programmes in different countries. The impact of these rules and their implications for behaviour can to some extent, however, be given a quantitative value through the calculation of replacement rates and effective marginal tax rates. It has often rightly been pointed out, of course, that the factors influencing labour market decision making are more complex than simple rational calculations of financial advantage, even if benefit recipients were in a position to make accurate calculations of this kind (see, for example, McLaughlin, Millar and Cooke, 1989). There are also difficulties involved in comparing benefit replacement rates across countries, since neither gross nor disposable income are independent of the processes of redistribution in different countries (Whiteford, 1995). Nevertheless, such a comparison does provide useful indicators of the incentive or disincentive effects built in to the structure of assistance payments.

Economic theory distinguishes between two factors that may be relevant to individual labour market decisions - the income effect and the substitution effect. The existence of social assistance means that a given level of income can be maintained without participation in the labour market (the income effect), while the withdrawal of benefits operates as a tax on earnings and reduces the cost of not earning (the substitution effect). However, if the level of social assistance is below the target level of income for an individual, the withdrawal rate may actually encourage further labour market effort, since the individual will have to work more hours to reach their income target (the income effect of the withdrawal rate).

Replacement rates are usually calculated by comparing the levels of benefit to some measure of income in work, thus showing what percentage of earnings is 'replaced' by benefits. They can thus be altered either by changing the rates of benefit or by altering the level of disposable income in work. In a number of countries, there are also important schemes to provide in-work benefits, with examples including Family Credit in the United Kingdom, Additional Family Payment in Australia, Family Income

Supplement in Ireland, the Earned Income Tax Credit in the United States, Family Support and the Guaranteed Minimum Family Income in New Zealand and a variety of Federal and provincial supplements in Canada. It is notable that these in-work benefits are most common in the English-speaking countries with extensive assistance schemes, and are mainly directed to families with children, although in a significant move the United Kingdom has begun the piloting of an income supplementation scheme for persons without children (Earnings Top-up). Such in-work benefits are an important component of the armoury of potential programmes to encourage workforce participation. However, the replacement rates that follow do not include calculation of the value of these in-work benefits, as the research was restricted to comparing those on social assistance with those on average earnings, and these programmes generally do not operate at that high an income level (see Whiteford and Bradshaw, 1994, for an analysis of the effect of in-work benefits for lone parents).

Table 4. shows estimates of replacement rates of social assistance (before housing costs) for a range of family types.[2] They are calculated by comparing the level of disposable income of persons receiving social assistance (using purchasing power parities) with the disposable incomes of the same household type where the head is earning average male earnings.[3] It needs to be emphasised that in countries with widely varying local assistance rates, the figures apply only in the specified location. Four separate states of the USA are included in order to illustrate the range of outcomes in difference jurisdictions.

For single people and couples (aged 35 years), replacement rates were very low in Greece and in Texas and Florida in the USA . They were also quite low in Pennsylvania, Germany, Canada (for single people), and the United Kingdom. Replacement rates were highest in Switzerland (Fribourg), Sweden, the Netherlands, Norway (Oslo) and Denmark. For couples with children the highest replacement rates were in the same countries (followed by Australia). For most other countries the presence of children raised the replacement rate substantially - to more than 100 per cent in Sweden and Switzerland. Overall, replacement rates in the UK were around two-third s of the way down the overall 'league table', before taking housing costs into account.

The effect of introducing housing costs is generally to increase replacement rates where there is additional housing cost assistance. In the case of Austria (Salzberg) and Finland the jump in replacement rates was quite substantial. In other cases, notably New York, Greece and Canada (for single people), replacement

Table 4. Estimated replacement ratios: social assistance as a percentage of net disposable income at average earnings, OECD countries 1992 (before housing costs)

	Single (35)	Couple (35)	Couple (35)+ 1 child (7)	Couple (35)+ 2 children (7, 14)	Lone parent + 1 child (3)
Australia	31	54	60	67	43
Austria	26	35	46	58	34
Belgium	39	47	52	53	56
Canada	19	40	47	53	45
Denmark	54	71	73	78	67
Finland	23	40	51	65	67
France	26	34	41	47	36
Germany	17	28	36	44	33
Ireland	29	41	47	55	44
Italy	42	56	65	64	56
Japan	25	36	46	58	44
Luxembourg	43	52	58	62	46
Netherlands	58	77	78	81	69
New Zealand	27	46	58	63	49
Norway	54	72	64	84	58
Portugal	44	43	45	45	68
Spain	26	28	32	36	35
Sweden	58	88	86	102	77
Switzerland	62	89	91	102	77
UK	21	31	42	51	38
USA - New York	27	39	52	62	48
USA - Pennsylvania	15	25	40	44	20
USA - Texas	6	12	23	43	28
USA - Florida	7	14	48	68	45

Note: Greece not included as it has no recurring general social assistance benefit. Information not available for Iceland and Turkey.

Source: Eardley *et al.* (1996).

rates fall sharply, reflecting high housing net costs in relation to the help available through social assistance. In the UK, replacement rates rise somewhat after housing costs, but its overall positio n in the ranking does not change much.

Replacement rates for lone parents are generally lower than for couples with children if the lone parent does not have to pay for child care when working. The exceptions are Belgium, Portugal and Switzerland. However, if the working lone parent has to pay for care of a child aged under three their replacement rates increase compared with a one-earner couple not requiring child care.

The finding that replacement rates after housing costs for some categories of recipients are over 100 per cent implies that beneficiaries are actually better-off than average full-time workers. However, there is a sense in which these figures may not accurately characterise the relative advantage of employment compared to benefit receipt. First, where high replacement rates are a consequence of taking into account housing costs, the calculations are based on a number of unavoidable assumptions which may not always emulate the real world. Secondly, in some countries employer social security contributions may have an impact on wages, so that gross and net earnings are systematically lower in countries with high levels of employer social security taxes than in countries with low or no employer social security contributions. It could be argued an individual in work is accruing entitlements to more generous pensions in retirement, while a recipient of social assistance is receiving no such future benefit. While it is difficult to put a value on such future benefits (Stahlberg, 1986), they imply that effective replacement rates are lower than those shown in this table .

Average effective tax rates and the poverty trap

The other component of an analysis of financial work incentives is the substitution effect associated with the withdrawal of benefits. This is usually analysed by looking at 'effective marginal tax rates' (EMTRs), which are estimated as the sum of the withdrawal rate on benefits and its interactions with any other form of benefit withdrawal, including tax and social insurance contributions. EM TRs are usually estimated for a small change in labour supply at the margin, looking for example, at what happens if incomes increase by £1 per week.

Here we look at average effective tax rates (AEMTRs), which are estimated over a wider range of income - the difference between zero earnings and average male earnings. This is likely to be a more realistic illustration of the choices available, since people cannot normally vary their work effort by £1 increments. Averaging marginal tax rates tends to disguise narrow income ranges, whe re marginal rates may be particularly high, but where these ranges are narrow the number of people directly affected by them is like ly to be small. This measure provides an indication of the disincentive effects of moving from a situation of complete 'dependence' on social assistance to a full-time job at average earnings. It thus gives an idea of the extent to which different assistance regimes have 'poverty traps' built into them. The calculation takes account of all relevant cash benefits available, plus changes in hous ing and health costs, as well as child care costs, where relevant.[4]

Table 5 shows average effective tax rates, again only before housing costs. Effective tax rates are lowest where benefit levels are lowest, since there is less assistance to be withdrawn. Correspondingly, effective tax rates are highest where benefits are relatively high, and exceed 100 per cent in those countries where replacement rates also exceeded 100 per cent. Effective tax rates are higher for people without children than for those without, although in many cases they are lower for lone parents than for unemployed couples with children. In a number of countries, child care costs add to effective tax rates. Housing costs also tend to increase effective tax rates in all countries apart from Portugal, Spain, and the USA. It should be emphasized again that in countries with local assistance schemes the AETRs apply in these areas and not necessarily nationally.

AETRs are different from replacement ratios, but comparison of Tables 4 and 5 and shows that the relation between the two is fairly constant, both between countries and across family types. The tables show that many of the schemes involve effective marginal tax rates at a level which could act as a disincentive to return to work. The UK, in this respect, performs relatively well, with marginal tax rates below the average for most family types.

Discussion: trends in work incentive policies

It was suggested at the beginning of this chapter that social assistance policy in most countries is increasingly directed towards getting employable recipients off benefits and into work. The preceding discussion has shown that while the general aim of limiting welfare dependency is broadly common to the industrialised countries, there is still considerable variation in detailed policy approaches across the major forms of assistance regime. On this basis it is possible to group countries into four sets.

Table 5. Average effective tax rates for assistance recipients moving into work on average earnings, OECD countries 1992 (before housing costs)

	Single (35)	Couple (35)	Couple (35)+ 1 child (7)	Couple (35)+ 2 children (7, 14)	Lone parent + 1 child (3)
Australia	48	63	68	73	54
Austria	50	55	60	65	50
Belgium	61	62	63	60	70
Canada	40	53	56	59	57
Denmark	76	82	83	85	81
Finland	38	52	58	69	71
France	47	50	53	54	35
Germany	49	51	54	58	57
Ireland	54	57	61	67	66
Italy	69	68	74	73	69
Japan	36	41	51	61	55
Luxembourg	58	60	63	62	52
Netherlands	78	87	87	88	81
New Zealand	46	61	70	74	63
Norway	68	79	79	87	64
Portugal	54	53	52	50	72
Spain	40	39	42	45	54
Sweden	69	91	89	102	69
Switzerland	74	92	94	102	83
UK	41	47	54	60	57
USA - New York	44	55	65	72	69
USA - Pennsylvania	28	38	53	66	59
USA - Texas	34	46	72	85	76
USA - Florida	7	14	48	68	45

Note: Greece not included as it has no recurring general social assistance benefit. Information not available for Iceland and Turkey.

Source: Eardley *et al.* (1996).

Countries with a past record of full employment (the Nordic countries, Switzerland, Austria and Japan): here work incentives have no t been a matter of major political debate (though they are emerging as such in Denmark and Sweden). Such policy shifts as have occur red in the Nordic countries are primarily of the incentive type, including child care provision, the Youth Allowance programme in Denmark and 'extraordinary work' programmes in Norway.

The limited social assistance regimes of southern Europe, plus Turkey: here the debate on work disincentives is less relevant. Social assistance for people working age is vestigial and its impact on local labour markets likewise slight. There has been some experimentation with work and integration schemes in Italy, Portugal and Spain, but their implementation has been patchy.

The remaining EU member states (excluding the UK and Ireland): here a growing concern with the 'new poverty' and social exclusion has fuelled experiments with integration programmes. The Revenu Minimum d'Insertion in France, Minimex in Belgium, and the re-integration programme in the Revenu Minimim Garanti in Luxembourg have all targeted young unemployed people and tied improved benefit levels to insertion in training and work experience schemes. However, this combined carrot and stick approach appears to have had only a marginal impact. In the Netherlands, with more generous benefits and typically weak links between social security and the labour mark et, there has been some tightening of work requirements for lone parents. Germany has not developed special insertion schemes, preferring to rely on its already well-established mechanisms for training and work placements.

The extensive social assistance states of the English-speaking world (including bi-lingual Canada): in these countries the relation between assistance and the labour market has assumed greater importance in policy debates. Yet even here Ireland is an exception, wi th few major proposals or policy changes. New Zealand has opted for a variety of measures to make claiming less attractive, notably absolute cuts in benefit levels. The remaining countries in this group have adopted a mixture of carrot and stick. The carrots include higher benefits and partial individualisation of income support for couples (Australia); a substantial extension of Earned Income

Tax Credit, more generous tapers and help with child care costs for lone parents (the USA); extra income disregards within Family Credit and a package of back-to-work provisions (the UK); and, in Canada, 'employment enhancing measures', a new child tax benefit an d time-limited wage supplements. The sticks have included more intensive requirements for job-search activity in all countries in th is group. In addition, Britain has introduced the new Jobseeker's Allowance, which further reduces the insurance element of unemployment protection and enhances job search requirements. In the USA, following the mid-term elections, debate and policy proposals became more punitive, with Republican congressional leaders calling for time-limited benefits for AFDC claimants, without federally-funded work programmes, and for public orphanages for those children whose parents cannot support them.

Overall, the pattern of responses to common economic and social pressures is complex. In many respects the differences are to be expected, given differences in labour markets, social assistance regimes, political complexion and broader social traditions. The prominence of work incentives in policy debates is certainly greater in countries with greater reliance on social assistance. Yet even wi thin this group policy approaches have been fairly distinct. It is also difficult to discern clear evidence of an association between the level of replacement rates or the stringency of work tests and the level of unemployment. If anything there is a tendency for countries paying higher social assistance benefits to have tougher work tests and lower levels of unemployment. Thus the Nordic countries tend to have relatively high levels of social assistance, high replacement rates but quite a severe means test with little or no disregards and strong arrangements to encourage labour participation - even by lone parents. It is perhaps also significant that these countries have relatively small-scale and locally-administered social assistance schemes. It may be difficult to combine strong labour participation policies when social assistance benefits are relatively low and also represent substantial elements of the benefit system for the unemployed. Alternatively, it may be easier to have benefits which are relatively high when they are not an important component of the benefit system for the unemployed.

Notes

1. The research was commissioned by the UK Department of Social Security, with additional support from the Social Policy Division of the OECD. Any views expressed are, however, those of the author and not necessarily those of either of the commissioning bodies. Tables 1, 2, 4 and 5 are © Crown Copyright 1996. The author wishes to thank the Controller of Her Majesty's Stationery Office and the Department of Social Security for permission to use this information. The tables must not be reproduced in any form without the permission of the Department of Social Security.

2. Benefit replacement rates are based on model family policy simulation techniques. Information provided by national expert informants allowed for the collection of data on earnings; national and local taxation; insurance contributions and benefits; contingency a nd assistance benefits; health, education and child care costs; and housing costs, for ten family types living in a specified location in each country. For details of the model family matrix exercise and discussion of its limitations, see Chapter 6 of Eardley et al., 1996.

3. Using average male wages probably results in the understatement of the real replacement rates of individuals in each country who are actually receiving social assistance, since it could be expected that many such individuals would earn less - perhaps substantially less - than average male earnings if they gained a job. This would be even more likely in the case of female lone parents. This abstraction is unavoidable since it was only possible to collect earnings data for cases at the one income level. In any case, the dispersion of earnings varies across countries.

4. An average effective tax rate (AETR) can be defined as follows:

$$AETR = \frac{\delta I \times 100}{\delta E}$$

where δI is the change in disposable income and δE is the change in earnings.

References

Bradbury, B. (1993) 'Family assistance, replacement rates and the unemployment of married men', Australian Bulletin of Labour, vol.1 9, no.12, pp114-132.

Bryson, A. and Jacobs, J. (1992) Policing the Workshy, Aldershot, Avebury. Commission on Social Justice (1994) Social Justice: Strategies for Renewal, London, Vintage.

Dean, H. and Taylor Gooby, P. (1992) Dependency Culture, Hemel Hempstead, Harvester Wheatsheaf.

Eardley, T., Bradshaw, J., Ditch, J., Gough. I.& Whiteford, P. (1996) Social Assistance in OECD Countries, Department of Social Security Research Report, London, HMSO.

Esping-Andersen, G. (1990) The Three Worlds of Welfare Capitalism, Cambridge, Polity Press.

Field, F. (1995) Making Welfare Work: Reconconstructing Welfare for the Millenium, London, Institute of Community Studies.

McLaughlin, E., Millar, J. and Cooke, K. (1989) Work and Welfare Benefits, Aldershot, Avebury.

Organisation for Economic Co-operation and Development (1988) The Future of Social Protection, Paris, OECD.

Organisation for Economic Co-operation and Development (1994a) New Orientations for Social Policy, Social Policy Studies No.12, Paris, OECD.

Organisation for Economic Co-operation and Development (1994b) Employment Outlook, July 1994, Paris, OECD.

Organisation for Economic Co-operation and Development (1995a) Employment Outlook, July 1995, Paris, OECD.

Organisation for Economic Co-operation and Development (1995b) OECD Economic Outlook, December 1995, Paris, OECD.

Saunders, P. (1995) 'Improving work incentives in a means-tested welfare system: the 1994 Australian social security reforms', Fiscal Studies, vol.16, no.2, pp47-70.

Scherer, P. (1978) 'The perverse additional worker effect', Australian Economic Papers, vol.17, no.32.

Stahlberg, A.-C. (1986) 'Social welfare policy - nothing but insurances?', Discussion Paper 6/1986, Stockholm, Swedish Institute for Social Research.

Whiteford, P. (1995) The Use of Replacement Ratios in International Comparisons of Benefit Systems, Social Policy Research Centre Discussion Paper No.54, Sydney, University of New South Wales.

Whiteford, P. and Bradshaw, J. (1994) 'Benefits and incentives for lone parents: a comparative analysis', International Social Security Review, vols.3-4/94, pp69-89.

15 Social Security in the Czech Republic: The Market, Paternalism or Social Democracy?

Mita Castle-Kanerova

The current debates about social policy in the Czech Republic highlight the increasing political significance of welfare in the East European transition to post-communism. From being an adjunct of economic reform when Klaus' Civic Democratic Party came to power in 1992 (rejecting the reform programme promulgated by the Federal government in 1989), social policy has become central to recasting the republic's political economy. As an election looms, Czechs voters are confronting issues similar to those faced by the European Union (EU) as economic uncertainty increases under the pressures of new technologies and global markets. But the dramatic changes experienced by the Czech Republic has made the question of whether and how an active social policy can co-exist with market-based restructuring much sharper and led to extensive debate over the nature of current government proposals and the future patterning of welfare provision.

Historically social democratic thinking has a strong tradition in the Republic and this, many hope, may foster a culturally specific development where policies of marketization are steered in the direction of 'prosperity without poverty'. Although this may sound naive to a western observer, the climate of change in the Czech Republic is such that these deeply felt traditions combined with an almost palpable fear of a return to paternalist 'socialism' cannot be ignored. Elsewhere in East Central Europe, moreover, there is growing evidence of a decline in support for pro-market political parties (Lewis, 1994; Bakos, 1994) and a growing realisation that the middle classes have not experienced the anticipated improvements in their living standards (Mokrzycki, 1991). Equally significant is the evidence of continued trust in the traditional institutions of state authority among the 'ambivalent citizens of the new democracies' (Rose & Haerpher, 1994).

In the Republic, the Klaus government claims to embody a radical departure from the centralised paternalism and state monopoly of the recent past, manifest not only in its neo-liberal economic policies, but in the sphere of social policy. Yet many opposition groups, whilst critical of economic developments, have attacked the government's social policy proposals for retaining central controls reminiscent of past paternalistic practices. It could be argued, however, that in many respects the social democratic slant of the government's social policy recommendations clash with its neo-liberal stance and commitment to privatisation. These apparent contradictions and the debate over the role of social policy in the new Republic are, perhaps, most visible, in the new social security measures which came into effect in January 1996.

Drawing on government documents and the emerging media debate about social policy issues, this chapter provides a preliminary assessment of this new system of social protection. It will first consider the socio-economic climate against which the new system of social security is being introduced. It will then outline its main features and briefly review the more general dilemmas over social welfare faced by the Czech Republic. The author acknowledges that the empirical base is somewhat narrow and its use not made easier by the difficulties of accessing reliable information across Eastern Europe. What is of importance, however, is the need to shift discussion away from the simple but tempting model of change from so-called 'totalitarianism' to 'democracy' and consider the complex ways in which notions of 'residualisation' and 'redistributive justice' cut across each other in a melting pot of policies.

The socio-economic context

In contrast to the vicissitudes experienced elsewhere, the Czech economy has remained remarkably healthy since the collapse of communism in 1989. According to official data, overall living standards in the Republic have risen while unemployment is far lower than in other East European countries, or in the EU as a whole. Average monthly incomes increased from 10.6 to 11.4 per cent between 1992 and 1994 (taking into account the index of expenditure), and by 6 per cent in 1995 (Socialni Politika 1/1995; Holanova, 1995). Unemployment has declined from 4.5 per cent in 1992 to 3.5 per cent in 1995 (Socialni Politika 1/1995), and the proportion of households below the officially defined social minimum and thus eligible for state income support is relatively low at 5.5 per cent (Zizkova, 1994). Unemployment among women is not significantly higher than among men (52-54 per cent), and the majority remain economically active, with only 5.4 per cent staying at home as housewives (Kalinova, 1995). Indeed, some observers claim that economic reform has strengthened women's labour market position, with 10 per cent seeing an improvement in their economic opportunities (Cermakova, 1995). Changes in the structure of employment, especially a three fold expansion of the tertiary sector between 1989 and 1994 have contributed to this (Tomes, 1995).

On the surface then the Czech experience appears to challenge the notion that East European countries face inevitable hardship on their road to a market economy and that the collapse of communism imposes yet another uniform pattern across the region. The government and its main policy-making arm, the Ministry of Labour and Social Affairs, has claimed much of the credit for the country' s favourable economic record, placing particular emphasis on its active employment policy. This is now disputed, notably by the Social Democrats (Buzkova 1995), and it should be acknowledged that low unemployment is partly a reflection of the low labour costs resulting from the stringent wage controls imposed between 1990 and 1992 under IMF and World Bank pressure and retained until 1995.

Moreover, there are signs that the country's economic profile may not be so secure and it is by no means clear that low unemployment, low inflation and low deficit budgets will remain permanent features of the economy. Non-governmental sources, and the trade unions, in particular project a distinctly less optimistic future. Thus trade union studies suggest the official figure of a 4 per cent growth rate in 1995 reflects a fast, temporary and often uncontrolled influx of foreign capital (sometimes of a speculative nature), with relatively low levels of long term investment. Short term demand has not been matched either by a rise in productivity (which has declined from 39 per cent of the EU level in 1989 to 33 per cent after 1992), or by any regeneration of the domestic productive economy (Pohledy 4/1995). Recent research suggests some 60 per cent of industrial enterprises are not economically viable (Heczko, 1994), and the government's estimate of the numbers of active entrepreneurs in the private sector has also been challenged (Hirsl, 1994). In addition, it is argued that three quarters of the private sector is composed of small businesses with no employees. Recruited primarily from the skilled working classes these small entrepreneurs have little economic clout and their interests are likely to remain those of 'petty bourgeois' artisans. The growth of the entrepreneurial middle strata is still fragile and hampered by high taxation as well as low earnings for the professional groups that do not give rise to savings and thus investment. The long recognised problem of over-employment, with some 20 per cent of the labour force in 'surplus activities' remains unresolved, and criticism of the mismanagement of state properties during privatisation has added to a growing sense of economic unease.

Other economic indicators are also beginning to cause concern. For instance, a number of studies have pointed to significant recent changes in patterns of social differentiation and consumption. The introduction of new tax measures (including VAT) in 1993, for example, was associated with a 20 per cent increase in prices and the simultaneous devaluation of people's savings. Despite counter-vailing measures (notably a 'levelling benefit'), real incomes in 1993 were 21 per cent lower than in 1990 (Hirsl et al., 1995) . By 1994 one survey found 64 per cent of households reported a worsening of their economic situation in comparison to 1989, 20 per cent reported some improvement, and only 9 per cent claimed a significant improvement (Hirsl et al 1995). There is also some evidence to suggest that consumption patterns are beginning to change with families making more use of home produced goods and services, re structuring their outgoings, spending less on culture and sports, and limiting their use of public services. (41 per cent of general households' income goes on food, and among pensioners it is 58.4 per cent, Lidove Noviny, 7.4.1995).

Perhaps more critically there are signs of increasing differentials in people's income and living standards resulting not only from changes in wage levels outside the state sector, but from the composite effects of voucher privatisation and restitution. In terms of wages, a new form of vertical differentiation is emerging. Whilst the top 10 per cent of wage earners saw their incomes rise by 9.6 per cent between 1992 and 1994, the lowest paid 10 per cent of the population experienced a decline of 1.7 per cent. When other assets are taken into account, after only four years of change, inequality in wealth in the Republic resembles that of Britain or the US (Hirsl et al., 1995). In 1993 another new form of differentiation began to emerge, between childless families and those with children. The communist regime had favoured the latter, but now, although population decline has reached an all time low, families are experiencing a decline in their incomes compared to those without children (Hirsl, 1994).

Szalai's (1995) study of the effects of market reforms in Hungary casts some light on the emergence of these apparently new forms of social differentiation and exclusion. Her investigation explodes the myth that the extremes of poverty are a product of recent market reforms. Rather she suggests the old system both promoted an illusion of social integration and enabled an alternative network of proto-market relationships to develop. Hence 'who got what' in the past depended on what the 'parallel' as well as the 'official' society offered and where different individuals and social groups managed to find their niche. Without access to informal networks and the informal economy, the poor under the old system lacked means of protection from hardship. Hence, she argues, those who 'lacked contacts with the informal world' and 'were in the past trapped in socialism have entirely fallen behind the main body of society' (p12). The current marginalization of the poor is therefore an extension of their previous social 'abandonment', and not a new phenomenon. What the old and the new regimes in East Central Europe share, however, is that they both treat the subject of poverty as politically taboo, presenting it as a 'technical matter of distribution' rather than a deeper socio-structural phenomenon (p2).

In the Czech Republic the growth of both old and new forms of inequality and insecurity have been masked by the apparent buoyancy of the economy and its low unemployment levels. But, as several independent observers, have noted this is partly due to the pre-emptive social policy measures introduced by the Federal legislation of 1990. It was then envisaged that those most vulnerable to unemployment would be young people under thirty and young families. Those who found themselves unemployed but had a child under four were offered a parental benefit, non-means tested and slightly higher in value than unemployment benefit (Tomes, 1995). Thus people on parental benefit effectively represent hidden unemployment, and there have been reports that the new Labour Exchanges 'recommend' parental benefit, especially to women with young children, instead of unemployment assistance. The government also seems to be relying on the deterrent effect of low unemployment benefit levels, fixed since 1992 at 60 per cent of average wage for the first three months and 50 per cent for the following three months when entitlement ends (Kalinova, 1995).

Indeed it has been acknowledged that the Republic's uniquely low unemployment levels were part of a governmental strategy to create a favourable social climate for carrying out other reforms (Kalinova, 1995) and thus involved a closely knit economic and employment policy that bore little resemblance to a free market approach. Thus many centrally planned regulations still apply, whilst the afore-mentioned wage regulations effectively lasted until June 1995. There is a degree of openness on the part of the government to admit that this was one means of controlling the pace of reforms and maintaining social peace. What is not so readily admitted is that both social reform and voucher privatisation have been used surreptitiously but deliberately to avert economic crisis.

Voucher privatisation in particular has fulfilled a crucial 'social' role in cushioning the effects of economic transformation. An estimated 70 per cent of the adult Czech population participated and by the end of 1994, one third had sold their shares, making private gains in the region of five times the average salary. This was not, as has sometimes been argued, a reflection of individual enterpreneurialism with long term productive investment in mind, but as a form of financial compensation in times of hardship (Hirsl et al., 1995). Nor should it be a surprise that the main beneficiaries, the new propertied classes, come from the sections of society who had access to material and political means under the communist regime, the nomenklatura and the more successful groups in the 'shadow economy'. Clear but tentative data is emerging to suggest that the nomenklatura has, through the privatisation process , come to occupy the most crucial and dynamic sectors of finance capital such as banking and insurance (Kabele & Potucek, 1994; Brom & Orenstein, 1994). But it is worthwhile noting that its behaviour is not necessarily like that of entrepreneurial classes under mature capitalism. Moreover the blend of these two strata is far from predictable and, rather than forming a 'new grand bourgeoisie ' (Hankiss, 1990), or the socially coherent 'new technocracy' envisaged by Szelenyi (1995), their interests may clash. Further uncertainty arises from the possibility that neo-liberalism is destroying the social and material privileges amassed by some social groups in the past. This view is shared by many, including some Czech governmental spokespeople, who argue that although they have put reasonably efficient systems in place, this may not be sufficiently attractive to the fragile professional middle classes who have been expecting a significant improvement in the quality of their life and who may be even loosing from the reforms. Hence a spate of recent prolonged strikes by doctors and threatened strikes by teachers.

It is in this uncertain environment, with an election looming, that the government has introduced a new social security system. As will be seen this bears many of the hallmarks of the transitional pressures faced throughout East-Central Europe and contains measures designed to encourage self-reliance and promote the state's 'hands off' approach to welfare. But it also marks an attempt to control the 'rampant' forces of the market and contain the possible havoc in people's lives resulting from its unfettered operations.

The new social security system

In the official documentation the new social security system is graphically represented by three Roman columns. The three independent pillars supporting the system are: social insurance, state social support, and social assistance. The social insurance element covers sickness benefit, pensions and the state's employment policy including unemployment benefit and the financing of both the Labour Exchanges and social security administration (Novela Socialniho Pojisteni, 1995). Contributions are compulsory for all those employed, with some exceptions for the self-employed (see below). Many critics insist that this scheme is a form of secondary taxation because it is as yet not financed through an independent Social Fund as promised in the political manifesto of 1992.

The 'second pillar' supporting those whose income falls below the defined social minimum is, in contrast, openly redistributive. The legislative documents declare this is a form of state support for the family, redistributing from those who have to those who have not, and from childless families to those with children. It is estimated that the social support system will affect 60 per cent the citizenry one way or another. (Duvodova Zprava, 1994; Vizek & Dlouhy, 1994; Visek, 1995a). Social assistance, on the other hand, has a residual role, dealing with poverty beyond that dealt with by the other 'two pillars'. It is strictly separated from state support, financed and administered at local level by self-governing authorities (though state grants will be given), and covers individual life situations of both financial and 'non-financial' hardship and need. This element of the new system is the least developed, and has attracted considerable criticism.

Together, however, the three 'pillars' mark a radical departure from the recent past. They also differ from some of the earlier proposals for reform. The communist system of social protection was heavily centralised. Provision was financed from the central budget and all benefits and services were nominally free with an undifferentiated deduction made at source. This system, built in the 1950's when living standards were being maintained through the use of state subsidies as a 'top up' to wages, linked together labour productivity, political loyalty and social security. The centralised wage policy was politically motivated, and bore little relation to either prices or labour market criteria, and sectors of industrial production deemed 'beneficial' to 'socialism' acquired preferential status and remuneration. But the acquisition of non-wage benefits and privileges became an important source of meeting people's needs. For some, this meant turning to the shadow economy; for others it meant dependency on what the state provided. The progressive increase in subsidies for housing and consumer goods, for example, reflected the system's need to legitimise itself and sustain the notion of social progress. For its critics, however, this seriously distorted the concept of welfare and social protection, with subsidies in effect becoming state benefits for the entire population, fostering what many now see as a 'dependency culture'.

The new social security system is being presented as a departure from this state welfare monopoly, designed to disaggregate wages and benefits and establish targeted and means-tested provisions. Responsibility for living standards is 'given back' to the individual, whilst the state retains its responsibility for those who fall through the 'safety net'. In many ways it forms part of a wider process of deregulation of the service sector, subsidy withdrawal and expenditure cuts. For instance, subsidies on public expenditure have been cut from 32 per cent in 1989 to 7 per cent in 1994; public expenditure on social security has fallen from 41.9 per cent to 35.1 per cent and on education from 14.3 per cent to 11.2 per cent in the same period. The health sector, on the other hand, saw an increase in funding from 16.2 per cent to 22.5 per cent as its privatisation got underway (Hirsl et al., 1995).

The new social security scheme itself follows several earlier versions, including those put forward by the Czechoslovak Federal Government of 1990/91 with the joint aim of liberalisation and democratisation. These proposals emphasised the need for separate funding of social security, decentralisation and regular valorisation of pensions and benefits to maintain social cohesion. They also embodied the widespread belief that preserving some elements of egalitarianism, redistribution and social solidarity would smooth the transition towards a new system. The Federal scheme also included a pledge to maintain tripartite discussions in all spheres of social policy, and the trade unions were invited to present their case. But after 1992 financial constrains began to override some of the earlier considerations. Policy-making shifted away from the philosophy of the Civic Forum and the broad political umbrella that formed the government after the Velvet Revolution and two key elements of the early proposals, the separate Social Fund and tripartite discussions, disappeared. There was, however, a real effort to learn from other European social security systems and this has filtered into current legislation. As will be seen this blends social democratic notions derived from Germany, Austria, Switzerland and Scandinavia in the form of social insurance and social support with means-tested social assistance governed by recent British precepts. But although the legislation in place since January 1996 marks the culmination of considerable discussion, it falls short of earlier promises and is not based on a general consensus.

Social insurance

Social insurance was the first of the social security changes to come into effect and had the longest gestation. It is designed to provide benefits during periods of interrupted employment (due to illness or unemployment) and in retirement. Insurance governing pensions is said to be motivated by the need to foster inter-generational solidarity. (It is estimated that by 2010 about 40% of the population will be of pensionable age.) It includes old age pensions, invalidity pensions, and widows and orphans pensions. A measure to raise the retirement age gradually by 2-4 months over the next ten years to 62 years for men and 57 to 61 years for women, depending on the number of children raised, is also in place. It is being argued that this is to bring pensions in line with European standards (Kral & Klimentova, 1995). The old age pension (which absorb 60-70 per cent of the funds) will be valorised in relation to th e growth of average wages (or every time that the cost of living goes up by more than 5 per cent). They are promised to remain at 56 per cent of an individual's net income (Kalinova, 1995; Odpovedi, 1995), but the trade unions and the Social Democrats calculate that this is not the case, with the current value of an old age pension being 43.3 per cent and declining (Arena, 10.4.1996). However, there is a definite tone of appeasement, and the valorisation threshold for old age pensions has been lowered from 10 per cent to 5 per cent in the last six months. Yet the expected deadline of January 1996 was postponed to April, yielding savings of four months.

Sickness benefits include provision for the loss of earnings during maternity leave (28 weeks); due to illness or injury (up to one year); or caring for a member of the family (9 days). It may reach 85 per cent of an individual's earnings ((Kral, 1994). The self-employed will be able to define his/her income level, but this must not be less than 35 per cent of the difference between profits and costs. Their sickness insurance is deemed not to be compulsory from 1.1.1994, but they contribute to other parts of the scheme (Novela, 1995, p47).

The insurance scheme is jointly funded by employees and employers contributions and, for the first time since 1948, the costs are 'transparent'. Employee contributions have been set at 8.75 per cent of individual income (an amendment from January 1996 takes into account income from earning such as financial bonuses or bonuses in kind). An employer pays 26.15 per cent towards the scheme (with a proviso of raising it to 30 per cent under certain circumstance). In terms of individual components employees contribute 1. 2 per cent towards sickness; 6.8 per cent towards pensions; and 0.75 per cent towards the state employment policy. Employers contribute 3.6 per cent towards sickness; 20.4 per cent towards pensions and 2.25 per cent towards employment policy (Novela, 1995). The main bone of contention though is that the social insurance scheme is not managed through a separate Social Fund as promised, but that contributions go into a special treasury account, and are therefore potentially liable to misuse.

State social support

The state social support system was devised to replace the ubiquitous state subsidies of the past and as such was hotly debated in parliament. It provides for nine benefits: income support, child benefit, parental benefit, carer's allowance, housing benefit, maternity grant, allowance to soldiers' families, travel allowance and a funeral grant. Originally all nine were to be provided on a flat rate basis. But in a famous compromise between the four coalition parties in the government in April 1995 child benefit, income support, housing benefit and the travel allowance were subject to means-testing and child benefit was more closely targeted. The scheme is said to be an expression both of the state's support for individuals and families with children and the redistributive role of social security. The Ministry of Labour and Social Affairs claims that the state has the right to expect a contribution from the well off towards the less well off, and from the childless to those with children on the basis of inter-generational solidarity and on the grounds that the children will in future contribute towards the pension funds of the childless (Visek, 1995b). It is also anticipated that citizens will generally behave in an ethical way, and only claim benefits if their material conditions justify it.

The benefits themselves are payable to individuals whose income falls below the official social minimum and are designed to meet basic nutritional needs and other 'essential personal needs of children and families'. All nine can be claimed as of right, although they will not be payable automatically and one has to apply for them on a yearly basis. They are to be made available through a new network of state-run regional benefit offices (totalling 370 outreach stations) with a newly trained staff of 3,000 replacing the benefit administration previously attached to enterprises.

The new state support benefits could be seen as part of the government's attempt to prevent vulnerable families falling below the poverty line and educating everyone in solidaristic social responsibility. But as the debates in the legislature and subsequent commentary show, the new benefit structure has attracted considerable criticism. Means-testing of four of the benefits has proved particularly controversial. This is not, however, because it introduced the concept of targeting into an East European welfare system, but because, according to various commentators, it was not bold enough. Thus some critics see the new provisions in many ways as a 'botched up' form of old-style state authoritarianism which fails to target the really needy. For example, it is estimated that child benefit, a key form of support (which has not yet been valorised and is consequently only worth 45% of its pre-1989 value) will be withdrawn from only 5 per cent of households, with a further 20 per cent experiencing a reduction. 50 per cent will not experience any change and only 25% will see some increase (Lidove Noviny, 29.5.1995).

Other commentators have raised different concerns, suggesting that whilst failing to reach the really needy, the scheme's relative generosity may threaten the nascent middle classes. What they need, it is argued, is the expansion of genuine productive economic activity within a stable legal environment, not restrictive, redistributive legislation which penalises wealth creation. The 'levelling' effect of the new social security system could, it is feared, lead to a situation in which the small class of the 'self-made rich' opted for self-provision, leaving the state to deal with the increasing number of the poor 'hanging around the government's neck'. (Konopasek, 1995). Such concerns about the redistributive role of the state have been echoed by analysts such as Tuma, the chief economist of a new financial company. In a key contribution to Lidove Noviny, he attributes the success of the Czech economy so far to the growth of conspicuous consumption by a few. The transfer of state property into private hands through restitution, voucher privatisation and the privatisation of state assets has, he argues, generated an artificial notion of affluence in which consumer spending by a minority has depleted the state coffers but not led to the productive use of capital. Alongside this is the continued problem of the 'shadow economy' with illegal employment, evasion of tax and foreign bank accounts (Tuma, 1995). For such writers then the new scheme seems counter-productive.

The scheme is also proving more complex and administratively demanding than anticipated. Not only are income support returns required four times a year in order to monitor claimants' financial circumstances and for means-testing, but household surveys are having to be conducted in order to determine the level of need. One such governmental survey in June 1994 found 66 per cent of the respondents experienced difficulty managing on their present income, 31.1 per cent had not experienced any major changes and only 3.7 per cent stated that they consider their standard of living better than the national average. The same survey noted that nearly 42 per cent of respondents thought it appropriate for the state to take responsibility for creating the right conditions for family functioning, and those most satisfied with their family circumstance are voters of the leading Civic Democratic Party (Tosner, 1994).

Social Assistance

The debate over the third element of the new social security system, social assistance, reveals further difficulties, especially in terms of its coverage, coercive elements and the viability of local administration. It is designed to help individuals deemed unable to help themselves because they are under age, have lost the capacity to provide for themselves due to ill-health or old age, or whose family has become 'dysfunctional' and whose income falls below the official social minimum (Niederle & Visek, 1995). This is currently set below the minimum wage, at 35 - 40 per cent of the average national wage, and provisions under the scheme are governed by legislation on 'social neediness' which specifies the safety-net minimum for households, individuals and children. It is estimated that the proportion of the population likely to qualify for assistance is relatively small (about 5.5 per cent), though it is admitted that a further 15-16 per cent live just above the threshold.

Under the social security act, responsibility for determining eligibility and devising the most suitable package of assistance has been vested with the local authorities, the community 'that knows best' (Visek, 1995). Each has responsibility for its residents and is obliged to provide basic support for the really destitute in the form of a daily meal, overnight accommodation and basic clothing. It is anticipated that they will develop a range of services as part of the 'assistance package', including not only bed and board but counselling, legal advice and loans. They also have discretionary power to 'top up' the assistance scheme with additional benefits for their residents (Zasady Zakona, 1995), though it is also hoped that local provision will be supplemented by the voluntary sector.

It is intended that the dual task of establishing eligibility and meting 'need' will be undertaken by specially trained local benefit officers, who are also to ensure that the 'package' is not 'demotivational' (Visek, 1995) and targeted at the really needy. Claimants are subject to a means-test related to their income over the previous six months. Those whose incomes fall below the social minimum but whose overall material circumstances, property or assets are deemed to provide a sufficient source of livelihood are not eligible for assistance. Similarly individuals who are out of work, but not registered as unemployed are ineligible, as are those who are not covered by compulsory medical insurance (Zakono Socialni Potrebnosti, 482/1991).

Though it is only in the process of being implemented the social assistance scheme has already given rise to considerable concern. First, it is widely known that many people do not register as unemployed with the Labour Exchanges. This partly stems from a reluctance to declare their material/property status to local officials, but it also reflects the continuing scale (and profitability) of the informal economy. It is also known that many private employers do not register their employees under the insurance scheme because of the mutual benefit of an informal employment agreement. The protection offered by the social assistance scheme to those w ho may fall pray to labour market fluctuations is thus both limited and uncertain.

Equally worrying for many commentators are the uncertain relations between the central state and local authorities in the Czech Republic and the ability of the latter to mop up poverty at the local level. Though the legislation envisaged joint funding by the central government and local authorities, with the former contributing on a per capita basis, the details have not yet been finalised and the overall financing of social assistance remains unclear. Moreover, whilst the state defines the legal rights of individuals and has the final authority to enforce the provisions, implementation as has been seen, remains with the localities. In most the mayors have assumed a distinct political role, pursuing policies which secure local electoral support, but often at the expense of minority groups or others perceived as 'undeserving'. Locally run social assistance, for some commentators, may thus focus on a narrow range of base provisions or, worse, exclude or minimise support for some groups such as members of the Romany population.

To concerns over the vagaries of local politics must be added those over the inadequacies of local administrative structures. A survey in October 1993 revealed, for instance, more than one third of local authorities lacked the necessary organizational base to undertake this new responsibility, while another third had only established a commission to 'look into it'. Only one quarter had allocated budgetary resources and were thus able to offer assistance. Many lacked the necessary personnel and local information and were unclear as to their accountability to state agencies. Non-statutory provision is in a similar embryonic state. Though there has been an 'explosion' of small scale grass roots voluntary activity, it is, as yet poorly co-ordinated and heavily dependent on female volunteers. Moreover legislation governing state-voluntary sector relations is incomplete, making self-financing and sponsorship difficult. Further concern has arisen over the role of the new benefit officers. Though it is anticipated most will have trained in social work, combining their 'assessment' and 'support' roles is unlikely to be easy and, given the historical legacy, they may well still be regarded as a continuation of the 'extended arm' of the paternalist state.

The social assistance part of the social security system is thus not only the most complex of the 'three pillars' but may, in future, become a real source of tension. Who, for instance, will mediate in situations where the local authority's provision based on what it can afford (or selects) conflicts with the state's commitment to equal responsibility for all its citizens? Will social problems be 'dumped' at local level or will the central authority be able to enforce its 'egalitarian' standards against vested local interests? (Vizek, 1995). In view of these issues the controversy surrounding this part of the social security scheme is both understandable and unlikely to be easily resolved (Zasady Zakona 1995).

Conclusion

The Czech social security system thus embraces a combination of different models, liberal and social democratic, punitive and solidaristic; paternalist and free market. Ultimately, however, controversy centres on the balance between paternalism and social market approaches. Though, as yet, the government's information

drives have had little impact (Socialni Politika 1/1996), the tendency from the top is clearly to control public spending whilst dis-
pelling public fears over pauperisation through publicising the
protection offered by the new social security system. The government's position has been expressed by Prime Minister Klaus at a
number of forums . He drew a specific distinction between 'solidarity among the citizens' and 'the state's care of the citizens' and
rejected the latter as an unhealthy option which drove people into
passivity (Klaus, 1995). Correlatively, he repudiated the notion
that solidarity among the citizens depends on securing reasonably
equal chances and opportunities in work, education, health and
other areas (Buzkova, 1995). Rather, he maintained that neither
education, health nor culture can be meaningfully included in
social policy.(Klaus, 1995). Indeed the term 'citizens' in his conception refers to taxpayers or benefit recipients in the
Bismarckian sense rather than the Beveridgian notion of
claimant-citizen.

The state's role in regulating social rights and duties does not
in itself constitute paternalistic behaviour and protectionist/pre-
ventive measures are a feature of many European welfare states.
But in the current social climate of East/Central Europe paternalism has strong negative connotations and is associated with the
state's misuse of its role as a distributor of social resources.
Though it claimed to guarantee certain rights and benefits the
communist state's re-distributive policies were fundamentally a
form of 'rationing' via a 'para-tax' on the entire population introduced to sustain and legitimate the government's power base
(Tomes, 1995). Benefits could be withdrawn from political dis-
senters (across the social spectrum) and preferential remuneration
(often of non -monetary kind) was used as a form of social control. The concept of re-distribution then was a charade and paternalism a substitute for lack of legitimacy.

Some Czech writers today consider the Klaus government dis-
plays similar tendencies (Konopasek, 1995), suggesting mone-
tarism and paternalism share a similar centralised approach to
financial controls. For the Social Democrats, the strongest opposition party , this is most visible in what they see as governmental mismanagement of the insurance funds. Rather than being
placed under separate independent administration as originally
intended, the Social Fund has remained under government control. The revenue raised, so t he opposition claims, has been used
to bolster the growth of the state apparatus whilst pensioners
have been 'cheated' of 20,000 Czech crowns each over the past
six years. (Arena, 10.4.1996). Moreover, although targeting was
supposed to 'solve' social deprivation, the problem of low

incomes remains, whilst claimants are subject to a series of new bureaucratic humiliations. This may recreate memories of the past regime in may people's minds rather than reassure them that they now live in a 'free and open' society. Indeed a real question mark needs to be placed over the democratic input at this stage, especially as the latest spate of legislative proposals include calls for tougher family laws, removal of some of the protective measures under the old labour law legislation, and a loosening of collective bargaining practices. The democratic agenda behind the social security system in the Czech Republic thus remains unclear. From the available evidence, the uniqueness of the Czech experience could yet be less an open challenge to pro-market policies than progressive democratisation from within.

References

Arena (1996) Czech TV programme featuring a debate on social policy, 10 April, Prague.

Bakos, G. (1994) 'Hungarian transition after three years', Europe-Asia Studies, vol.6, no.7, pp1189-1214

Brom, K. & Orenstein, M. (1994) 'The privatized sector in the Czech Republic', Europe-Asia Studies, vol.46, no.6.

Buzkova, P. (1995) 'Co je a neni socialni politika? Klausovy protiklady', Sondy, vol.44, 13 November, p1.

Cermakova, M. (1995) 'Gender, spolecnost, pracovni trh', Sociologicky Casopis, vol.44, 13 November, p1.

Duvodova Zprava (1994) MPSV, Praha, pp64-111. Hankiss, E. (1990) East European Alternatives, Oxford, Oxford University Press.

Heczko, S. (1994) 'Systemove zmeny v ekonomice i spolecnosti.', Pohledy no. 6, pp1-5.

Holanova, E. (1995) 'K Vyvoji peneznich prijmu domacnosti a zivotnich nakladu za 1.-3.ctvrtleti 1994', Socialni Politika, vol.21, n o.3, pp7-8

Hirsl, M. 'Vyvoj zamestnanosti, realnych prijmu a nazoru na zivotni uroven v Ceske Republice', Pohledy, no.4, pp4-9.

Hirsl, M., Rusnok, J.,& Fassmann, M. (1995) 'Zprava o socialni politice a vyvoji socialnich podminek v Ceske Republice, 1989-1994', Pohledy no.1/2, pp1-16.

Kabele, J. & Potucek, M. (1994) Formovani a implementace socialnich politik v Ceske Republice jako politicky proces, Unpublished study for Start, Prague.

Kalinova, L. (1995) 'Tendence vyvoje zamestnanosti a nezamestnanosti v Ceske Republice', Socialni Politika, vol.21, no.3, pp14-16.

Klaus,V. (1995) 'Principy zdrave socialni politiky', Sondy, vol.31, 14 August, p1.

Konopasek, Z. (1995) 'Bezva finta, ktera by se nemusela vyplatit', Lidove Noviny 5 April, p8.

Kral, J. (1994) 'Nove v nemocenskem pojisteni', Socialni Politika, vol.20, no.4, pp4-5.

Kral, J. & Klimentova, J. (1995) 'K pripravov anemu zakonu o duchodovem pojisteni', Socialni Politika, vol .21, no.3, pp2-5.

Lewis, P.G. (1994) 'Political institutionalization and party development in post-communist Poland', Europe-Asia Studies, vol.46, no. 5. pp 779-799.

Lidove Noviny (1995) 'Prijmy rostly pomaleji nez zivotni naklady', 7 April.

Lidove Noviny (1995) 'S valorizaci minima porostou i davky.' 29 May

Machonin, P. (1996) 'Vyvoj ceske spolecnosti v letech 1989-1995, jeji soucasny stav a vyhledy ocima sociologa', Pohledy, vol.4., no. 1, pp1-7.

Mokrzycki, E. (1991) 'Dedictivi realneho socialismu a zapadni demokracie', Sociologicky Casopis, vol.27, no.6, pp 751-757.

Niederle, P. & Visek, P. (1995) 'K novemu pojeti socialni promoci', Socialni Politika vol.2. no1. pp10-11.

Novela Socialniho Pojisteni (1995), Zizkova, M. MPSV, Bilance, Praha.

Odpovedi Na Otazky KtereVas Zajimaji (1995), government leaflet, Vodicka,J., MPSV, Praha

Pick, M. (1995) 'Statni rozpocet pred volbami 1996', Pohledy, vol.3, no.4, pp1-6.

Rose, R. & Haerpher, Ch. (1994) 'Mass response to transformation in post-communist societies', Europe-Asia Studies, vol.46, no.1, pp3 - 28.

Socialni Politika (1996) 'Co ukazalo setreni informovanosti o statni socialni podpore', vol.22, no.1, pp11-12.

Szalai, J. (1995) 'Power and poverty', unpublished paper,presented at workshop on ' Problems of political psychology of the post-communist era', Budapest, 18-19 October.

Szelenyi, I. (1995) 'The rise of mangerialism: the "new class" after the fall of communism', Keynote address to the Second European Sociological Association Conference, Budapest, 30 August.

Tomes, I. (1995) unpublished personal interview, Prague, November.

Tosner, J.(1994) 'Rodina 1994', Socialni Politika, vol.20, no.10, pp11-12.

Tuma, Z. (1995) 'Co ma spolecneho John M. Keynes a ceska transformace', Lidove Noviny 11 April, p111.

Visek, P.(1995a) 'K problematice statni socialni podpory', Socialni Politika, vol.21, no.2, pp4-6.

Visek, P. (1995b) 'Proc je treba oddelit pri poskytovani socialni pomoci vykon statni spravy od pusobnosti somospravy', Socialni Politika, vol.21, no.2, pp11-12.

Visek, P & Dlouhy, J.(1994) Nad Diskusi o Statni Socialni Podpore MPSV, Praha, pp1-6.

Zizkova, J.(1994) 'Chudoba a moznosti jejiho reseni', Socialni Politika, vol.20, no.10, pp15-17.

Zakon o Socialni Potrebnosti (1991), 482, MPSV, 6 November,Prague.

Zasady Zakona o Socialni Pomoci (1995), MPSV, pracovni verze, 6 April, Prague, pp1-64.

16 Is There an Italian Welfare State?

Robert Sykes

To the outside world Italy has a somewhat contradictory character. The country is a major player in the international economy
especially in the fields of clothing, automobiles, agricultural products, petrochemicals, and white goods. Although not commonly
recognised, the Italian economy has enjoyed fairly continuous
growth through the 1970s and 1980s reaching a sustained
growth rate of 3 per cent in the 1990s and it is now, arguably,
the fifth largest in the world. On the other hand, Italy is also
fraught with government instability, massive public debt, corruption scandals in government and public administration, large
regional differences in living standards, and a continuing presence
of the Mafia and associated criminal organisations which perme-
ate many aspects of Italian society .

This complexity and contradiction has contributed to the relative lack of study by non-Italians of most areas of Italian society.
This is certainly so with regard to the study of welfare provision
and social policy. It would appear that the Italian case has either
been regarded by non-Italians as a bizarre and peculiar 'one-off'
offering little useful comparison with other social policy regimes,
or that the inherent complexities and particularisms of Italian welfare structures and processes have dissuaded all but a few Italian
academics from analysing them. Though there is a growing Italian
literature on welfare (for example, Ascoli, 1984; Cotesta, 1995;
Ferrera 1984 and 1993), social policy as an academic discipline

does not, as yet, exist. For all these reasons Italian social policy lacks an extensive analytical literature. With these constraints in mind this chapter is intended to provide a broad overview of social welfare in Italy, and, in so doing, contribute to the growing number of country-focused studies which are needed to underpin the theoretical frameworks of comparative analysis.

The chapter's initial focus is the development of state welfare since the Second World War and the key distinctive features of Italian social welfare provision, namely: clientilism, regional and local variations, and the role of the non-profit sector[1]. It then considers current attempts to simultaneously address these features as problems and to undertake a broader restructuring of state welfare along the market-oriented lines being pursued elsewhere in Europe. Thus the chapter's title 'Is there an Italian welfare state?' may be seen as containing three sub-questions around which the discussion is organised: (a) Is there an (i.e. a unitary) Italian welfare state? (b) Is there an Italian welfare state, i.e. to what extent is the state (singly or in combination with other providers) the provider of welfare in Italy?, and, (c) Is the Italian welfare state system being residualised in the 1990s?

The Development of the Italian Welfare State

The post-war development of the welfare system in Italy can be divided into three phases: the period from the end of the Second World War until the late 1960s, the establishment of a true welfare state in the 1970s, and the period from the 1980s to the present day . One theme, however, links the three periods and continues to characterise the Italian welfare system today:

> ' ...the system has developed according to an incremental and particularistic approach, without any rationalisation or restructuring to fill the needs and the wants...of different social groups'. (Ascoli, 1987, p111).

The 1950s and 1960s

The Italian state is formally charged within the constitution to provide all citizens with care, assistance and education. Yet in the immediate post-war period various political and economic factors severely limited the extent to which such commitments were translated into universalist provision. Various writers have pointed out (e.g. Ascoli 1984,1987; Ferrera, 1984; Furlong, 1994; Ginsborg, 1990; Sassoon, 1986) that the political settlement by which the post-Fascist Italian state was established under pressure from the Allies, and especially the USA, involved the exclusion from government of the leftist political parties, the Socialist Party (PSI) an d the Communist Party (PCI), in an attempt to prevent a feared Communist take-over. One effect of this sponsored political settlement was effectively to hand political hegemony to the Catholic-based Christian Democratic party (DC), who have remained a dominant for ce in Italian politics ever since. The key to the post-war government's economic policy then was to keep wage rates down so as to be able to compete in world markets (Ginsborg, 1990) while extending welfare benefits to selected groups thus ensuring their political support. Various governments led by the DC sought to sustain consensus amongst the middle classes and proprietors whilst at the same time engaging in a policy of extensive public works and public subsidies to agriculture. Health insurance funds were established for farmers (1956), artisans (1957), and traders (1960) accompanied by the extension of old-age pensions to the same groups -1957,1959, and 1966 respectively (Ascoli, 1987, p119). On the other hand, the working classes saw their standards of living held down.

In the 1960s, however, the strength of the unions began to grow and increasing industrial unrest and more generalised social protest in the major cities of the North led the government and employers to realise that a new form of political settlement was required. In government the Socialists (PSI) and the Christian Democrats moved closer together in the so-called 'opening to the left' as calls for reform from various sections of Italian society especially students, workers, the women's movement, and immigrants from the South grew. In 1962 compulsory secondary schooling to the age of fourteen was introduced, though the content of the curriculum remained archaic and the organisation of schooling was left untouched. Meanwhile strikes and demonstrations became almost daily occurrences and pressure for further reform built up. Despite government promises agrarian reform, the introduction of a national health service, fiscal reform, labour market reform and reform of the inefficient state bureaucracy all failed to materialise. Growing social and political unrest culminated in the 'hot autumn' (autonnocaldo) of 1968-69. Initially the protests, based largely upon students who came from the ceti medi (middle classes), had little effect. Those of workers at key industrial centres such as FIAT in Turin proved a more significant threat to Italy's economic and political stability, however. The trade unions gained significant power in this situation as did the Communist Party both with regard to economic and social policy and the government began to respond (Ginsborg, 1990).

A new 'consensus' over the need for more extensive welfare provision emerged, symbolised in the 1969 Pensions Act. This brought a significant increase in old age pensions (pensioni di anzianita), especially for ex-workers in manufacturing industry. Pensions were indexed to the cost of living and a 'social pension' introduced a provision of last resort for those over sixty-five. The more important development , however, was the introduction of new rules for disability pensions: henceforward only five years of contributions were necessary of which only one needed to be employment-related. Medically-documented physical invalidity was no longer required for the receipt of a disability pension. Residence in an 'economically disadvantaged area', i.e. an area of chronic high unemployment, became a basis for application for a disability pension after five years of contributions to the National Institute for Social Security (INPS).

The Pensions Act of 1969 marked a turning point in that it reflected the demands of the leftist parties and trades unions an d as such framed the subsequent development of statutory welfare in Italy. It led to the improvement of pensions benefits for low-in come groups and the working classes without adversely affecting the benefits of previously favoured groups (Reginoni,1984) and ensured that the disability pension became a major feature not only of social welfare provision but also of the government's labour market policies and the new political settlement. These pensions became, in effect, a means of 'buying-off' political and social discontent in areas of very high unemployment and under-employment, principally in the Mezzogiorno. In short it was a classic case both of the political bargaining (trasformismo) and piecemeal policy change which came to characterise the Italian welfare state. However, the legislation also established a financial millstone for the Italian economy which later became a major focus of welfare state reform. Furthermore, in the field of pensions as elsewhere the increasing complexity and discretionary nature of many benefits provided fertile ground for the growth of a patronage system or clientilism (clientilismo) between those governing the welfare bureaucracies (both officials and political party agents) and welfare beneficiaries.

The 1970s

These characteristic features became more embedded with the proliferation of state welfare provision in the 1970s. Continuing pressure from trades unions, the PCI, workers groups, women's groups, informal social movements, and increasing political terrorism provided the background to this legislation and the associated escalation in social expenditure.

Alongside the increases in expenditure and areas of provision, an important change in the structure of social policy administration also occurred in the 1970s: twenty two years after it had been provided for in the Constitution, regional government was fin ally established in the spring of 1970. Each regional government gained its own elected council with greater powers than either the communes (local authorities) or provinces. These included the right to legislate upon as well as to administer a wide range of services including housing, health, and other social welfare services (Furlong, 1994; Sassoon, 1986; Allum, 1995).

Various acts were introduced to regulate the housing market in 1977 and 1978. A number of acts designed to help young people in the labour market were introduced in the same period (Youth Employment Acts 1977, 1978), as was a Vocational Training Act (1978) which required regional governments to collect local labour market information and to provide generalised vocational training. The Public Child-Care Centres Act (1971), the Family Law Act (1975), the Public Women's Advice and Aid Bureaux Act (1975) are further examples of the spread of legislation in the 1970s (Ferrera, 1984; Ascoli, 1987). But the expansion of state involvement in social welfare was, perhaps, most characteristically reflected in the 1978 National Health System Act. This appeared to set up a universalist health system. A single health insurance management system was to cater for all citizens, health provision was decentralised to the regions, and local health units (unita sanitarie locali-USL) were established in which there was to be citizen's participation in management.

Thus, on the face of it, the new provisions of the 1970s, added to previous schemes, provided a comprehensive range of welfare facilities to all Italian citizens while the state had gained financial responsibility for a welfare system whose cost rose as a percentage of GDP from 16.8 per cent in 1960 to 29.1 per cent in 1980. While the late 1960s saw an extension of provision to new social groups without attempting to alter the particularist ideology of earlier policies, the rhetoric of the '70s legislation seemed to mark a change towards a more universalist welfare ideology. The reality was both less extensive and less universal than this formal, legislative picture suggests. In the case of housing, social care and education, for example, the implementation of policy fell far short of legislation (Saraceno & Negri, 1994). Funds were not forthcoming from central government for the regions or communes to carry out their responsibilities. Houses and schools were not built. Only some regions, usually in the Centre and the

North, actually delivered most of the services as required by law and requested by their citizens. Administrative inefficiency and bureaucratic procedures of Byzantine complexity often meant that moneys which were received from central government remained unspent (Furlong, 1994). Despite a formal commitment to universalist principles, the Italian welfare state remained shot through with particularist provisions and processes and service delivery experienced by various citizens was far from being universalist or unitary.

By the end of the 1970s the presence of particularism in the form of clientilism and regional differences arguably made the Italian welfare state fundamentally non-unitary despite claims to universalism. These features were further complicated by the role of the Catholic church in the provision of welfare services. It is now time to draw out these particularistic characteristics more clearly.

Clientilism and trasformismo

The process whereby an intermediary or 'patron' acts on behalf of his 'client' in order to secure a benefit or service, be it material, administrative, pecuniary or otherwise from a landlord, a political elite, or, more recently, an official of the local or nation al state stretches back to the feudal period in Italy. The patron expects, in return for his successful intermediation, some form of support from his client at a later date. Whilst this describes the basic process of exchange at the heart of clientilism it can take many forms other than the simple one-to-one 'patron-client' link. The system has become institutionalised in the twentieth century so as to involve, in addition to the client, political parties at national and local levels, local government officials, and the boards of bodies such as the local health units and pensions authorities. As we shall see below, insofar as they, too, are affected by the need to bargain with political parties and the government for funding and other support, both Catholic welfare agencies and other non-profit organisations (NPOs) are also part of this clientilistic process.

Clientilism as it affects welfare access and delivery primarily involves the political parties. As various writers have indicated (e.g. Furlong, 1994; Allum, 1995), the liberal political elite which governed the country from unification in 1870 was very weak. It was confronted by a political elite in the South which was fundamentally opposed to the new central state's authority, and it had to contend with significant economic inequalities between the

North and the South. The government's political instability and lack of legitimacy led it to seek the support of various interest groups in return for social and political benefits. The quid pro quo was an allocation of public funds. This pattern of patronage to secure political support, was subsequently adapted and made more pervasive by the Fascist regime. After the second world war it continued, and though primarily exercised at a local level, clientilism involving the political parties intermingled with the process of coalition building in order to retain power (trasformismo) by subsequent Italian governments. As Ranci (1994) summarises it: 'a regime of fragmented negotiations between local and central authorit ies has permeated both the public administration and the political arena, making clientilist inter-mediation the most incisive way t o obtain public benefits' (p273).

How does clientilism work in practice? In some senses it is almost impossible to discover precisely because the process is kept private, and it is neither in the interests of the 'citizen-client' not the political party patron and the appropriate bureaucratic officials to make the process public. Clientilism became a central feature of the decentralised social welfare system after the 1970s. The political parties invaded the realms of civil society - and effectively controlled the distribution of resources (Ciccaro ne, 1995; Saraceno & Negri, 1994). As an illustration of the process, jobs in local and regional government, including those with responsibility for the delivery of welfare, were the subject of lottitazione - a share out of posts between the political parties depending upon bargains struck and local strengths. The USLs are prime examples of this process - in 1985 the DC had 57 per cent of the USL presidents, and the PSI 20 per cent (Ginsborg, 1990). From a claimant's perspective the growth of regional and local political networks for the distribution of welfare benefits mirrored the particularistic character of social policy at national level. It matte red less that one was a citizen with certain social and political rights to welfare services than that one could access local political party patronage networks. Services such as housing and health care, and the speed at which an individual citizen actually received claimed legitimate benefits habitually depended upon access to the role of local political party officials acting as intermediaries. The very precise and restrictive legislation which characterises Italian public life and was designed to reduce such discretionary behaviour had, in practice, generated a slow and inefficient public bureaucracy. Private negotiations and discretionary administrative procedures were, and are, considered necessary by the various actors in the welfare field so as to overcome the inertia and in efficiency of the system. So, as a number of writers have pointed out (e.g. Furlong, 1994; Ranci, 1994), modern Italian welfare clientilism comes less from an absence of regulation and more from excessive legislation which has increased the discretionary power of bureaucrats and politicians.

Whilst clearly illegitimate the clientilistic practices involving ordinary citizens do not usually involve money or material benefit but rather electoral support in return for the services rendered. Nevertheless, clientilism and corruption have often overlapped, as the tangentopoli scandals of the 1990s have shown. Clientilism can thus be described as an integral feature of the Italian welfare system, though it may also be regarded as a feature of other 'southern' welfare states such as Portugal, Spain and Greece (see Ferrera,1996 and Conclusion below).

Spatial and regional differences

Regional differences in welfare service delivery need to be set in the context of spatial differences in Italy's social and economic structure. Italy has a very uneven pattern of economic development and, consequently, an uneven pattern of unemployment, poverty, a nd other forms of social disadvantage. Unemployment, for example, has risen nationally from 10 per cent in 1990 to 11.8 per cent in 1994. These aggregate figures conceal very large regional variations, however. Whereas in the Northern and Central regions of Italy the overall unemployment rate ranged between 4.3 per cent and 8.9 per cent, in the South and Islands the rates ranged from 21.9 per cent in Sicily to 23.1 per cent in Campania. When considering female and youth unemployment (people under twenty five) the contrasts and their social policy implications are even starker. Rates for female unemployment range between approximately 7 per cent and 15 per cent, and for youth unemployment between approximately 16 per cent and 28 per cent in the Northern regions. Female unemployment rates range from 20 per cent (Puglia) and 32.3 per cent (Campania) in the Southern regions, whereas youth unemployment ranges between 41.2 per cent in Puglia and a massive 60 per cent in Campania (Eurostat, 1995, Table 3.28).

The significance of these figures is two-fold. First, as the Italian economy develops the gap between the North and South continues to widen both in terms of employment and patterns of social deprivation. Secondly, the Mezzogiorno continues to suffer economically and otherwise despite the massive influx of funds to the South made by central government since the 1960s and 1970s. Thus if one lives in certain parts of Italy one is much more likely both to suffer economic and social disadvantage and to require forms of social assistance and support from the welfare system. However, the evidence shows that in these same regions public administration including welfare provision is more likely to be riven with clientilism, inefficiency and corruption (see for example Sassoon, 1986 pp210-220; Ginsborg, 1990; Boccella, 1994).

The devolution of most areas of welfare provision to regional government in 1970 may have seemed to place access and control of such provision closer to the citizen, as indeed did the creation of the USLs in 1978. Once again, however, it appears that in some regions, notably Emilia-Romagna, Tuscany and Umbria in the North and Centre, welfare services have become relatively accessible, and open to genuine local management, whereas in others, notably Campania, Calabria and other Southern regions, welfare services are poorly-funded, poorly-managed and controlled by the local political elites. In short, if you are an Italian seeking welfare support it matters very much where you live and what the political complexion of your local commune or region is - all Italians are not equal when it comes to social welfare.

Having looked at two features of the particularist character of the state-provided welfare in Italy, it is now time to consider the second sub-question raised at the beginning: what other bodies provide welfare services beside the state in Italy?

State and Non-State Welfare

So far no mention has been made of the single largest competitor to the Italian welfare state, namely the Catholic church. The Church has resisted the growth of state welfare almost from its inception in 1870 regarding welfare as part of its own sphere. Indeed, it has been one of the more powerful political forces with which governments have had to bargain either directly or through representation of its interests by political parties, especially the DC. In fact the Church effectively is the non-profit welfare sector in Italy. It represents 70 per cent of private care institutions, 50 per cent of private hospitals, 58 per cent of vocational training centres, 75 per cent of private elementary schools and 48 per cent of private high schools (ISTAT figures quoted in Ranci, 1994, p279) . Whilst religious bodies are significantly involved in welfare provision in a number of other countries, rarely if ever is the monopoly so overwhelmingly held by one church.

So what of other NPOs besides the Catholic church? The answer is that, until very recently, it is very difficult to identify true NPOs which are distinct from either church or state. It has already been argued that politicisation of civil society is a key feature of Italian state welfare: this also extends in many respects to the private and voluntary welfare sectors. Whilst it is fair to say that other European countries have a close interpenetration of voluntary, for-profit private and state welfare (e.g. France and Germany) the Italian case does, once again, appear to have a special character in this regard. In the first place, a large proportion of NPOs are not, in fact, institutionally separate from the government. Rather, as IPABs (Istituzioni Pubbliche di Assistenza e Beneficenza) they have a charter which allows them to deliver services on behalf of the state. Secondly, the internal management o f many of these IPABs and other NPOs is controlled from outside by public authorities, political parties and the Catholic church. Thirdly, most of the non-religious NPOs providing public services have been set up and supported by political parties and owe their al legiance to them.

Thus while Italy is not alone in have a blurred distinction between the public, private and voluntary sectors in welfare pro vision, it is unique in the sense that all three sectors are affected by and forced to work within the peculiar pattern of clientili sm and political bargaining which we have previously described (Ranci, 1994; Kuhnle & Selle, 1992). Non-profit welfare organisations have suffered from pressure to distribute their services on clientilistic rather than universalist criteria. The process works both ways, however. One of the most notorious examples of corruption uncovered by recent mani pulite (clean hands) investigations was of an IPAB administrator who used his position to accumulate bribes to finance the Italian Socialist Party, PSI.

In the 1980s and 1990s there has been a weakening of the authority of the Catholic church in the field of social and welfare matters, evidenced by the defeat of its campaign to repeal abortion and divorce laws, the rise of non-religious social movements and the general growth of secularism and individualism (Ascoli, 1992). Many of these new voluntary organisations have been given resources by the church, but have resisted church interference and managed to develop an independent role. It is with regard to many of the 'new' problems, such as AIDS, drug abuse, and immigrant problems that they have developed a presence. Legislative changes have al so encouraged the development of a whole range of NPOs (Saraceno & Negri, 1994). Nevertheless, and despite these changes, it could b e argued that the non-profit welfare sector in Italy constitutes an important particularistic link between the political parties and their clienteles.

Recent Developments: the 1980s and 1990s

These distinctive features of the Italian welfare system had been set by the beginning of the 1980s. Indeed, Italy appeared to share many of the features of state welfare provision found in other western European countries by this time. However, whilst other Western European countries were attempting to control their welfare expenditures, Italy continued to engage in a process of massive expansion both of provision and expenditure in the 1970s.

The composition of social expenditure between different policy areas differed from the norms in other European countries, however: the relative level of health and education expenditures is close to other European countries, but expenditures on housing, family allowances and unemployment are much lower, and levels of pensions are higher (see Table 1 below). Moreover, as Ferrera points out (1984, p71), the period between 1965 and 1980 saw an increasing imbalance between revenues and government expenditure of which social expenditure took an increasing proportion. This became more visible during the 1980s as the

Table 1: Composition of Public Expenditure in 1980

	Italy	France, Germany UK	USA
Total Public Expenditure of which:	100	100	100
Public Social Expenditure	61.9	67.1	57.2
a) Public goods and Services	28.9	31.3	27.2
Of which			
Education	12.1	12.2	17.1
Health	13.0	12.6	7.6
Housing	2.4	4.9	1.2
b) Income maintenance	33.8	35.8	30.0
Of which			
Pensions	26.1	20.5	20.5
Illness	1.5	2.5	0.3
Family Allowances	2.2	3.6	1.5
Unemployment Benefits	0.7	2.3	1.2

Source: Adapted from OECD figures cited in Ascoli (1987) p114

Italian economy underwent restructuring (Graziani & Boccella, 1994; Sassoon, 1986; Collicelli, 1995). After an initially poor beginning to the decade when inflation reached an annual rate of over 21 per cent in 1980, which only reduced to 15 per cent by 1983, the Italian economy began to improve markedly. Though employment fell in the manufacturing sector and unemployment overall began to rise (from 7.6 per cent in 1980 to 10.6 per cent in 1985), this was the period of rapid growth in the small to medium size firms at the heart of the new Italian economy and of the services sector.

How, then, did this economic change affect Italian social policy? In the first place, the benefits and costs of economic growth were very unequally distributed. The concentration of economic activity in the North and Central regions of Italy meant that unemployment, especially amongst young people, poverty and other measures of social disadvantage worsened in the South whilst those in the prosperous regions benefited. At the same time, prosperity brought with it an increase in the diversity and complexity of demands for welfare and welfare provision grew (Collicelli, 1995). Whilst the institutional and legislative changes in state welfare provision introduced in the 1970s remained largely unchanged, the consequences of structural economic change led both to the use of exist ing provisions to cope with new problems, such as increasing and chronic unemployment in both the North and the South, and to the development of 'new' client groups and new demands. One effect of economic restructuring, for example, was a fall in demand for industries such as car manufacture. The FIAT works in Turin saw large numbers of skilled workers being laid off or made redundant and the cassa integrazione scheme, first introduced in 1975, was increasingly used both to provide support for such workers and to avoid social and political unrest in the large Northern cities. The fund was generated from a levy on employers and paid out at a rate of 80 per cent of former wages having been applied for by the relevant trade union. The fund was payable locally for between three months and two years, and centrally after this for a period of up to ten years. This scheme benefited only certain unionised occupational groups, however, and the remainder of the workforce was able to call only upon a very limited unemployment fund. Another example concerns the increasing use of existing 'disability' pensions, regardless of whether a claimant was actually suffering some form of disability or not, as a form of social insurance to those living in what the Italian state officially designated as 'economically disadvantaged areas', the Mezzogiorno in particular (Ascoli, 1987; Chamberlayne, 1992).

Meanwhile, poverty was 'rediscovered' in Italy. In the late 1980s, a government commission discovered that whilst the level of poverty was less than 9 per cent in the North, the figure rose to 26 per cent in the South, exceeding 35 per cent in Calabria (Negri, 1994). Moreover, poverty was taking new forms which appeared to require new responses. Changes in Italian society such as the increasing involvement of women in paid labour, the growth of single-parent families, increasing numbers of elderly people, the grow th of immigrant populations etc. have complicated the patterning of disadvantage and inequality. Furthermore, as Censis (Centro Studi Investimenti Sociali, an independent Italian social research organisation) has shown, the type of demands for welfare have become increasingly sophisticated and fragmented (see Cotesta, 1995 passim.). Welfare clients and potential welfare clients have begun, often through user-groups and welfare pressure groups, to expect not only quantity but also quality of provision. Thus pressure increas ed throughout the 1980s for expansion of social welfare provision which, given the politicised nature of the Italian welfare state, was difficult to resist. At the same time, however, pressure was building for the government to take action to curb social spending as the economy moved deeper into crisis. So the structure of social welfare established in the 1970s became more complex (and more expensive) in the 1980s. Though attempts were made to curb costs and to shift more and more responsibilities to the regions, there was no significant restructuring of welfare, and the system continued to expand. It is against this background that the upheavals of the 1990s have to be understood.

As Italy moved into the late 1980s and the 1990s the country has witnessed what, even for it, has been unprecedented economic and political upheaval. In this period Italy has experienced a period of radical criticism of the political status quo and, within it, the role of the dominant post-war political force, the Christian Democrats (DC). It seems that the political hegemony of the Christian Democrats and the legitimacy of the political and administrative system, including the Italian welfare system, are now seriously if not fatally weakened.

The early 1990s[2] saw the growth and electoral success of political parties of the centre-right such as Forza Italia and the Northern League, leading to the installation of Silvio Berlusconi (leader of Forza Italia), as prime minister after the March 1994 elections. The financial scandals revealed by the mani pulite investigations in the early 1990s showed enormous corruption in major cities across the country involving the PSI and DC, parties which were the major coalition partners in government for most of the 1960s, 1970s and 1980s. The Berlusconi government foundered when the support of one of its coalition partners, the Northern League, was withdrawn and a caretaker government of non-elected officials led by Lamberto Dini took over. The previous leaders of both parties , Giulio Andreotti (DC) and Bettino Craxi (PSI) along with Berlusconi were all put under investigation for alleged involvement in illegal political activity involving corruption, fraud and bribes. The so-called tangentopoli ('bribesville') allega-tions and investigations often involved corruptiori surrounding the activities of local social welfare agencies, and/or contracts for buildings such as hospitals. Typically, local party officials or 'party-sponsored' public administrators associated with PSI and DC were found to hav e accepted large sums on behalf of their par-ties for contracts or other 'favours'.

Whilst these scandals continued, Italian governments tried to reduce the country's national debt and the ratio of debt to GDP so as to regain control of expenditure, especially social expendi-ture. As 1996 and the EU Inter-governmental Conference approached , the Italian government struggled hard to meet the convergence criteria for Economic and Monetary Union set down at Maastricht. Meanwhile, and despite continuing growth in GDP, national rates of unemployment rose: from 10.5 per cent in January 1994 to 12.1 per cent in January 1995 (Istituto Centrale di Statistica (ISTAT) figures). It is in the context of these political, economic and social pressures that we need to consider changes to the Italian welfare system in the 1990s.

Successive budgets attempted to reduce public and especially welfare spending. The 1996 budget proposed by the Dini gov-ernment aimed to reduce the public sector deficit from 7.4 per cent to 5.9 per cent of GDP, and to reduce the debt to GDP ratio to 122 per cent, still double the EU norm. This was to be achieved by a mix of minimal spending cuts and an increase in taxation and other revenues. The Dini government being com-posed of non-elected 'experts' was very weak in the face of the other political parties and the trades unions, and there was pres-sure both from critics on the right (Berlusconi etc.), and the Italian public for a general election. Despite this weakness, however, the government achieved a major structural reform of one of the major and most expensive parts o f the Italian welfare state: pen-sions.

The Italian national pension fund, INPS, has needed to call for ever more support from the state over the last twenty years. As indicated above, a key feature of old-age pensions in the Italian system was that the level of payments was based only on the last five years of working life. Along with other anomalies from the political bargains struck in the 1960s, and the aforementioned use of 'invalidity pensions' as a form of pay off for lack of jobs in the South, pensions payments have become the most pressing financial burden within the social expenditure budget. In 1990, INPS needed to call on the government for transfers of 54 billion lire - 24.7 per cent of its outgoings. By 1995 these figures had risen to 72.2 billion lire, or 26.5 per cent of outgoings (Lane, 1995). In addition to the inherently inefficient actuarial base of the pensions schemes, the problem is exacerbated by the changing ratio of payers to recipients in the state system. In the 1960s some 19.1m. people were paying into the INPS scheme and only 6.9m. were drawing pensions, a ratio of 2.8 contributors to every recipient. The ratio has now dropped to below 1:1. The Dini government managed, with trade union and employer support to move the state pensions scheme to a basis that pensions paid will depend upon contributions m ade during the full working life (but see Graham, 1995). Also seniority pensions, pensioni di anzianita, previously payable after only thirty five years' contributions, are to be phased out. Yet these changes are all unlikely to be fully effective until ten or twenty years hence, since the weakness of the Dini government and the strength of the trades unions has meant that the pensions deal will only be phased in gradually. This has been one price for the unions' concessions on wage indexation, the so-called scala mobile. However, the use of private pensions to supplement state schemes is unlikely in the near future. The private pensions funds' assets are only about 100,000 billion lire in Italy (as compared with £2,000,000 billion in the UK), and the county's stock exchange and tax system are not structured in such a way as to encourage Italians, except perhaps high earners, to use private pensions for their cover (Lane, 1995).

Turning to other aspects of the welfare state, it is clear that a number of legislative moves made in the early 1990s were designed to shift it away from the practices and problems of the past. Laws passed in 1990 and 1991 are likely to have a significant, if as yet uncertain effect upon the delivery of welfare in Italy. The first of these was aimed at changing the institutional framework of public administration at the local, i.e. regional, commune, city, level so as to give greater devolved power to these authorities. It was also aimed specifically at counteracting clientilist practices either by making administrative documents available to citizens, or by transferring administrative decisions from elected politicians to professional managers. As Saraceno and Negri point out the '..development of such a system at local and national level may assure that the granting of social assistance benefits and services are no longer left to the discretion of individual administrators and social workers' (1994, p24).

Secondly, certain laws passed in 1991 concerned the non-profit, non-state sector in social welfare. Volunteer groups are subject to a range of regulation from government but may, in return, benefit by being able to buy property, to accept donations, to ent er into agreements with local government for welfare delivery, to gain tax exemptions and so on. 'Through this law, funding of social assistance services and activities by non-public actors... is for the first time explicitly supported and facilitated in Italy.' (Saraceno & Negri, 1994 p25). Similarly, social co-operatives are encouraged, through financial and other advantages, to act in concert with local administrations to organise social, health and educational services and get people back into the labour market.

Finally, legislation in 1992 has had a number of consequences for the Italian National Health Service. Firstly, regions have had their responsibilities increased especially vis-a-vis the USLs which are to be grouped together in larger units. The intention of central government is to increase efficiency and cut costs, though many experts doubt that this will be acieved. Secondly, public hospitals are also to be reorganised so that some will become separate from their local USL and become aziende ospedaliere or enter prises. Such enterprise hospitals will enjoy a high degree of management, financial and administrative autonomy and be allowed, for example, to re-invest budget surpluses. Thirdly, market forces are to be introduced within hospitals. For example, hospitals must provide space for doctors to carry out their private practice, and must have a 6-12 per cent quota of beds for private patients. Furthermore, the state may pay for some of the costs of private medical treatment, and private associations are to be allowed to shop within the public health service for the best package in price and quality of medical care for their private patients. The introduction of prescription charges via 'tickets' in 1992 extended a process begun in the 1980s so that now only the elderly poor, the permanently disabled and the 'certified poor' may be exempted from payment. This measure alone has generated enormous popular dissatisfaction across Italy (Saraceno & Negri, 1994; Vicarelli, 1994).

It is clear that in the 1990s state welfare provision in Italy is undergoing significant change even if it is difficult as yet to estimate quite what the overall effect will be. It is too early to say whether the state system will become residualised, and, in any case, it needs to be remembered that a significant proportion of welfare delivery has been achieved through the Catholic church and other NPOs alongside public provision ever since the growth of the post-war welfare state. It does, however, appear that the 'welfare mix' discussed so much in Britain and other capitalist welfare systems of late is beginning to be developed in Italy, albeit in a characteristically Italian way. The Italian welfare state is unlikely to disappear in the near future but it is being subjected increasingly in the 1990s to market forces, to demands for new services and decentralisation, to demands for greater openness an d accessibility, to demands for greater efficiency and depoliticisation, and, ultimately, to changes in the underpinning welfare philosophy (Ascoli, 1994; Cotesta, 1995).

Conclusion

This short overview has attempted to summarise some of the key features of the Italian welfare system by focusing upon the short but eventful development of the state welfare system. It has shown how the system is, as elsewhere, inextricably linked to the political, economic, and social life of the country. Certain features such as the overwhelming particularism, clientilism and politicisation, plus the role of non-profit organisations make apparently similar moves such as decentralisation and privatisation resonate very differently in Italian welfare circumstances compared with, say, Germany, the UK, Sweden or France (but compare Chamberlayne 1991 & 1992). A recent paper by Ferrera (1996) has usefully drawn attention to what he calls the 'southern model' of welfare. He argues for the analytical importance of the Spanish, Greek, Portuguese and Italian welfare systems in their own right rather than as 'deviations' from the models of welfare regimes proposed, for example, by Esping-Andersen (1990) and Leibfried (1992). For Ferrera, South European welfare states are distinguished from the: 'the highly homogenous, standardised and universalistic welfare states of northern Europe', in so far as the former:

> rest on a closed, particularistic culture and on a 'soft' state apparatus, both still highly imbued with the logic of patron-client relationships which has been the hallmark of this area of Europe (Ferrara, 1996 p29).

Recently-developed models of social welfare systems, especially Esping-Andersen's, have undoubtedly moved the exercise of comparative social policy analysis forward significantly. Yet, as so often in the social sciences, we find that complex and contradictory social realities resist our attempts to simplify and categorise. As one of the largest welfare systems in Europe and the world it is strange that in comparison with the systems of northern Europe Italy enjoys so little serious attention outside its own boundaries.

Hopefully, however, this chapter has indicated not only that the Italian welfare system is a complex and fascinating phenomenon, but that it also raises questions both at an empirical and a theoretical level for comparative social policy analysis.

Notes

1. Informal and voluntary welfare is a vital part of the Italian welfare system but is not dealt with here for reasons of space and focus

2. Much of the material for this section on the 1990s is derived from sources in the Italian and English press, in particular The Financial Times, The Guardian, The Economist and La Repubblica. Except where specifically indicated, however, the figures quoted are f rom official sources such as the Italian government, ISTAT the Italian Statistical Service, EUROSTAT and the OECD.

References

Allum, P. (1995) State and Society in Western Europe, Polity, Cambridge.

Ascoli, U. (ed) (1984) Welfare State all'italiana, Laterza, Bari-Roma.

Ascoli, U (1987) 'The Italian Welfare State: Between Incrementalism and Rationalism', in R. Friedman, N. Gilbert & M. Sherer, M. (ed s) Modern Welfare States, Brighton, Wheatsheaf.

Ascoli, U. (1992) 'Towards a partnership between statutory sector and voluntary action? Italian welfare pluralism in the 90s', in S. Kuhnle & P. Selle (eds) Government and Voluntary Organisations, Aldershot, Avebury.

Ascoli, U. (1994) 'Le prospettive dello stato sociale', in P. Ginsborg (ed) Stato Dell'Italia, Milan, il Saggiatore/Bruno Mondadori.

Bocella, N. (1994)'Squilibri territoriali' and 'Mezzogiorno piu lontano del Nord', in P. Ginsborg (ed) Stato Dell'Italia, Milan, ilS aggiatore/Bruno Mondadori.

Chamberlayne, P. (1991) 'New directions in welfare? France, West Germany, Italy and Britain in the 1980s', Critical Social Policy, n o.33: pp 5-21.

Chamberlayne, P. (1992) 'Income maintenance and institutional forms: a comparison of France, West Germany, Italy and Britain 1945-19 90', Policy and Politics vol.20, no.4 pp299-318.

Ciccarone, G. (1995) 'Incentivie controlli nel regime italino di welfare state: teorie dei contratti e risultanze campionarie', in V. Cotesta (ed) Il Welfare Italiano, Roma, Donzelli Editore.

Collicelli, C. (1995) 'Crisi del welfare state ed evoluzione della domanda: tra selezione e conflitto', in V. Cotesta (ed) Il Welfare Italiano, Roma, Donzelli Editore.

Cotesta, V. (ed) Il Welfa re Italiano, Roma, Donzelli Editore. Cotesta, V. (ed) (1995) Il Welfare Italiano, Roma, Donzelli Editore.

Esping-Andersen, G. (1990) The Three Worlds of Welfare Capitalism, Cambridge, Polity Press.

Eurostat (1995) Basic Statistics of the European Union, 32nd Edn,. Luxembourg, Office for Offical Publications of the European Communities,

Ferrera, M. (1984) Il welfare state in Italia: sviluppo e crisi in prospettiva comparata, Bologna, Il Mulino.

Ferrera, M. (1993) Modelli di solidarieta, Bologna, Il Mulino. Ferrera, M. (1996) 'The 'Southern model of welfare', Journal of European Social Policy vol.6, no.1, pp17-37.

Furlong, P. (1994) Modern Italy: Representation and Reform, London, Routledge.

Ginsborg, P. (1990) A History of Contemporary Italy, London, Penguin.

Graham, R. (1995) 'Boost for Dini as far left splits on pensions', Financial Times 15 June 1995.

Graziani, A. & Boccella, N. (eds) 'Il sistema economico' in P. Ginsborg (ed) Stato Dell'Italia,Milan, il Saggiatore/Bruno Mondadori.

Kuhnle, S. & Selle, P. (eds) (1992) Government and Voluntary Organisations, Aldershot, Avebury,

Lane, D. (1995) 'Survey of Italy (10): Pensions to be reined in', Financial Times 28 July 1995.

Leibfreid, S. (1992) 'Towards a European Welfare State', in Z. Ferge & J.E. Kolberg (eds) Social Policy in a Changing Europe, Westview, Boulder.

Negri, N. (1994) 'Vecchie e nuove forme di poverta', in P. Ginsborg (ed) Stato Dell'Italia,Milan, il Saggiatore/Bruno Mondadori.

Ranci, C. (1994) 'The role of the third sector in welfare policies in Italy', in P. 6 & I. Vidal (eds) Delivering Welfare, Barcelona , CIES.

Reginoni, R. (1984) 'Il sistema pensionistico: risorse e vincoli', in U. Ascoli (ed) Welfare State all'italiana, Bari-Roma, Laterza.

Saraceno, C. & Negri, N. (1994) 'The changing Italian welfare state', Journal of European Social Policy, vol.4, no.1 pp19-34.

Sassoon, D. (1986) Contemporary Italy, London, Longman.

Vicarelli, G. (1994) 'Il sistema sanitario' and 'Le USL verso un nuovo modello di gestione della salute', in P. Ginsborg (ed) Stato Dell'Italia, Milan, il Saggiatore/Bruno Mondadori.

17 Social Policy and the Clinton Presidency

Gillian Peele[1]

When President Clinton took office as President of the United States in January 1993, he was not merely the first Democratic President for thirteen years, but one who had campaigned for the presidency on domestic rather than foreign policy issues. Instead of President Bush's concentration on foreign and security policy, Clinton promised to address issues of relevance to ordinary Americans - notably the economy, jobs, health care and welfare reform.

It was hardly surprising that welfare reform and social policy generally should be on a Democratic President's political agenda. There was concern that American society and the federal government needed to address problems of poverty, crime, homelessness, health care and unemployment which were visible on the country's streets as much as in the volumes of official statistics. Equally significantly there was a concern that many of the United States' established welfare and social security programmes faced an uncertain financial future and that a radical review of these programmes was long overdue. In addition to the generalised sentiment in favour of action in these areas, there was an awareness, reinforced by liberal advocacy groups, that a Democratic administration had the opportunity through its appointments as well as its policy decisions to reverse Republican and conservative approaches in a range of sensitive areas such as health, education and abortion.

President Clinton himself was eager to address the substantive social policy issues which he, like many Democrats, felt had been neglected in the period of Republican dominance. The question, however, was whether large complex issues like welfare reform and national health care could be successfully addressed by the new administration. For, whatever the rhetoric of President Clinton's electoral campaign and indeed of his inaugural address, there were powerful political and institutional factors constraining his freedom of action to enact an agenda of wide-reaching social reform. In this chapter therefore I shall first examine the political and ideological factors which have constrained President Clinton's handling of social policy. I shall then very briefly highlight some of the most controversial aspects of his social policy record. Finally I shall attempt to draw some general conclusions about his achievements in this important field of domestic policy-making.

A Weak Mandate?

Any American president's capacity to shape the immediate political agenda will depend on the specific circumstances of his election and the public perception of his political strength. Clinton came to office with a weak mandate. Only 42 per cent of American voters had cast their vote for him and, although this was sufficient to gain him the electoral victory in a three-way race with George Bush and Ross Perot, it was hardly the clear endorsement which Presidents need at the beginning of their incumbency to secure support for their programmes. The perceived weakness of this electoral mandate was, moreover, rapidly compounded by low presidential popularity ratings, which reflected a combination of early administrative errors and doubts about Clinton's personal integrity (Drew, 1994).

Clinton's position within his own party was fragile. He was very much a 'New Democrat', a product of the party's efforts through the Democratic Leadership Council to make the Democrats electable at the national level by dissociating the party from the demands of its minority constituencies. The Democratic Leadership Council and its associated think-tank , the Progressive Policy Institute (P.P.I.), were the source of many of the policy ideas and stances embraced by the Clinton transition team and the newly elected Clinton administration.

During the campaign Clinton marked out his difference from traditional liberal Democrat policies. He announced that the era of big government (and high taxing and spending) was over; and he acknowledged that many traditional welfare programmes needed to be reviewed. He deliberately distanced himself from

some of the radical black agenda and adopted conservative positions on crime and capital punishment. He tapped into new
approaches to traditional problems - such as the need to link work
requirements (popularly known as 'workfare') and retraining to
the receipt of welfare benefits and to private sector approaches to
government which emphasised cost-effectiveness and value-for-
money (King, 1995; Osborne and Gaebler, 1992). Instead of
spending on the relief of poverty Clinton was more interested in
investment in the economic and social infrastructure through tax
incentives to research in the field of high technology and educational and training measures. The policy stances which Clinton
took in the 1992 campaign were, as the introduction to Mandate
for Change put it, part of the Democratic 'reclamation of the middle class' which began with the start of the 1990s. Clinton, it was
suggested, had built 'a new coalition reaching out to all sectors of
the party, including the large minority who voted Republican in
the 1980's', a coalition resembling 'the pre-1965 New Deal to
Great Society alliances' (Lipset and Schram, 1993, px xv).

Yet, as Clinton's subsequent experience in government was to
prove, this analysis of the 1992 election as a redefining election
and a sign of a new consensus in American politics was somewhat
optimistic. It was difficult for him to translate his 'New Democrat'
philosophy into tangible policy and in consequence he frequently
found himself losing control of the policy agenda. The tensions
within the diverse Democratic coalition emerged as soon as difficult social policy issues were addressed, not least because there
were fundamental differences between the interests and values of
middle class Reagan Democrats and important Democratic constituencies such as blacks and feminists. These differences
emerged even as Clinton was constructing his administrative team
in a way which was calculated to reflect the diversity of the
American people, as the controversy over his nominees to be
Attorney General and to head the Civil Rights Division of the
Department of Justice demonstrated (Peele, 1994).

Moreover, although Clinton had been able to win the presidency as a centrist New Democrat, in Congress there was much
more support and sympathy for traditional Democratic policies.
Indeed the Congress elected with President Clinton in 1992 (the
103rd Congress) was in many respects unusual. The absolute
number of Democrats had declined but more striking was the
degree of turnover that had occurred in the membership. Not
since the Watergate babes of 1974 had so many freshmen
appeared on Capitol Hill as a result of voluntary retirements and
electoral defeats (Pomper, 1993). And as became apparent many
of these freshmen were very sensitive to the new public concern

about the deficit. Women also did particularly well in the election of 1992 causing it to be dubbed 'the year of the woman', although many of those women first elected to the House in 1992 subsequently lost their seats in 1994 (Cook et al., 1994) .

Clinton's political position was also constrained by the fact that all policy initiatives had to be set against the background of the budget deficit which appeared to preclude an enhanced federal role. There is room for debate about how significant the deficit really is in the context of the American budget as a whole. Certainly as a proportion of GDP it was small by comparison with some other countries. But by 1992 it had become a symbolic issue which could be exploited both by independent candidates such as Ross Perot and by right-wing Republicans. Democratic candidates in 1992 also found that the deficit issue was one that concerned electors . It was tangible - and very quantifiable - evidence of the federal government's inability to put its own house in order.

Republican presidents Reagan and Bush as well as Congress had attempted to address the deficit by cutting back on many federal spending programmes. But their room for manoeuvre was limited because only a small amount of the federal budget is discretionary spending . Without addressing the major question of entitlement programmes, not merely was the federal government locked into commitments to social spending which could rise automatically with demographic change; but it had to admit its inability to control some 35 cents of every tax dollar spent by the federal government.

Despite the increasing popular salience of the deficit issue, Clinton had side-stepped it during the campaign, promising rather vaguely to cut it in half. He was , however, forced to deal with it after the election as it increasingly impinged both on his concrete policy plans and on his political strategy. The debate about the significance of the budget deficit was given a new twist after the 1994 mid-term elections when Republican majorities in both chambers of Congress sought to reduce the $2000 billion deficit to zero by the year 2002. As a result social policy was essentially driven by deficit politics, although both the Republicans and the Democrats sought to disguise the fact.

Social policy and American values

A second powerful set of constraints of President Clinton's freedom of manoeuvre in the field of social policy was provided by the distinctive American tradition of social policy (Ashford, 1986). The United States has been seen as a 'welfare laggard' and, as

Peters (1994) has emphasised , the fact that many of the programmes that do exist are means-tested makes them seem even
more meagre by comparison with those provided in many other
western democracies. Although there is much room for argument
about how far American values and cultural patterns by themselves can account for the United States' slow and incomplete
commitment to extensive welfare provision for its citizens, there
is no doubt American political culture, marked as it is by individualism, voluntarism and hostility to bureaucracy offers an unrecep-
tive climate for government-led welfare reforms (Skocpol, 1995).
Despite the massive bursts of federally-inspired reforms of the
1930's New Deal and the 1960's Great Society programmes,
popular attitudes to welfare programmes were ambiguous.
Typically programmes which could be seen as contractual or contributory and which benefited majorities in the society remained
popular. Thus Social Security - the old age pension provision -
introduced in the 1935 Social Security Act has retained overwhelming political support and indeed has been seen as untouch-
able despite the problems associated with its funding.
Programmes which were contributory and targeted at minority
groups such as the unemployed and dependent children were
much less popular and were frequently denigrated as 'welfare
hand-outs'. This distinction between entitlements such as social
security payments and welfare had been enshrined in American
welfare policy at the time of the New Deal. But it reflects an
extremely profound element in popular consciousness which distinguished between the 'deserving' and the 'undeserving' poor
(Katz, 1989).

Discussion of America's social welfare programmes was also
clouded by a failure to recognise the extent to which they were
financially precarious. The social security programme in particular was in jeopardy because of demographic change. But
Medicare was also imperilled and indeed the debate about how to
rescue Medicare was to dominate much of the 1994-1996 period. The popularity of many of the most costly programmes made
even restricting inflation adjustments (COLAS) or taxing entitlements highly controversial.

Hostility to government regulation and bureaucratic intervention compounded generalised suspicion about welfare programmes so that efforts to address poverty in the United States
frequently ran into a triple road block. Welfare programmes were
seen as inherently undesirable because they undermined the
virtues of self-help and created a class of welfare dependants, an
underclass. They were also undesirable because they were costly
and had to be paid for out of general revenue i.e. taxation. And

they were dangerous because they expanded collectivism and the tentacles of Washington.

It should be emphasised that these cultural patterns would have produced difficulties for any president trying to reform key areas of American social policy. President Clinton was in a particularly unhappy situation because one of his key themes (reform of the system of medical provision) generated suspicion from the right and centre, while his welfare reform proposals excited suspicion on the left of the Democratic Party and among those pressure groups organised to protect the poor. Not surprisingly perhaps concrete policy proposals on health care and welfare reform were slow to appear and by the time they had appeared the Clinton presidency had lost much of its political clout.

Institutional complexity and policy-making

Finally, President Clinton found himself constrained by the institutional framework of the American political system which created multiple obstacles to coherent policy-making. Thus although the President could set the policy making agenda, Congress played a substantial role in the process of translating that agenda into legislation. Congress itself is constrained by its own internal processes and by its members' receptiveness to the ebb and flow of public opinion, as mediated by the welter of pressure groups and the press . Congress in the 1990's is an intensely partisan body. The media has become increasingly adversarial. The Republican loss of the presidency in 1992 created an oppositional stance among Republicans in Congress, an attitude that was especially marked in the House of Representatives under Newt Gingrich's leadership. The Republican capture of both chambers of Congress in the 1994 mid-term elections inevitably legitimised Republican perceptions that Clinton had no mandate. Simple opposition to the administration's agenda was replaced by an effort on the part of the Republicans to set its own policy agenda especially on such salient issues as the budget and welfare reform.

The separation of power between executive and legislature in the United States is not the only institutional complication to coherent policy-making. Especially relevant to the character of social policy is the fact that the American system is a federal system and the states exercise a good deal of influence in matters of social policy . Indeed Reagan and to a lesser extent Bush had tried to expand the state's role in the social policy as part of their larger project of redistributing power between Washington DC and the states.

The federal system created additional important actors in the policy process and injected variety and divergence at all stages of administration and implementation. From the period of the Nixon presidency Republican administrations had attempted to encourage greater devolution of power from Washington to the state. Reagan in particular had attempted to promote a 'new federalism' which would see the transfer of many welfare responsibilities to the states. The attraction of this policy for Republicans was that it all owed a simultaneous reduction of the federal role and made likely more restrictive policies, since many states were more conservative in their attitudes to social policy than was the federal government. But the emphasis on the state contribution to welfare policy was not always done in the belief that it would produce cuts in substantive provision . Indeed Clinton has encouraged experimentation with welfare policy by individual states under a system of waivers for federal mandates, although many governors believe that they should have even more flexibility to devise their own approaches to welfare problems.

For their part the groups which spoke for the recipients of welfare benefits frequently opposed greater state autonomy in welfare provision and challenged the federal waivers in the courts. For example, the use of family caps on welfare payments was challenged in the courts by the American Council on Civil Liberties, a sponsoring group of the Child Exclusion Coalition, a broad based group formed in 1994 to resist the trend (Washington Post 24 May 1994). Thus, although it initially seemed that the President would be able to avoid the problems presented by divided government which had marked American politics for much of the post-1968 period, he had to face the policy complexity produced by the fragmented American system. And he by no means had an automatic guarantee that legislation proposed by him would be acceptable to Congress. Unfortunately for Clinton, the period of a Democratic controlled Congress was short-lived. The 1994 mid-term elections produced an unexpected Republican sweep of both the House and the Senate. The capture of the House by the Republicans under Newt Gingrich's leadership was especially problematic for the President. For Gingrich had secured his victory on the basis of the Contract with America, a document calling for a revolutionary change in the role of government. It is important to be clear what the Contract with America was and what it was not. It was not a manifesto which convinced voters. Quite the contrary -most voters had never heard of it. Rather it acted as a mandate, a unifying platform which Newt Gingrich could use to bind his freshmen representatives together. The period of Clinton's presidency must therefore be divided into two logical halves : the first in which, bathed in the glow of electoral victory and with at least a nominal majority in both houses of Congress, he could press on with his own agenda; the second in which he faced an ideologically abrasive Republican majority in Congress. In the second half of his presidency Clinton's strategy was essentially to allow the Republicans to make the running though reserving to himself the right to criticise and block Congressional initiatives.

Clinton's first two years

The immediate impact of a Democratic president and a Democratic Congress was felt in the ability to pass previously vetoed legislation. Thus the Family and Medical Leave Bill was signed as the first legislation of Clinton's presidency in February 1993. This legislation, which Clinton said exhibited his commitment to 'putting people first' (the title of his manifesto) guaranteed up to 12 weeks per year of unpaid leave for cases of medical or other emergency. The point of the bill was that it reflected the needs of working parents especially women who had become an increasingly important factor in the American economy. For as Clinton pointed out the percentage of mothers with children under 18 who were working had risen from 35 per cent in 1965 to 67 per cent in 1992 (Clinton, 1993). Control of the presidency also allowed the new president to make some changes to sensitive policy areas by executive order. As a result restrictions on research using foetal tissue, the 'gag rule' (Title X of the Public Health Services Act) , the ban on abortions in military hospitals and the ban on importing the abortifacient pill RU486 were all lifted in the first month of Clinton's presidency.

The ideological tensions within the Democratic coalition and the uncertain ideological compass of the new administration were apparent from Clinton's cabinet appointments. Despite the centre-right tilt of the administration, Clinton chose as his Secretary of Health and Human Services Donna E. Shalala, a left-of-centre academic. However, as Shalala knew from her appointment, the key issues that might appear in her jurisdiction - health care reform and welfare reform - were so important that her responsibility for developing policy would be shared. Hillary Clinton was expected to play a key role in health care reform, while social welfare cut across the interests of Labor Secretary, Robert Reich. Other key appointments in the new administration were David Ellwood, a Harvard academic who wanted to enhance training and education but who also had long been a critic of a system which made it economically advantageous to be on AFDC and

Medicaid rather than taking lower paid work. Ellwood along with Mary Jo Bane were appointed to the Department of Health and Human Services and given key roles in the evolution of welfare policy.

Inevitably social policy for Clinton had to be placed in the context of his economic strategy. The economic programme which he devised at the beginning of his administration was an imaginative effort to reconcile the pressures of deficit reduction with the desire to enhance some federal spending, while redirecting the taxation system in a way which would make the richer sections of society bear the burden. The Clinton programme, which aimed to cut the deficit by $493 billion over 5 years, envisaged tax increases of $246 billion over 5 years. From the beginning it was noticeable how difficult Clinton found it to make radical cuts to programmes. In the proposals which emerged from this early economic strategy Clinton cut out only five programmes completely and left untouched all the major social spending programmes. Clinton's first budget (and the stimulus package which accompanied it) underlined how constrained Clinton was as a policy-setter. Congress rejected the stimulus package and forced major changes in the budget in a manner which was politically damaging for the presidency.

As far as major social policy issues were concerned, Clinton's hot issue of 1993 was health care reform. As Clinton declared , it was time 'to make sense of America's health care system' (Clinton, 1993). It was not inevitable that Clinton would make this such a major item of his legislative agenda and indeed in the campaign he appeared to have become interested in it largely because his rivals for the Democratic nomination, Bob Kerrey and Paul Tsongas, had highlighted the issue. In government however Clinton feared that other democrats such as Edward Kennedy and Harris Wofford (whose surprise victory in Pennsylvania was largely attributed to the issue)would introduce their reforms (Drew, 1994).

The problems of the American health care system have been much discussed and there had been several attempts in the recent past to overhaul it. Indeed the health care debate illustrates very well how the complexities of social policy-making in the United States, as a politically weak president attempted to achieve a radical and comprehensive reform in conjunction with a Congress which was at least as concerned about the role of government and the deficit as about extending medical coverage to all Americans, made any reform, let alone a major and comprehensive one, problematic.

Cost and coverage were the key issues of the health reform debate and they were, of course, inseparable. One of the weaknesses of the American system of health provision was coverage since it was reckoned that only 85 per cent of the American public was covered by healthcare insurance. Disproportionately it was the working poor, blacks and the unemployed who lacked cover. Thus while it was reckoned in 1992 that some 73.6 per cent of whites had medical insurance, nearly 38 per cent of blacks had no insurance (Paton, 1994). Some efforts had been made to plug the gaps in coverage - for example by the introduction of federal finance through Medicaid and Medicare in 1965 as part of the Great Society effort to cope with the problems of poverty. But the gaps remained and had policy consequences such as the markedly different infant mortality rates as between blacks and whites.

But any extension of coverage would be costly and the question arose as to who would bear that cost. If, as seemed likely, i t would be the federal government, what were the implications for federal spending? Even without an extension of coverage, the search for cost control of medical treatment was bound to occur, given that the United States already spent more of its income (14 per cent) on health than any other nation and that health care costs by themselves would drive up the deficit. (It was reckoned in 1993 that Medicaid and Medicare costs would rise by 67 per cent in the next five years.)

A number of factors contributed to the high cost of American health care. First the demographic factor meant that more elder ly people were surviving longer and consuming expensive health care. Secondly inflation in the health care sector ran higher than in other areas, not least because the federal government had no way of limiting the fees paid to health care providers and physicians. Thirdly the advance of science and technology meant that ever more expensive products were available and fuelled demand for them. Finally, powerful pressure groups - both providers of medical services and consumers of them - had developed a vested interest in the status quo.

Clinton announced his decision to address health care reform early in his presidency - on January 25th 1993. Yet the process which he used to develop the reform (a task force under Hillary Rodham Clinton working alongside an interagency working group) was unwieldy. Together with his uncertain political strategy for building and maintaining a coalition behind reform this ensured that opponents of reform had time to strengthen their position with the public and with Congress (Mann and Ornstein, 1995; Barer et al,. 1995).

The actual details of the complex Clinton health plan (which was not enacted) are now of less importance than its guiding principles. Clinton found he had an ideological split in his party between those who wanted to rely on the market to control costs through regulated or managed competition (the DLC approach and that favoured by the influential Jackson Hole group of health policy reformers), and those who favoured direct government intervention to extend coverage and attempt to control expenditure. Clinton's plan mandated employers to provide health care insurance for most workers and their families but injected federal subsidies to help individuals pay their share of insurance costs and to help small businesses. It aimed to control costs by capping the annual insurance premium payable and by encouraging competition through regional health alliances which would pool insurance premiums and in theory push down the cost of medical provision. Quality would be monitored by a national regulatory authority(the National Health Board) and pre-existing schemes such as Medicare and Medicaid would be incorporated into the new arrangements.

Although the initial public reception was favourable it became clear that the plan lacked the votes to get through Congress. There were several reasons for the failure (Ranade, 1995). Heavy responsibility must be apportioned to the President himself for the timing and manner of the reform. It must also be said that an effort to enact such a bold and radical reform from a position of political weakness made it likely that no reform would be successful. If Clinton had been content to pursue incremental as opposed to comprehensive reform he might have done better. Coverage for example could have been extended in small steps. Ultimately however the American political system frustrated Clinton. Policy making is a shared activity and Congressional participation in the process meant that once the administration's bill had gone to Congress it would be the legislature's priorities and processes that would determine the outcome.

Welfare reform

Although health care reform had absorbed much of the initial energy of the Clinton administration, welfare reform was also on the agenda (Norris and Thomson, 1995). In the campaign Clinton had promised to 'end welfare as we know it' and in May 1993 set up a welfare reform task force. (By comparison with the byzantine structure of the health care task force which involved about 500 people, the task force charged with welfare reform was only some 32 strong.) At the same time the National Governors

Association, the American Public Welfare Association (which represents state welfare directors) and the National Conference of State Legislatures had put together a welfare task force that was expected to work informally with the Administration group (Kosterlitz, 1993).

Some of Clinton's approach to welfare reform could be gleaned from his early economic package. Clinton emphasised spending that constituted an investment in the future such as expenditure on compensatory education programmes like Head Start and on the Women's, Infants and Children' Program (WIC). But he also placed much store on the Earned Income Tax Credit putting some $21 billion into his reconciliation package of 1993. And, as a 'New Democrat', he was interested in emphasising individual responsibility and new (or recycled old) ideas of linking the receipt of benefits to willingness to work. The emphasis on willingness to work as a precondition of receiving welfare benefits was part of a revised approach to social policy which had an influence beyond the United States (King, 1995). Such ideas provoked intense fury on the left of the Democratic Party who argued that they hurt vulnerable groups. Clinton came under fire not merely from spokesmen of the black constituency, such as Jesse Jackson, but also from those like Senator Moynihan who suspected that Clinton's interest in welfare reform owed more to electoral tactics than to interest in the substantive issues involved.

The absorption with health care reform had deflected Clinton from immediate consideration of welfare reform, although many observers such as Senator Moynihan thought welfare reform the more pressing issue. Although rumours about what might be in Clinton's welfare reform proposals abounded in early 1994, the administration's plan was only announced in June 1994. It had been delayed in part because of deep divisions inside the administration. As anticipated it tilted towards the right and attempted to address the issue of personal responsibility. States were given an enhanced role and additional autonomy in their distribution of benefits. As well as giving states additional responsibility for collecting support for child support from absent fathers, Clinton , in a move which civil rights activists thought would unleash the floodgates of restrictive legislation at the state level, included in his proposals a plan to allow states to deny additional benefits to women who had children while on benefit. (Claiborne, 1994). New Jersey, for example, had introduced what was known as a 'family cap' in 1992 though data suggested that denial of benefit had little impact on subsequent decisions to have children (Carney, 1995).

Other aspects of Clinton's welfare proposals were equally explosive. Although the provision that recipients of welfare had to undertake training in order to increase their capacity for work could be seen as part of the new approach to using welfare constructively, a two year limit was placed on unemployment assistance. Limiting the possible time that could be spent on welfare had become a popular policy prescription; but the White House had not resolved the issue of what to do about those who had undertaken further training but still could not find work at the end of two years. The two year limit on cash assistance was seen as marking a clear dividing line between 'New' and 'traditional' (i.e. liberal) Democrats. Clinton it seemed, having moved towards the left on health care reform, was now moving right in his search for a credible welfare reform policy.

The slow pace of Clinton's welfare policy-making meant that Congress was unlikely to be able to deal with the president's proposals in that Congress. As the mid-term elections approached, the debate about social policy began to be conducted in a very different tone. And the unexpected sweep of the House and Senate by the Republican Party made Clinton the first Democratic President since Truman to face a Republican controlled Congress and transferred the initiative from the White House to Capitol Hill.

Divided government again

The Republican Party which won the mid-term Congressional elections of 1994 was itself a coalition influenced by a number of new forces in American politics. In particular social conservatives and the religious right, as organised through the Christian Coalition and groups such as the Traditional Values Coalition, exercised a substantial influence. More generally there was a concern in Republican ranks with 'values', by which was generally meant a renewed emphasis on the family and traditional moral attitudes(Carney, 1995) . This, together with the concern for the deficit, meant that social policy would be high on the new Republican Congressional agenda but in a very different form from that of President Clinton. Instead of seeing the federal government as an essential instrument in the relief of poverty, the Republicans wanted to reduce the role of the federal government in family decisions. Thus Congress saw the introduction of such bills as the Parental Rights and Respnsibilities Act sponsored by Grassley and Largent and renewed efforts to abolish the Department of Education.

The new Republicans in Washington wanted action and in their first one hundred days the emphasis was on the implementation of the Contract with America, the document which Gingrich had campaigned on and which he claimed gave him his mandate. The Contract w ith America deliberately omitted divisive social issues from its remit, focusing instead on political and fiscal issues such as the requirement for a balanced budget and welfare reform (Lavery, 1995). But it was followed by a Contract with the American Family whic h had the effect of keeping the religious right's social agenda before the public.

The advent of a Republican Congress meant that Republicans would make much of the running on welfare reform for the last two years of the Clinton presidency. Many of the policy proposals suggested by Republicans - for example limiting the time spent on welfare, linking welfare to a work requirement and structuring welfare benefits in a way that acted as a disincentive to unmarried mothers to have further children out of wedlock - were increasingly common currency among Republicans and Democrats. Increasingly also the public mood seemed to be shifting in favour of a more conservative approach to welfare. For example a poll taken in April 1995 by Yankelovich for CNN-Time asked whether respondents favoured or opposed a five year limit on the amount of time a welfare recipient could receive cash payments (National Journal 29 July 1995) 74 per cent of the public were in favour of such a limit with only 21 per cent opposed and 5 per cent unsure.

Discussion of welfare issues did however reveal stark partisan differences. For Democrats reform of welfare was reform of a system they had largely built . For Republicans the welfare system was increasingly a symbol of all that was wrong with America and they wished to remove the federal role. For Democrats the demands of deficit reduction and the needs of social policy created an intense problem. For Republicans the overriding goal was deficit reduction, however harshly the cuts might fall.

For the president there were some advantages in the new situation. Clinton took the opportunity of his 1995 State of the Union address to reassert some of the centrist themes which had dominated his 1992 campaign and which had become blurred during the first two years of the presidency. Thus he called for a new covenant with the American people and urged an overhaul of welfare as well as tougher action against illegal immigrants. He also acknowledged that health care reform would have to proceed on a consensual step-by-step basis.

Although the president could no longer drive policy, he retained influence through his ability to veto legislation sent up to him by Congress, a constitutional power he was to use increasingly in the battle over the budget and appropriations. And, although Republicans controlled both the House and the Senate, this did not mean that legislation on contentious subjects was any easier to steer through Congress, not least because of divisions between the House and the Senate on many issues and between moderates and conservatives in the G.O.P. ranks. (Although some Senators such as Phil Gramm were every bit as draconian in their approach as their House colleagues, some Senators were very sensitive to the policy implications of cuts and Senators from growth states were wary of methods of calculating block grants based on retrospective funding figures.)

Clinton used the veto to stall a welfare measure which would have turned the responsibility for funding welfare almost entirely to the states by transferring the federal funding for anti-poverty programmes to block grants. It would also have imposed a five year time limit on the use of federal money and allowed states the right to reduce that time limit further to two years. The bill also restricted the distribution of welfare to immigrant families - a proposal which had gained increasing cross-party support but which, apart from its harshness to children and welfare recipients, presented peculiar difficulties to states such as California and Texas. The Republican measure also capped welfare spending and ended the guarantee of assistance to any eligible family (Washington Post 1996). (House Republicans aimed to cut $230 billion from federal spending over seven years by transferring 336 categorical aid programmes to block grants). The problem with block grants, which some Republican governors such as Governor Thompson of Wisconsin and Weld of Massachusetts were extremely enthusiastic about, was that they not merely reduced the federal government role in welfare provision but were calculated to drive down spending at the state level. Moreover not all states were equally enthusiastic about taking over the responsibility for welfare.

Clinton's response to these Republican initiatives was to temper the cuts, arguing for ones smaller than those advocated by the G.O.P. Although some Democrats thought this strategy smacked too much of electioneering, it was difficult to see how Clinton could have ignored the debate completely.

The President and Congress also did battle over the future of Medicare. The spiralling costs of Medicare made it an attractive target for G.O.P. budget-cutters but they were reluctant to attack such a popular programme, given the power of such groups as the American Association of Retired Persons. However, a report from the Medicare Trustees in April 1995 suggested that Medicare might be bankrupt by the year 2002. This report gave Republicans an opportunity to present their cuts as part of an effort to 'save Medicare' (Schneider, 1995). The Republican Medicare proposal was vetoed by Clinton in 1995 after a long fight in which Republicans claimed that they were offering a plan better able to save the system than the Democrats' who put forward cuts of $54 billion dollars over seven years- roughly a third of those sought by the G.O.P.

Conclusions

The optimism that constructive social reform might be achieved in the United States had largely evaporated even before Clinton's hold on the policy agenda was weakened by the 1994 midterm elections. The Clinton administration failed to deliver major social policy reform when it had the best chance of doing so, and part of the blame must be placed on the president himself. But the failure to generate substantial reform must also be placed in the context of a society where there were increasingly deep divisions about how to address social issues and extensive concern about the deficit. And in so far as there was a discernible public mood, it was one that was conservative-leaning rather than liberal, opposed to federal intervention rather than supportive of federal initiative. In these circumstances it is likely that the kinds of policy reform that will be successful will be small and incremental ones not radical and comprehensive ones (like Clinton's original health care initiative). In contrast to paralysis at the federal level, it is tempting to seek compensation in the surge of state activity. But many of the experiments at the state level require evaluation and it remains to be seen how far the initial enthusiasm of the states for replacing the federal role in the relief of poverty will be sustained. If there is a second term of the Clinton presidency, it is likely to be politically more skilled and less ambitious in policy terms. Paradoxically, however, such a presidency might be able to deliver more than the first term presidency, although it will undoubtedly be inadequate to the needs of the contemporary United States.

Note

1. I am grateful to Mr. Kenny Baer of Pembroke College, Oxford for discussing the role of the Democratic Leadership Council with me.

References

Ashford, D. (1986) The Emergence of the Welfare States, Oxford, Basil Blackwell.

Barer, M.C. with Marmor, T.C. & Morrison, E.M. (1995) 'Health care in the US: on the road to nowhere (again)?', Social Science and Medicine, vol. 41, pp453-460.

Carney, E.N. (1995) 'Rush to judgement' National Journal, 15 July.

Carney, E.N. (1995) 'Family Time', National Journal, 29 July.

Claiborne, W. (1994) 'Reluctant allies oppose Clinton family cap welfare proposal', Washington Post, 27 May.

Clinton, W. J. (1993a) Public Papers of the Presidents: William J Clinton, 15 February.

Clinton, W. J. (1993b) 'Remarks on health care reform', Public Papers of the Presidents. William J. Clinton, vol.1, 25 January.

Cook, E.A., Thomas, S. & Wilcox, C. (1994) The Year of the Woman: Myths and Realities, Boulder Colorado, Westview Press.

Drew, E. (1994) On the Edge: the Clinton Presidency, New York, Simon and Schuster.

Katz, M.B. (1989) The Undeserving Poor: From the War on Welfare to the War on Poverty, New York, Pantheon.

King, D.S. (1995) Actively Seeking Work? The Politics of Unemployment and Welfare Policy in the United States and Great Britain, Chicago, Chicago University Press.

Kosterlitz, J. (1993) 'Changing of the guard', Washington Post, 15 May.

Lipset, S.M. & Schram, M. (1993) 'Interpreting the 1992 Election,' in W. Marshall, & M. Schram (eds) Mandate for Change, New York, Berkeley Books for the Progressive Policy Institute.

Lavery, K. (1995) 'The contract with America', Public Money and Management, vol. 15, pp 5-7.

Mann, T. & Ornstein, N. (1995) Intensive Care: How Congress Shapes Health Policy, Washington D.C., AEI/Brookings.

Norris, D. F. & Thomson L. (eds) (1995) The Politics of Welfare Reform, London, Sage.

Osborne, D. E & Gaebler, T. (1992) Reinventing Government: How the Entrepreneurial Spirit is Transforming the Public Sector, Reading , Mass., Addison-Wesley.

Paton, C. (1994,1995) ' Health policy: The analytics and politics of attempted reform', in G. Peele et al., (eds) Developments in American Politics 2 London, Macmillan and New Jersey, Chatham House.

Peele, G. (1994; 1995) 'The Supreme Court and the Constitution', in G. Peele, C.J. Bailey, B. Cain, & B.G. Peters (eds) Developments in American Politics 2, London, Macmillan and New Jersey, Chatham House.

Peters, B. G. (1994,1995) 'Social policy', in G. Peele et al., (eds) Developments in American Politics 2, London, Macmillan and New Jersey, Chatham House.

Pomper, G. M (1993) The Election of 1992, Chatham, N.J., Chatham House.

Ranade, W. (1995) 'US health care reform', Public Money and Management, vol. 15, pp9-16.

Schneider, W. (1995) 'Who's really Medicare's best friend?', National Journal, 6 May.

Skocpol, T. (1995) Social Policy in the United States: Future Possibilities in Historical Perspective, Princeton, Princeton University Press.

Washington Post National Weekly Edition, 12-18 February 1996 ('Going their own ways').